D1559596

Between Law and Narrative

Gorgias Dissertations in Biblical Studies

51

Gorgias Dissertations (GD) make available to scholars and the public outstanding doctoral dissertations in various disciplines. The series provides a valuable service to the scholarly community as it disseminates unique academic perspectives that would otherwise remain inaccessible. Gorgias Press has successfully introduced many young scholars as published authors to the academic world through the dissertation series.

Between Law and Narrative

The Method and Function of Abstraction

Bernon P. Lee

gorgias press

2010

Gorgias Press LLC, 180 Centennial Ave., Piscataway, NJ, 08854, USA

www.gorgiaspress.com

Copyright © 2010 by Gorgias Press LLC

2010   ⌐

ISBN 978-1-59333-912-8   ISSN 1935-6870

Library of Congress Cataloging-in-Publication Data

Lee, Bernon.
   Between law and narrative : the method and
function of abstraction / by Bernon Lee.
        p. cm. -- (Gorgias dissertations ; 51)
   Includes index.
   1. Law (Theology)--Biblical teaching. 2.
Jewish law--Interpretation and construction. 3.
Bible. O.T. Leviticus--Criticism, Narrative. 4.
Bible. O.T. Numbers--Criticism, Narrative. I.
Title.
   BS1199.L3L44 2010
   222'.1306--dc22
                                    2010012623

Printed in the United States of America

To Connie

TABLE OF CONTENTS

ACKNOWLEDGEMENTS

This book is a slightly revised version of a dissertation submitted in 2003 to the Biblical Department of the Toronto School of Theology. I am grateful to the friendly staff at Gorgias Press for facilitating its publication: George and Christine Kiraz, Katie Stott and Jasmaile Eumnath. William Katip and Grace College have my thanks for contributions to the cost of publication.

Many have contributed to the gestational process behind the composition of the dissertation and its revision in this volume. I am grateful for the stimulating discussion of fellow students in seminars at the Toronto School of Theology and the Department of Near and Middle Eastern Civilizations at the University of Toronto, all of whom made postgraduate study a rewarding and enjoyable experience. Professor E.J. Revell introduced me to current discussions of Classical Hebrew syntax. The seminal ideas behind the dissertation were tested first in a seminar on the forms of biblical law under the direction of Professor Paul E. Dion. The Late Professor Gerald T. Sheppard helped with directions for initial explorations in the confluence of literary theory and biblical studies. For the investment of these teachers in my intellectual edification I am grateful.

The Late Professor Brian Peckham guided me through several drafts of the dissertation. His critical judgement has saved this work from numerous oversights. Brian's gentle demeanour, infused with brilliant insights and the spirit of encouragement, haunts my memory. I miss him.

Professor Glen Taylor was my advisor through my program of research. I have benefited as much from his erudite criticism as from his unfailing support and good humour through difficult times. Glen's humility and graciousness (as expressed by his insistence on carrying my suitcases up two storeys to my apartment, the selfless hospitality that greeted me upon my arrival at Wycliffe College in the University of Toronto) continues to inspire me and to characterise our relationship.

Together with the other members of the dissertation committee already mentioned (Professors Taylor, Peckham and Sheppard), Professors Marion Taylor and Dennis Olson are to be thanked for their suggestions for improvement to the dissertation. Responsibility for remaining deficiencies falls squarely upon me.

Thanks are due to various colleagues at institutions I have had the privilege of being a part, whose friendships made for scintillating and convivial discourse on matters relating to biblical literature and religious studies: Brent Sandy, Skip Forbes, Mark Norris and Tiberius Rata of Grace College; Gary Long, Juan Hernández Jr., Mike Holmes, Victor Ezigbo, Christian Collins-Winn, Sara Shady, Dan Yim and other members of the community on the third floor of the Academic Center at Bethel University. Where conversations strayed beyond subject matter relating to that of this book, my pleasure only increased.

My scholarly pursuits are possible because of familial support, financial and moral. I am grateful for the unfailing encouragement of my parents, Hubert Lee and Ho Kwan Peck. Of Zechariah and Mattya's provision of times of refreshment from the rigours of research and writing I bear fond memories.

Foremost among those deserving of gratitude is my wife. The magnitude of Connie's love and dedication, from her affectionate attention through times of despondency to reminders to partake of meals, is unmatched. I cherish our life together. This work is dedicated to her.

LIST OF ABBREVIATIONS

AB	Anchor Bible
BA	*Biblical Archaeologist*
BHRG	*A Biblical Hebrew Reference Grammar.* Christo H.J. van der Merwe, van der, Jackie A. Naude and Jan H. Kroeze. Biblical Languages: Hebrew 3. Sheffield, 1999.
BHS	*Biblia Hebraica Stuttgartensia*
BJS	Brown Judaic Studies
BO	*Bibliotheca orientalis*
FAT	Forschungen zum Alten Testament
GBH	*Grammatik des Biblischen Hebräisch.* Wolfgang Schneider. 6th ed. München, 1985.
GKC	*Gesenius' Hebrew Grammar.* Edited by E. Kautzsch. Translated by A.E. Cowley. 2d ed. Oxford, 1910.
Hist.	*Historia*
HS	*Hebrew Studies*
HUCA	*Hebrew Union College Annual*
IBHS	*An Introduction to Biblical Hebrew Syntax.* B.K. Waltke and M. O'Connor. Winona Lake, 1990.
ICC	International Critical Commentary
JANESCU	*Journal of the Near Eastern Society of Columbia University*
JBL	*Journal of Biblical Literature*
JNSL	*Journal of Northwest Semitic Languages*
Jöuon	Jöuon, P. *A Grammar of Biblical Hebrew.* Translated and revised by T. Muraoka. 2 vols. Subsidia Biblica 14/1–2. Rome, 1991.

JQR	*Jewish Quarterly Review*
JSOT	*Journal for the Study of the Old Testament*
JSOTSup	Journal for the Study of the Old Testament: Supplement Series
KHC	Kurzer Hand-Commentar zum Alten Testament
Midr.	*Midrash*
NICOT	New International Commentary on the Old Testament
NRSV	New Revised Standard Version
OTL	Old Testament Library
Pesiq. Rab Kah.	*Pesiqta de Rab Kahana*
RB	*Revue Biblique*
SBLDS	Society of Biblical Literature Dissertation Series
Sem	*Semitica*
LXX	Septuagint
Syr.	Syriac
TDOT	*Theological Dictionary of the Old Testament.* Edited by G.J. Botterweck and H. Ringgren. Translated by J.T. Willis, G.W. Bromiley, and D.E. Green. 8 vols. Grand Rapids, 1974-
Tg. Onq.	*Targum Onqelos*
Tg. Neof.	*Targum Neofiti*
Tg. Ps.-J.	*Targum Pseudo-Jonathan*
TWOT	*Theological Wordbook of the Old Testament.* Edited by R.L. Harris, G.L. Archer Jr., and B.K. Waltke. 2 vols. Chicago, 1980.
VT	*Vetus Testamentum*
VTSup	Supplements to *Vetus Testamentum*
WBC	Word Biblical Commentary
WMANT	Wissenschaftliche Monographien zum Alten und Neuen Testament
WTJ	*Westminster Theological Journal*
ZAH	*Zeitschrift für Althebräistik*
ZAW	*Zeitschrift für die alttestamentliche Wissenschaft*

CHAPTER ONE
READING NARRATIVE AND LAW

The act of reading, according to Wolfgang Iser, consists of postulating connections between parts of texts where no explicit connection exists (1978, 182). The overall system of a given text contains "blanks" which require a filling out in order to create the interaction of the various components. This, according to Iser, is the act of readerly ideation; an assumption of connectivity between textual portions placed in close proximity. While the connections between segments within the text occur with varying degrees of clarity, the compulsion for readers to seek out the links remains consistent because of the co-existence of the parts within the whole of the text. It is the act of combination that facilitates completion in the object of reading, the totality of meaning. Toward this end, the blanks become triggers for the process of organization. The failure to forge the connections is a failure to grasp the internal coherence of a literary work.

THE OBJECTIVES OF THIS WORK

Bringing Iser's insights to bear upon the confluence of narrative and law in Leviticus and Numbers, the present work seeks to forge thematic connections between the two forms of discourse.[1] The

---

[1] 'Theme' and its adjectival derivative 'thematic' have reference to a concept—capable of expression in a word, phrase, or sentence—qualifying or contained within a unit of text. The term is used often in this broad sense within this volume. The term is applied also with a more specific meaning with reference to a segment of narrative defining a series of events, effectively cutting them off from preceding and following

mere coincidence of narrative and law, in accordance with Iser's judgement, would invite the reader to make connections of theme between the content of the laws and that of the adjacent narrative.[2] The current work envisions that the narratives are not mere occasions for legal promulgation: the arbitrary creation of slots within the unfolding drama of the narrative in which laws of edifying import for a community of readers may be inserted. On

---

events (the process of selection). In such cases, theme (as a static quality) combined with the dynamic sequential element of narrative (the temporal sequence of events in stories) creates the feature of plot in narrative. As the following brief description of the concept of 'abstraction' explains, the expression of theme over a series of successive events (the dynamic sequential element of narrative) consists of moments of movement toward the completion of the sequence of events capable of receiving a specified thematic qualification (a word, phrase, or sentence standing as summary for the series of events).

   [2] In her introduction to the criticism of narrative, Mieke Bal defines a narrative text as "a text in which an agent relates ('tells') a story in a particular medium, such as language, imagery, sound, buildings, or a combination thereof" (Bal 1997, 5). Stories are defined by the fact that they contain events caused and experienced by actors, related by chronology and logic. But narrative texts also contain sentences that do not relay events; thus, Bal also employs the term 'narrative' in a stricter sense with reference to those sentences in a narrative text representing events (transitions from one state to another) in designating material of a non-narrative nature (Bal 1997, 31–5). The laws as representations of speech embedded within sentences spoken by the independent and omniscient narrator in the portrayal of events falls within the category of non-narrative material (Bal 1997, 60). In keeping with Bal's definitions, it may be more accurate to describe the goal of our undertaking as the comparison of two distinct components within narrative texts. It is the comparison of the temporal and logical element of progression in the events of narrative texts, with the legal prescriptions embedded in acts of speech. The laws may be recognized as the prescriptions dealing with characters and circumstances beyond the confines of a single moment in the narrative; thus, the laws by definition have a focus that is typical, and not specific. The laws address classes of character and circumstance of which narratives offer specific exemplars.

the contrary, laws function as comments about narratives, and narratives as dramatic representations of those comments. Such an understanding of the connections between law and narrative would go beyond the fact that the laws are acts of speech embedded in the narratives, the words of actors in the unfolding drama. The communicative content of the laws may not be confined by subordination to an event of speech within a series of events narrated by the omniscient and independent narrator; the laws may constitute also comments of the narrator to the reader— a way of making an observation about the significance of surrounding narrative—without a participant within the narrative as intermediary. While the laws may be expressed through the words of participants in the narrative, they are also another component in the narrator's ensemble of forms within a larger structure of communication working to define the thematic import of the content of that communication. The present work postulates that sets of legal prescriptions in the selected material from Leviticus and Numbers are terse statements designating thematic matter expressed over the course of sections of the surrounding narrative: summary statements for passages of narrative. This extraction (through brief formulation) of thematic concepts governing and characterizing a series of events in narrative is referred to, within the confines of this study, as the procedure of abstraction in the process of reading narrative. Essentially, the procedure of abstraction as a whole entails alteration in the process of combination through which meaning is achieved in narrative: the constitution of theme through a sequence of events in narrative is exchanged for representation in a concept divested of its sequential and dynamic quality in narrative through abstraction. The term 'abstraction' and the nature of the alteration in the process of thematic combination in the formation of meaning may be understood with reference to a two-fold process.

The first step in the thematic abstraction of narrative is founded upon the observation that narratives generally display events in a chronological progression, with semantic increments at various pivotal points adding up to a full thematic expression at its conclusion. Narratives relating stories of, for example, crime and punishment contain moments where a significant advancement toward denouement (the discovery of a vital clue pointing to the guilty party, the arrest of the culprit) occurs. It is only with the conclusion (the execution of the perpetrator of the crime) that the thematic qualification of summary for the stretch of narrative (crime and punishment, act of judgement) may apply. Such a series of events in a stretch of narrative displaying thematic coherence is transformed often by summary into single prescriptive clauses or sentences displaying similar thematic content. Essentially, the laws contain statements that extract the thematic essence in a stretch of narrative with reference to a word, phrase or sentence that may stand to qualify the series of events in a given portion of the narrative. Alternatively, the laws may designate the events defining the beginning and the end of the series of events in the narrative: the act of transgression and that of punishment in a portion of narrative depicting an act of judgement.[3]

A second aspect of the procedure of abstraction occurs wherever groups of legal prescriptions on disparate topics exists as a body. In such cases, thematic coherence is achieved through observation of the common denominator in the various individual components. The common denominator, through repeated representation in all the groups of laws, comes to the forefront of a reader's attention. This second aspect of abstraction represents a shift from the syntagmatic process in the constitution of theme in narrative, to a paradigmatic process in law. While the first component in the process of abstraction extracts the key movements sustaining a stretch of narrative, the second component of abstraction may bring specific details significant for the thematic import of the narrative to a reader's attention by repetition through the body of law. Overarching themes of general import and their complementary concepts governing law and

---

[3] This may be designated as abstraction by the device of explicitly depicting the bi-polar structure of a stretch of narrative with a coherent theme (e.g. A man who strikes another leading to death [transgression] shall be put to death [execution]; just as he did to the other [transgression], so shall it be done to him [execution]). Alternatively, a law may invoke a term (e.g. 'judgement') standing to qualify the proximate portion of narrative, thereby invoking the bi-polar series of motifs indirectly.

narrative become prominent through multiple doses of exposure in the components of the legal passage.

Knowledge of the inner-workings of abstraction provides a method for the comprehension of the aesthetic principles involved in the collocation of narrative and law. Such an understanding of abstraction in relation to the properties of narrative produces a mode of interpretation, the operations of one literary manoeuvre, in reading law and story. The corpus of Leviticus and Numbers will provide several examples of the abstraction of narrative in law.

AN OUTLINE OF THE TASK

The rest of the first chapter explores examples of specific attempts to link narrative and law in the Hebrew Bible with reference to elements of theme. Subsequently, a review of developments within narratology of the precise conjunction of theme and the element of temporal sequence in the events of narrative takes place. The definition of a method and its attendant concepts for the first step in the process of abstraction comes into view.[4]

Subsequent to the review of scholarship of outlining the theoretical underpinings for the suggested approach to narrative and law in the Hebrew Bible, attention will turn to specific cases for illustration (chs. 2, 3). The division of the analysis into two chapters reflects the degree of clarity in the thematic links between the laws and the narrative. The cases where the degree of thematic continuity between law and narrative is clear come first (ch. 2). Those cases requiring greater effort on the part of the reader come later in chapter three. The selected portions of text for analysis are Lev 10:1–20, 24:10–23, Num 9:1–14, 15:1–41, 27:1–11, and 36:1–13. That these texts combine narrative and law is, of course,

---

[4] The precise description of the second component in the process of abstraction, the definition of common elements of theme in groups of laws, is best left to the portion of the volume dealing with specific cases (chs. 2, 3). This is the case because of the fact that the second component in the process of abstraction is not attested widely in the theoretical formulations of narrative structure to date. The specific application of the second component to the laws of Leviticus and Numbers may be seen with greater clarity with reference to specific examples from the text.

essential to the topic under discussion. Another criterion stands behind the selection. This volume identifies a function for the combination of law and narrative: the procedure of abstraction in law which extracts the thematic import of a series of events in narrative. The focus is upon the mechanics behind the process of reading, a description of the path readers tread in the act of interpretation. How did readers get what they got out of these passages of narrative and law in the history of their interpretation? In keeping with the nature of the objective, it is fitting that the selection of texts should begin with those widely recognized as discrete literary units espousing the thematic integration of law and narrative.[5] The degree of scholarly agreement on the integration of the two types of discourse in these texts provides the occasion for the exploration of the process of comprehending narrative in conjunction with law, the proposed procedure of abstraction, in these texts. While indications of the thematic links beyond the boundaries of the selected passages shall be observed in the introduction to each passage under examination, the amount of detail intrinsic to the procedure of investigation requires focus. Such links cannot be pursued extensively within the confines of this work.

The fourth chapter is devoted to the clarification of syntactical matters arising from the analysis of the selected texts. The focus of syntactical analysis on the legal prescriptions occurs in the course of demonstrating the second component in the process of abstraction; the identification of common elements in a body of laws proceeds from an awareness of plurality—sets of commands on distinct topics—within the larger corpus. Arguments for topical divisions and sub-divisions within the laws are made with appeal to semantic distinctions and structures of syntax. The fourth chapter undertakes the verification of claims regarding syntax made in the

---

[5] Verses 1–31 and 37–41 in Num 15 may be an exception. Yet, observations of thematic continuity within the chapter are not absent (see Keil and Delitzsch 1865, 104; Davies 1995, 161); particularly forceful and convincing are those put forth by Olson (1996, 91–6). My analysis will draw out even more relationships within the textual corpus.

analysis of the legal prescriptions against the collection of laws in Leviticus and Numbers.

The final chapter of the book draws conclusions from the preceding analyses. The fifth chapter begins with a summary of the mechanics of abstraction and its functions as these are demonstrated in the analysis of the selected texts. Subsequently, the discussion turns to explore the significance of the abstraction of narrative as a literary device in biblical literature, and as a method of thought and experience beyond the practice of reading. The wider implications of the abstraction of narrative as a feature of cognition are contemplated in the conclusion to the book.

THE SETTING OF THIS WORK
WITHIN BIBLICAL SCHOLARSHIP: SOME REPRESENTATIVE VIEWS

The assumption that the laws of Leviticus and Numbers are thematically integrated with the narratives apart from a chronological progression from the events at Sinai toward those on the brink of entering the promised land has not always been made in modern biblical scholarship. In many texts containing laws, the atomistic tendency of approaches concerned with the history of the text raised doubts concerning the thematic coherence of the promulgations as a group. In searching for the boundaries between sources in the text and locating the historical, cultural, and geographical location of various traditions and the socio-literary conventions behind the various forms of discourse, focus fell upon inconcinnities within the final form of the text bearing testimony of its history. In the pursuit of detail and precision in establishing the diachronic dimension of the text, attention, by and large, turned from the final form.

Martin Noth's comment on the selection of laws in Numbers 15, one that is uncharacteristic of the bulk of his work, represents an extreme in the historical criticism of the Hebrew Bible; he denies any purpose behind the selection and placement apart from editorial whim (1968, 6). More recently, scholars concerned with the transmission of the text have turned to the concerns of redactors in bringing textual portions from disparate periods together as a single textual entity. In considering the perspectives of redactors, historical criticism maintains a dual focus upon the elements of diversity in the text constituting the collage of Israel's developing literary traditions, as well as the forces of synthesis and integration bringing the parts together.[6]

A burgeoning stream of scholars seeking to locate the laws of the Hebrew Bible within the context of the surrounding narrative has appeared.[7] The growing interest in methods of interpretation focused upon the aesthetic principles underlying the structure of the text has little concern for the history of the text. This group attempts to understand the redactional aims which have brought the various components together in the final form of the text. It is within the setting of this emerging interest that the present work finds its location. The works of Olson, Sprinkle, and Stahl are three attempts at the synthesis of law and narrative. Collectively, they may be deemed to be representative of the ethos of a larger movement in biblical scholarship within the study of biblical law.

Dennis Olson's treatment of selected legal texts occurs under the auspice of a larger undertaking. He considers the theological framework of Numbers to be a transition from the generation of the exodus to that of the one entering the promised land: a transition on transit through the wilderness. The former generation is that of the census list of chapter one and the list of Numbers 26 enumerates the new generation (Olson 1985, 125). Within this wider framework, as one particular study shows, the laws of Numbers 15 effect a transition of concern from the old to the new generation: a transition already witnessed in the dispossession of the present generation from the promise of land in the narrative of chapters 13–4 (cf. 14:21–5). God's attention, in chapter 15, turns away from the chastisement for the present generation in

---

[6] In the study of biblical law, the use of earlier texts in later ones in order to anchor legal innovations—transformations in legal tradition dealing with circumstances beyond the anticipation of earlier legislation—in the prestige of earlier works has generated much interest. Examples of such application may be found in studies by Fishbane (1985, 1986), Levinson (1991, 1997, 2008) and Stackert (2007).

[7] Surveys of the various approaches practiced within this growing stream of scholarship, especially with regard to narrative, have been written by, among others, Robert Culley (1985) and David Gunn (1987).

chapter 14 to the infusion of hope with the presumptive gesture that the future generation will possess the land indeed (Olson 1985, 172). This transition is inherent to the content of the laws. The conclusion of the laws in Num 15:41 makes explicit reference to the generation of the exodus: the one barred from entrance into the land because of misgivings narrated in Numbers 13–4 (Olson 1985, 171). But the laws are also oriented to posterity by reference to their application in the new country (Num 15:2b) throughout the generations to come (Num 15:14, 15, 21, 23, 38). For Olson, the case of the man caught gathering wood on the Sabbath (Num 15: 32–41) is a case of transgression committed with blatant disregard (with a 'high hand') for divine authority. Details pertaining to the degree of guilt and the specific form of punishment are not anticipated in earlier legal formulations (Exod 31:14; 35:2). The case is an example of an application of an old law in a new setting (Olson 1985, 171). This exercise is essential to the continued affirmation of divine legal proclamation in later generations and, being so, is taken up thus by the theme of transition (Olson 1985, 172). Olson's proposal for a thematic correspondence between chapters 13–4 and 15 rests on numerous keyword associations first observed by Gordon Wenham (הארץ [throughout Num 13, 14; 15:2, 8]; מצרים [Num 14:3, 4, 19, 22; 15:41]; העדה [10 times in Num 13–4; 15:24–5]; סלח [Num 14:19–20; 15:25–6, 28]; ראה [Num 13:18, 33; 15:39]; עין [Num 13:33; 15:39]; תור [7 times in Num 13–4; 15:39]).[8] Repeated words encourage thematic associations within the larger literary complex; the thematic mimicry by the laws in Numbers 15 of events in the narrative of chapters 13–4 is strengthened.[9]

---

[8] The textual references cited by Olson (1985, 171) may be found on p. 126 of Wenham's commentary on Numbers (1981).

[9] Olson also identifies the narrative of Num 16 (the rebellion of Korah, Dathan and Abiram) as another example of sin with a 'high hand' in addition to the transgression of Num 15:32–6 (1985, 173–4). As such, it strikes a note of thematic correspondence with the law of Num 15:30–1.

Joe Sprinkle's study of the function of Exod 20:22–23:33 may be summarized best with a glance at the chiastic structure deemed to be operative in the complex of narrative and law in Exodus 19–24.[10]

A   Narrative, the Covenant offered (ch. 19)
B   General regulations, the Decalogue (20. 1–17)
C   Narrative, people's fear of God (20.18–21)
B'   Specific regulations (20.22–23.33)
A'   Narrative, the Covenant consummated (ch. 24)

The outermost brackets (A, A') show the progression in the narrative portions: the offer of the covenant is accepted by Israel. The center of the chiasmus (Exod 20:18–21), as Sprinkle attests, is a resumptive statement of Exod 19:16–9. The verses of Exod 20:18–21 explain the fear recorded by the narrator in Exod 19:16–19 from the human point of view. For Sprinkle, the placement of the people's fear at the centre of the chiasmus sustains the fear of God, a sense of awe, as the "operating principle" that binds the individual narratives and laws as a unit; the awesome display accompanies the call to a covenantal relationship and motivates Israel's acceptance of it. The placement of an explicit statement about the people's fear at the center is meant to provoke reflection on the proper perspective from which to approach an understanding of the covenant (Sprinkle 1994, 26–7); the fear of God is the appropriate (and perhaps, also the only possible) response to the display of majesty. Entwined amidst the narratives are the laws given as divine speech. The Decalogue is an authorial summary of the specific regulations of Exod 20:22–23:33 placed in the mouth of God.[11] The Decalogue exemplifies the operating principle of the larger narrative complex of Exodus 19–24: it describes the course of behaviour which ought to be the natural

---

[10] The following presentation of Sprinkle's identification of chiasmus in Exod 19–24 is reproduced from p. 27 of Sprinkle's study of the Covenant Code (1994).

[11] Sprinkle's term for this phenomenon is "free direct discourse" (1994, 26). Thematic correspondences displaying the shift toward specifics between Exod 20:2–17 and 20:22–23:33 may be found on pages 25–6.

consequence of a healthy fear of God (Sprinkle 1994, 196).[12] Under the governance of the general operating principle exemplified in the chiasmus of Exodus 19–24, other overlapping chiastic structures lend cohesion to the laws of Exod 20:22–23:33 (Sprinkle 1994, 200–1). As with Olson's reading of Numbers 13–5, the laws of Exod 20:1–17 and 20:22–23:33 are considered exemplars of the thematic forces that hold the surrounding narrative units together.

Nanette Stahl understands the proclamation of law in the Hebrew Bible as occurring at moments of transition in the relationship between humans and the divine. Such moments are fraught with tension: an ambivalence in the nature of the relationship resulting in a complex and even contradictory representation (Stahl 1995, 12). In speaking of such moments, Stahl writes:

> The view that emerges is at the same time optimistic and celebratory yet deeply pessimistic and disillusioned. As presented in biblical narrative, every attempt on the part of the deity to establish a relationship with humanity—or to initiate change after some failure—is fraught with the tension between promise and jeopardy. (Stahl 1995, 12)

In the midst of such tension, law becomes a vehicle for the expression of this duality. Stahl's reading of Exodus 19 in conjunction with the Decalogue in the following chapter for example identifies an underlying tension in the narrative. The narrative represents God's desire for intimacy with Israel (Exod 19:4–5, 6); and, at the same time, the threat of fatality for humans inherent to such proximity to the deity (Exod 19:12–3, 21, 24).[13] The contradiction between these concepts requires synthesis, which takes place through the mediation of Moses (Exod 20:16). According to Stahl, the coexistence of divine immanence and transcendence in the narrative of Exodus 19 is depicted in the

---

[12] Perhaps, this is the gist of the initial promulgations centering on the divine person in the Decalogue (Exod 20:2–11), which Sprinkle considers a summary of the larger legal corpus of Exod 20:22–23:33 (1994, 25).

[13] In both preceding instances, the textual references in brackets are Stahl's (1995, 52).

thematic tension within the Decalogue (1995, 54). The first four prescriptions (Exod 20:3–11) deal with divine majesty and omnipotence in the relationship with Israel. The fifth (Exod 20:12; the commandment to honour father and mother) is transitional: it emulates the divine-human relationship without designating it explicitly. The second half (Exod 20:13–7) deals exclusively with matters pertinent to the function of human society; no direct mention of divine governance is made. In this manner, law imitates, and in doing so designates, the coexistence of contradictory elements in a preceding segment of narrative.

The three aforementioned cases share a concern for the present form of the biblical text combining law and narrative. All seek to identify themes in narratives and to show their intersection with those of the laws. For Olson, Numbers 13–4 and 15 represent a renewal of hope for the new generation. Sprinkle sees awe in the presence of God inspiring Israel's move to seal the covenant in Exodus 19–24. Stahl's reading of Exodus 19–20 uncovers a portrayal of divine immanence and transcendence. Olson and Sprinkle take the added step of appeal to formal devices (keyword associations and chiasmus respectively) for the justification of thematic coherence.[14]

The present work shares the concern for the final form of the text and the identification of themes reflected in the three studies above. However, this study differs in its concern for the concept of abstraction in law, and the concomitant attention to the integration of theme and the aspect of temporal succession in the events of the narrative. For the exposition of the theoretical underpinnings sustaining such a view of narrative, attention now must turn to the

---

[14] In a similar vein of thought, James W. Watts (2007, 103–7) has found a pattern of compliance with divine command in the inaugural sacrifices of Lev 8:1–9:24, reinforced by a verbal refrain alluding to such compliance (Lev 8:4, 5, 9, 13, 17, 21, 29, 34, 36; 9:6, 7, 10). By his observation, apart from the misadventure of Nadab and Abihu, the following narrative of Lev 10:1–20 echoes the theme of compliance (2007, 106–8).

development of the concept of plot in narrative theory.[15] Particularly, the work of scholars collectively identified under the descriptive labels of Russian Formalism and French Structuralism, who have made advances with respect to plot in narrative, will prove fertile ground.

METHOD AND THEORY:
THE CONCEPT OF PLOT IN NARRATOLOGY

To visit the cinema is to experience the art of the storyteller. To describe the experience of a film in order to promote the film is to attend to plot. Without giving the story away in its entirety, one must offer sufficient details from the unfolding action so as to communicate the subject matter of the film. Incidental details are left out in preference for those events depicting pivotal moments in the film, moments of significance for the major theme(s) of the drama. While the summary of the pivotal moments in succession may be accomplished in a single descriptive sentence, one would be hard-pressed to promote the film through a depiction of the complications which produce suspense. The ingenuity of the plot, as it seems, consists of the artistic arrangement of a theme of interest through a chronological sequence of events. When such

---

[15] Narratology, as defined by Bal (1997, 3), is "the theory of narratives, narrative texts, images, spectacles, events; cultural artifacts that 'tell a story.' Such a theory helps to understand, analyse, and evaluate narratives. A theory is a systematic set of generalized statements about a particular segment of reality. That segment of reality, the corpus, about which narratology attempts to make its pronouncements consists of 'narrative texts' of all kinds, made for a variety of purposes and serving many different functions". From Bal's definition of narrative texts and narratology, it may be seen that the theory of narrative casts a wide net, encompassing numerous distinct methods and examining a host of phenomena in narrative texts. The requirements of this study are more particular; the ensuing discussion concentrates on developments in Formalism, Structuralism, and reader-oriented criticism pertaining to the element of plot. The following survey of perspectives on said subject is not exhaustive, but selective of works representative of trends in discourse on the subject.

ingenuity is sufficiently projected through the rhetoric of a review, reviewers strike a note of aesthetic agreement with their audience.

Similarities abound where narrative texts are concerned. In describing the essence of narrative, the outline of its plot is foremost in the mind of one who would attempt to recommend a novel or an epic poem.[16] A summary of a given stretch of narrative would entail the selection of key actions in chronological sequence thought to be representative of the plot within the unit of choice.[17]

---

[16] It is difficult to attempt a description of the concepts underlying the dynamic quality of narrative texts without the use of words pertinent to the subject matter in common usage. However, the disparate use of such terms by various theorists requires further definition for the purposes of this work. Plot, as the term is used henceforth in this volume, is the combination of the element of temporal succession in the events of the narrative and theme. Theme, as already stated, is a statement—a word, phrase or sentence—qualifying a series of events as a constituent of plot. With its bi-partite composite nature, plot is an essential component of narrative texts. This description of plot corresponds with that of Scholes and Kellogg in their chapter on plot in narrative (1966, 207). Where the thematic definition endemic to plot isolates a segment of the narrative text as a unit, distinguishing it from the subject matter of surrounding material, that segment of text is referred to as a narrative sequence. Narratives may be perceived as a series of narrative sequences, each susceptible to summary by reference to theme. The series of narrative sequences are capable of combination at higher levels: a narrative sequence depicting an act of ensnarement (beginning with the laying of a trap, and concluding with capture) may form the closing bracket—as an act of retribution—in a larger block of narrative moving from transgression to punishment.

[17] Henceforth, the term 'chronological sequence' (also 'chronological succession' and 'chronological progression') or any one of its adjectival derivatives (e.g. chronologically sequential) emphasizes the quality of strict temporal succession in the events of narrative without necessarily excluding a thematic unity to the sequence of events. Where the term is used to the exclusion of theme (and hence, the negation of plot), such use will be made explicit in expression or in the context of antithesis to the element of theme. The term 'narrative sequence', in contrast, always refers to a motivated sequence of actions. It should be noted as well that the terms 'event' and 'action' are used interchangeably throughout this

Such considerations led Scholes and Kellogg to define plot "as the dynamic, sequential element in narrative literature" (1966, 207). Turning to the analogy of the comic book, they postulate that a sequence of pictures would have a plot if arranged "in a meaningful manner" with "dynamic sequential" progression. The further qualification "in a meaningful manner" highlights another essential element in the formation of plot: theme. All narratives entail the representation of events in succession. Beyond the sole element of temporal succession in the events of narrative, it may be stated that only those events bound by a descriptive term or clause depicting a theme receive representation in narrative texts. The selection of events is not a random choice of acts related solely by the progression of time. Unrelated acts beyond the boundaries of an established theme must be kept to a minimum or eliminated. The hallmark of plot in narrative is thus "selectivity" and "movement" (Scholes and Kellog 1966, 211). Mere chronological sequence on its own is insufficient for the genesis of a narrative sequence, a stretch of the narrative susceptible to a formulation of theme.

The exclusion of either chronological sequence or theme would cause the degeneration of plot and the narrative would decompose. The loss of chronological sequence would result in the treatise; the loss of theme would leave us with the chronicle. Further qualification for the use of chronological sequence and theme in narrative is required. While the former is essential to narrative, it is possible to present textual units out of the larger chronological sequence of the work as a whole. While the representation of chronological sequence would remain a fundamental component within each unit (and by and large in the entire story), its perception on occasion must follow the reconstruction of the order of events in the world of the text after reading the story to its end. Boris Tomashevsky distinguishes between 'plot' and 'story' by recognizing the ability of the former to take certain units out of the general chronological progression of

---

introductory chapter. Both terms designate the inception of states and actions proper, the building blocks for theme and plot in narratives.

the 'story' in its presentation (1965, 67).[18] A narrator's strategy may account for such deviations.[19] For example, the motive for an

---

[18] This definition of 'plot' in opposition to 'story' is integral to the methods of Formalism, as represented by Shklovsky (1990, 147–70) and Tomashevsky (1990, 66–7). The use of the term 'plot' in the present work maintains a concern for the dynamic element in narrative, without designation of the element of temporal discontinuity in the representation of events in narration. 'Plot' in the present study, therefore, accords with 'story' as deployed by Shklovsky and Tomashevsky. Consequently, the term 'narrative sequence' designates the textual boundaries for a group of events bound by thematic coherence and displaying chronological progression upon the reconstitution of order, after a reader has encountered all the components of the narrative sequence. Tomashevsky's formulations regarding the dynamic quality of narrative follow a similar tack. The element of temporal discontinuity in the order of the presentation of events hardly occurs within the narrative sequences selected for scrutiny in the present work.

[19] Meir Sternberg has provided numerous examples of temporal discontinuity in biblical narrative (1987, 264–320). It is a foundational proposition of the Formalist credo that the mechanics of literary form are the substance of literary art. Endemic to the expression of literary art is an affinity for drawing attention to its own devices. For practitioners of Formalism, interpretation cannot ignore the inner-workings of the medium of communication; attention to the art of narrative is to be aware of its devices (the means by which narrators control the pace of unfolding events and the order in which readers encounter them). Selden and Widdowson's evaluation of Russian Formalism in its formative stages arrives at the conclusion that the movement considered the content of literary works, the plethora of human experience, to be insignificant in itself for the constitution of the work (Selden and Widdowson 1993, 27). These items are merely the raw material from which literary devices fashion a work of art. The Formalist position on the primacy of form over content in the approach to reading may be seen in Shklovsky's proposal that the process of 'defamiliarization' is essential to literary art (Shklovsky 1965, 12–3). The literary piece seeks to lead a reader's perception away from normative modes of comprehension in order to attend to the form of the presentation: the devices, for example, of repetition, tautological parallelism, and the retardation of action in narrative.

action may be withheld in order to create the element of surprise for the reader. Such a device plays with the order of time and cause; the latter is related to theme in that the ultimate goal of the cause-effect sequence exemplifies the theme of the narrative unit.[20] The thematic component receives its full definition at the conclusion of the narrative sequence. As such, causality is the bond that holds each component captive to the full definition of the theme in the narrative sequence. In other words, the causal link between the various events is nothing less than the manifestation of theme through the narrative sequence. While Tomashevsky's distinction between 'plot' and 'story' allows for lapses in the representation of chronological sequence in the presentation of events in narrative texts, it is his identification of causality in narrative sequences that clarifies the syntagmatic expression of theme in narrative sequences. Chronological sequence and theme become mutually dependent when they intersect in narrative. Causality is the bond between the two elements. Narrative sequences, thus, are by definition teleological.

If it is the case in narrative sequences that chronologically sequential actions exemplify themes, then themes impose limits on the sequences. The addition of other actions to a narrative sequence could change the theme of the unit by subsuming the original theme under a wider descriptive term to account for the additional events. In light of such observation, it is easy to see why Scholes and Kellogg, following Aristotle's lead, state that narrative plots require "a beginning, a middle, and an end" (1966, 211). Using the example of historical narrative, they assert that the historian must identify a theme in the past and remove all matters beyond the boundaries of the theme (both within and beyond the period of the subject matter at hand). The thematic boundaries which govern the termination of a narrative sequence also define its beginning. The limits at both ends of a narrative sequence, by virtue of the unit's thematic unity, are quite obvious in the reading process according to Shklovsky:

---

[20] Indeed it is the loss of causality precisely that results in the 'pointless' exposition which, according to Tomashevsky, is the chronicle (1965, 66).

If we consider any typical story-anecdote, we shall see that it represents something complete and finished. If for example, we look at the successful answer by which a person extricates himself from a certain predicament, then we will discover a motivation for the predicament, the hero's answer, and a definite resolution. Such is the structure of stories based on "cunning" in general. . . . We witness here a definite completed circle of plot structure, which at times deploys descriptions or characterizations, but which, in itself, represents something completely resolved. As I have said above, several such stories may form a more complex structure by being incorporated within one framework, that is, by being integrated into one plot structure. (Shklovsky 1990, 68)

The "completed circle of plot structure" becomes quite recognizable in the reading process because of the pronounced complementary nature of either extremity in the narrative sequence.[21] Consequently, following Shklovsky's observations, the integration of such a structure within a wider framework would require the genesis of a more complex overarching structure. Such an identification of a new narrative sequence would include additional events preceding and following the narrative sequence covered by the original formulation.

In view of the bi-polar nature of narrative sequences and their diachronic expression of theme, theorists seeking to transcribe the structure of narrative often focus on transformations between the states at the poles. Working with biblical texts, Robert Culley has identified, among other varieties, narrative sequences which he terms 'punishment sequences' (1992, 57–63) and 'reward sequences' (1992, 70–1). The transcriptions for the two sequences are in the following respective order: Wrong-Punished; Good Deed-Rewarded (Culley 1992, 58, 70). An example of the first may be found in 2 Kgs 2:23–5. A group of boys insults the prophet

---

[21] The identification of such boundaries as espoused by Shklovsky is, of course, the direct result of authorial "selectivity" as previously described by Scholes and Kellogg (1966, 211), and Tomashevsky (1965, 66).

Elisha, the prophet pronounces a curse upon them, and then a bear attacks the youth. The narrative sequence begins with an action identified as a transgression. This deed sparks a causal sequence leading to retribution. Culley's transcription represents the diachronic (as well as, through the experience of reading the text, syntagmatic) and bi-polar structure of the narrative sequence. The naming of the sequence as a 'punishment sequence' expresses the theme of the unit. Similarly, the appellation 'reward sequence' aptly describes the theme in Exod 2:15–22 (an example of the second transcription from above). Moses assists the daughters of a Midianite priest at a well, and he is subsequently rewarded with one of the daughters as a bride. The diachronic progression is similarly expressed by Culley's transcription as a movement from a good deed to a reward (1992, 71).

Culley's proposal that a narrative sequence is a bi-polar sequence with the second element fulfilling the expectation raised by the first along a causal nexus (Culley 1992, 53) demonstrates the relationship between chronological sequence and theme along with the restrictions imposed by theme in narrative sequences. Further critical examination of theoretical formulations of narrative structure focuses on the procedure for the combination of events (or groups of events) within narrative sequences. While present discussion has established the bi-polar structure of narrative, attention must turn now to the movement between the poles.

THE MOVEMENT BETWEEN THE POLES

The work of Claude Lévi-Strauss on myths and the development of his ideas in the work of A.-J. Greimas clarify the nature of the journey between the poles. Lévi-Strauss begins with the observation that entities in binary opposition often compose the "universe of the tale" (1976, 135). Within these mythic narratives, individual concepts take their semantic significance in opposition to another concept. In analyzing the narratives of the Plains Indians, he takes the pair 'eagle-wolverine' to signify the opposition of a celestial predator and a chthonic hunter (Lévi-Strauss 1976, 136). In opposition with a different element, the image of the eagle would have different significance. For example, the pair 'eagle-owl' might instead project the contrast of a daytime predator with a hunter by night.[22] Projecting such a relationship upon the syntagmatic progression in myths, Lévi-Strauss proposes that narratives may be understood as transitions between pairs of concepts in binary opposition. The transition becomes a way of mediation between two contrary concepts. In a critique of Vladimir Propp's work on Russian folktales, Lévi-Strauss identifies Propp's sequence Prohibition-Violation as a pair in binary opposition: the violation is a reversal of the prohibition (Lévi-Strauss 1976, 137). The two elements define a sequence in tandem whereby—not unlike aforementioned observations by Shklovsky and Culley—the second member corresponds to the first as a complementary half. Elsewhere, Lévi-Strauss analyses the Oedipus story as giving expression to the binary oppositions 'over-emphasized bonds of kinship' versus 'de-emphasized bonds of kinship', and 'chthonic genesis of humanity' versus 'autochthonic genesis of humanity' (Lévi-Strauss 1967). While the interest of Lévi-Strauss has to do

---

[22] Structuralism, a movement with which Lévi-Strauss and Greimas identify, brings the study of literature within the purview of Semiotics, the study of the process of signification. The contribution of Structuralism is the postulation that the transaction between 'sign' and 'signified' occurs within a network of relations, which the reader brings to the process of reading. An illustration offered from traffic control is the role of the sign of a red light within the network of red, green and yellow lights, which a driver must comprehend (Selden and Widdowson 1993, 105). The signified values—'stop', 'go', and 'prepare to stop'—similarly occur within a network where each entity receives its definition with reference to the others. The quality of *différance*, the realization of a concept within a system of opposition, is central to Structuralism. Where the chain of events in narrative is concerned, the functional relationship of an act of transgression to one of retribution differs from its relationship to an act of exoneration. The first set of binary concepts tells a story of judgement; the latter outlines a story of escape. For a concise description of the foundational concepts behind structuralist methodology, see Gregor Cambell's entry "Structuralism" in *Encyclopedia of Contemporary Literary Theory: Approaches, Scholars, Terms* (1993).

with contrary, or even contradictory, concepts inherent to the cultural and mythological constructions of various human groups (customary conceptions often beyond the immediate motivational logic of the text), his basic proposal of an initial concept being integrated and transformed into a contrary concept in the mythic process, as it will be seen, may be applied to narrative texts as a literary tool for analysis.[23]

A.-J. Greimas takes up and expands upon the work of Lévi-Strauss in his construction of an actantial model for narrative texts consisting of actantial pairs in binary opposition (Sender vs. Receiver; Subject vs. Object; Helper vs. Opponent).[24] The driving force behind the movement between the binary pair of a narrative sequence may be perceived as the subject's desire for the object value. An application of the Greimasian actantial model in Hebrew narrative may be seen in Jobling's reading of 1 Samuel 13–31 (Jobling 1978, 4–25).[25] The character David's (Subject) quest for the object value of kingship is the driving force behind the narrative:

---

[23] Shklovsky, with justification, argues strongly against such methods which take their bearing from socio-economic forms and religious conceptions at the expense of plot development within the story itself (1990, 18–20). He refers specifically to the attempt by some to explain Odysseus' hidden presence in a room full of contestants for his wife's affection as a depiction of the custom whereby a man's relatives have a right to his wife's affections. Shklovsky's counter-argument seeks an explanation for the rage of Odysseus which would seem out of place in such a depiction of custom (1990, 20).

[24] The adoption of a system of binary oppositions in the structure of narrative by Greimas is explained in essays from the two volumes *On Meaning* (1987, 63–83) and *Structural Semantics* (1983, 222–56). Detailed description of his actantial model for narrative may be found in the same works (1987, 106–20; 1983, 197–221).

[25] The following diagram comes from p. 15 of Jobling's book (1998). It has been modified to clarify its relation to the actantial model defined by Greimas (the actantial roles are within brackets).

Yahweh (Sender)—Saul's kingship (Object)—David (Receiver)

Philistines, Jonathan (Helper)—David (Subject)—Saul, Jonathan (Opponent)

Sender initiates the action by conveying Object to Receiver. Subject, who is the protagonist is assisted by Helper and opposed by Opponent. These actantial roles may be assumed by more than one personality or even by non-persons, since the roles are viewed as abstract actantial forces within the narrative. According to Jobling's application, the character Jonathan falls within both categories Helper and Opponent. As an aide to David he assumes the role of the former; but when he is identified with Saul as his heir, he stands as an opponent to David.[26] Just as the actants in the narrative sequence occur as classes in binary opposition, so do formulations for states of affairs at each end of the narrative sequence: the binary concepts in opposition which sustain the narrative are two-fold:

1. Human monarchy is alien to Yahwism, but
2. Israel is a human monarchy under Yahweh.

1. Monarchy is inherently dynastic, but
2. Israel's monarchy is not traced from her first king. (Jobling 1978, 17)

In both formulations David's quest for the throne is mitigation between the opposing statements, a smoothing over of an otherwise blatant contradiction.[27] Jonathan's role is especially

---

[26] Jobling points to several cases (1 Sam 16:21, 22; 17:57; 19:7) where Jonathan's regal appearance stands as an indication of his opposition, in terms of plot, to David's quest for the throne. In contrast, 1 Sam 20:13 shows an abdication on the part of Jonathan in David's favour (Jobling 1978, 13).

[27] Elsewhere, Greimas's examples of binary opposites sustaining narrative sequences seem less contradictory and more complementary. Consider the pairs 'mandating' versus 'acceptance' and 'communication' versus 'reception'. The sense of binary opposition as used by Greimas covers both relationships depicting the forging of a semantic entity in

pronounced in the second formulation regarding dynastic succession. The rules of dynastic succession exclude David as a candidate for the throne. An exception occurs when a monarch exercises the initiative to abdicate in favour of another; Jonathan, in his capacity as heir, performs this abdication for David's benefit (Jobling 1978, 17–18). The journey from Saul's decline to David's ascension is a journey of mediation between the opposing propositions which sustain the narrative with Jonathan as the instrument of mediation.

Jobling's application of theories formulated by Lévi-Strauss and Greimas is informative in two aspects. Firstly, the actantial model proposed designates opposing forces competing for alternative conclusions to the narrative sequence. This fact is clear from the actantial opposites Helper and Opponent; each party seeks to negate the purposes of the other in order to establish its own. A second significant factor is that the existence of such opposing forces in a narrative sequence implies the existence of moments of risk in the narrative, points where one alternative is eliminated in preference for the other. These points carry the burden in the definition of a narrative's theme. Will a narrative sequence depict an act of justice or a miscarriage of justice, obedience to prohibition or defiance?[28] The theories of Boris Tomashevsky and Roland Barthes regarding the graded progression of plot in narrative take up these observations.

Perhaps Tomashevsky's attempt (1965) is the first to describe a system of graded movement in a narrative sequence. He begins by reducing narratives to their smallest thematic elements; he names these units 'motifs' and distinguishes between 'bound

---

correspondence with one another. For a summary and application of Greimas's method of analysis for narrative, see Jean Calloud's *Structural Analysis of Narrative* (1976). A list of various binary oppositions in narrative sequences is supplied on pages 17 and 18.

[28] Culley's transcription of narrative sequences comes to mind. The designation of theme, as encoded in the name of the sequence, is wholly dependent on the quality of the second member in the sequence, the decisive indicator of the final state of affairs.

motifs' and 'free motifs' (1965, 67–8).[29] The former are essential to the portrayal of plot and, consequently, to a summary of the narrative. Free motifs may be omitted in summary. Among bound motifs, Tomashevsky distinguishes between 'dynamic' and 'static' motifs: the former bring change to the situation in a narrative by advancing its designated theme; the latter do not (1965, 70–1). Dynamic motifs are bound motifs by virtue of the fact that they alter the direction of the plot and, in doing so, define the theme. Static motifs may be bound or free. While static motifs are often free because they offer no change in the situation, one must acknowledge that the initial bound motif must be static since it stands at the beginning of the sequence establishing the initial situation. Tzevetan Todorov likens the static motif to an adjective, and the dynamic motif to a verb (1981, 51–2). While the verb depicts motion, the adjective declares a state. Whereas bound motifs form the skeletal outline of a narrative sequence, free motifs are attached to a preceding bound motif offering an expansion of the bound motif, forestalling advancement to the next bound motif (Tomashevsky 1965, 69). The free motif represents an identifiable event (capable of receiving thematic qualification) or series of events offering movement in the story without the advancement of the plot. The free motif is often subordinate to the preceding

---

[29] Tomashevsky defines the motif simply as the smallest irreducible component of "thematic material" in a narrative: the on-set of evening, the slaying of an old woman, the death of a hero (Tomashevsky 1965, 67). Presumably, the term refers to the smallest unit of theme in narrative, beyond which further division is impossible or impractical. While the relationship of motifs as thematic components within narratives is maintained, the use of the term in the present work in the formulation of a series of motifs does not negate the possibility of further reduction into component parts. Motifs are the component parts (thematic qualifications for events or groups of events) of a narrative sequence. The thematic appellation for the narrative sequence may in turn constitute a single motif within a series making up a larger narrative sequence. Motifs, as conceived within this study, exist within relationships of subordination to specified narrative sequences. The use of the term here does not imply that the unit of action represented is the smallest irreducible member in a hierarchy.

bound motif—being susceptible of classification as a component of the bound motif—without removing any element of risk standing to block the path to the completion of the narrative sequence.

Shklovsky offers an example of the function of plot retardation endemic to the occurrence of the free motif (1990, 30–1) in a tale of a rooster and a hen. The narrative sequence is suspended between the incident of the rooster swallowing a pin, and the resolution to that problem through the swallowing of water. Between these acts, the hen runs to the sea to seek water where it is told to procure tusks from the badger in exchange for the water. The hen proceeds to the badger who demands acorns in exchange for tusks. This pattern is repeated until the demands of one of the parties down the line of hosts to the suppliant is satisfied. The hen, through a process of reversal which supplies each trading party with its demand, secures the water. The initial effort of the hen is the inception of the solution to the problem; it constitutes movement toward the resolution for the problem. The attainment of the water marks a second increment in the movement toward resolution. However, everything in between these two points retards the movement of the hen's initiative prolonging its consummation; this is a function of the free motif. The intervening material may be summarized as the hen's effort to procure water, an extensive repetitive expansion of the initial act of visiting the sea which is a bound and dynamic motif.

Tomashevsky's system exposes the graded movement of plot within a narrative sequence by identifying the pivotal moments in the narrative sequence. Following this initial effort, Roland Barthes offers a similar description of movement between the poles of a narrative sequence with at least one advantage. Barthes makes an initial distinction between 'functions' and 'indices'. 'Functions' designate the sequence of events in narratives; these form a syntagmatic series. 'Indices' point to concepts of a non-sequential nature: matters pertaining to personality and atmosphere that stand alongside the sequence of events (Barthes 1975, 246–7).[30] Within

---

[30] It is possible, of course, for an event to act as both 'function' and 'index' in the narrative. Consuming a shot of bourbon may be part of a

the category 'functions', Barthes further distinguishes the two sub-categories of 'nuclei' and 'catalyses'. These correspond respectively with Tomashevsky's bound and free motifs. As pivotal moments in a narrative sequence, nuclei open, maintain, or close an alternative route for the continuation of the narrative. As such, nuclei represent moments of choice on the part of the author (Barthes 1975, 248). Using the example of a telephone ringing, Barthes identifies the ringing of the telephone and the picking up of the receiver as nuclei in a brief recognizable narrative sequence. The alternative to the second nucleus which is to leave the telephone unanswered would take the narrative along a different route. The alternative to the first (the telephone does not ring) would eliminate the entire narrative sequence as it stands. Every action in between the nuclei (e.g. the setting down of a cigarette, rising from the chair) is a catalysis; these actions may be multiplied to extend the duration between nuclei. According to Barthes, catalyses prolong the tension of a narrative sequence, delaying the fulfillment of meaning in a designated segment of the narrative sequence; this description of the function of catalysis accords with Tomashevsky's understanding of the function of free motifs. Catalyses postpone the definition of the narrative sequence by multiplying the distance between nuclei (in a sequence of more than two, each nucleus represents an increment towards the ultimate definition of the narrative sequence). In accordance with the proposal of Scholes and Kellogg regarding selectivity and movement in narrative, Barthes's description of nuclei identifies meaning in a narrative sequence with the conclusion of that sequence. In keeping with insights gleaned from the actantial model of Greimas, the proposal by Barthes accomplishes definition for the narrative sequence through the elimination of alternative possibilities of realization which may be suggested within the narrative sequence.

Over Tomashevsky's formulation, the advantage of the method of Barthes is its identification of the vantage point from which a reader identifies a narrative sequence. For Barthes, the naming of a sequence occurs when a sequence of nuclei coheres

---

narrative sequence depicting a meeting over drinks (function), as well as designation for the socio-economic status of the consumer (index).

under a descriptive term.[31] He cites the example of ordering a drink, receiving it, consuming it, and paying for it (Barthes 1975, 253). The preceding series designates a closed sequence because the addition of anything prior to ordering the drink and posterior to paying for it would depart from the label *consommation*. Barthes, essentially, describes the process of determining the theme of a narrative sequence; the name of a narrative sequence is the expression of its theme, the statement of description encompassing the procession of events between the poles of a narrative sequence. In the formation of larger units of narrative, the name of a narrative sequence may be taken up as a component within another narrative sequence, a second term encompassing a larger chunk of narrative text. Barthes assigns the series Encounter-Solicitation-Contract the name Request. As a function, Request finds its fulfillment in the consequent function Aid.[32] Request, in turn, may be reduced to its composite nuclei: Encounter-Solicitation-Contract. A nucleus of Request, the series of events covered by the name Encounter, spawns its own composite nuclei: Approach-Hailing-Greeting-Installation.

---

[31] Todorov would write the thematic coherence of the individual nuclei into the formulation of narrative structure. Todorov's system is built on the analogy of the sentence. The pivotal functions (Tomashevsky's 'bound motifs') of a narrative sequence are formulated as propositions with subjects and predicates (adjectival ['static', by Tomashevsky's definition] or verbal ['dynamic', by Tomashevsky's definition]). For Todorov, the complete sequence consists of five propositions with static propositions at each end. The initial proposition defines a stable situation which is subsequently disrupted; the narrative ends with a static proposition which is the reestablishment of a stable condition. The final situation is not identical to the first; but neither are the two completely different (Todorov 1981, 51). The predicate of the final proposition must be an incomplete repetition (or, as he prefers, transformation) of the first. The grammatical and lexical similarity, by Todorov's design, reflects thematic coherence; the difference shows movement within the narrative sequence (Todorov 1971, 233).

[32] The diagram below is adapted from one occurring on p. 255 of the essay by Barthes (1975).

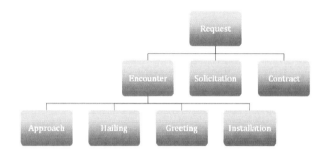

The diagram above outlines a hierarchy of concepts: each member in a series of nuclei subordinate to an overarching descriptive term in turn governs its own series of nuclei. The ascent of the hierarchy entails the encounter of descriptive terms covering increasingly larger segments of events in the narrative.

The nature of the task of reading described so far in following the arguments of Culley, Tomashevsky, and Barthes is to name a narrative sequence and to identify its nuclei at the conclusion of the narrative sequence. Noteworthy is the fact that the application of a label may occur also in the course of reading through a narrative sequence. Keeping the example of Request by Barthes, it may be seen that the alteration of the final nucleus from Contract to Refusal (Encounter-Solicitation-Refusal instead of Encounter-Solicitation-Contract) would produce a new name for the sequence: Rebuff instead of Request.[33] Should Aid still follow further on in the story, the newly named narrative sequence Rebuff would fall away as a nucleus of Request. Rebuff and Request are thus mutually exclusive functions in mutually exclusive narrative sequences occurring as alternative possibilities for readers making their way through the narrative. A reader could conceive of numerous mutually exclusive thematic propositions in the course of the narrative sequence apart from the negation of a thematic

---

[33] Admittedly, the choice of the term Request is somewhat misleading as its application assumes assent on the part of the party receiving the request.

proposition.[34] The generation of numerous labels beginning with the identification of Encounter as a nucleus is possible. These projected labels would fall away in the process of reading to leave one label at the conclusion of the narrative sequence. Furthermore, the possibility of coexistent labels sharing one or more nuclei (in name or by virtue of the fact that the labels encompass the same events) in a narrative sequence also exists. This fact increases the task of readers from choosing between single possibilities in mid-sequence to choosing between groups of possible labels. A request including a response could also be a narrative sequence functioning as a test of character. The group of events previously labeled Solicitation and Contract would be renamed Inquiry and Affirmation respectively with the act of solicitation functioning as a tool for discernment. The subsequent agreement in response to the act of solicitation ascertains the character of the party receiving the request for assistance:

Request	Discernment (of character)
Encounter-Solicitation-Contract	Encounter-Inquiry-Affirmation

---

[34] Moving away from the Formalist dictum of literary device being tied to literary form in texts, Structuralists insist that readers work in partnership with the prompting of texts in endowing meaning upon sequences of events in narrative. Authors and readers draw upon a plethora of structures and codes supplied by literary sources and the wider experience of human culture (Selden and Widdowson 1993, 103). The postulation by Barthes of orchestrated projections for the final shape of a narrative sequence clearly envisions an active role for the reader. As a movement, reader-oriented theories of literature rise as a reaction to the treatment of literary texts as objects that could and should be interpreted apart from the reader's experience of reading (Schellenberg 1993, 170). Interpretation, on the contrary, is subjective navigation within limits set by texts and/or communities of interpretation. In evaluating the response of a reader, Stanley Fish (1980a, b), for example, argues for meaning in the text as an event, not an object. Critics must therefore anticipate a reader's misconceptions and tentative conclusions based on inadequate data in the course of reading.

The positive outcome of the quest for help (also functioning as an inquiry of character) brings a promise of assistance (Contract) as well as the identification of a helper (Affirmation). Thus conceived, the initial nuclei in a sequence are susceptible of becoming components of a narrative sequence with a different label either by keeping their names or only their content, the events covered by the labels. Different labels dwell upon different, but compatible, aspects of theme in the same narrative sequence. The exercise of generating mutually exclusive and coexistent labels for narrative sequences with their component nuclei shows the intricate operations at work in a reader's mind in the course of a narrative sequence.[35] Examples from literature are abundant.

Detective stories often encourage the production of mutually exclusive labels and coexistent labels for narrative sequences in the initial description of a crime. In the course of the narrative, a reader may be led to adopt a false rendition of events or to focus on a rendition of less importance; consequently, readers place false labels onto, or overlook labels for, narrative sequences which would otherwise explain a crime.[36] As a rule, indeterminacy remains

---

[35] Literary convention may intercede in order to exclude certain options. Todorov, in commenting on *The Quest for the Holy Grail*, observes that the exploits of Galahad never end in failure (1977, 130–1). From the beginning he is designated as "the Good Knight, the invincible, the one who will complete the quest of the Grail, the image and reincarnation of Jesus Christ" (Todorov 1977, 131). For Todorov, it is the logic of ritual that governs such narrative types (1977, 133). The narrative is merely the constitution of "a rule which is already present", an exposition of that which is foretold.

[36] For Tomashevsky, such orchestrated mis-readings are a confusion regarding motivation (1965, 80). It is possible to make the further distinction between the (mis-)guided adoption of false motivation and the projection of a line of motivation coexistent with the descriptive label that comes to the forefront later on in the story. The coexistent label—the descriptive term denoting the projected line of motivation—conceals the 'truth' (the description for the series of events that comes to apply later in the story) through its immediate availability to the reader through innuendo in the course of reading.

at the end of the initial portrayal of the crime; the labels remain obscure.[37] As noted by Todorov, the detective's exposition consists of a return to events previously narrated (1977, 135). Details are corrected or explained in greater depth in order that the true significance of various narrative sequences may come to light. Dangling motifs set loose in the course of the narrative are confirmed or debunked. New labels characterizing narrative sequences replace or come alongside old ones picked up previously.

In biblical texts, chapter eight of 1 Samuel presents an example of coexistent labels applicable to part of a narrative sequence. The narrator's notation of the crimes of Samuel's sons in verse three leads us to believe that Israel's request for a king is solely an appeal for the removal of corruption in leadership. God's interpretation in verse seven identifies an illegitimate parallel motive behind the request: the rejection of Israel's God as king. The same act of speech by the elders, a pivotal point in the narrative sequence, receives two different but compatible characterizations (the removal of corrupt leadership may be retained as a real concern in spite of the darker agenda) with the first obscuring the second by its initial prominence. Coexistent labels for the same act lead to coexistent labels for the narrative sequence of 1 Samuel 8 as a whole; it is both appeal and rebellion in the same stroke with divine concession at the end. By the

---

[37] The knowledge that the conclusion of the initial description will yield few conclusions increases the reader's propensity for the generation of possible scenarios from the scattered clues in the course of the narrative. In fact, the preference for the least likely solution displayed by the genre pushes for an increase in the number of formulations to include those on the margins of likelihood. Within the genre of the detective story, the pleasure of the reader lies at the confluence of anticipation (from within the initial narration of a crime) and retrospection (at the conclusion of the final exposition). In line with the opinions of Iser (1980, 52–7) and Fish (1980b, 70–82), it may be affirmed that the experience of reading is a process, an entanglement in the web of shifting interpretative perspective.

conclusion of the narrative sequence, both labels are formed and set side by side as coexistent elements of the text.[38]

The generation of hypothesis in the process of reading is anticipated in the category of operation designated as the 'hermeneutical code' by Barthes. In contrast to his 'proairetic code' which classifies groups of events under a term of description at the conclusion of a narrative sequence, the 'hermeneutical code' encompasses all suggestions of enigma in the process of reading (Barthes 1974, 19, 62, 75–6). The hermeneutical code, therefore, attends to the arousal of desire for conclusion and solution.[39] The

---

[38] The suggestion that readers generate labels in digesting the content of narrative sequences is not a facile reduction of narratives to bearers of singular, non-negotiable meanings. This is evident from the case just seen. In keeping with the approaches of Poststructuralist literary commentary, Barthes deemphasizes the traditional conception of the role of the 'author' in the genesis of meaning, opting for a model that shares that responsibility with readers. Readers do not discover preexisting significance in texts, they are 'scriptors' engaged, along with writers, in an on-going production of meaning endemic to, and evolving through, every reading of a text. Scriptors become the venue where texts previously read coalesce, generating a veritable source of words and ideas capable of drawing out latent, even contradictory, meanings in the text under scrutiny through interaction (Barthes 1981, 37; Barthes 1986, 53). The meaning of a text, for Barthes, is never fixed, and various readers are engaged in incessant bouts of negotiation between various groups of texts in the quest for meaning in acts of interpretation. Frank Kermode, following the lead of Barthes, sees the modern novel as the apogee in the design of polyvalent texts that elicit projections of coherence, even as they frustrate closure in such projections (1983, 81–2). Readers remain suspended. Such is the power of literature to ask questions about life without supplying definite answers, and, as Kermode states elsewhere, to lead readers to examine the modes of deception in discovering inconcinnities in their projections of meaning (1983, 105–6). As Barthes has pointed out, all texts admit a degree of polyvalence. The third chapter of this volume, specifically, explores multiplicity in the interpretation of passages of narrative and law.

[39] Jonathan Culler's description of this desire for conclusion is well illustrated: "After a severe quarrel hero and heroine may either be

maintenance of the enigma is the exacerbation of the desire: the distancing of answer from question, of predicate from subject (1974, 76). When applied to the unfolding of a narrative sequence with an identifiable label at its conclusion, the hermeneutical code governs every readerly conjecture prior to the terminus.[40]

In brief, it may be said that the observations on the graded movement of plot through the critical review of theoretical models for narrative structure are significant for the study of the interaction between narratives and legal texts in Leviticus and Numbers. Following the working hypothesis that a series of legal prescriptions may collectively portray an identifiable theme in a proximate narrative sequence, it becomes important that a method of identifying theme in narrative sequences be set in place. The identification of pivotal points (Tomashevsky's 'bound motifs' and the 'nuclei' of Barthes) in a narrative sequence with an identifiable descriptive term designating the thematic accomplishment from one end of the narrative sequence to the other is such a method.

---

reconciled or go their separate ways, and the suspense which the reader may feel at such moments is, structurally, a desire to know whether the quarrel is to be classified as a testing of love or as an end to love. Though the action itself may be presented with all the clarity he could wish, he does not yet know its function in the plot structure. And it is only when the enigma or problem is resolved that he moves from an understanding of action to an understanding or representation of plot" (Culler 1975, 211).

[40] As noted by Culler (1975, 210), Bremond confuses the hermeneutical code and the proairetic code in his insistence that a model for narrative structure include the possibilities at each moment of choice (1964, 20–3; 1966, 66–7). For Bremond, the elementary sequence consists of three points: *virtualité, actualisation,* and *but atteint.* The last two are points of bifurcation; the opposite possibilities that the potential is not actualized and that actualization encounters failure are included in Bremond's scheme. While Bremond's essays are a reminder of mutually exclusive thematic formulations in the process of reading, it averts confusion to consider the classification of alternative narrative sequences in the course of reading apart from each other, and apart from those established at the end of the narrative sequence.

The efforts of Tomashevsky, Barthes, and, to a lesser extent, Culley are representative of the aforementioned method. Due to the fact that the task at hand merely requires the identification of thematic concepts that hold a series of actions and states together as identifiable units of meaning in the course of reading, more ambitious schemes which correlate actantial roles (Greimas, Jobling) and transcribe narrative structures strictly according to the grammatical constraints of the sentence (Todorov) are not necessary.

The sequential perspective (the difference between Barthes's 'proairetic' and 'hermeneutical' codes) from which a postulation of theme comes will be significant in the following textual analyses as well. The precedence of a group of prescriptions to a narrative sequence invites readers to impose upon the narrative sequence the overarching theme of the prescriptions. The application of the theme would be formulated as a question through the course of the narrative. In contrast, the reversed sequence (with the precedence of the narrative sequence) would be similar to an operation in accordance with the function of the proairetic code espoused by Barthes; the theme of the laws may be imposed as a coexistent theme or a corrective to that expressed at the conclusion of the narrative. In either case, the application occurs after a reader has read through the narrative sequence. Where thematic conjecture finds confirmation (or negation) at the end of the narrative sequence or in the thematic expression of a following set of laws, interaction between the two 'codes' occurs. Complications in this interactive process (for example, when conjecture from within the narrative sequence finds confirmation, not at its conclusion, but in a set of laws outside the narrative sequence) produce the rich texture of the text which is the conflict of divergent perspectives of interpretation.[41]

---

[41] The brief analysis of 1 Sam 8 outlined one such complication. There, duplicity on the part of Israel's elders was shown by the clash of interpretative perspectives (taking divine perspective as dominant over those of the elders). In the hypothesis regarding the role of law within narrative, the thematic expression of a set of laws following a narrative sequence may stand as a corrective to a more ambiguous thematic

THE EXPRESSION OF THEME
APART FROM NARRATIVE SEQUENCE

It has been said that a series of laws with an identifiable theme may bear thematic resemblance with a proximate narrative sequence. The discussion thus far has described the structural collaboration of chronological sequence and theme in the formation of plot in narrative. It remains to be explained how thematic structure in narrative sequences may be reconfigured as prescriptive clauses. Since the focus of our task is the description of a relationship between types of discourse (narrative and law), the transferability of theme between the different vehicles for its expression is significant.

It has been noted by Todorov that an entire narrative sequence may be substituted for another (1981, 52). The process is not unlike the occurrence of a relative clause providing qualitative elaboration on a preceding noun phrase (Todorov 1977, 71). Within the structure of a story, a secondary narrative proceeding from the mouth of one of the characters (hence, its subordination to the primary narrative) may mimic thematic structures in the primary narrative in its attempt to characterize events described in the primary narrative. Todorov provides an example from the *Decameron* (1981, 52–3). The character Bergamin travels to a foreign city in response to an invitation to a feast by Messire Cane. The latter cancels the invitation at the last moment leaving Bergamin with the burden of having to pay for his own consumption at the feast. Happening upon Messire Cane on another occasion, Bergamin, having changed the names of the various participants, portrays the aforementioned events in a tale. He adds the fact that the host was so filled with remorse that he compensates his guest

---

expression in the narrative sequence. The course of the narrative may throw up several invitations to conjecture in keeping with the thematic coherence portrayed by the laws; but these conjectures remain unconfirmed at the conclusion of the sequence. Hence the complicated situation arises in that conjecture fails to find confirmation at the end of the narrative sequence, but a set of laws following hint that the reader's initial inclination may not have been off the mark.

with gifts. Messire Cane notes the allusion and compensates Bergamin. The subordinated narrative, through mimicry, explicitly points to a thematic structure in the first part of the primary narrative, the travesty of justice. In doing so, it precipitates remedy through incrimination. This explicit identification of a narrative sequence depicting an act of injustice is the argument calling for its inclusion within a larger sequence with the addition of repentance and compensation. Within such a scheme, as Todorov notes, the subordinated narrative achieves its purpose.

> But what is the internal significance of embedding, why are all these means assembled to give it so much emphasis? The structure of narrative provides the answer: embedding is an articulation of the most essential property of all narrative. For the embedding narrative is the *narrative of a narrative*. By telling the story of another narrative, the first narrative achieves its fundamental theme and at the same time is reflected in this image of itself. The embedded narrative is the image of that great abstract narrative of which all the others are merely infinitesimal parts as well as the image of the embedding narrative which directly precedes it. (Todorov 1977, 72–3)

If it be the case that the thematic mimicry of narrative by another narrative can achieve a pointed argument by a character for a course of action, would not the brevity of a shorter unit of text (a sentence or even a clause) attain greater precision? Could not a sentence or phrase achieve greater prominence by virtue of its intensity, the product of the crystallization of a theme previously spread out over the course of a narrative sequence? Todorov mentions that proverbs are often substituted for narratives as embedded arguments for a thematic structure in the primary narrative. The reader's perception of events in the story is shaped through the timely interjection of a gnomic saying with all the force of a cultural construct of tradition behind it. Todorov also mentions the possibility of a greater degree of coercion achieved through reference to a law in the midst of narrative (1977, 77).[42]

---

[42] Herein lies the distinction between the summary of a narrative sequence for the promotion of a novel and the naming of the sequence

Public perceptions of lawful behaviour, the repository of custom, are brought to bear upon the interpretation of events in narrative. To these thematic abstractions of narrative sequences, Shklovsky, in suggesting that the prophetic statement designates an event in the future as the precursor for a series of acts leading to the fulfillment of the prediction, adds one more example (1990, 54). While the act of prediction may stand at the head of a narrative sequence with its fulfillment at the end, the prophetic statement itself may designate a narrative sequence beginning with a precondition and ending with the completion of the foreseen final state of affairs (when X does Y, then N will come to pass).[43] Where proverbs and prescriptive utterances are concerned, a quick browse through the children's section of a bookstore may yield a series of brief didactic sayings with accompanying narratives for the purpose

---

for reasons of argumentation. The former must preserve, to a certain degree, explicit mention of the 'bound motifs' in order to portray the aesthetic elements of the narrative; the latter need only typecast the narrative under a particular moral/logical category.

[43] See Culley's section on announcement-fulfillment sequences (1992, 71–5). The story of Adrastus and Atys in *The Histories* by Herodotus (*Hist.* 1:34–44) is an example from Greek historiography. Croesus, the Lydian monarch, declines the request of his son Atys for permission to participate in the hunt for the boar of the Mysian mountain-country; a dream of the king foretells the death of his son through the instrument of an iron weapon. The content of the prediction is reported through the explanation of the king for his decision, in addition to the words of the narrator. In response to his son's argument that a boar possesses no iron weapon, the king relents from his restriction. Croesus, in the spirit of caution, sends the suppliant Adrastus to watch over Atys. While the prophetic announcement of death through a weapon of iron offers no explicit outline of an initial state of affairs leading to the fulfillment of the prophecy, the brandishing of spears at the sight of the boar elicits readerly expectation of a tragic consequence in keeping with the prophetic announcement (*Hist.* 1:43). The ill-fated Atys is slain in error by the spear of his designated guardian, Adrastus. The appearance of the weapon poised to strike becomes the opening motif in a narrative sequence named in a prophetic vision of death through an iron weapon.

of illustration: make hay while the sun shines; what goes up must come down; slow and steady wins the race.[44]

Turning to the Hebrew Bible, we find many brief statements of various types which are capable of expansion into narrative sequences. Some of these occur within narrative sequences which exemplify their themes. Two examples will suffice to illustrate the point. The challenge to Baal by Joash to exact retribution for the destruction of his altar in Judg 6:31 contains within its formulation clear designation of a bi-polar structure capable of generating a narrative sequence (ירב לו כי נתץ את־מזבחו). The assumption intrinsic to the jussive clause ירב לו is that an act of transgression against the deity ought to provoke retribution. However, the absence of retribution leaves this prospective narrative sequence unrealized: the initial member (the destruction of Baal's altar) of the prospective bi-polar structure is without retribution as a counterpart. Thus, the challenge to Baal to assume divine status (אם־אלהים הוא) meets with no response. A passage from 2 Sam 12 provides a second case in point. The prophetic pronouncement of 2 Sam 12:14b by the prophet Nathan (גם הבן הילוד לך מות ימות) comes to fulfillment in the following verses. God initiates the fulfillment (v. 15) which David attempts to block through supplication and fasting (v. 16) to no avail (v. 18). The prophetic pronouncement provides a bi-polar structure beginning with birth (הילוד לך) and ending with death (מות ימות) to which the ensuing narrative sequence adheres. In light of the prophetic announcement, the narrator's report on the birth of the child is the harbinger of death in the royal household.

---

[44] Jerome Brunner (2002, 20) refers to such an utterance as a 'coda': "a retrospective evaluation of what it might all mean, a feature that also returns the hearer or reader from the there and then of the narrative to the here and now of the telling". While proclaiming the descriptive function of such utterances, Brunner maintains the possibility, in some cases, of ambiguity within such statements. A precarious balance is struck between clarity and obfuscation, leaving as open the possibility of an "invitation to problem finding" in story-telling as the possibility of "problem solving".

That the legal prescriptions of the Hebrew Bible share the ability of predictive and proverbial statements to summarily condense a narrative sequence into a single clause or sentence is manifest. The clause from Exod 21:12 (מכה איש ומת מות יומת) designates the opening and closing actions of a potential narrative sequence of recognizable thematic coherence; an act of judgement upon a crime. An example of a conditional formulation preserving a similar bi-polar structure capable of sustaining a narrative sequence may be seen in Exod 21:20: וכי־יכה איש את־עבדו או את־אמתו בשבט ומת תחת ידו (crime) נקם ינקם (punishment). While conditional formulations preserve the element of temporal sequence between the protasis and the apodosis, they remain a rough outline (perhaps, only with the bound motifs) for a longer narrative sequence. In both cases, it is the concentration of the theme within a shorter unit of text which makes it explicit.[45] Essentially, all brief statements containing the seeds of a narrative sequence function by removing or reducing to a minimum the element of chronological sequence while retaining the element of theme. Hence, the ability to identify the bound motifs of a narrative sequence (those that define the descriptive label for the sequence) becomes essential in the genesis of proverbial, prophetic, or legal statements seeking to reflect the thematic content of a narrative sequence. All such condensations

---

[45] While much of the work of Calum Carmichael dwells upon the cryptic encapsulation in laws of the subject matter of narrative through figurative modes (see, for example, his chapter "Laws as Miniature Narratives" [1996, 49–61]), his observation of the ability of terse gnomic sayings to capture the essence of a story (1996, 49) pertains to our discussion. It might be noted that the connections Carmichael sees between laws and narratives would be more pronounced if not for the distance between the material. The relationship, for example (see Carmichael 1996, 54), between the exhortation to love one's neighbour (Lev 19:18) and Joseph's willingness to transgress against Egyptian custom in dining with his brothers (Gen 43:32) would be obvious, even certain, with the collocation of the material. Proximity, by Wolfgang Iser's estimation, would set readers on a quest for connections between passages, even picking up on links of greater obscurity (1978, 182).

of narrative explicitly, or implicitly, allude to the graded progression of plot in narrative sequences.

Of course, by implication, not all such condensations of narrative directly designate the bi-polar structure of a narrative sequence. Some of the examples mentioned above only designate one member of the poles; the presence of the other member must be inferred. 'Slow and steady wins the race' only designates the final motif of the narrative sequence: the end of the race. The beginning of the sequence must be supplied by the imaginative efforts of the reader interacting with the concept of a race. This last case is not unlike those without any explicit representation of either extremity in a narrative sequence. In accordance with the proposal by Barthes that any label implies a limited narrative sequence, a law or a proverb would activate a bi-polar narrative structure by mentioning any descriptive term covering such a structure. A commandment against stealing could designate the term 'theft'; implicit to the concept would lie the potential for a narrative sequence beginning with temptation as an event and ending with an act of despoliation. While the explicit designation of a narrative sequence by reference to its bi-polar structure is distinctive, the link with a narrative sequence by reference to an encompassing descriptive label is not impossible.

One last comment on a possible complication in the relationship between narrative sequences and the brief statements which capture their theme, especially with regard to laws, may be made with reference to Lev 10:9. While the inception and conclusion of a narrative sequence is discernible in the law, it must be transformed into a positive statement in order to identify accurately a narrative structure beginning with a transgression and ending with retribution (If you consume strong drink . . . you shall die).[46] The negative formulation of the original prohibition points to a narrative sequence that does not occur. This difficulty arises because of the fact that laws are not primarily concerned with

---

[46] The presumption is that a narrative sequence consisting of a transgression leading to punishment is desired. It would be rare to find a narrative sequence outlining the aversion of penalty through the avoidance of transgression.

describing narrative sequences. If laws designate structures capable of expansion into narratives, these structures are subordinate to the purposes of legal rhetoric. Hence, legal prescriptions following a narrative sequence may prohibit the actions described in that narrative with the addition of the negative particle before the syntactical components designating the narrative sequence. The fact that the proximity of the two textual units betrays a purposeful interactive link demands a degree of flexibility in the method of tracing the correspondence between representatives of the two discourse types.

The examples mentioned suggest a mode of interaction between narrative sequences and laws. The aim is to demonstrate a method for approaching the relationship between the two types of discourse. Specifically, the review of various models for narrative structure seeks to identify a method which is respectful of narrative structure defined in accordance with observations on the graded movement between the boundaries of a narrative sequence, the accomplishment of plot in narrative. It will be seen that the means of thematic abstraction and the syntactical devices employed reveal flexibility within the wide parameters outlined thus far. In the following analysis of specific cases, the passages requiring a greater degree of imagination on the part of a reader come later (ch. 3). Such complications in the act of interpretation are due to pronounced discrepancies between thematic formulations—whether pertaining to those existent upon conclusion, or between those forged mid-way through a passage and at conclusion—occuring within a designated passage. The analysis of passages of narrative and law displaying a higher degree of thematic coherence comes first.

CHAPTER TWO
READINGS IN NARRATIVE AND LAW: THE SIMPLE CASES

The proposition set forth in the previous chapter is that laws may summarise proximate narrative sequences by extracting themes displayed over the course of narrative sequences, and expressing these themes in brief statements (a phrase, a clause or two clauses). On occasion, a second step in the process highlights common aspects of the theme extracted from the narrative by repeating formulations of the theme or accompanying concepts complementary to the theme throughout the body of laws. The common elements of the laws emerge with a higher level of visibility, drawing attention to different aspects of the common theme linking law and narrative. This, in brief, is the abstraction of narrative within adjacent bodies of law. The present chapter proceeds with the description of the procedure of abstraction in passages of law and narrative in Leviticus and Numbers.

By and large, the units of text selected are classified (simple or complicated) according to the degree to which they engage the imagination of the reader in interpretation. Complicated cases are passages requiring greater effort in forging thematic identity between what appear to be discordant parts within the whole; the act of ideation, espoused by Iser, is drawn into application with accelerated rigour. Intimately entwined with the process of interpretation is thematic coherence. The interpretative imagination becomes more absorbed in passages displaying a higher degree of thematic indeterminacy. Thematic coherence in a textual unit is constituted at two levels in the text. At the first level, narrative sequences and legal passages must demonstrate thematic unity apart from each other. At the second level, both types of discourse must combine in the formation of a joint thematic definition.

Failure at one or both of these levels results in the thematic indeterminacy of a textual unit. Where such failure occurs, readers must decide to accept one thematic definition over another mutually exclusive option, effectively designating one discordant element as an orchestrated mis-reading designed to enhance the effect of the final interpretation, where the designated 'correct' reading is revealed. Where the discernment of such an editorial strategy proves impossible, two alternatives present themselves. Readers may choose, as one option, to recognize a haphazard arrangement in the formation of the textual unit. This choice in interpretation understands the passage to consist of disparate topics without any overarching unity in theme. The second option is to seek once again a rhetorical strategy behind the indissoluble thematic antithesis within the passage. Such thematic indeterminacy may signal an invitation to readers to participate in the experience of the interpretative dilemma, effecting a degree of readerly self-examination with a view to the conflicting perspectives in the text. In all the anticipated responses to the thematic indeterminacy of a passage above, the reader's imagination becomes engaged by wrestling with alternative signals of theme emerging from the process of reading. Where the quest for thematic coherence or a reason for dissonance fails within the parameters of the portion of text, the efforts of readers may turn to the examination of the wider context to seek explanation for such perceived thematic inconcinnities.

Efforts to comprehend the mechanics, both semantic and grammatical, behind the combination of narrative and law begin with the cases that require a lesser degree of readerly engagement: the simple cases.

THE CASE OF LEVITICUS 24:10–23

The textual unit of Lev 24:10–23 opens with a quarrel between an individual of mixed ancestry (Israelite and Egyptian) and an Israelite. The former abuses the divine name in the heat of the moment; he is placed under arrest subsequently while the community seeks divine direction in the matter. God issues the command that the culprit is to be executed with the pelting of stones; the community complies with the divine exhortation, and the individual is put to death.

The Wider Literary Setting of Leviticus 24:10–23

Most commentators offer scant suggestion with regard to the place of the textual unit in the predominantly prescriptive material of the book. Wenham (1979, 308–9) and Hartley (1992, 397), for example, refrain from offering an explanation for the placement of this narrative. Both scholars refer to the suggestion that the compiler's arrangement reflects the historical sequence of events, an understanding adopted by Harrison (1980, 220). Harrison's suggestion places the book closer to the realm of the chronicle where strict chronological sequence displaces any concern for theme. In contrast, Bertholet notes that the prescriptions of Lev 24:1–9 stand in contrast with those of the preceding chapter. The laws of Leviticus 23 are concerned with details of worship applicable throughout the year, whereas Lev 24:1–9 prescribes procedures for specific festivals (Bertholet 1901, 83). Presumably, the events and laws of Lev 24:10–23 would come under a similar spirit of contrast against the prescriptions of Leviticus 23.

More recently, Douglas has identified the thematic structure of the book as a whole as being in the shape of a ring (1993, 8–12; with diagram on p. 11). Leviticus 19, a collection of laws mostly having to do with just dealings, stands as the thematic center of the book and the fulcrum in the structure. Leviticus 26 picks up the subject matter of Leviticus 19, and marks a conclusion to the book. Leviticus 27 is a latch that returns the subject matter (on things and persons consecrated to God) to that of the beginning (sacrificial portions [chs. 1–7] and people [chs. 8–9] consecrated to God). Thus, by the end of Leviticus 27, the ring is fully formed. Moving away on both sides from the fulcrum which is Leviticus 19, corresponding thematic units forge symmetrical agreement between the two halves of the ring. Within this arrangement, the unit of Lev 24:10–23 stands in correspondence with the material of chapter ten in the book. The former deals with the desecration of the divine name and the latter, with the desecration of the sanctuary.

Milgrom, in agreement with the assessment of Douglas, points to an additional link between the two narratives. Chapter five describes procedures of rectification for the inadvertent (vv. 14–6) and unwitting (vv. 17–9) desecration of the sanctuary as well as the inadvertent desecration of the divine name (vv. 20–6). Chapter ten narrates the willful desecration of the sanctuary; thus, the textual unit is a thematic complement to Lev 5:14–9 cast in the form of narrative. But this editorial act of completion leaves Lev 5:20–6 (dealing with the inadvertent desecration of the divine name) without a corresponding complementary element. In view of this lack, the narration of the willful desecration of the divine name in Lev 24:10–23 becomes a distant element of completion for Lev 5:20–6, as chapter ten is for Lev 5:14–9 (Milgrom 2001, 2106).

In view of the related functions of Lev 10:1–20 and 24:10–23 (in relation to Lev 5:14–26), an explanation for their separation is in order. Douglas addresses this issue: the narratives (Lev 10:1–20; 24:10–23) represent the screens of the tabernacle in a reader's virtual promenade through the tabernacle in reading Leviticus. In accordance with this structural correspondence between text and tabernacle, the narratives are located at the points where a reader would encounter the partitions between the segments of the tabernacle (1999, 222–31, 241–4; 2004, 149). In accordance with the tripartite division of the tabernacle, the first part of the book (Lev 1:1–17:16) deals with matters pertaining to the court of sacrifice. The second part (Lev 18:1–24:9) contains instructions concerning persons permitted in (Lev 21:1–22:16), and items designated for (Lev 24:1–9), the outer portion of the tent containing the incense altar. The last portion (Lev 25:1–27:34) concerns the redemption of items belonging to the resident of the holiest portion of the tabernacle. In reading through the book, one proceeds toward the inner recesses of the tabernacle. Within such an arrangement, the intrusion of the narratives (Lev 10:1–20; 24:10–23) designates specific locations in the reader's movement around the tabernacle. Thus, both Douglas and Milgrom demonstrate that the placement of Lev 24:10–23 is not random. The passage is thematically integrated, despite being separated from its related portions of text in the interest of literary patterning, the devices of a larger organization of theme.

The Literary Structure of Leviticus 24:10–23

While explanations for the placement of Lev 24:10–23 are few, recognition for its internal structure is abundant. The passage depicts an act of judgement with the laws prescribing retribution for the abuse of the divine name and other transgressions. The thematic expression of the passage may be seen, so noted by Douglas (1999, 206), in the names of the participants and a tribe

(שְׁלֹמִית, דִּבְרִי, and דָּן): all the names include the concept of retribution or judgement. The similar focus of the narrative and the laws on retributive justice prompted Elliger to describe the narrative as an aetiological account for the laws (1966, 330). The same observation leads Bertholet to propose that the narrative is either an expression of the art of Haggada or a Midrash on the laws (1901, 84).

In varying degrees, commentators have pointed also to the chiastic structure from verse 13 onward with the law of talion (v. 20a), a prominent expression of retribution, at the center of the structure. This structure binds the laws closely to a portion of the narrative (vv. 13, 23). Thomas Boys may have been the first to notice chiasmus in the passage.[1] Subsequent notification of this structural feature includes, among others, those of Wenham (1979, 312), Fishbane (1985, 101), Welch (1990, 7–9), Hartley (1992, 405–6), Jackson (1996, 119–20), and Milgrom (2001, 2128–9). The following diagram is part of Milgrom's recent outline of structure in Lev 24:13–23 as seen in his commentary (2001, 2129):

---

[1] John Forbes (1854, 39) cites the observations of Boys.

A   And YHWH spoke to Moses, saying: (v. 13)

    B   Take the blasphemer outside the camp; and have all who were within hearing lean their hands on his head; then have the whole community stone him (v. 14)

       C   And the Israelites speak thus: (v. 15a)

          D   Anyone who curses his God shall bear his punishment; (v. 15b)

                 a   but if he (also) pronounces the name of YHWH, he must be put to death. (v. 16aα)

                     x   The whole community shall stone him; alien as well as citizen, (v. 16aβ, bα)

                 a'   if he has (thus) pronounced the Name, he must be put to death. (v. 16bβ)

          E   If anyone kills any human being, he must be put to death (v. 17)

            F   But anyone who kills an animal shall make restitution for it, life for life (v. 18)

               G   If anyone maims another. as he has done so shall it be done to him: (v. 19)

                   X   fracture for fracture, eye for eye, tooth for tooth. (v. 20a)

               G'   The injury he has inflicted on the person shall be inflicted on him. (v. 20b)

            F'   One who kills an animal shall make restitution for it; (v. 21a)

          E'   but one who kills a human being shall be put to death. (v. 21b)

          D'   You shall have one law for the alien and citizen alike; for I, YHWH your God (have spoken). (v.22)

       C'   Moses spoke (thus) to the Israelites. (v.23aα)

    B'   And they took the blasphemer outside the camp and pelted him with stones. (v. 23aβ)

A'   The Israelites did as YHWH had commanded Moses. (v. 23b)

Milgrom's formulation is unique in its recognition of the internal chiasmus within unit D. The palistrophe sets the prescription which stipulates the death penalty for abuse of the divine name for both native and sojourner (v. 16aβ, bα) at the center of unit D. Unit D' restates the inclusive aspect of the law in unit D within the larger structure of inversion. Without diminishing the central focus of the larger chiasmus (v. 20a), the statement of inclusion within unit D achieves prominence. The prominence of this statement, along with the explicit mention of the culprit's ancestry (v. 10aβ), leads many to consider ancestry as one of the factors prompting Moses to seek divine counsel for an appropriate response (among others, Fishbane 1985, 103; Budd 1996, 337; Milgrom 2001, 2111).

Terms and Definitions

Throughout the examination of the selected texts, the identification of the narrative sequence is confined to those clauses depicting the sequence of events in the passage. The representation of the narrative sequence excludes the legal prescriptions presented in direct speech. The aim of the exercise is to evaluate the interaction of law and narrative; toward the accomplishment of this task, the two types of discourse should be treated separately in the initial stages of the analysis. Also excluded generally in the evaluation of the narrative sequence is the syntactical expression of the non-legal portions of direct speech; these parts of the text will be examined in detail only where they are significant for the semantic structure of the narrative sequence. Here and throughout the study, a distinction is drawn between legal prescriptions and instructions specific to a given occasion in the narrative and confined to specific individuals in application. Legal prescriptions tend to address situations deemed recurrent over an extensive duration involving roles (not individuals) defined by the situation specified.[2]

---

[2] Sophie Lafont (1994, 95), with reference to modern standards, adopts a similar criterion for the identification of legal statements in the ancient Near East: "The idea of a timeless, general and impersonal rule is a feature admitted unanimously by modern doctrine. It helps to sharpen the definition of the law, to catch its technical distinctive aspect. *Stricto*

In general, all forms of direct speech will be excluded from the detailed grammatical and semantic analysis of the text with respect to the descriptive category of a narrative sequence. Notwithstanding this policy, the semantic import of the portions of speech will be noted for the fact that they define the acts of speech reported in the narrative, distinguishing between different thematic appellations (e.g. threat, counsel or judgement). Prior to each discussion, the relevant texts will be presented with the translation of the New Revised Standard Version (NRSV). Deviations from this translation for the sake of clarification in argument will be indicated.

The Hebrew text (MT) will be presented clause by clause. In narrative texts, a textual selection may incorporate more than one narrative sequence. In view of this fact, the notation of verses by numerical reference within parentheses in the translation marks the lower limit of a specified narrative sequence. Although these enumerations of verse occur within the translation, they correspond to the verse numbers of the published Hebrew text *(BHS)* where the latter system of enumeration is not in agreement with the various translations into English. Within the specified narrative sequence, each clause in the Hebrew text of the presentation will receive a number in order to facilitate reference. For the sake of clarity in cross-reference between the Hebrew text and the translation, the portion of the translation corresponding to a specific (numbered) clause in the Hebrew text presented will receive the same numerical value (*without* enclosing parentheses); this number stands at the *beginning* of the relevant portion of the text in translation.[3] A somewhat similar system occurs in the

---

sensu, positive law is general and legislates for the future; it is not a personal or temporary rule." A second criterion hinges upon the authority of the proper institution of the state, a function assumed by reference to divine origins for law in biblical texts. An argument for the laws of the Hebrew Bible as legally binding statements in ancient Israel is beyond the scope of this study. The concern here, merely, is for the definition of a mode of discourse within a larger literary corpus.

[3] Be careful to distinguish within the translation between the numerals designating the narrative sequence, and those designating the translation

presentation of legal prescriptions. A difference lies in the fact that the legal prescriptions will be divided into separate command sets in accordance to the dictates of syntax and semantics (groupings by topic); beyond this single feature of distinction, the format for the presentation of the legal prescriptions is in accord with the format for narrative sequences. Notations of verse numbers in accordance with the printed Hebrew text (*BHS*) occur after each command set in the English translation within parentheses. Within the Hebrew text presented in the adjacent column, each individual clause of every command set receives a number presented without enclosing parentheses, standing before the clause it designates. The corresponding portion of text in the translation receives the same number, standing prior to the portion of text the number designates without enclosing parentheses.

The analysis following the presentation of the text of narrative sequences and legal prescriptions will refer to clauses by the verse numbers designating the command set (within parentheses, occuring at the end of the material they designate), with the numerical reference for the individual clause following within brackets (no enclosing parentheses, standing before the designated clause in the Hebrew text and the corresponding portion of the translation). Independent syntactical constituents are sequences of words occuring without predication. Neither the entire entity nor any of its components is a constituent of a clause, participating as

---

of a designated clause in the Hebrew text presented in the adjacent column. Numerical designations for narrative sequences are within parentheses. These numbers or sequence of numbers occur at the end of the passage they designate; a break in the text follows in cases where more material follows in the presentation. Numbers designating the translation of a clause specified in the Hebrew text presented stand, without enclosing brackets, before the material they designate. The object of analysis is the Hebrew text of the passage. Consequently, the language and grammar of the Hebrew text take precedence over the lexical and grammatical choices of the translation. The numerical designation of the corresponding segment in the translation to the enumerated clauses of the Hebrew text in the display is an approximation, offered as a lexical aid to the Hebrew text.

or with links to the subject, object or modifier within a clause. In this sense, independent syntactical constituents may be said to be independent of a clause. By virtue of their independence from a clause, independent syntactical constituents receive separate numerical designation, setting them apart from the surrounding clauses.[4] Excluded from this category are cases of extraposition. An extraposed member, in contrast to an independent syntactical constituent, is connected with a clause in its immediate vicinity by the presence of a constituent within that clause sharing the same referent as that of the extraposed member. A series of three dashes (–––) indicates the omission of one clause or more in the presentation of the text. In the textual presentation of narrative sequences, these omitted portions are passages of direct speech contributing to the formation of the motivational significance of the speech-act. A series of three dots (. . .) shows that a word or phrase (or even an embedded clause; see below) has been omitted within a clause receiving numerical designation. All abbreviations or remaining specialized use of terms will be explained in the course of the analysis.

Within the chosen scheme of presentation by individual clauses, relative clauses subordinate to words or phrases within a clause are distinguished from clauses subordinate to a clause or a group of clauses; the former are considered embedded clauses offering semantic expansion on an entity within a clause. Relative clauses of such type are presented as constituents of the subordinating clause; these relative clauses occur as part of the subject, object or modifier within the subordinating clause. Relative clauses of this type do not receive numerical notation apart from the clauses containing the constituents governing their subordinate status. The definition of a clause is the minimal syntactical unit where predication occurs. The identifying criterion of predication follows, among others, that of *GBH* (§§44.1.1.1–3) and *BHRG* (§§12.1–5). With regard to the definitive guidelines of *BHRG*, the definition of the clause employed for the present study is confined to the sub-category 'simple sentence' (*BHRG* §12.5.1). The

---

[4] While this feature of the format of presentation is equally applicable in narrative sequences, it simply does not occur in the selected texts.

alternative category 'complex sentence' allows for the combination of two clauses in a relationship of subordination, where the subordinate clause is governed by the entirety of the other clause (not by a specific constituent in the other clause; see *BHRG* §12.1.3). This exclusion of the qualities of the 'complex sentence' is in accordance with the qualification 'minimal' in the working definition of a clause undertaken for the present study.

The Narrative Sequence

The narrative sequence in Lev 24:10–23 consists of a series of ten consecutive imperfect clauses (henceforward, also referred to as wayyiqtol clauses) interspersed by three conjunctive clauses and a subordinate clause.[5]

1 ויצא בן־אשה ישראלית	1 (2) A man whose mother was
(2) והוא בן־איש מצרי	an Israelite and whose father
בתוך בני ישראל[6]	was an Egyptian came out
3 וינצו במחנה בן הישראלית	among the people of Israel;
ואיש	3 and the Israelite woman's son
הישראלי	and a certain Israelite began
4 ויקב בן־האשה הישראלית	fighting in the camp. 4 The
את־השם	Israelite woman's son blasph-

---

[5] Within the present study, the term 'conjunctive clause' refers to a clause employing a coordinating conjunction (ו or או). In the case of ו, the conjunction must not be part of a consecutive verbal form (the consecutive imperfect form or the consecutive perfect form). The term 'consecutive clause' (wayyiqtol clause or weqatal clause) should not imply strict temporal or logical succession in the events portrayed; this connection has been shown to be false in recent studies on the consecutive imperfect clause (Washburn 1994; Buth 1995). The term 'consecutive clause' is a formal category (referring to wayyiqtol and weqatal clauses), part and parcel of Biblical Hebrew grammatical parlance.

[6] This line is part of the first clause in the series. The two portions are separated by the interceding verbless clause of v. 10aβ (10–23 [2]). The parentheses enclosing the numerical designation for 10–23 (2) in the Hebrew text and the translation in the presentation of the narrative sequence indicates the enclosure of 10–23 (2) within 10–23 (1).

5 ויקלל
6 ויביאו אתו אל־משה
7 ושם אמו שלמית בת־דברי
למטה־דן
8 ויניחהו במשמר לפרש להם
על־פי יהוה
9 וידבר יהוה אל־משה לאמר

emed the Name 5 in a curse. 6 And they brought him to Moses— 7 now his mother's name was Shelomith, daughter of Dibri, of the tribe of Dan— 8 and they put him in custody until the decision of the Lord should be made clear to them. 9 The Lord said to Moses, saying:

---

10 וידבר משה אל־בני ישראל
11 ויוציאו את־המקלל
אל־מחוץ למחנה
12 וירגמו אתו אבן
13 ובני־ישראל עשו
14 כאשר צוה יהוה את־משה

10 Moses spoke thus to the people of Israel; 11 and they took the blasphemer outside the camp, 12 and stoned him to death. 13 The people of the Lord did 14 as the Lord had commanded Moses. (vv. 10–23)

Apart from the unit of direct speech introduced by 10–23 (9), the clauses departing from the series of consecutive imperfect clauses are 10–23 (2, 7, 13, 14). Among these deviations from the series of consecutive clauses are conjunctive verbless clauses (10–23 [2, 7]), a conjunctive verbal clause (10–23 [13]; waw-X-qatal)[7] and a subordinate clause (10–23 [14]).

The semantic-pragmatic significance of verbless clauses and waw-X-qatal clauses within chains of consecutive imperfect clauses has been documented well in several studies on Biblical Hebrew syntax focused on structures beyond the clause. Niccacci, in speaking of waw-X-qatal clauses, lists the functions of this type of clause as the provision of antecedent and circumstantial information. The waw-X-qatal clause also may indicate contrast or specification with a preceding clause in a series of wayyiqtol clauses (Niccacci 1997, 172–5). For Niccacci, the verbless clause is the syntactic equivalent of the clause with a finite verb in second

---

[7] The element 'X' represents another constituent of the clause apart from a particle of negation.

position (waw-X-qatal or waw-X-yiqtol); the latter is designated a 'compound nominal clause' by Niccacci (1997, 181). Buth identifies focus and contextualization in narrative as functions of waw-X-qatal clauses (1995, 84–93). In Biblical Hebrew, the function of focus places salient information in a prominent position within the clause.[8] Contextualization, on the other hand, expresses departure from the series of wayyiqtol clauses in order to introduce a new episode; the syntactical element standing prior to the verb may or may not designate the following topic (Buth 1995, 89–90). Also identified by Buth is the designation of a climactic episode by transition from a series of consecutive imperfect clauses to waw-X-qatal clauses. The transition accentuates the peak by retarding the flow of action in the narrative; the effect is not unlike the occurrence of retarded motion in film. The attention of the reader is riveted to the flow of events (Buth 1995, 91). Kotze, in an effort to offer greater definition for the qualification 'circumstantial sentence' as a structural feature of narrative texts, pays attention to any departure from the consecutive imperfect clause. The operative criterion of any formal structure that may render the consecutive imperfect form an impossibility (finite verb in second position, absence of the conjunction ו, or the use of another type of conjunction) brings subordinate clauses and verbless clauses within the purview of his investigation (Kotze 1989, 112).[9] Within narrative, Kotze offers the following as functions for departure from the consecutive imperfect series of clauses: concomitant state of affairs or action; information on an antecedent; particularisation/closer or additional explanation; flashback (Kotze 1989, 121–2). Kotze's analysis of 1 Samuel 1–12 reveals the dominant role of verbless clauses in the enactment of a

---

[8] Niccacci makes a similar distinction (as with Buth's functional category 'focus') by identifying such waw-X-qatal clauses as placing emphasis on the component X. The function of contrast is an example of such a statement of emphasis (Niccacci 1997, 176)

[9] Niccacci's approach to Biblical Hebrew syntax similarly recognizes grammatical subordination (the presence of a subordinating conjunction) as one way of representing discontinuity from the main line in narrative texts (1994a, 127–8; 1997, 198–200).

circumstantial paragraph providing additional information on a character in the narrative. It is evident that the functions of clauses in the narrative sequence of a non-wayyiqtol type have received much attention and definition in existing studies of Biblical Hebrew syntax.

Returning to the passage at hand, it may be observed that the two conjunctive verbless clauses 10–23 (2, 7) offer additional information on characters: the first identifies the blasphemer's ancestry (Egyptian by patrilineal heritage), and the second provides his mother's name, family (the name of the maternal grandfather), and tribe. The first piece of information is significant in that it immediately raises the question as to whether the law against the abuse of the divine name applies in this case. Gerstenberger objects to the relevance of this contingency for the narrative sequence on the basis of the statement of inclusion in Deut 23:9 (1996, 361). However, the analysis of plot in narrative must take into consideration the information available (or not available) at a given point in the literary corpus with regard to the sequential progression in the final form of the biblical text. Prior prohibitions against the inappropriate use (לשוא) of the divine name (Exod. 20:7) and verbal attacks against God (Exod 22:27)[10] do not specify the inclusion of the non-Israelite within the scope of the law. The prohibitions also lack the prescription of a form of punishment for transgression. With regard to the second conjunctive verbless clause (10–23 [7]), it should be noted that the clause alludes to the theme of the narrative sequence as a whole. As previously noted in the work of Douglas (1999, 206), the names שלמית (Retribution), דברי (Lawsuit), and דן (Judgement)[11] are all suitable thematic

---

[10] It is assumed that the object of קלל in 10–23 (5) is God (M. Sanh. 7:5). The divine name is omitted to avoid the collocation of the tetragrammaton and קלל. The law in v. 15 (within direct speech introduced by 10–23 [9]) placing blame upon the one cursing God (or gods) makes it all the more likely that divinity is the victim of revile in 10–23 (5).

[11] The terms within brackets are those of Douglas (1999, 207). The connection of שלמית with retribution is made with reference to שְׁלָמָה. דברי is associated with דְּבָרָה. Douglas also refers to Gen 49:16 to

appellations for the narrative sequence; the act of naming, of course, constitutes the definition of the narrative sequence. The disruption of the series of consecutive imperfect clauses in 10–23 (7) brings a higher degree of visibility to a theme of the narrative sequence.

The final two clauses of the narrative sequence 10–23 (13, 14) also admit deviation from the series of consecutive imperfect clauses: the clause 10–23 (13) is a conjunctive clause of the type waw-X-qatal. In addition to the aforementioned functions of this type of clause in relation to wayyiqtol clauses, it has been noted that the waw-X-qatal clause may indicate conclusion in a unit of narrative. Niccacci (1994b, 181, 189) demonstrates such a function with reference to Gen 2:25; Kotze prescribes a similar function in 1 Sam 4:18b (1989, 123). The qualification 'conclusion' for 10–23 (13) is appropriate for its position at the end of the narrative sequence. Moreover, the clause, in tandem with 10–23 (14), stands as a summary of the preceding clauses (10–23 [11–2]) which narrate the specific details of Israel's compliance with God's bidding. The subordinate clause 10–23 (14) maintains disruption from the series of consecutive imperfect clauses in order to establish the correspondence of the congregation's actions to divine imperative.[12]

---

associate the tribal name of דן (presumably, in addition to its etymological roots) with the act of judgement. Gerstenberger, in contrast, associates the mother's name with another nuance of the root שׁלם: peace. The effect of this association is the removal of any blame on the Israelite side of the culprit's ancestry (Gerstenberger 1996, 361). However, his suggestion (but also Milgrom [2001, 2110] with reference to Judg 14:1–20, 16:1–4, and 18:30) that the tribe of Dan might cast an air of unorthodoxy (cf. Judg 17–8) even on the Israelite side of the ancestry runs counter to the characterization suggested for the name שׁלמית by Douglas. The proposal of Douglas is to be preferred for the thematic cohesion it identifies in all three names.

[12] The syntactical prominence afforded to the comparative clause 10–23 (14) cannot be understated. As part of the statement of summary (10–23 [13–4]), the clause makes an explicit claim for a fact witnessed by the report on the community's compliance. The report of 10–23 (11–2) repeats the beginning and end of the verbal sequence expressing God's

The narrative sequence moves swiftly from an infraction of divine law to the penalty for that violation. The significant moments which define the theme in the narrative sequence, the bound motifs (the 'nuclei' in the terminology of Barthes), may be expressed by the following sequence of terms: Transgression-Inquiry-Instruction-Retribution. Each term may govern a series of clauses in the text. In conjunction with the content of Exod 20:7 and 22:27—the conjunctive verbless clause 10–23 (2) points to deficiencies in the prescriptions from Exodus—the lack of a prescribed penalty for the transgression and the question of the applicability of the ruling for an individual of mixed ancestry blocks the movement from Transgression to Retribution. The binary pair Inquiry-Instruction removes the barrier, allowing the final motif of the series (Retribution) to occur. The accomplishment of thematic closure is underlined by the clauses 10–23 (13–4); with closure, the definition of the narrative sequence as an act of judgement, so aptly represented in the personal names of 10–23 (7), is formed. Thus, the deviations from the series of consecutive imperfect clauses have significance beyond the functions commonly identified for such deviations: information on participants in 10–23 (2, 7), and conclusion in 10–23 (13–4). The legal prescriptions occur under the motif Instruction; the commandments facilitate the removal of the doubt concerning previous legislation that retards the completion of the narrative sequence. That the aforementioned function occurs with the promulgation of the laws is clear; but the manner in which the justification and explanation for the judgement occur bears closer analysis.

The Legal Prescriptions

The legal prescriptions cover a variety of topics. Not all of the topics are relevant immediately to the subject matter of the narrative sequence. Verses 15b and 16 represent the sole material concerned with the issues of the narrative sequence: the abuse of

---

judgement on the blasphemer introduced by the act of speech designated by 10–23 (9): הוצא המקלל . . . ורגמו אתו כל־העדה (v. 14). The summary statement gives expression to an already tacit correspondence between command and fulfillment (Instruction-Retribution).

the divine name. Verses 17 and 18 deal with homicide and the slaying of a beast respectively. Verses 19 and 20 attend to the matter of injuries inflicted upon a person. Verse 21 returns to the subject of the slaying of humans and beasts. Verse 22 ensures that the preceding rulings are understood as being relevant for natives and sojourners.

The legal prescriptions of the passage are divided into separate command sets in accordance with syntactical and semantic criteria. The analysis following the presentation of the text will consider each command set on an individual basis before examining their arrangement as a group in relation to the narrative sequence.

1 אִישׁ אִישׁ כִּי־יְקַלֵּל אֱלֹהָיו	1 Anyone who curses God 2 shall bear the sin. 3 One who blasphemes the name of the Lord shall be put to death; 4 the whole congregation shall stone the blasphemer. 5 Aliens as well as citizens, when they blaspheme the Name, shall be put to death. (vv. 15b–6)
2 וְנָשָׂא חֶטְאוֹ	
3 וְנֹקֵב שֵׁם־יהוה מוֹת יוּמָת	
4 רָגוֹם יִרְגְּמוּ־בוֹ כָּל־הָעֵדָה	
5 כַּגֵּר כָּאֶזְרָח בְּנָקְבוֹ־שֵׁם יוּמָת	
1 וְאִישׁ כִּי יַכֶּה כָּל־נֶפֶשׁ אָדָם	1 Anyone who kills a human being 2 shall be put to death. 3 Anyone who kills an animal shall make restitution for it, life for life. (vv. 17–8)
2 מוֹת יוּמָת	
3 וּמַכֵּה נֶפֶשׁ־בְּהֵמָה יְשַׁלְּמֶנָּה נֶפֶשׁ תַּחַת נָפֶשׁ	
1 וְאִישׁ כִּי־יִתֵּן מוּם בַּעֲמִיתוֹ	1 Anyone who maims another 2–3 shall suffer the same injury in return: 4 fracture for fracture, eye for eye, tooth for tooth; 5 the injury inflicted 6 is
2 כַּאֲשֶׁר עָשָׂה	
3 כֵּן יֵעָשֶׂה לּוֹ [13]	
4 שֶׁבֶר תַּחַת שֶׁבֶר עַיִן תַּחַת עַיִן שֵׁן תַּחַת שֵׁן	

---

[13] The two clauses 19–22 (2, 3) have been combined in the translation; the separation of the material in order to reflect the order of the clauses in Hebrew is not feasible. The dash connecting the numerical designation of this portion in the translation reflects the combination of these two clauses in the translation.

5 כאשר יתן מום באדם   the injury to be suffered. 7 One
6 כן ינתן בו   who kills an animal shall make
7 ומכה בהמה ישלמנה   restitution for it; 8 but one who
8 ומכה אדם יומת   kills a human being shall be put
9 משפט אחד יהיה לכם   to death. 9 You shall have one
10 כגר כאזרח יהיה   law 10 for the alien and the
11 כי אני יהוה אלהיכם   citizen: 11 for I am the Lord
                              your God. (vv. 19–22)

A Note on Inter-Clausal Syntax in the Legal Prescriptions

The description of syntax within the legal prescriptions requires greater detail than the identification of clauses apart from a designated main line clause-type. In texts with an orientation toward the future, the main line clause is often considered to be the consecutive perfect (weqatal) clause.[14] Yet, the legal prescriptions of Leviticus and Numbers often contain lengthy passages without a consecutive perfect clause; the main line in such cases seems not to emerge. In the system of classification employed for the following analysis of legal prescriptions, the grammatical features within clauses often considered to pose disruption to the so-called main line series of consecutive perfect clauses are placed within a

---

[14] Such is the conclusion of, among others, Niccacci (1994a, 131; 1994b, 177–8; 1997, 189–90), Longacre (1992, 181–8; 1994, 51–5), Buth (1995, 97–9), and Gentry (1998, 13–4). The study of syntactical structure beyond the level of the clause in Biblical Hebrew proceeds often with reference to the pragmatic category variously called 'prominence' or 'relief'. The qualification 'pragmatic' refers to the portion of grammar solely concerned with the situation of communication (Buth 1995, 78); in Biblical Hebrew grammar, this distinction often refers to the function of a formal construction within the system of grammar prior to interaction with the referential universe (the world of the text). As a pragmatic category, 'relief' frequently outlines the contours of a text through the binary opposition designated by the terms 'main line' and 'secondary line' (but also foreground/background, and continuity/discontinuity). Descriptions of the theories behind, and their applications within, the nascent discipline of Biblical Hebrew text-syntax may be found in van der Merwe (1994) and Lowery (1995).

hierarchy; the hierarchy reflects the degree of syntactical disruption inherent to each type of clause on a graded scale. The postulation of a graded system of syntactical sequence or disjuncture between clauses provides a finer definition for continuity and discontinuity within any text consisting of a variety of clause-types. Broadly speaking, the degree of syntactical disjuncture between clauses is classified according to the nature of the conjunction and its absence or presence within the clause. Asyndetic clauses pose the highest degree of disjuncture because of the absence of any form of conjunction. By virtue of their departure from the sequence of main (i.e. independent) clauses (grammatical hypotaxis), subordinate clauses pose a similar degree of syntactical disjuncture as asyndetic clauses. Conjunctive clauses (in prescriptive texts, often waw-X-yiqtol clauses) and consecutive clauses express a lesser degree of syntactical discontinuity. Between conjunctive clauses and consecutive clauses, the latter type expresses a greater degree of syntactical continuity. Consecutive clauses often depict— though not exclusively—events in temporal and logical succession in legal prescriptions; quite frequently, these prescriptions dictate procedures. The unique pragmatic stature of the consecutive perfect form in prescriptive texts is the accomplishment of the apparent combination of the conjunction ך and the perfect verbal form (qatal) in the formation of an autonomous morpho-syntactic category; the form is not simply the perfect verbal form following ך.[15] The absence of a finite verb in the clause, the use of a

---

[15] So noted by Niccacci (1994a, 128) and Longacre (1992, 178, 181). The correlation of the weqatal form with the use of the imperfect (GKC §112b; Jöuon §§119c–d)—for example, with the on-set of negation—and differences in the placement of the tone from that of the perfect form (GKC §49h; *GBH* §24.4.2; Jöuon §43a) are marks of the consecutive perfect form's distinction. Hypothetical reconstructions (Rainey 1986) of the historical development of the consecutive imperfect form (wayyiqtol) postulate a link with a prefixed preterite form (yaqtul), which stands in contrast with the longer form (yaqtulu) thought to be the precursor of the Biblical Hebrew imperfect form (yiqtol). This morpho-syntactic distinction is thought to abide in Hebrew between the verbal forms wayyiqtol and yiqtol. For Blake (1944, 271–2), the pairing of wayyiqtol

conjunction other than ו, or the imposition of a negative particle often necessitates the departure from a sequence of consecutive clauses to the use of a conjunctive clause. Conjunctive clauses are those employing a coordinate conjunction (e.g. ו, או) apart from the formation of a consecutive verbal form (weqatal, wayyiqtol). The function of the disruption inherent to the transition from a consecutive perfect clause to the waw-X-yiqtol (conjunctive) clause has been the subject of several studies (Niccacci 1997, 172–8; Longacre 1992, 181–8). Niccacci, for example, judges the function of the transition to be the expression of a secondary line of communication depicting circumstance, comparison, contrast, specification, or comment in relation to events on the main line of narrative texts. By and large, variation between these four types of clause (asyndetic, subordinate, conjunctive and consecutive clauses) map out the terrain of legal prescriptive texts forging syntactical continuities and discontinuities for a diverse host of functions. Other grammatical features contributing to the disruption of inter-clausal linkage will be noted in the course of the analysis.[16]

Two principles govern the effect of the syntactical disjuncture of a given clause. Firstly, the perception of discontinuity within the text is the accomplishment of change: the disjuncture of asyndeton is felt when it is preceded or followed by clauses displaying a greater degree of syntactical continuity. Such transitions are the essence of texture within the syntactical structure of the text, inviting investigation of the system of

---

with qatal leads, by inverse analogy in the development of the language, to the similar correlation of weqatal with yiqtol. The latter dichotomous coupling ensures the distinction between qatal and the consecutive verbal form weqatal.

[16] This brief introduction to the theoretical foundations behind the syntactical analysis of the legal prescriptions must suffice for now as attention turns to the practical task of describing the syntax of the selected passages. More thorough explanation for the method behind the task with reference to representative examples of the current state of inquiry into Biblical Hebrew syntax occurs in a subsequent chapter (ch. 4). Chapter 4 also will verify the proposed system of syntax against a larger textual corpus: all the legal prescriptions of Leviticus and Numbers.

communication producing the change. A second operative principle is the fact that the prominence of a clause achieved through syntactical disjuncture may have significance for a series of clauses, or only for itself. The former feature of syntactical disjuncture marks the initiation of a unit or sub-unit of text within a series of laws on a single topic.[17] The latter usage draws attention to a single clause in order to set it apart from the clauses of its vicinity; among other functions, such use of syntactical disjuncture propels an emphatic statement of contrast to the forefront of a series of prescriptions.

Verses 15b–6

Turning to the passage of prescriptions at hand, it may be seen that, against the syntactical structures of continuity and discontinuity in the clauses of verses 15b–6, the coherence of sub-groups within the command set and other transitions in the communicative context between clauses or groups of clauses emerge with clarity. Syntactical disjuncture is the achievement of the system of inter-clausal relations as an autonomous category; however, it is the task of semantics to interpret the significance of the disruption. Thus, the interpretation of syntactical structure—including the aforementioned distinction between the significance of syntactical disjuncture for a series of clauses and a single clause—occurs at the intersection of syntax and semantics.[18] The

---

[17] On rare occasion, the syntactical disjuncture of a clause may perform both functions. The clause may mark the beginning of a series of commands on a new topic; but it may also stand apart—along with a series of following clauses with an equal degree of syntactical disjuncture, perhaps a series of syntactically prominent clauses expressing overarching principles—from a group of clauses later on in the same command set displaying a greater degree of syntactical cohesion (with a higher degree of syntactical continuity).

[18] This point has been stated by Niccacci (1994b, 178–9), and demonstrated with reference to examples in narrative from Gen 1:1–3:24 (1994b, 184, 187–8). Significant to Niccacci's argument for the legitimate role of semantics in the interpretation of syntax are cases where the departure from a series of consecutive imperfect clauses may either signal

first clause 15b–6 (1) portrays a condition which is followed by a consecutive perfect clause (15b–6 [2]) expressing the prescription (ונשא חטאו). In addition to the fact that the first clause of the command set (15b–16 [1]) is subordinate, syntactical disjuncture at the beginning of the legal passage is achieved through the presence of the extraposed subject איש איש expressing distribution (every man).[19] As a grammatical constituent beyond the boundaries of the

---

the on-set of a new episode, or the close of an episode with a statement of conclusion; it is the content of the clauses that determines their interpretation. However, the independence of syntax from semantics is preserved by the fact that syntactical variation remains a formal indicator of the pragmatic constraints of organizing information within texts: not all clauses capable of interpretation as circumstance, comparison or comment may be set apart with a higher degree of syntactical discontinuity. It is in recognition of the partnership between syntax and semantics that the term 'semantic-pragmatic' is used at various points in this study to qualify its analytical stance.

[19] As is the case in *BHRG* (§§34.5, 46.1.2c [3]), the term 'extraposition' refers to grammatical constituents occurring beyond the boundaries of the clause with a constituent of the clause sharing a common referent and designating the extraposed entity's syntactical role within the clause. Common terms for the designated syntactical phenomenon include 'dislocated construction' or 'pendens construction'. Following the definitions for the syntactical feature by Franz J. Backhaus (1995, 1–2), the location of the extraposed member beyond the boundaries of the clause may be determined by the existence of the grammatical constituent within the clause acting as co-referent with the extraposed entity, and the syntactical separation of the two elements with the extraposed constituent standing at the margin of the clause. This degree of separation is often indicated—although not without exception—by the intercession of a conjunction, interrogative pronoun or particle of exclamation standing to mark the upper boundary of the clause. However, it should be noted that such elements (conjunctions, interrogative pronouns etc.) standing to govern the clause may stand on rare occasion prior to an extraposed constituent indicating the relationship of the extraposed constituent as a satellite of the clause; the extraposed member does function through its resumption within the clause as a syntactical component of the clause. Such variation in the

clause of which it is a satellite, its placement before the clause interrupts the lexical succession forged by that clause with the preceding clause.[20] Following the consecutive perfect clause 15b–6 (2), a conjunctive imperfect clause (waw-X-yiqtol) effects a higher degree of syntactical disjuncture from the previous consecutive clause in restating the substance of the preceding conditional prescription (15b–6 [1–2]) in a new formulation. The last two clauses of the set of commands are asyndetic verbal clauses (15b–6 [4, 5]). The first asyndetic clause expresses the mode of execution

---

location of the conjunction or the interrogative pronoun reveals its specific function, not so much to establish the boundary of the clause but to effect syntactical separation between the extraposed member and its resumptive co-referent within the clause. In the case before us, the subordinating conjunction כִּי separates the extraposed member אִישׁ אִישׁ from the verbal conjugation יְקַלֵּל which encodes the subject of the clause, the role of the extraposed member within the clause. Without the syntactical separation enforced by the conjunction, 15b–6 (1) would be a subordinate clause with the grammatical subject expressed in an independent nominal formation (not part of the verbal morpheme) standing before the verb. While *BHRG* (§40.9I [1]) admits the possibility that such intercession of the subordinate conjunction does not indicate extraposition (1999, 300), it is prudent to follow *IBHS* (§38.2d) in allocating a function for the formal deviation and regarding such cases as those of extraposition. Subsequent analysis will reveal a consistent function for the recognition of extraposition in such cases in contributing greater definition and coherence to the syntactical structure of texts. While the term 'extraposition' may designate constituents standing prior to (left-dislocation), or following (right-dislocation) the clause, the occurrence of the term, unless otherwise stated, will refer to the former syntactical feature. This abbreviated reference occurs in view of the fact that extraposition with left-dislocation is the statistically dominant feature in the analysis of the selected passages between the two variants. Consequently, the subsequent verification of the analysis with reference to the larger corpus of Leviticus and Numbers (ch. 4) will focus also on extraposition with left-dislocation.

[20] It should be noted that 17–18 (1), which begins the following command set on the slaying of human and beast, also has an extraposed subject (וְאִישׁ) standing before the clause.

for the blasphemer, and the second states that the legislation applies equally to sojourner and native. Together, these last two asyndetic clauses are a response to the outstanding questions impeding the flow of the narrative sequence toward its fulfillment. When the series of inter-clausal connections within the command set are viewed in conjunction with the semantic import of the laws and that of the narrative sequence, an interpretation for the syntax of the command set emerges. A graded system of syntactical disjuncture reveals the links, breaks and statements of salience within the command set of verses 15b–6. Syntactical subordination with extraposition (15b–6 [1]) marks the initiation of the command set; a consecutive clause (15b–6 [2]) proceeds with the prescription. Relative to the weqatal clause 15b–16 (2), a higher degree of disjuncture (waw-X-yiqtol) marks the end of the initial conditional prescription (15b–6 [1–2]) and the beginning of the next law (15b–16 [3]). Asyndeton, expressing an even higher degree of syntactical disjuncture, intervenes raising the visibility of the last two clauses (15b–6 [4, 5]) as semantic input significant for the progression of the related narrative sequence: the clauses address the deficiencies in the prescriptions in Exodus brought to light by the circumstances of the narrative sequence.

The topical coherence of the command set is clear: blasphemy and its penalty are the subject of concern. Furthermore, the topical unity of the command set is indicated by the collocation of קלל and נקב within the command set (15b–6 [1, 3, 5]). The two verbs are a mutually informative pair lending precision to the description of a single act of speech: the divine name is invoked within the context of derision. Within the close quarters of the command set, the event denoted by each verb implies the virtual presence of the other in the same prescription (Milgrom 2001, 2118).[21] The strength of this argument by Milgrom

---

[21] Milgrom, with reference to Saadiah Gaon, takes both קלל and נקב in 15b–6 (1, 3) respectively—each term on its own—to be synecdochical expressions for the full expression in Lev 24:11aα (with both verbal roots deployed in tandem). The view that the two clauses of Lev 24:11aα are mutually descriptive has been expressed also by Dillmann (1897, 656), Hoffmann (1906, 313), Weingreen (1972, 119), Livingston (1986, 353),

lies in the absence of any negative connotation to נקב apart from
קלל. To claim a negative connotation for the mere mention of the
divine name is to forbid the taking of an oath by inciting God as
witness by name, an act attested without any hint of illegality on
numerous occasions within the biblical corpus (Judg 8:19; 1 Sam
14:39, 45; 19:6; 1Kgs 22:14; 2 Kgs 5:16, 20, etc.).[22] Further
indication of the complementary relationship within 15b–6 (1, 3)
may be found in Hartley's (1992, 410) observation that the penalty
for the second law is a specific expression (מות יומת) of the first
(ונשא חטאו): suffering the penalty of death is one way of being
made to bear (the consequences of) one's crime. In terms of
literary patterning, Milgrom has demonstrated the literary pattern
of chiasmus within the command set, with the material of 15b–6
(4) and a portion of 15b–6 (5) at its point of focus (2001,
2129): רגום ירגמו־בו כל־העדה כגר כאזרח.[23] The placement of
this material at the center of the structure lends weight to the
proposal from the examination of the syntactical structure that the
clauses 15b–6 (4, 5) are prominent and significant for the narrative
sequence. One final point bears significance for the analysis.
Thinking in terms of the bi-polar structure that expresses the
theme of the narrative sequence (Transgression-Retribution), it
may be seen that the command set portrays this structural
progression in increasingly smaller syntactical units as the reader
moves through the command set:

Levine (1989, 166), and Hartley (1992, 409). The crime, as stated in Lev
24:11aα, actually consists of the pronouncement of the divine name
within an act of derision. The collocation of the terms as a lexical pair in
the prescriptions of 15b–6 (1–3) serve to strengthen further the bond
between the laws.

[22] The various witnesses of LXX, *Tg. Onq.*, *Tg. Neof.* (with the further
qualification בגדפין), Syr. and *m. Sanh.* 7:5 attest to the fact that נקב
specifically denotes pronounciation. The versions in Greek translate with
ὀνομάζω, while the Aramaic versions use פרש for MT's נקב.

[23] The chiasmus has been demonstrated in the diagram previously
reproduced from Milgrom's commentary on a preceding page.

Transgression	Retribution	Syntactical Unit
אִישׁ אִישׁ כִּי־יְקַלֵּל אֱלֹהָיו	וְנָשָׂא חֶטְאוֹ	Sentence (two clauses)
וְנֹקֵב שֵׁם־יְהוָה	מוֹת יוּמַת	Clause
כַּגֵּר כָּאֶזְרָח בְּנָקְבוֹ־שֵׁם	יוּמַת	Clause

The laws are, in essence, a summary statement indicating the extremities which define the plot of the narrative sequence. The movement through verses 15b–6 (excluding 15b–6 [4]) may be seen as a graded crystallization of the thematic expression of the narrative sequence; each increment shortens and, in so doing, clarifies the theme of the narrative sequence.

Verses 17–8

Just like the last command set, the command set of verses 17–8 begins with a subordinate (conditional) clause employing an extraposed subject (אִישׁ) standing before the clause (17–8 [1]). The proclitic conjunction ו of 17–8 (1) maintains a link—albeit one of diminished capacity, given the subordinate status of the clause and the presence of extraposition—with the preceding clause (15b–6 [5]). The syntactical link is almost certainly motivated by factors beyond the immediate relationship of the two clauses; the connection is between the two command sets (vv. 15b–6 and 17–8).[24] The following asyndetic clause 17–8 (2) expresses the apodosis

---

[24] A similar function may be prescribed for the conjunction ו at the beginning of the following command set (vv. 19–22). Together, the conjunctions append the two other command sets to the first (vv. 15b–6) to form the legal passage of Lev 24:10–23. The act of distinguishing between conjunctions linking syntactical entities larger than the clause from those forging links between clauses is challenging: the conjunction ו straddles both functions. Essentially, interpreters must decide which clauses belong together before they relate with other clauses or groups of clauses. In the case at hand, the conjunction ו standing at the inception of a series of clauses bound by topical unity and separated from previous

of the first prescription: the penalty of death is to apply. The
sustained degree of syntactical disjuncture in 17–8 (2) is perceived
in relation to the greater degree of syntactical continuity

---

material by semantic criteria and other syntactical features within the
initial clause, would be a syntactical link effecting inclusion on behalf of
the entire series as a block. In identifying the inception of such a
syntactical block, A.F. den Exter Blokland writes: "In general continuity
associates with economy in language. Comparatively more information is
required to deal with discontinuity than with continuity. Normally the (re-
)introduction of a new subject requires extra information at least in the
form of its thematization. But once a new subject is introduced a passage
can often manage subject changes without thematization. A lexical subject
change therefore is consistent with a higher level of continuity than an
explicit subject change. On the other hand, thematizing the subject, while
it remains the same, seems to supply superfluous information. A relative
lack of economy, however, is consistent with discontinuity. The seemingly
superfluous additional information seems, in fact, to signal relative
discontinuity, a loosening of cohesion as compared to the continued use
of the same subject without thematization" (den Exter Blokland 1995,
150). Applying den Exter Blokland's method to the interpretation of the
command set vv. 17–8, it may be said that the amount of information
regarding the subject in the conditional clause 17–8 (1) satisfies den Exter
Blokland's criteria of "extra information" expressing "thematization" for
the identification of thematic discontinuity. The following clause, 17–8
(2), provides little information on the subject, which must be supplied
with reference to 17–8 (1); this factor draws 17–8 (1) and 17–8 (2)
together as a block to be distinguished from 15b–6 (5). Hence the
conjunction ו of 17–8 (1) forges linkage on behalf of the block (17–8 [3] is
included by conjunction and the syntactical disjuncture of subordination
in the clause following 17–8 [3]). Den Exter Blokland's principle is
applicable also in cases where syntactical disjuncture does not coincide
with an ostensible change in topic: the asyndetic clauses 15b–6 (4, 5) and
17–8 (2) mark a high degree of syntactical disjuncture within command
sets of topical unity. However, all these clauses contain pronominal
references to participants, who stood as grammatical objects in previous
clauses. The high degree of anaphora indicates topical cohesion in spite of
syntactical disjuncture; hence, interpreters must search for other functions
for syntactical disjuncture apart from that of topical delineation.

(conjunction) expressed in the following clause (17–8 [3]). Syntactical disjuncture in 17–8 (2) occurs to effect prominence for this clause within the command set; the element of urgency inherent to the pronouncement of the penalty of death is the motivation for syntactical prominence. Another grammatical feature contributing to the expression of urgency is the emphatic use of the infinitive absolute standing before the finite verb (GKC, §113n; Jöuon, §123e; *BHRG*, §20.2.1). The third clause of the command set 17–8 (3) is connected to the rest of the set by conjunction (waw-X-yiqtol), appending to the command set the requirement for restitution in the case of the destruction of an animal.

Apart from syntax, the topical coherence of the set is expressed by its singular concern with the taking of life (נכה). As with the former set of commands, the representation of transgression and recompense within each prescription moves from a larger syntactical unit to a smaller entity, from two clauses (17–8[1, 2]) to one (17–8 [3]).

Verses 19–22

The command set beginning with 19–22 (1) is similar to those seen so far: a subordinate (conditional) clause with extraposed subject initiates the set. The apodosis in the initial conditional formulation is unique in that it (the apodosis) also consists of protasis and apodosis (19–22 [2] is subordinate to the following clause). As previously noted, the ו of 19–22 (1) identifies the entire command set as the third member in a series of three command sets. In spite of asyndeton in 19–22 (3), the pronominal reference to the subject of 19–22 (2) in 19–22 (3) and the adverbial particle כן (referring back to כאשר עשה in 19–22 [2]) bind both clauses together (19–22 [2, 3]). Both clauses (19–22 [2, 3]) in turn are bound to 19–22 (1) by the sustained anaphoric reference (by pronominal reference in לו and the representation of the subject implicit to the verbal morpheme עשה) to איש (in 19–22 [1]).[25]

---

[25] The high degree of syntactical disjuncture within the initial clauses of the command set (and also 19–22 [5, 6]), as it will be seen, reflect the

The following formulaic series (19–22 [4])—each member consisting of a noun with prepositional phrase—may be regarded either as three asyndetic verbless clauses, or as syntactical constituents below the level of the clause (nouns and prepositional phrases not part of a clause). The versions in Greek (LXX), as well as other ancient witnesses, maintain the absence of the finite verb. While Greek often omits the copulative verb (εἶναι) in proverbial statements (Smyth 1920, §944; Blass and Debrunner 1961, §127), the omission of ἔσται (the expected form in 19–22 [4]) is rare in Hellenistic usage (Blass and Debrunner 1961, §128.4). Moreover, a survey of the other occurrences of the formula of talion reveals that the phrase of the type 'X תחת/ב X' functions as an adverbial adjunct to a fientive verbal predicate wherever it occurs in conjunction with a verb (with נתן in Exod 21:23–5; with שלם above in 17–8 [3]). The deployment of the formula apart from the grammatical function of an adverbial adjunct to a verbal predicate in 19–22 (4) would be a different use of the formula from these aforementioned cases.[26] The combination of the foregoing

---

rhetorical intent of the entire legal passage. For now, it may be observed that subordination (19–22 [2]) and asyndeton (19–22 [3]) make prominent the principle of equivalence endemic to the prescription (19–22 [2,3]). This partnership between syntax and rhetoric persists in 19–22 (4).

[26] Two factors work against the inclusion of the formula of talion as an extended adverbial adjunct to יֵעָשֶׂה in the preceding clause 19–22 (3). Firstly, the major accent of disjuncture *silluq* (on לוֹ at the conclusion of 19–22 [3]) sets the formula of talion apart from the clause 19–22 (3). In contrast, *silluq* at the conclusion of נפש תחת נפש in 17–8 (3) draws the formula into the clause of which it is a member. Similarly, the occurrence of *silluq* in the same phrase in Exod 21:23b draws the first member of the extensive formula within the purview of the clause (Exod 21:23b). The separation of the first member (נפש תחת נפש)—through the selective placement of *silluq*—from the rest of the series occupying the next two verses (from עין תחת עין to חבורה תחת חבורה) suggests the understanding that the formula of talion is a constituent of the clause (adverbial adjunct) beginning at Exod 21:23b. A second factor is that the formula of talion would be superfluous as an adverbial adjunct in 19–22 (3), in light of the fact that the clause, without the formula, already

observations leads to the conclusion that the various nominal groupings of 19–22 (4) should be considered syntactically independent entities. The phrases express the principle of equivalence inherent to the comparative sentences (19–22 [1–3]; 19–22 [5–6]) which occur at both ends of the formula of talion. The exclusion of 19–22 (4) from membership within a clause is disruptive to the syntax of the command set; the formulaic series stands out by not being integrated within the system of syntax conveying lexical movement (of various degrees of facility) from one clause to the next. Without the element of predication and without anchor within an adjacent clause as a constituent of the clause (functioning as, or as part of, the subject, object or modifier within the clause), independent syntactical constituents are an affront to the hierarchy of syntactical categories constituting the text (phrase, clause, paragraph). The series of phrases in 19–22 (4) usurps the role of clauses in the manner it relates to the surrounding clauses; instead of acting as a constituent within a clause, it engages directly the surrounding clauses as elements of syntax within the text. Consequently, in considering the flow of the text as a sequence of propositions encapsulated by clauses, independent syntactical constituents project an especially high degree of syntactical prominence. Unlike extraposed members standing before the clause of which they are a satellite, independent syntactical constituents—not being connected to a clause with a syntactical role within the clause—usually do not bring a quality of syntactical disjuncture to the following clause; the syntactical prominence is confined to the independent entity.

The clause 19–22 (5) is a subordinate (comparative) clause followed by an asyndetic clause (19–22 [6]). The substance of 19–22 (5, 6) is similar to that of the preceding prescription (19–22 [1–3]); the significance of the high degree of syntactical disjuncture in

---

expresses the correspondence between crime and retribution. Another example of the formula of talion without a verb is found in Deut 19:21b. In Deut 19:21, the formula of talion is separated from the preceding clause (ולא תחוס עינך) by a major accent of disjuncture ('atnah). In terms of content, the formula of talion clearly cannot be included as a grammatical constituent of the preceding clause in Deut 19:21a.

these clauses has been explained. The decision to interpret 19–22 (7–11) as part of the present command set despite the obvious topical transition in 19–22 (7) is based on the fact that the following two prescriptions (19–22 [7, 8]) are conjunctive clauses (waw-X-yiqtol). This form of linkage (conjunction) expresses a higher degree of syntactical continuity between individual prescriptions within command sets up to this point; thus the link with 19–22 (6) is syntactically pronounced. The combination of the prescriptions of 19–22 (7–11) regarding topics previously treated separately within distinct command sets seems to signal the initiation of a new criterion for the combination of commands beginning with 19–22 (1): a criterion allowing for the combination of different topics. The significance (and hence, the argument) for this proposal of a new criterion for the combination of commands in verses 19–22 must await the consideration of the interaction between all the command sets of the prescriptive passage. The command set ends with two asyndetic clauses and a subordinate (causal) clause. The clauses 19–22 (9, 10) disrupt the newly acquired syntactical continuity in the preceding two clauses (19–22 [7, 8]) in order to express with prominence a response to one of the outstanding questions raised through the reading of the narrative sequence: the applicability of the law against the abuse of the divine name for an individual of mixed ancestry. The prominence of this response was seen previously in the asyndetic clause 15b–16 (5). A final subordinate clause (19–22 [11]) expressing the identity of God as the foundational impetus for the body of legislation closes the legal discourse.

While 19–22 (1) embarks on new subject matter distinct from that of the previous command set, the topical integrity of the set is apparently compromised with the on-set of 19–22 (7). Against the larger backdrop of the other command sets, verses 19–22 begin by adding a new subject matter to those of preceding command sets (injuries involving humans; 19–22 [1–6]); the command set moves on to combine the new subject with two of those already witnessed in previous command sets (19–22 [7, 8]; cf. 17–8 [1–2, 3]). The command set verses 19–22 is unique also in two other aspects. Firstly, it bypasses the intermediate level of a single clause (down from the level of the sentence) in its initial reduction of the 'distance' between the motifs of transgression and retribution moving from conditional sentence (19–22 [1–3]; 3 clauses) to groups of nouns and prepositional phrases (adverbial adjuncts) without any expression of predication (19–22 [4]). Secondly, the command set replays the syntactical reduction of the nexus between deed and consequence by reverting to a level beyond the single clause (19–22 [5–6]; 2 clauses) in its portrayal of the sequence of motifs. Subsequently, the prescription for the procedure of judgement is reduced to single clauses (19–22 [9, 10]) within the command set.[27]

Coherence of Narrative and Law in Leviticus 24:10–23

In prescribing a penalty for the abuse of the divine name, the command set verses 15b–6 demonstrates the bi-polar structure sustaining and, consequently, defining the narrative sequence. The prescription abstracts the thematic content progressively built up over four motifs (Transgression-Inquiry-Instruction-Retribution) by effectively reducing it to two (Transgression-Retribution). In syntactical terms, the thematic progression expressed over several clauses in the narrative sequence is reduced to two clauses in the prescription of 15b–6 (1–2). Syntax and semantics collaborate in the process of thematic abstraction. Subsequent prescriptions in the set (15b–6 [3, 5]) reduce further the thematic movement to single clauses. As the syntactical units expressing this progression of theme in the narrative sequence shrinks, the visibility of the theme is heightened.

A similar operation in the following command set (vv. 17–8) activates the next stage of abstraction: the first stage removes

---

[27] The clauses 19–22 (9, 10) may be considered representatives of the movement from transgression to retribution although they do not denote explicitly the bi-polar entities constituting the extremities of the formulation Transgression-Retribution. The procedure (משפט אחד) being prescribed in both clauses is, by proximity to the prescriptions of 19–22 (5–8), a procedure of retribution. With reference to the theoretical formulations of Barthes concerning narrative sequences, this is a case where a name (משפט אחד in conjunction with the thematic import of the preceding prescriptions) implies a sequence of motifs. The final clause of the command set (19–22 [11]) must, of course, be excluded from such classification.

theme from its extended sequential expression (the element of chronological progression in narrative). The next stage forces the placement of that abstracted value of theme within a larger semantic category through the comparison of the command sets on different subject matter (vv. 15b–6, 17–8). The second stage in the procedure of abstraction is a move toward generalization; it is the generation of a thematic statement or series of motifs capable of representing the laws from both command sets while reflecting the plot of the narrative sequence. This general category of theme emerges as the common element between the two command sets encountered at this point in reading. In fact, this second stage of abstraction is essential for producing the formulation Transgression-Retribution; the earlier extraction of the bi-polar sequence of motifs sustaining the narrative sequence in the first command set (vv. 15b–6)—the earlier stage of abstraction—might suggest names for the motifs more specific in nature (Abuse of Divine Name-Execution).

With the initiation of the third command set (19–22), the second stage of abstraction is reinforced with one more variation of circumstance expressing the abstracted theme. The heightened reduction of the syntactical unit (down to single phrases) embodying the Transgression-Retribution continuum draws attention to a specific aspect of the larger semantic category uniting the subject matter in all three command sets. This precise aspect of the general theme encompassing narrative and law is the fact that the retribution befits the crime (tit for tat). In essence, incremental concentrations of a theme capable of expansion into a narrative sequence receive the identification of a common aspect in one extreme syntactical reduction (19–22 [4]). This similarity is not immediately visible prior to verses 19–22; its clarification is the accomplishment of the principle of talion.[28] In association with the

---

[28] The accomplishment of a general principle through the formula of talion (X תחת X) here is acknowledged widely (Budd 1997, 338; Hartley 1992, 411; Westbrook 1986, 67; Frymer-Kensky 1980, 232; Fisher 1982, 584; Wenham 1979, 312). Bernard Jackson, however, argues against seeing in the formula the expression of an abstract principle, finding in such recognition of symbolism within the expression the imposition of modern

fact that the formulaic series of 19–22 (4) is at the center of the chiastic structure of the passage (as demonstrated by several commentators), the thematic concentration afforded by syntactical reduction establishes the prominence of equilibrium between crime and punishment for the laws and the passage as a whole; the syntactical prominence of 19–22 (4) renders the heightened thematic concentration of the formulaic series that much more outstanding to the reader's eye. Now that the process of abstraction has established the similarity between all the various prescriptions in spite of their dealing with diverse subject matter, the command set verses 19–22 proceeds by repeating, and thereby including within the set, the subject matter of the preceding set (vv. 17–8; penalties for the slaying of humans and beasts). The emergence of the common thematic principle underlying all the command sets and the narrative sequence is the occasion for the dissolution of the previous topical boundaries dividing the command sets. The topical plurality of verses 19–22 is indicative of this shift in the perception of the laws.

The significance of this accomplishment in the laws for the interpretation of the narrative sequence is the perception of a current of thought motivating the divine legal judgement: judicial equity. This perception of the spirit of justice behind the new ruling, the prescription of retribution in keeping with the gravity of the crime, facilitates the adavancement of the narrative sequence from Inquiry to Retribution. The rhetorical goal of the legal

---

methods of linguistic practice (Jackson 2006, 195). Jackson, rather, finds in the formula, and its variation, more direct expression. According to him, the formula X תחת X denotes quantitative equilibrium in retribution or recompense; the notion of a 'substitution' of equitable proportion for loss is the expressed contribution of the formula (Jackson 2000, 278–80; Jackson 2006, 196–9). The variant formula כ...כאשר, on the other hand, expresses equivalence in the quality of retribution. Jackson, despite said reservations, finds in the literary structure of Lev 24:10–23, the occurrence of chiasmus as well as the collocation of both formulae, the expression of an abstract principle of equivalence (Jackson 2006, 206). Literary patterning, therefore, communicates that which the precise content of both formulae does not.

passage is accomplished. Noteworthy also is the fact that the statement of equilibrium, through the inclusion of the sojourner in three formulations of the movement from crime to punishment (15b–6 [5]; 19–22 [9, 10]), extends to cover similar acts by the sojourner within its purview. Thus, the offending sojourner of the narrative sequence is equally subject to the appropriate penalty; equity abides in legal pronouncement across boundaries of race. Through the rhetoric of the laws, the divine legal pronouncement on the novel situation of an individual of mixed ancestry caught in the act of blasphemy is shown to be the required measure in the restoration of equity. Through the same art in the arrangement of the laws, the legal decision is shown to be in accord with a principle already operative in other laws.

THE CASE OF NUMBERS 9:1–14

The passage of Num 9:1–14 relates the celebration of the Passover prior to the departure from Sinai. A group from among the Israelites finds itself unable to participate in the event due to defilement from contact with a corpse. In response to the protest against exclusion, Moses seeks divine counsel in order to resolve the problem. Allowance is made for the celebration of the Passover, one month after the stipulated period, for those unable to keep the original date due to defilement or absence on a distant journey. Allowance is made also for the sojourner to participate in the event. The legal pronouncements are supplementary to, and thereby reminiscent of, those in Exodus 12.

The Wider Literary Setting of Numbers 9:1–14

The passage is chronologically dislocated from its context: the statement of Num 1:1 depicts God addressing Moses on the first day of the second month in the second year of the departure from Egypt, whereas Num 9:1 initiates an account of events in the first month of the same year. The chronological dislocation is often thought to be the result of interpolation in the process of redaction. Levine, for example, understands the opening temporal statement of Num 9:1 to have been in place prior to the addition of the temporal statement at the beginning of the book (1993, 295). Noth sees a post-exilic hand in the legal accommodation of those on a distant journey in Num 9:1–14 (1968, 71). Gray (1906, 82–3) considers the reason for the insertion of the material at this juncture in the book to be the fact that the designation for the allowance of a second celebration is in the second month—a period which concurs with the temporal statement in the narrative at the beginning of the book. Gray's proposal subjects the progression of the narrative to the order of Israel's cultic calendar; hence, by his reckoning, the designation of the supplementary Passover for (the 14th day of) the second month of the cultic calendar dictates that the account of its establishment come after events covered by the chronological designation of Num 1:1 (the 1st day of the 2nd month), despite the temporal statement of the passage beginning at Num 9:1 (the 1st month in the year). However, Gray's proposal leaves the report of the normative observance of the Passover on the 14th day of the first month (Num 9:5), which ought to come before the date specified in Num 1:1, outside the temporal scheme. More likely are the proposals of Budd (1984, 97) and Milgrom (1990, 67) for the temporal dislocation of Num 9:1–14. Both scholars advocate that the returned focus on the Passover in Num 9:1–14, a foundational event in God's intervention with Israel, stands to mark the departure from Sinai just as the original event which inspired the rite initiated the departure from Egypt.[29] The paradigm reinforces recognition of divine initiative in Israel's deliverance and agenda, the stated purpose for the commemoration of the Passover (Exod 12:17, 42).

The internal coherence of the passage is clear from its thematic distinction from the surrounding material. The preceding chapter outlines procedures for the ordination of Aaron and his sons; and the following passage, Num 9:15–23, relates Israel's departure from Sinai.

The Narrative Sequence

The narrative consists of two members: verses 1–5 and 6–14.

---

[29] Milgrom (1990, 67) sees a function of distinction in structural mimesis: the prescription for the annual rite is separated from the original event. Thus, Num. 9:1–14 relates the first act of commemoration.

1 ‏וידבר יהוה אל־משה
במדבר־סיני בשנה השנית
לצאתם מארץ מצרים בחדש
הראשון
לאמר

1 The Lord spoke to Moses in the wilderness of Sinai, in the first month of the second year after they had come out of the land of Egypt, saying:

---

2 ‏וידבר משה אל־בני ישראל
לעשת הפסח
3 ‏ויעשו את־הפסח
בראשון בארבעה עשר יום
לחדש
בין הערבים במדבר סיני
4 ‏ככל אשר צוה יהוה את־משה
כן עשו בני ישראל

2 So Moses told the Israelites that they should keep the Passover. 3 They kept the Passover in the first month, on the fourteenth day of the month, at twilight, in the wilderness of Sinai. 4 Just as the Lord had commanded Moses, so the Israelites did (vv. 1–5).

1 ‏ויהי אנשים אשר היו טמאים
לנפש אדם
2 ‏ולא־יכלו לעשת־הפסח ביום
ההוא
3 ‏ויקרבו לפני משה ולפני אהרן
ביום ההוא
4 ‏ויאמרו האנשים ההמה אליו

1 Now there were certain people who were unclean through touching a corpse, 2 so that they could not keep the Passover on that day. 3 They came before Moses and Aaron on that day, 4 and said to him,

---

5 ‏ויאמר אלהם משה

5 Moses spoke to them,

---

6 ‏וידבר יהוה אל־משה לאמר

6 The Lord spoke to Moses, saying:

(vv. 6–14).

The first narrative sequence is carried by three consecutive imperfect (wayyiqtol) clauses (1–5 [1, 2, 3]) and one asyndetic verbal clause employing a perfect form (1–5 [4]). The motif which initiates the sequence is an exhortation; the content of the speech in Num 9:2–3 defines the motif represented by the initial verbal clause of the passage (1–5 [1]).[30] The fulfillment of the exact specifications of the exhortation (1–5 [3–4]) brings the narrative sequence to a close. The thematic import of the narrative sequence may be expressed by the sequence of motifs Exhortation-Compliance.

Noteworthy is the semantic import of the final clause in the sequence (1–5 [4]). The clause, on its own, encapsulates the entire thematic formulation from command to fulfillment in its expression:

Exhortation	Compliance
ככל אשר צוה יהוה את־משה	כן עשו בני ישראל
Just as the Lord had commanded Moses,	so the Israelites did.

In the demonstrated fashion, the clause may be considered a summary of the first narrative sequence as a whole. The transition

---

[30] The divine speech introduced by 1–5 (1) consists of three asyndetic clauses. The effect of the asyndeton is a choppy speech of three utterances strung together in a loose formation. The initial verbal form (וְיַעֲשׂוּ) in the speech is problematic. A conjunctive clause with an inital imperfect form is rare as the first clause in a unit of speech (Revell 1987, 28; Niccacci 1990, 187). The prefixed verbal form at the beginning of the clause with conjunction ו (weyiqtol) is modal (often expressing a wish or purpose) following a preceding clause employing an imperfect (other than weyiqtol) or imperative form. The insertion of εἰπόν (assuming אֱמֹר before וְיַעֲשׂוּ) by LXX recognizes this syntactical fact as being normative. Another possibility is to follow *Tg. Onq.* and Syr. in omitting the conjunction; thus, the verb would be a jussive form initiating a prescriptive series. An explanation for the presence of the conjunction in the consonantal text of the Hebrew is found in the somewhat speculative suggestion by Dillmann (1886, 46), that the form was originally a consecutive imperfect form (wayyiqtol) transposed through the process of redaction. The pointing of the text in MT is an attempt to render the clause coherent in its present context.

to such a statement of conclusion motivates the prominence of the clause through its departure from the series of consecutive imperfect clauses, even as the clause clarifies the identified thematic structure supporting the narrative sequence.

The second narrative sequence (vv. 6–14) may be understood, following one possibility, as a chronologically displaced portion of the narrative sequence in verses 1–5. This interpretation would suppose that the event of 1–5 (4) occurs at a point in time following the events implementing the supplementary celebration (6–14 [1–6]). The implication inherent to this understanding of the text is that the summary statement of compliance (1–5 [4]) includes the events of the enactment of the supplementary celebration of the Passover (6–14 [1–6]). Another possibility for interpretation is to regard verses 6–14 as a second narrative sequence incorporating the exhortation in 1–5 (1) as its initial motif. By this interpretation, the clause 1–5 (1) performs the dual role of expressing the inciting motif of exhortation for both verses 1–5 and 6–14. The conclusion with an act of compliance, like the one in verses 1–5, would be understood as being present at the end of verses 6–14. Thus, both events (the exhortation and the act of compliance) are projected as being present virtually in the series of clauses of verses 6–14, the second narrative sequence.[31] According to this other possible interpretation, the second narrative sequence (vv. 6–14) expresses a second cycle of the initial narrative sequence with a complication of plot: an obstruction to compliance occurs because of the presence of those unable to perform the Passover. Both possible interpretations understand the narrative sequence of verses 6–14 as being dependent on that of verses 1–5. However, without any overt indication of a disruption to the order of events in 6–14 (1), it

---

[31] The nature of the projection on the part of the reader required differs between the postulation of the exhortation and the compliance in verses 6–14. The former may be regained by looking back to 1–5 (1), the exhortation initiating the first narrative sequence. In contrast, the compliance with the call to celebrate the Passover in verses 6–14 must be inserted by conjecture on the analogy of the act of compliance in the first narrative sequence; the absence of any statement to the contrary allows for this act of conjecture on the part of the reader.

is preferable to take verses 6–14 as a separate (albeit dependent) narrative sequence occurring after the events of verses 1–5 with the following formulation of a series of motifs: [Exhortation]-Inquiry (concerning an obstacle)-Resolution-[Compliance].[32]

Six clauses carry the second narrative sequence (6–14 [1] includes an embedded relative clause). As in Lev 24:10–23, the content of the portions of direct speech (including the legal prescriptions) define the motivational significance of the narrative clauses denoting speech. The series of consecutive clauses is broken once in order to express negation through the conjunctive clause 6–14 (2). Apart from the fact that negation necessitates the departure from the series of consecutive clauses, 6–14 (2) also expresses the barrier to the conclusion of the narrative sequence with an added measure of visibility. It is the presence of this barrier that provides the impetus for the motif Inquiry, leading to Resolution.[33]

---

[32] The square brackets indicate motifs imported from the narrative sequence of vv. 1–5; these motifs may be understood as having a virtual presence in vv. 6–14.

[33] Scholars proposing syntactical systems expressing features from the perspective of 'prominence' (the identification of foreground and background information in various discourse types) are divided with regard to the status of narrative clauses where the sole constituent separating the verb from the conjunction is the particle of negation (i.e. a waw-X-qatal clause where, contrary to the definition adopted for this study, 'X' is the particle of negation). Longacre considers all clauses of negation in narrative as background information by virtue of the fact that such clauses denote non-events (1989, 76–7; 1992, 178–80); being so, they can hardly be punctiliar and sequential, two character traits which, by his judgement, establish the consecutive imperfect clause (except for those deploying the verb הָיָה) as the foreground clause-type in narrative. In contrast, Niccacci distinguishes between waw-X-qatal clauses and negative clauses of the type envisioned (waw-X-qatal, where 'X' is the particle of negation). He considers the latter a foreground clause (by his terminology, a 'main-line' clause) in narrative by appealing to the fact that it is the only possible way to negate a consecutive imperfect clause (Niccacci 1995, 551). Niccacci's insistence on the criterion of syntax offers a welcome

The Legal Prescriptions

The legal prescriptions follow the command for Moses to transmit the divine address to the people (דבר אל־בני ישראל לאמר) with the laws as the precise content of that address. All the laws concern the performance of the Passover although their details extend beyond the immediate issue of the narrative sequence: the inability of those defiled through contact with a corpse to partake of the Passover. Syntactical divisions within the text and the identification of distinct units of topic collaborate in the definition of three command sets: verses 10b–2, 13, and 14.

1 איש איש כי־יהיה־טמא לנפש	1 Anyone of you or your
או בדרך רחקה לכם או לדרתיכם	descendants who is unclean
2 ועשה פסח ליהוה	through touching a corpse,
3 בחדש השני בארבעה עשר יום	or is away on a journey,
בין הערבים יעשו אתו	2 shall still keep the passover

---

corrective to Longacre's dependence on semantic criteria (with the result that consecutive imperfect clauses of the root היה are considered background material despite their bearing no formal distinction from other consecutive imperfect clauses). However, it remains a fact that negation renders the consecutive imperfect clause impossible; thus, the imposition of the particle of negation produces a formal distinction from the consecutive imperfect clause requiring analysis. Den Exter Blokland has understaken a study within the corpus of 1–2 Kgs (1995, 224–61). In line with the conclusions of Andersen (1994, 78), he finds no reason to consider the conjunctive clause with negation a foreground narrative clause along with the consecutive imperfect clause. Den Exter Blokland discerns that the former often stands as a statement of conclusion (either by itself or as part of a series of non-consecutive imperfect clauses) to a preceding series of consecutive imperfect clauses offering comment by way of contrast (1995, 253–61). Thus, formal and semantic-pragmatic criteria suggest that negated clauses occupy a category of prominence apart from consecutive clauses. While it is the case that Longacre's semantic criterion of punctiliar and sequential action in the foregroung of narrative is not valid, the observation that clauses of negation constitute non-events—a value coming to expression through the pragmatic category of prominence—is not insignificant.

4 עַל־מַצּוֹת וּמְרֹרִים יֹאכְלֻהוּ
5 לֹא־יַשְׁאִירוּ מִמֶּנּוּ עַד־בֹּקֶר
6 וְעֶצֶם לֹא יִשְׁבְּרוּ־בוֹ
7 כְּכָל־חֻקַּת הַפֶּסַח יַעֲשׂוּ אֹתוֹ

to the Lord. 3 In the second month on the fourteenth day, at twilight, they shall keep it; 4 they shall eat it with unleavened bread and bitter herbs. 5 They shall leave none of it until morning, 6 nor break a bone of it; 7 according to all the statute of the passover they shall keep it. (vv. 10b–2)

1 וְהָאִישׁ אֲשֶׁר־הוּא טָהוֹר
   וּבְדֶרֶךְ לֹא־הָיָה
2 וְחָדַל לַעֲשׂוֹת הַפֶּסַח
3 וְנִכְרְתָה הַנֶּפֶשׁ הַהִוא מֵעַמֶּיהָ
4 כִּי קָרְבַּן יְהוָה לֹא הִקְרִיב בְּמֹעֲדוֹ
5 חֶטְאוֹ יִשָּׂא הָאִישׁ הַהוּא

1 But anyone who is clean and not on a journey, 2 and yet refrains from keeping the passover, 3 shall be cut off from the people 4 for not presenting the Lord's offering at its appointed time; 5 such a one shall bear the consequences for the sin. (v. 13)

1 כִּי־יָגוּר אִתְּכֶם גֵּר
2 וְעָשָׂה פֶסַח לַיהוָה
3 כְּחֻקַּת הַפֶּסַח וּכְמִשְׁפָּטוֹ כֵּן יַעֲשֶׂה
4 חֻקָּה אַחַת יִהְיֶה לָכֶם וְלַגֵּר
   וּלְאֶזְרַח הָאָרֶץ

1 Any alien residing among you 2 who wishes to keep the passover to the Lord 3 shall do so according to the statute of the passover and to its regulation; 4 you shall have one statute for both the alien and the native. (v. 14)

Verses 10b–2

The command set of verses 10b–2 begins with the subordinate clause 10b–2 (1) expressing the condition which the law addresses. The extraposed subject אִישׁ אִישׁ standing before the clause complements subordination in effecting the syntactical disjuncture appropriate to the beginning of a command set. Two categories of person are the specific concern of this law: the individual defiled through contact with a corpse, and the one travelling afar. Two prepositional phrases offer further qualification for the extraposed subject at the beginning of the clause: לכם או לדרתיכם.[34] A consecutive clause (10b–2 [2]) proceeds with the prescription following the condition layed down by the initial subordinate clause. With the exception of 10b–2 (6), the remaining prescriptions (after 10b–2 [2]) consist of asyndetic verbal clauses. These remaining clauses of the command set, including 10b–2 (6), offer additional detail to the initial prescription with preposed condition (10b–2 [1–2]); the issues of timing and procedure for the consumption (and disposal) of the sacrifice are of concern (10b–2 [3–6]). The specifications repeat portions of the initial precriptive passage offering instruction on the procedure for the Passover in Exodus 12. The final command (10b–2 [7]) stands to summarize the catalogue of specifications; all the instructions for the Passover apply. The movement to such a high degree of syntactical disjuncture following the consecutive clause 10b–2 (2) renders each specification in the catalogue of auxiliary detail to the main prescription of the command set (to observe the Passover) prominent. Within the catalogue only the prohibitions (10b–2 [5, 6]) are grouped together by conjunction in 10b–2 (6). This measure of relative syntactical continuity occurs in order to denote the unity of 10b–2 (5, 6) within the list.

As a command set, verses 10b–2 is distinctly focused on prescribing a second Passover for those unable to observe the first. The following command set (v. 13) deals with the individual neglecting the regular (first) Passover without good cause. The initial law (10b–2 [1–2]), by invoking the performance of the Passover, is summarily descriptive of the thematic passage of the second narrative sequence within the span of two clauses.[35] Two

---

[34] According to Kellermann (1970, 124), the alternative of taking the prepositional phrases in conjunction with רחקה בדרך would require דורות, in this instance, to mean 'households' (cf. Isa 38:12; Ps 49:20). The rendition of LXX, ἐν ταῖς γενεαῖς ὑμῶν, contradicts such an interpretation for דרותיכם (cf. Isa 38:12; the Greek version has τῆς συγγενίας μου for דורי).

[35] This is a case where the invocation of a term or phrase (עשה פסח) is an index for an established series of motifs (Exhortation-Compliance)

subsequent laws (10b–2 [3, 7]) similarly express the thematic content of the second narrative sequence in single clauses; thus, the syntactical unit denoting the thematic content of the narrative sequence (particularly, the second one)[36] in its entirety (from Exhortation to Compliance) contracts in the course of the command set. Closer scrutiny of 10b–2 (3–7) yields greater structural detail. The material in between 10b–2 (3) and 10b–2 (7) describe specific acts pertaining to the performance of the Passover: the clauses list various components of the action encompassed by יעשו אתו in 10b–2 (3, 7). As such, the group of laws of 10b–2 (3–7) form a list of additional detail moving from the general to the specific and back, with the general statements (at each end) constituting thematic statements of the second narrative sequence. The series of specific components to the rite in 10b–2 (4–6) ensures that a major contribution of the command set, so clearly set forth in the final clause of the command set, does not pass unnoticed: ככל־חקת הפסח יעשו אתו. The clauses of 10b–2 (3–7) are a catalogue of specification in relation to 10b–2 (1–2), with their own variations in the degree of specificity.

Verse 13

The command set verse 13 begins with a conjunctive clause (waw-X-qatal); an extraposed subject with an attached series of relative clauses   (אשר־הוא טהור ובדרך לא־היה וחדל לעשות הפסח)

---

in the proximate narrative sequence. While the designation is less effective than the explicit mention of the individual motifs governed by the phrase, the proximity of the narrative sequence displaying the sequence of motifs clarifies the connection between the sequence of motifs and the term. Admittedly, the connection is particular to the context of Num 9:1–14: it is the collocation of the subject matter of the narrative sequence and the structure of motifs underlying the plot that produces the connection in the reader's mind within the passage.

[36] The restriction of the application to the second narrative sequence is due to the temporal designation of 10b–2 (3), which designates the time frame for the supplementary Passover. Also, the subordinate clause 10b–2 (1) clearly designates the supplementary celebration by mentioning those excluded from participating in the festival at its original designated period.

represents a degree of syntactical disjuncture corresponding to the beginning of the last command set.[37] The syntactical coherence of the command set verse 13 becomes evident with the transition to a higher degree of syntactical continuity in the following clauses: the consecutive clauses 13 (2, 3). The subordinate clause 13 (4) is intrusive. The clause supplies a reason for the penalty just proclaimed in 13 (3): the designated period for the offering has not been observed. The asyndetic verbal clause 13 (5) maintains a high degree of syntactical disjuncture in order to declare the culpability of the errant party. The clause 13 (5) achieves the status of a statement of general qualification for the command set as a whole: the command set is shown to be a series of clauses denoting the punishment of a transgressor. Asyndeton sets 13 (5) apart from the prescribed penalty for the neglect of the Passover (13 [1–3]) as a general quality of the laws capable of motivating the legislation as a whole. In this manner, 13 (5) may be seen to have a function similar to the motive (subordinate) clause 13 (4).

The command set verse 13 may be seen as an appendix to the previous command set emphasizing the limits of exception afforded by the allowance for a second celebration of the divine act of deliverance; the single motive clause of the command set (13 [4]) stipulates the precise nature of the crime as the failure to observe the rite at its designated time (בְּמֹעֲדוֹ; i.e. the normative time frame of the Passover). However, the concern over the consequence of non-compliance with the stated period for the rite without good reason deviates from the concern of the previous command set over the correct procedure for the observance of the Passover. The syntactical coherence of the command set verse 13 reflects its distinction in topic from the preceding command set (vv. 10b–2).

Verse 14

The syntactical structure of the command set verse 14 is familiar: the command set begins with a subordinate clause outlining a

---

[37] The conjunction prior to the extraposed constituent, as observed by Kellermann, governs the whole command set (v. 13) introducing a second member following the first command set, vv. 10b–2 (Kellermann 1970, 127–8).

condition (14 [1]), and proceeds with a consecutive clause (14 [2]) to complete the first prescription.[38] The final two commands addressing the same topic consists of asyndetic verbal clauses (14 [3, 4]). The syntactical disjuncture of asyndeton lends prominence to these last two commands. The first of the two (14 [3]) echoes a statement which similarly received the prominence of asyndeton in the command set verses 10b–2: the applicability of the proper procedure in the performance of the rite of Passover (10b–2 [7]). The second prescription of the two (14 [4]) proclaims the inclusion of the sojourner; this statement may be considered to be the additional contribution (to the legal corpus) of the command set as a whole within a single clause. The motive for syntactical prominence in these last two clauses of the command set (14 [3, 4]) must await the overall analysis of the legal prescriptions in conjunction with the narrative sequence.

The command set is distinct in topic by virtue of the fact that it focuses solely on the status of the sojourner with regard to the Passover. As a group, sojourners, having submitted to the rite of circumcision (Exod 12:43–9), are distinguished from other classes of foreigners (שכיר and ותושב) with respect to Passover

---

[38] A reason may be sought for the interpretation of the syntactical discontinuity of 13 (1) as topical transition (to a new command set) instead of the interpretation adopted for the asyndetic clause 13 (5). In response, it may be said that the decision to recognize a topical boundary at the beginning of 14 (1) is, once again, made with reference to guidelines espoused by den Exter Blokland. The introduction of a new subject (גר) with the injection of a significant amount of information of an introductory nature (the conditional statement of 14 [1, 2]) effects a degree of discontinuity from the preceding clauses. In contrast, 13 (5) reveals its connection with preceding material through its designation of the subject with a qualifying demonstrative pronoun (האיש ההוא). A similar explanation may be made for the choice of 13 (1) as the initial clause of a new command set. As noted by Niccacci, syntactical discontinuity is a function of grammar; it is often the role of semantics to evaluate the significance of syntactical disjuncture (1994b, 179).

observance.[39] With regard to the thematic progression of both narrative sequences, the prescriptions of verse 14 are representative in the fact that they name the narrative sequences (עשה הפסח), as opposed to designating their motifs explicitly. With increasingly brief units of syntax—from two clauses in 14 [1–2] to one in 14 [3])—the prescriptions extract the theme of the narrative sequence from its extended chronological sequence. As with the command set of verses 10b–2, a similar graded process of thematic abstraction and distillation occurs here in the command set verse 14.

Coherence of Narrative and Law in Num 9:1–14

The narrative sequences depict all of Israel (including the גר) performing the first Passover rite following the original event. With increasing syntactical brevity, the command sets of verses 10b–2 and 14 portray the thematic progression of the two narrative sequences in Num 9:1–14; the laws abstract the thematic essence portrayed over several clauses in the narrative sequences fostering clarity through condensation. In the legal prescriptions, various features of syntax expressing disjuncture (two subordinate clauses and one conjunctive clause with clause-initial extraposition) set boundaries between command sets dealing with different topics. In advocating the integrity of each command set, structures of syntax draw attention to semantic interaction between parts of the legal passage.

Within each command set, syntactical disjuncture (in the case of Num 9:1–14, asyndetic verbal clauses) lends emphasis to specific details pertinent to the presentation of theme in each command set, or simply expresses a heightened degree of urgency. Vital features stand out awaiting comparison between command sets. Just like the legal prescriptions of Lev 24:10–23 which bid the reader identify the common denominator in all the command sets, verses 10b–2 (+ 13) and 14 reveal a larger concept of more general application

---

[39] Harrison (1992, 161) and Budd (1984, 98) point to the distinct status of the sojourner among groups of foreigners where Passover observance is concerned. For a detailed description of the sojourner's status, see Milgrom's excursus on the subject (1990, 398–402).

encompassing both command sets: the command sets are concerned with the inclusion of two marginal groups in the Israelite community (those ritually unclean or away on a journey, and the sojourner) where the celebration of the Passover is concerned. In addition to the common concept of general application, the asyndetic clauses in both command sets lend prominence to a second common element between the two command sets: both command sets advocate the performance of the Passover rite according to all the established statutes and prescribed procedures (10b–2 [7 + 3–6]; 14 [3]). The statement emerging from the combination of verses 10b–2 (+ 13) and 14 receives coverage in two asyndetic clauses of the latter command set (v. 14) which conclude the legal prescrip-tions: כחקת הפסח וכמשפטו כן יעשה חקה אחת יהיה לכם ולגר הארץ The laws are divine response to human inquiry and thematic summaries of the adjacent narrative sequences. The laws respond to the inquiry by invoking one abstract concept behind the laws, the spirit of inclusion, while underlining the importance that the procedure should conform with the established guidelines. These principles are essential to the combined reading of both narrative sequences in Num 9:1–14.

THE CASE OF NUMBERS 27:1–11

Num 27:1–11 tells the story of the daughters of Zelophehad seeking an inheritance in their father's apportionment of land. The patrilineal pattern of inheritance would leave Zelophehad, not having any sons, without the ability to perpetuate his name by association with a portion of land. Moses receives a request from Zelophehad's daughters for an exception to the normal practice of inheritance. Divine initiative grants the request and proceeds to establish a principle for future problematic cases regarding inheritance: a hierarchy is established to determine the specific beneficiary within the clan.

The Wider Literary Setting of Numbers 27:1–11

The incident follows the census of Num 26:1–65, which forms the basis for the division of the land to be received by Israel (Num 26:52–65). The placement of the passage of Num 27:1–11 facilitates continuation on the subject of inheritance (Gray 1906,

397). It should be noted that the association of inclusion by name within the census and the possession of land in chapter 26 persists in Num 27:1–11: the argument of the daughters equates the loss of the allotment of land (אֲחֻזָּה) with the withdrawal (גָּרַע) of their father's name from the list. This association of a name with the possession of land within the context of Numbers 26 and 27 has been observed by numerous commentators: among others, Calvin (Bingham 1984, 255), Harrison (1980, 354–5), Davies (1981, 141–142), Olson (1985, 174–5), Milgrom (1990, 231), Ashley (1993, 545–6) and Levine (2000, 341) take note of the connection. Davies and Milgrom make reference to several other attestations of such an association: 1 Chr 2:34–5, Neh 7:63, Ezra 2:61, 2 Sam 14:4–7, and Ruth 4:10.

A larger and consistent literary agenda uniting the passages from Numbers 26 to the end of the book has been identified by Levine. In his view, the census of chapter 26, the issue of the inheritance of Zelophehad's daughters (chs. 27, 36), explanation for the route to Canaan (ch. 33), and the geographical delimitation of the land all share a concern for the new generation of Israelites emerging from the wilderness (Levine 2000, 54–5). Within this context, Calvin's remark that the request of Zelophehad's daughters is a statement of confidence in Israel's impending possession of the land is not without significance (Bingham 1984, 256). The confidence of the new generation is its distinguishing mark from that of the old which culminated in the rebellious demonstrations of Numbers 13 and 14. The observations of Calvin and Levine complement Olson's thesis (1985, 83–124) that the book, as a whole, may be understood as a transition of focus from the old generation (Num 1–25) to the new (Num 26–36). Within this scheme of interpretation, Num 27:1–11 is a component in the renewed hope of Israel with its returned focus on claiming the land promised by God. As Olson observes, the futuristic perspective inherent to the dramatic progression of the episodes concerning the daughters of Zelophehad (Num 27:1–11; 36: 1–13) forms a bracket around the latter portion of the book introduced by the census of Numbers 16. Through its infusion with the dramatic episodes within the bracket, the futuristic perspective defines the agenda of the latter half of the book through a three-fold focus on the possession of the land, its distribution, and the on-going interpretation of a legal tradition established by a divine act in the past (Olson 1985, 175–6).

The thematic coherence of Num 27:1–11 is quite clear; the (re)quest for an appropriate procedure for inheritance permeates the narrative and the laws of the unit. The characterization of the passage as midrashic (Budd 1984, 300) or aetiological (Levine 2000, 342) betrays a perception of thematic unity; the narrative demonstrates the application of, or explains, the laws. Although the agnatic principle of inheritance outlined in the laws (Num 27:8–11) is operative in the divine concession to the daughters of Zelophehad (Num 27:7), the laws in effect extend to cover circumstances beyond the content of the request of the daughters (so noted, Noth 1968, 211; Fishbane 1985, 103–4; Ashley 1993, 542–3). The analysis will show that this legal expansion does not compromise the thematic coherence of the passage, but instead acts to enrich it.

The Narrative Sequence

The narrative sequence of Num 27:1–11 is no different from those of the preceding cases: a chain of consecutive imperfect (wayyiqtol) clauses expresses the sequence of events.

1 ותקרבנה בנות צלפחד בן־חפר בן־גלעד בן־מכיר בן־מנשה למשפחת מנשה בן־יוסף 2 ואלה שמות בנתיו מחלה נעה וחגלה ומלכה ותרצה 3 ותעמדנה לפני משה ולפני אלעזר הכהן ולפני הנשיאם וכל־העדה פתח אהל־מועד לאמר	1 Then the daughters of Zelophehad came forward. Zelophehad was son of Hepher son of Gilead son of Machir son of Manasseh son of Joseph, a member of the Manassite clans. 2 The names of his daughters were: Mahlah, Noah, Hoglah, Milcah, and Tirzah. 3 They stood before Moses, Eleazer the priest, the leaders and all the congregation, at the entrance of the tent of meeting, and they said,
4 ויקרב משה את־משפטן לפני יהוה 5 ויאמר יהוה אל־משה לאמר	4 Moses brought their case before the Lord. 5 And the Lord spoke to Moses, saying: (vv. 1–6)

Five clauses sustain the narrative sequence. The conjunctive clause 1–6 (2) is the sole departure from the series of consecutive imperfect clauses; the conjunctive clause introduces a list of names. The introduction to Zelophehad's daughters fulfills a well-documented function of the verbless clause—as a disruptive feature in a series of consecutive imperfect clauses—in Biblical Hebrew prose: participant introduction (so noted by, among others, de Regt [1999, 275–9, 281–2]). However, the disruption of the sequence of consecutive clauses is motivated by factors beyond the function of participant introduction. The order of the names is a match with the order in the census list (Num 26:33b). While the imitation simply may be compliance with the requirements of protocol (Harrison 1992, 354–5), it is in effect—along with the ancestral outline of Zelophehad in 1–6 (1)—an allusion to the census list of Numbers 26.[40] With a single stroke the related issues of landholding and the continuity of a namesake, the essence of the census, have been brought to the forefront of the narrative in Num 27:1–11.[41] The stage having been set by narratorial initiative, the claim of the daughters introduced by the act of speech in 1–6 (3) acquires a concrete dimension: the objection to the withdrawal (גרע) of Zelophehad's name is not just an objection to the loss of the inheritance bearing his name, but the erasure of his name from the census list.[42] The divine response introduced by the act of speech in 1–6 (5) acquiesces to the request of the daughters.

---

[40] While the order of the names varies in Num 36:11 with the resumption of the issue of inheritance and the daughters of Zelophehad, the list remains intact.

[41] Epigrahic evidence matches the names of the daughters to places in Syria-Palestine (Lemaire 1972, 13–20). Some have seen in this fact another motive for the list of 1–6 (2) apart from that of allusion to the census of Num 26: the passage, as a whole, aims to provide explanation and justification for Manasseh's holdings west of the Jordan (Gray 1906, 392, 398; Snaith 1966, 127; Levine 2000, 55, 342, 344).

[42] The allusion to the census through the list of Zelophehad's daughters has been noted by numerous commentators (Noth 1968, 211; Budd 1984, 300; Olson 1985, 174, 175; Levine 2000, 341, 346; Ashley 1993, 541). However, it is only Levine that recognizes

By allusion to the enactment of the census, the narrative sequence centers the argument of the daughters around the familial unit under Zelophehad's name, which must now act to receive its allotment by divine initiative within the tribe (Num 26:55b). The absence of a son to Zelophehad (ובנים לא־היו לו), a legitimate heir, produces an obstacle to an otherwise smooth transition from the claim of the family (1–6 [2]) to the allotment of an inheritance (1–6 [5]).[43] The series of motifs in the narrative sequence may be expressed by the following formulation: Claim-Allotment (of

---

למה יגרע שם־אבינו מתוך משפחתו (v. 4aα) as referring to the actual impending removal of Zelophehad's name from the registration list of the census (2000, 346).

[43] A secondary impediment may be assumed by the effort of the daughters to exclude their father from Korah's rebellious faction (v. 3). Presumably, the mistaken identification of Zelophehad with this group would lead to the confiscation of his allotment through the identification of the act as a crime of considerable severity (Weingreen 1966, 521; de Vaulx 1972, 319–20). Weingreen, with comparative reference to the alleged crime of Naboth in 1 Kgs 21:1–16, suggests the identification of the crime of treason as the judgement the daughters seek to avert. By contrast, the daughters proclaim that their father had perished by his own error. Speculation abounds as to the nature of this error. Rabbi Akiba thought it to be the sin of the one gathering wood on the Sabbath in Num 15 (b. Sabb. 96b). Holzinger suggests the divine act of retribution in response to human disobedience in the garden (Gen 3:22) as a possible object of reference (1903, 137). Calvin considers the same option, but rejects it as an 'unnatural' choice (Bingham 1984, 257). Perhaps, the distance between the two passages of scripture rendered the possibility of a connection remote in Calvin's estimation. Most modern commentators take the referent of "his own sin" (בחטאו) to be the error of Israel which receives the divine judgement of exclusion from entrance to Canaan in Num 14:22–3 (Gray 1906, 398; Noth 1968, 211; Weingreen 1966, 518, 521; Snaith 1969, 186; Budd 1984, 301; Milgrom 1990, 231; Ashley 1993, 542, 545). The proximity of the aforementioned episode makes the last option most probable. Other sources of rabbinic exegesis understand the specific reference to "his own sin" to have the further implication of excluding the act of inciting others to rebellion from Zelophehad's transgression (Sipre [Num] 113; b. B. Bat. 118b).

Inheritance). Furthermore, it may be noted that the very act of speech (1–6 [2]) which establishes the initial motif (Claim) alludes to a previous event leading to the claim: אבינו מת במדבר. Although without representation in the clauses expressing the sequence of events in the narrative, this event, by reference in direct speech, is present virtually; it is the death of the father that leaves the tract of land open to claim.[44] Consequently, the formulation may be re-written as: [Demise]-Claim-Allotment (of Inheritance).[45]

The Legal Prescriptions

Previous analysis of the legal portions of the selected texts has proceeded with the separate treatment of each command set. The legal prescriptions of Num 27:1–11 share similarities in structures of syntax between each command set, producing a regular texture throughout the passage of laws with significance for the scheme of interpretation. Consequently, the analysis of the present legal passage should consider the command sets simultaneously. The numbering of the clauses in the presentation of the Hebrew text and the denotations of verse numbers in the translation will continue to mark the boundaries between command sets.

The legal prescriptions are preceded by divine instruction for Moses to accommodate the request of Zelophehad's daughters: the allotment of their father's portion (Num 27:7). The divine voice turns then to instruct Moses to address the community in proclaiming a system for the distribution of the inheritance where an immediate heir is not available (Num 27:8a). The legal prescriptions are the content of that proclamation.

1 אִישׁ כִּי־יָמוּת	1 If a man dies, 2 and has no
2 וּבֵן אֵין לוֹ	son, 3 then you shall pass his
3 וְהַעֲבַרְתֶּם אֶת־נַחֲלָתוֹ לְבִתּוֹ	inheritance on to his daughter.

---

[44] For other cases displaying male succession as the normative mode of inheritance, see Gen 29:24, 29, Judg 1:13–5, and 1 Kgs 9:16.

[45] As with the formulation for the narrative sequences of Num 9:1–14, the square brackets indicate the virtuality of the motif they enclose.

(v. 8b)

1 וְאִם־אֵין לוֹ בַּת
2 וּנְתַתֶּם אֶת־נַחֲלָתוֹ לְאֶחָיו

1 If he has no daughter, 2 then you shall give his inheritance to his brothers. (v. 9)

1 וְאִם־אֵין לוֹ אַחִים
2 וּנְתַתֶּם אֶת־נַחֲלָתוֹ לַאֲחִי אָבִיו

1 If he has no brothers, 2 then you shall give his inheritance to his father's brothers. (v. 10)

1 וְאִם־אֵין אַחִים לְאָבִיו
2 וּנְתַתֶּם אֶת־נַחֲלָתוֹ
לִשְׁאֵרוֹ הַקָּרֹב אֵלָיו מִמִּשְׁפַּחְתּוֹ
3 וְיָרַשׁ אֹתָהּ
4 וְהָיְתָה לִבְנֵי יִשְׂרָאֵל לְחֻקַּת
מִשְׁפָּט
5 כַּאֲשֶׁר צִוָּה יְהוָה אֶת־מֹשֶׁה

1 And if his father has no brothers, 2 then you shall give his inheritance to the nearest kinsman of his clan, 3 and he shall possess it. 4 It shall be for the Israelites a statute and ordinance, 5 as the Lord commanded Moses. (v. 11)

A subordinate clause employing the extraposed element אִישׁ before the clause (8b [1]) introduces the first condition. The role of the extraposed member within the clause is expressed by its resumption (as subject) within the verbal morpheme יוּמַת. The interceding particle of conjunction marks the status of the noun אִישׁ as an extraposed constituent standing prior to the clause. A higher degree of syntactical continuity proceeds with the protasis (8b [2]): the conjunctive verbless clause of negation 8b (2) follows the initial subordinate clause with extraposed member. As a clause without a finite verb, 8b (2) stands apart from the syntactical continuum expressed by the following consecutive clause (8b [3], flowing from the initial subordinate clause (8b [1]). Despite the higher degree of syntactical continuity of 8b (2) in comparison with 8b (1), the disjuncture of the conjunctive clause 8b (2) is perceived in relation to the following consecutive clause 8b (3).[46] Conjunction

---

[46] The command set at hand (v. 8b) provides excellent illustration of the principles behind the interpretation of inter-clausal syntax. The degree of syntactical disjuncture (whether marking a topical boundary or raising the visibility of a single clause) must be determined by reference to the semantic import of the clause in relation to the surrounding clauses.

sets the negative import of 8b (2) apart from the series of events
(8b [1, 3]) bearing the procedure of inheritance in the first
command set. The primary difficulty addressed by the prescription
is the expression of 8b (2): the absence of a son as heir. The
consecutive perfect clause 8b (3) completes the first command set.
The subordinate verbless clause 9 (1) marks the initiation of the
next command set addressing a variant circumstance.

Two factors distinguish the first command set from the
others. Firstly, the commencement of the first command set
employs the additional disjunctive feature of extraposition at its
inception. Subsequent command sets within the passage dispense
with the feature of extraposition as an additional expression of
syntactical disjuncture at their beginning. It seems the case that
among clauses of the same type (in this case, subordinate clauses),
the additional feature of extraposition may mark the initiation of
the main topic with the initiation of sub-topics being left to those
clauses without the element of extraposition. The second
distinction between the first command set and the others support
such an interpretation of the syntax. The initial command set is the
only one introduced by כִּי; all subsequent command sets take the
conditional conjunction אִם. Both observations of syntax betray the
unique relationship between the conditional statements of the
command sets. As the passage stands, 8b (1) is an integral part of
the conditional statement in each subsequent set. In fact, the
conditional statements through each command set are cumulative:
each conditional statement adds a new condition to the
accumulated mass of the previous one. This relationship between
the command sets is given expression through the interaction of
the conditional (subordinate) conjunctions כִּי and אִם: the former

_____

Conjunction in 8b (2) conveys syntactical continuity in relation to
subordination with extraposition in 8b (1). However, a degree of
disjuncture is perceived (within 8b [1–2]) when the following consecutive
clause (8b [3]) is brought into consideration. The element of negation in
8b (2) allows the conclusion that the degree of syntactical disjuncture of
conjunction in the clause is the dismemberment of 8b (2) from the series
of fientive verbal clauses of 8b (1–3 [minus 2]): the elevation of a single
clause is the effect of syntactical disjuncture in 8b (2).

establishes the foundational condition while the latter introduces additional variations.[47] The absence of the additional element of syntactical disjuncture afforded by a clause-initial extraposed constituent in the subsequent command sets expresses a degree of coherence between the command sets. Despite this element of coherence between the command sets, the fact that each subsequent conditional statement renders the prescription in the apodosis of the last command set impossible makes each command set distinct; the syntactical disjuncture of the subordinate clauses mark these distinctions. The final command set (v. 11) is also unique. The commands, unlike those of the other command sets, end with a comparative (subordinate) clause (11 [5]) designating the prescriptive procedure as a command issued through Moses.

Apart from the minor (albeit significant) differences listed above, the command sets proceed from clauses expressing a higher degree of syntactical disjuncture (subordinate clauses) to those expressing continuity (consecutive clauses). Only in one case (v. 11) does the command set end by reverting to a higher degree of syntactical disjuncture (subordination in 11 [5]). The syntactical uniformity of the group clarifies the divisions between command sets lending cadence to the order in the legal passage.

All the command sets begin with an event precipitating the necessity for the transfer of property: the death or absence of an individual. The persistence of this event throughout all the

---

[47] The establishment of the initial condition followed by subsequent variations by the addition of more conditions in Num 27:8b–11 has been noted by Ashley (1993, 542). Grammarians have noted the secondary function of אִם in relation to כִּי in a sizable proportion of cases where the two conjunctions occur together (GKC §159*bb*; *BHRG* §40.9). Revell (1991, 1278–84) provides a more detailed analysis of the interaction between the two conditional particles. His analysis finds that אִם frequently provides contrasting and even mutually exclusive alternatives when following a conditional statement introduced by כִּי. This use of אִם is implicit in its basic function as an indicator of one among two or more possibilities (Revell 1991, 1280). Where such other possibilities are not explicitly mentioned, they may be inferred by context. By contrast, כִּי often introduces an independent condition (Revell 1991, 1281).

conditional statements of the command sets is indicated, as previously mentioned, by the cumulative significance of אִם in relation to כִּי within the context of the passage of laws. The verbless clause of negation (expressed by אֵין) in each conditional statement expresses a barrier to the legitimate completion of the transfer. For the command sets of verses nine, ten and eleven, the verbless clause of negation represents the most recent additional barrier: the absence of the next candidate within the hierarchy. Consecutive clauses (8b [3]; 9 [2]; 10 [2]; 11 [2–3]) in each command set overcome the obstacles and address the necessity precipitated at the beginning of the set. In essence, the command sets are skeletal outlines—representations of a series of motifs— capable of expansion into narrative sequences similar to the narrative sequence of Num 27:1–11: [Demise]-Claim-Allotment (of Inheritance).[48] In the legal prescriptions, the command sets expressing these bi-polar formulations of theme move from longer units of syntax (8b [1–3]; three clauses) to shorter units (9 [1–2]; 10 [1–2]; two clauses each). The return to a longer syntactical unit in the final command set (11 [1–5]; 5 clauses)[49] produces a structure

---

[48] While the legal prescriptions include the motif Demise, it is informative that the instructions addressing the specific circumstances of the narrative sequence in vv. 7–8a omit it. Directly engaging the request of the daughters, the divine response of vv. 7–8a begins by acknowledging the event immediately preceding it (the death of Zelophehad), and thus provoking, the response to the specific circumstances: the event encoded within the motivational scheme of the narrative sequence as Claim. The formulation of the instructions of vv. 7–8a in the terms of such a scheme would yield the apocopated variant Claim-Allotment (of Inheritance).

[49] In the command set of v. 11, the bi-polar formulation of a theme akin to that of the narrative sequence is represented by the first three clauses (11 [1–3]); the subsequent clauses 11 (4–5) report the establishment of a new statute of procedure (לְחֻקַּת מִשְׁפָּט) for Israel. Despite the exclusion of the last two clauses from the parameters of the formulation, the command set still represents the return to a longer syntactical unit (three clauses as opposed to two) for the formulation of the narrative's theme.

of concentration for the theme of narrative and law within the command sets in the middle of the legal passage.

In addition to the syntactical uniformity of the command sets, the command sets also display a common preference for the closest available relative as the designated recipient of the inheritance in accordance with a stated hierarchy. The effect of the juxtaposition of the command sets in the legal passage is the identification of this common denominator in all the command sets.

Coherence of Narrative and Law in Numbers 27:1–11

The command sets are abstractions of the narrative sequence: they identify the bound motifs sustaining the narrative sequence at its poles (Demise and Allotment), representing these motifs in brief series of clauses. Despite the fact that the party receiving the inheritance varies from one command set to another, the general categories (i.e. the names applied to characterize the events) for the events forming the series of motifs remain the same; it is a movement from the death of the head of the family to the allotment of the inheritance for the next-of-kin. Consequently, a thematic element binding the clauses of the narrative sequence in Num 27:1–11 emerges with greater clarity. The especially compact expression of the thematic element at the center of the series of command sets provides focus, even as the repetition of the thematic element from one command set to another creates emphasis. The thematic coherence of narrative sequence and legal prescription is unmistakable. From the series of command sets bearing the same element of theme a second similar trait emerges: the fact that the closest relative available is to be the beneficiary of the inheritance. This secondary development in the process of abstraction—the emergence of the guiding principle in the movement between Demise and Allotment—is the accomplishment of the collocation of the command sets forcing the identification of similar traits, the basis for the collection of laws.

The result of readerly movement between narrative sequence and law is the placement of the narrative sequence within a broader category, which may have remained obscure without the interaction with the legal passage. From a rhetorical point of view, the divine ruling in favour of the daughters of Zelophehad becomes ensconced in a principle of operation capable of generating and justifying procedures well beyond the circumstantial confines of the situation in Num 27:1–11. In effect, the divine concession to the daughters is shown to be in line with the original principle which awards the land holdings of the deceased to the son, the next-of-kin.

THE CASE OF NUMBERS 36:1–13

Num 36:1–13 follows Num 27:1–11 in pursuing the issue of inheritance and the daughters of Zelophehad. A group of elders from Zelophehad's clan in the tribe of Manasseh come forward to meet Moses. With reference to the judgement of Num 27:1–11, they point to the possibility that, through marriage of the daughters, landholdings from the tribe of Manasseh could pass over to other tribes. By deference to divine command, Moses responds to the elders by making it a requirement that the daughters of Zelophehad marry within their tribe. Subsequently, similar restrictions are issued to all Israel in anticipation of similar situations in the future. The daughters of Zelophehad comply with divine requirement by marrying the sons of their uncles.

The Wider Literary Setting of Numbers 36:1–13

The connection with the previous episode of Num 27:1–11 is blatant; the patriarchal heads make reference to God's decision to allow Zelophehad's daughters to claim their father's inheritance in Numbers 27 (Num 36:2). An issue of interest for biblical scholars is the separation of Num 36:1–13 from Num 27:1–11. In view of the close connection in terms of the development of plot, why do these passages occur so far apart in the final form of the text? Noth regards Num 36:1–13 to be an appendix to Num 27:1–11 included at the end of the book (1968, 257). Noth's reference to the process of redaction in the text leaving a preexisting block of material intact is preceded and followed by the similar comments of Gray and Budd respectively. Gray, with Budd's approval (1984, 384), envisions a later hand adopting the style of P inserting a supplement (minus Num 36:13) to the legislation of Num 27:1–11 (Gray 1906, 477).

The consideration of the nature of the material in between the passages by Olson (1985) produces a reason for the separation of the two bodies of text.[50] The two passages form an inclusio enclosing events involving the generation of the second census (Num 27:12–35:34). An atmosphere of hope surrounds the dominant themes of the events in between, which mostly deal directly with the possession of the land or assume a situation of residence in the land (Olson 1985, 175). The content of the enclosing frame—the prospective aspect of the legal promulgation—defines the theological agenda behind the editorial process of the collected material within the framework. This optimism of the second generation contrasts with the dour perspective of the previous generation, which culminates in the loss of the privilege of settlement. Olson's observation of an optimistic futurism endemic to the events following the second census of Numbers 26 finds support in Ashley's identification of Num 36:1–13 as part of a block of material (Num 33:50–36:13) concerned directly with the land promised by God (1993, 659). The concentration of laws dealing specifically with the land (Num 33:50–36:13) spearheads the movement toward the possession of the land. In incorporating Ashley's observation, Olson's inclusio may be seen to pack a futuristic punch toward the end of the material contained by the inclusio (Num 27:12–35:34). Even the progression within the enclosed material reflects the orientation of the block as a whole toward the future.

The clauses of Num 36:1–13 also forge a connection with previous material in geographical terms. The summary statement of Num 36:13 marks the end of a series of commandments with reference to Israel's location on the plains of Moab. The geographical reference recalls Israel's initial arrival in Moab in Num 22:1 and, in conjunction with that notification, groups the commandments of the interceding material as a unified block sharing the plains of Moab as the locus of promulgation (Gray 1906, 478; Milgrom 1990, 299; Ashley 1993, 659, among others). Levine sees in Num 22:1 a statement of transition to the

---

[50] The following observation of structure had been mentioned previously in connection with the discussion of Num 27:1–11.

Transjordanian phase of Israel's sojourn (2000, 159). The transition signals the impending end to Israel's wandering: a development coinciding with the dispossession of a generation lacking in vision (Num 14:21–3) and the inauguration of one with hope in heart (Num 26). Thus, it may be seen that the geographical reference of Num 36:13 forges a connection between the movement toward the promised land and the passing of a generation. The shift of focus toward the land also is inherent in the futuristic perspective of Num 36:1–13 and 27:1–11 (along with the larger block of Num 33:50–36:13).

As is the case with Num 27:1–11, the coherence of Num 36:1–13 as a literary unit is evident: the laws are closely associated with the concern for the loss of tribal parcels of land in the narrative. As a literary unit, Num 36:1–13 is distinguished from previous subject matter in Num 35:1–34, which provides instructions for the establishment of cities of refuge and their operation.

The Narrative Sequence

A total of ten clauses constitute the narrative sequence of Num 36:1–13. Consecutive imperfect clauses bear the bulk of the burden relaying the series of events in succession. Four clauses depart from the series of consecutive clauses. Of these four clauses, one is a subordinate clause (1–13 [5]) and three are asyndetic clauses (1–13 [6, 8, 10]). The asyndetic clauses are verbal clauses with the exception of 1–13 (10).[51]

---

[51] A relative clause expanding upon the predicate of the verbless clause 1–13 (10), however, employs a finite verbal form. The relative clause, by virtue of its subordination to a noun phrase within the clause, is excluded from the analysis of inter-clausal syntax in the narrative sequence.

1 וַיִּקְרְבוּ רָאשֵׁי הָאָבוֹת
לְמִשְׁפַּחַת בְּנֵי־גִלְעָד בֶּן־מָכִיר
בֶּן־מְנַשֶּׁה
מִמִּשְׁפְּחֹת בְּנֵי יוֹסֵף
2 וַיְדַבְּרוּ לִפְנֵי מֹשֶׁה וְלִפְנֵי
הַנְּשִׂאִים
3 וַיֹּאמְרוּ

1 The heads of the ancestral houses of the clans of the descendants of Gilead son of Machir son of Manasseh, of the Josephite clans, came forward 2 and spoke in the presence of Moses and the leaders, the heads of the ancestral houses of the Israelites; 3 they said,

———

4 וַיְצַו מֹשֶׁה אֶת־בְּנֵי יִשְׂרָאֵל
עַל־פִּי יְהוָה לֵאמֹר

4 Then Moses commanded the Israelites according to the word of the Lord, saying,

———

5 כַּאֲשֶׁר צִוָּה יְהוָה אֶת־מֹשֶׁה
6 כֵּן עָשׂוּ בְּנוֹת צְלָפְחָד[52]
7 וַתִּהְיֶינָה מַחְלָה תִרְצָה וְחָגְלָה
וּמִלְכָּה
וְנֹעָה בְּנוֹת צְלָפְחָד לִבְנֵי
דֹדֵיהֶן לְנָשִׁים
8 מִמִּשְׁפְּחֹת בְּנֵי־מְנַשֶּׁה בֶן־יוֹסֵף
הָיוּ לְנָשִׁים
9 וַתְּהִי נַחֲלָתָן עַל־מַטֵּה
מִשְׁפַּחַת אֲבִיהֶן
10 אֵלֶּה הַמִּצְוֺת וְהַמִּשְׁפָּטִים
אֲשֶׁר צִוָּה יְהוָה בְּיַד־מֹשֶׁה
אֶל־בְּנֵי יִשְׂרָאֵל בְּעַרְבֹת מוֹאָב
עַל יַרְדֵּן יְרֵחוֹ

5–6 The daughters of Zelophehad did as the Lord had commanded Moses. 7 Mahlah, Tirzah, Hoglah, Milcah, and Noah, the daughters of Zelophehad, married sons of their father's brothers. 8 They were married into the clans of the descendants of Manasseh son of joseph, 9 and their inheritance remained in the tribe of their father's clan. 10 These are the commandments and the ordinances that the Lord commanded through Moses to the Israelites in the plains of Moab by the Jordan at Jericho (vv. 1–13).

———

[52] The translation combines the clauses 1–13 (5, 6), inverting the order of their occurrence. The numerical designation for this portion of the text in the translation (5–6) is a reflection of this fact.

The initial departure from the series of consecutive clauses
(1–13 [5]) picks up the narrative following the communication of
divine will by Moses in direct speech (introduced by 1–13 [4]). The
subordinate clause 1–13 (5) performs the function of comparison:
the clause expresses the compliance of Zelophehad's daughters
with divine restriction. The apodosis to the comparative clause 1–
13 (5) is an asyndetic clause (1–13 [6]). The syntactical disjuncture
of the two clauses (1–13 [5, 6]) establishes the prominence of the
report of conformity to divine will. As a statement of compliance,
1–13 (5–6) reveals a connection of cause and effect with the
command given in 1–13 (4). This connection is given expression by
lexical correspondence (the use of similar phrases) between 1–13
(5) and 1–13 (4): Moses issues a command according to divine
proclamation (1–13 [4]), and Zelophehad's daughters comply with
the divine command to Moses for the people (1–13 [5]).

(1–13 [4]) וַיְצַו מֹשֶׁה אֶת־בְּנֵי יִשְׂרָאֵל עַל־פִּי יְהוָה לֵאמֹר

(1–13 [5]) כַּאֲשֶׁר צִוָּה יְהוָה אֶת־מֹשֶׁה

Through the inversion of the lexical sequence מֹשֶׁה←יְהוָה in
1–13 (4) and the resurgence of the verb צוה, 1–13 (5) forges its
connection with 1–13 (4). The clause 1–13 (5), as part of the
statement raising the prominence of the obedience of the daughters
(1–13 [5–6]), emphasizes the divine origin of the instruction
through its placement of יְהוָה as subject of the verb (instead of
מֹשֶׁה as in 1–13 [4]).

The third departure from the series of consecutive clauses is
the asyndetic verbal clause 1–13 (8). The clause reports the fact that
the daughters of Zelophehad took husbands within Manasseh. The
previous clause, 1–13 (7), is a consecutive imperfect clause
reporting that the daughters married their cousins; the asyndetic
clause 1–13 (8) interrupts the series of consecutive clauses (1–13 [9]
resumes the sequence of consecutive clauses) in order to establish
the significance of the marriage for the progression of the plot: the
danger of Manasseh losing territory to the other tribes through the
marriage of Zelophehad's daughters has been averted. It is
noteworthy that the divine instruction to Moses concerning the
marriage of Zelophehad's daughters explicitly mentions this

restriction: אַךְ לְמִשְׁפַּחַת מַטֵּה אֲבִיהֶם תִּהְיֶינָה לְנָשִׁים (Num 36:6b). In the narrative sequence, the specific manner in which the restriction is observed (1–13 [7]) by marrying cousins is reported as part of the sequence of consecutive clauses. Syntactical disruption occurs with the clause responding directly to the divine pronouncement of Num 36:6b. In this manner, 1–13 (8), like 1–13 (5–6), strives to establish the compliance of Zelophehad's daughters with divine instruction through the added visibility of syntactical disjuncture. The majority of the disruptions to the series of consecutive clauses rallies around a single feature of the narrative sequence: the fulfillment of divine imperative.

The final clause of the narrative sequence is 1–13 (10). As an asyndetic verbless clause, 1–13 (10) offers summary as closing statement to the book of Numbers as well as to the particular narrative sequence. The wider structural significance of this clause has been discussed in the introduction to the literary significance of the textual unit for the book.

The narrative sequence begins with the appeal of the elders of Gilead to Moses regarding the previous ruling of Num 27:1–11. Moses, after consultation with God, addresses the concern of the elders. The daughters of Zelophehad subsequently act in compliance with the divine ruling. The narrative sequence may be expressed by the following sequence of motifs: Appeal-Intercession-Redress. The second motif of the sequence (Intercession) represents a significant progression toward the final motif (Redress) which addresses the thematic progression set in motion by the initial motif (Appeal). The fact that 1–13 (5, 6, 8) in the preceding syntactical analysis of the narrative sequence depart from the sequence of consecutive clauses lends gravity to the final motif in the formulation (Redress). However, the observation that the content of 1–13 (5, 6, 8) is a response to the act of divine intercession through Moses in 1–13 (4)—whether the connections are forged with 1–13 (4) itself or with components of the speech introduced by 1–13 (4)—shows a higher degree of emphasis on the connection between the motifs Intercession and Redress than between Appeal and Redress. Thus, the divine intervention, in conjunction with the closing events of the narrative sequence (Intercession leading to Redress), emerges with elevated status within the sequence of motifs.

That the narrative sequence as a whole may be described as the successful effort of a tribe in assuming retention of its territorial allotment may be seen in the way the obstacle to the completion of the sequence is formulated.[53] A glance at the inter-clausal syntax of the appeal of the elders (the content of the speech introduced by 1–13 [3]) reveals the significance of syntax for the rhetoric of the appeal, which sets the sequence of motifs in motion.

1 את־אדני צוה יהוה לתת את־הארץ בנחלה בגורל לבני ישראל 2 ואדני צוה ביהוה לתת את־נחלת צלפחד אחינו לבנתיו 3 והיו לאחד מבני שבטי בני־ישראל לנשים 4 ונגרעה נחלתן מנחלת אבתינו 5 ונוסף על נחלת המטה אשר תהיינה להם 6 ומגרל נחלתנו יגרע 7 ואם־יהיה היבל לבני ישראל 8 ונוספה נחלתן על נחלת המטה אשר תהיינה להם 9 ומנחלת מטה אבתינו יגרע נחלתן	1 The Lord commanded my lord to give the land for inheritance by lot to the Israelites; 2 and my lord was commanded by the Lord to give the inheritance of our brother Zelophehad to his daughters. 3 But if they are married into another Israelite tribe, 4 then their inheritance will be taken from the inheritance of our ancestors 5 and added into the inheritance of the tribe into which they marry; 6 so it will be taken away from the allotted portion of our inheritance. 7 And when the jubilee of the Israelites comes, 8 then their inheritance will be added to the inheritance of the tribe into which they have married; 9 and their inheritance will be taken from the inheritance of our ancestral tribe (vv. 2–4).

---

[53] The connection between the sequence of motifs, Appeal-Intercession-Redress, and the retention of the tribal allotment is one forged within the particular context of this narrative sequence. The designated motifs outline a story concerning an act of legal intervention; within the context of Num 36:1–13, the protection of the tribal landholding is the content of the intervention. Later, it may be seen that the laws designate the series of events by employing a term at home in the specific context of the narrative.

After an asyndetic clause (2–4 [1]) initiates the unit of speech, the recovered information forming a prelude to the enunciation of the problem at hand persists with the conjunctive clause 2–4 (2). Together, the two clauses 2–4 (1–2) are a reference to the previous ruling in Numbers 27 setting the foundation for the projected sequence of events producing the problem (2–4 [3–5]; consecutive perfect clauses).[54] The series of consecutive clauses (2–4 [3–5]) is broken with a return to a conjunctive clause in 2–4 (6); the clause restates the event of particular concern from the preceding series of consecutive clauses (Manasseh's loss of territory). A subordinate (conditional) clause 2–4 (7) introduces an additional statement to the complaint: even the Jubilee will not see the return of this territory to Manasseh.[55] The conditional statement beginning with 2–4 (7) proceeds with a consecutive clause (2–4 [8]) before a conjunctive clause (2–4 [9]) intercedes with a degree of syntactical disjuncture. Once again, the disruption at 2–4 (9) of that which could be a single series of consecutive clauses occurs in order to state an event of concern for the speaker: Manasseh's loss. The

---

[54] In addition to marking the initiation of the unit of speech, the relatively higher degree of syntactical disjuncture in 2–4 (1), as well as 2–4 (2), in comparison to the following consecutive clauses sets 2–4 (1–2) apart from the following series of clauses.

[55] Noth considers the reference to the laws of the Jubilee in Lev 25:8–17 a contradiction to the rhetoric of the complaint: one would expect the Jubilee to be an occasion for the return of the lost parcel of land to Manasseh (Noth 1968, 257). Snaith, in recognizing the law of Jubilee to govern only transactions of sale, finds the statement of 2–4 (7–8) out of place for its concern with land lost through inheritance. Against the views of Noth and Snaith, it should be noted that the impotence of the law of Jubilee in the case at hand is the precise purpose for its mention here in Num 36:1–13. The occasion of the Jubilee for the restoration of equity in landholdings can bring no redress to Manasseh's loss (Dillmann 1886, 222; Holzinger 1903, 173; Gray 1906, 478; Ashley 1993, 659; Levine 2000, 578). The proposition by de Vaulx that the reference to the Jubilee speaks of an unknown law confirming the transfer of all property through marriage (1972, 405) is quite unnecessary. The rhetorical scheme in Num 36:2–4 supplies an adequate context for the reference to the Jubilee.

syntactical prominence of select clauses in the speech of the elders elevates the source of malcontent.

The Legal Prescriptions

The singular topical focus of the series of laws limits the number of command sets to one; subsequent examination of the syntactical flow between the clauses will support this observation from semantic criteria. Unlike previous cases where legal portions were separated from other prescriptive material in direct speech through the intervention of a secondary reference to a unit of speech (see Lev 24:15a and Num 27:8a), the present case makes no syntactical distinction between the two categories. In fact, it is difficult to ascertain the point at which the transition occurs in the prescriptions. Commentators often take Num 36:8a (6b–9 [5] in the numerical scheme for clauses in the following presentation of the text) to be the beginning of the address directed at the nation as a whole (Noth 1968, 257; Ashley 1993, 659). However, it should be noted that the preceding two clauses (6b–9 [3, 4]) already concern the larger community (בני ישראל). Thus, it is the case that prescriptive material addressing the specific circumstance of the narrative sequence (Num 36:6aβ, 6b) flow into legal prescription with little interruption in the progression of thought (marriage of the daughters within the tribe will disrupt the possibility of inappropriate property exchange within the nation). In light of the subtlety of this transition to legal prescription, the presentation of the text and the following analysis must consider together the two types of prescription. The prescriptions follow upon a statement of quotation of divine promulgation (Num 36:6a) in the response of Moses to the elders of Gilead and all Israel.

1 לטוב בעיניהם תהיינה לנשים	1 Let them marry whom they think best; 2 only it must be into
2 אך למשפחת מטה אביהם תהיינה לנשים	a clan of their father's tribe that they are married, 3 so that no
3 ולא־תסב נחלה לבני ישראל ממטה אל־מטה	inheritance of the Israelites will be transferred from one tribe to another; 4 for all Israelites shall
4 כי איש בנחלת מטה אבתיו ידבקו בני ישראל	retain the inheritance of their ancestral tribes. 5 Every daughter
5 וכל־בת ירשת נחלה	who possesses an inheritance in

ממטות
בני ישראל ממשפחת מטה
אביה
תהיה לאשה
6 למען יירשו בני ישראל
איש נחלת אבתיו
7 ולא־תסב נחלה ממטה
למטה אחר
8 כי־איש בנחלתיו ידבקו
מטות בני ישראל

any tribe of the Israelites shall marry one from the clan of her father's tribe, 6 so that all Israelites may continue to possess their ancestral inheritance. 7 No inheritance shall be transferred from one tribe to another; 8 for each of the tribes of the Israelites shall retain its own inheritance.
(vv. 6b–9)

The asyndetic verbal clause 6b–9 (1) initiates the series of prescriptions allowing the daughters of Zelophehad to marry whom they please. Asyndeton persists beyond the first clause of the command set; the asyndetic clause 6b–9 (2) states a restriction to the initial allowance. Muraoka identifies two related functions for the particle אך: asseverative-emphatic and restrictive-adversative. The common element in the two categories is the fact that the particle brings prominence to the word or clause which it qualifies (Muraoka 1985, 129–30). The case from 6b–9 (2) falls, by Muraoka's judgement, within the category restrictive-adversative. As a feature of inter-clausal syntax imposing a higher degree of disjuncture, asyndeton complements the emphatic use of the particle אך. Following the pronounced restriction of 6b–9 (2) with a measure of syntactical prominence, the series of prescriptions proceeds with a higher degree of syntactical continuity: the clause 6b–9 (3) is a conjunctive clause.

With the on-set of 6b–9 (3), the issue at hand spreads beyond the circumstances involving Zelophehad's daughters to encompass a common concern for every tribe within the nation. Henceforward, conjunctive clauses, on the whole, link the commands forming the rest of the prescriptive discourse in the passage (6b–9 [3, 5, 7]). The series of conjunctive clauses are punctuated by subordinate clauses providing two statements of motive (6b–9 [4 and 8]) and one purpose clause (6b–9 [6]); unlike previous cases where subordinate clauses marked topical transitions, here they cause syntactical disruption solely for reasons of explanation for the legislation.

The legal prescriptions of the passage are uniform in their object of concern: all inheriting daughters of Israel must marry within their tribe (6b–9 [5]) in order to prevent the loss of one tribe's landholding to another (6b–9 [3, 7]). The subordinate clauses reinforce this reasoning (6b–9 [4, 6, 8]). The subordinate clauses which exude syntactical prominence in establishing motive and purpose are also summary thematic statements for the narrative sequence; the narrative sequence recounts series of actions tantamount to the retention of an allotment of land, moving from human appeal (Appeal) to divine redress of inequity (Redress). This designation of the narrative's theme in the subordinate clauses is not shared by the prohibitions (6b–9 [3, 7]) and the single exhortation (6b–9 [5]) of the legal prescriptions. The clause 6b–9 (5) only depicts the act concluding the narrative, and the prohibitions (6b–9 [3, 7]) omit mention of the series of motifs in the narrative sequence or of a phrase capable of denoting the series of motifs in conjunction with the dramatic development of the narrative sequence.

A summary of the semantic composition of the legal section must include mention of the chiastic structure placing the command of 6b–9 (5) at its center along with the purpose clause 6b–9 (6). The outer ring of the structure consists of the almost identical sets of clauses 6b–9 (3–4) and 6b–9 (7–8).

ולא־תסב נחלה לבני ישראל

A: 6b–9 (3–4)

ממטה אל־מטה
כי איש בנחלת מטה אבתיו
ידבקו בני ישראל

X: 6b–9 (5–6)

וכל־בת ירשת נחלה ממטות
בני ישראל ממשפחת מטה אביה
תהיה לאשה
למען יירשו בני ישראל
איש נחלת אבתיו

A': 6b–9 (7–8)

ולא־תסב נחלה ממטה למטה

אחר
כי־איש בנחלתיו ידבקו
מטות בני ישראל

The central location of 6b–9 (5–6) lends prominence to the full legal prescription embracing the precise detail giving rise to the problem: female inheritance. It may be said that 6b–9 (5–6) constitutes a specific legal statement addressing more closely the events of the narrative sequence; the statement is flanked by laws prohibiting an action (the transfer of tribal allotments) resulting from a variety of possible causes. The experience of reading through the laws of 6b–9 (3–8) entails a movement from a general formulation, to a specific pronouncement, and back then to the general statement.

Coherence of Narrative and Law in Numbers 36:1–13

Within the plot of the narrative sequence, the legal prescriptions are divine response to the appeal of the elders of Gilead. As representations of the bi-polar sequence of motifs expressing the thematic progression of the narrative sequence, the subordinate clauses of the legal prescriptions (6b–9 [4, 6, 8])—the clauses expressing the reason for the legislation—express concepts, statements of theme, capable of reduction to the series of motifs bearing the narrative sequence. Thus, the subordinate clauses disrupt the syntactical flow of the laws in order to present abstract statements of theme inherent to the narrative sequence; the subordinate clauses reduce the sequence of motifs expressed over the space of nine clauses in the narrative sequence (excluding the summary statement for the entire book in 1–13 [10]) to single clauses collectively designating the series of motifs. The distinct topical focus of the narrative sequence emerges with even greater clarity in the laws.

SUMMARY: THE INTERACTION OF NARRATIVE AND LAW IN THE SIMPLE CASES

A function of syntactical disjuncture in the legal prescriptions reviewed is to demarcate topical boundaries between various sets of commands. In the texts reviewed, subordinate clauses, asyndetic clauses and clauses employing extraposition function to effect syntactical disjuncture. The syntactical demarcation of such boundaries assists readers in recognizing semantic boundaries; the parts (individual command sets) which form the whole (the legal passage) receive notice. This feature in the process of reading is essential for the process of abstraction as defined in the preceding analysis. The common semantic category emerges alongside an awareness of the unique contributions of each command set: the reader's search for the basis for the combination is activated by realization of plurality within the whole. While such acts of comparison between command sets often are essential for deriving the formulation of motifs underlying adjacent narrative sequences, they are also instrumental in pointing out other principles or concepts governing the laws and the narratives.[56] In Lev 24:10–23, Num 9:1–14 and 27:1–11, the thematic definitions applied to narrative sequences achieve standing within principles underlying adjacent legal prescriptions emerging through the comparison of the various command sets; within such readerly acts of ideation (to use Iser's term), recognition of the parts and the whole are concomitant acts of reading. As an act of divine response to human dilemma in the narrative sequences, the laws take on additional weight through the exemplification of a principle. Equity and consistency permeate the body of laws. This is the fruit of abstraction.

---

[56] While such concepts and principles (often given prominence in syntactically obtrusive clauses) shown to govern entire groups of prescriptions and narrative sequences are thematic, only some are capable of formulation within the stipulated series of motifs governing the narrative sequence. This distinction was noted throughout the analysis. The principle of equity between crime and punishment in Lev 24:10–23 (שׁן תחת שׁן) is clearly amenable—susceptible to demonstration of completion through the series of motifs—to the stipulated series of motifs Trangression-Execution; but the principle of inclusion in the Passover legislation of Num 9:1–14 is not visible in the series of motifs Exhortation-Compliance. Essentially, not all themes find expression in the completion of a sequence of events in narrative. Even in narrative—as they are in laws—themes may exist within every event of the series forming the narrative sequence; inclusion is inherent to Exhortation and Compliance in Num 9:1–14. Such themes in narrative would be apprehended as the paradigmatic feature within the flow of motifs. In any case, thematic abstraction through the apprehension of common concepts within command sets can draw attention to such concepts in law and narrative.

A second function of syntactical disjuncture is to effect a degree of emphasis on the content of single clauses. In examples witnessed thus far, emphasis effects urgency in the pronouncement of a sentence for an act of transgression, or prominence for a statement of thematic significance for the group of laws and the narrative sequence. The bi-polar formulations of plot (in narrative) and additional concepts of a dominant nature culled from the act of comparison between command sets often receive the prominence of syntactical disjuncture in individual clauses. The subordinate clauses of the legal prescriptions of Num 36:1–13 are an example of prominence through syntactical disjuncture for the terse thematic formulation of the accompanying narrative sequence. These formulations are abstract statements of the thematic categories binding the events of the narrative sequence as a series. This function of abstraction—the extrapolation of the foundational motifs carrying the narrative sequence—is a feature Num 36:1–13 shares with the other passages of law. In the cases of Lev 24:10–23, Num 9:1–14 and 27:1–11, the additional establishment of common elements through the interaction of several command sets leads to the interaction of laws with narrative sequences as reformed thematic appellations for the sequence of motifs, or as pointers to particular concepts resident in the narratives. An act of judgement receives a statement of qualification as an act establishing equality between deed and recompense (Lev 24:10–23); the performance of the Sabbath is shown to be inclusive in its outlook (Num 9:1–14); and an award of inheritance is shown to adhere to the principle of the closest relative (by the definition of agnatic succession) to the deceased as the designated heir.

The procedure of abstraction within the laws combines formulations of a syntagmatic and paradigmatic nature: whereas the isolation of a series of motifs follows the progression of the narrative sequence (syntagmatic), the identification of the larger thematic category is performed by juxtaposing series of similar thematic formulations in law (paradigmatic). The procedure of abstraction, aided by the devices of syntax, produces summary statements of general import capable of designating lines of plot within adjacent narrative sequences. Where co-existent bi-polar formulations may exist, such statements constitute acts of selection: the choice of elevating one formulation of plot over another in the narrative. As such, the laws become communications by which readers receive direction regarding the specific formulation of theme and its component motifs they are to take note.

CHAPTER THREE
READINGS IN NARRATIVE AND LAW:
THE COMPLICATED CASES

The measure of a textual unit's degree of complexity may be defined by the degree to which the passage taxes the reader's interpretative imagination in defining the thematic coherence of the material: complicated texts require much effort at interpretation. The following two cases require a higher degree of participation in the reading process. Portions of passages (narrative sequences or laws) seem to defy incorporation within thematic definitions for preceding or following material; and when an effort toward accommodation is successful, it requires the adjustment or elimination of previous formulations of theme. Where such conflicting interpretations occur, the resolution may not be at hand. In previous cases, narrative sequences and legal prescriptions collaborated, with legal prescriptions offering thematic clarification in terse statements for structures of meaning inherent to narrative sequences. In the passages ahead, the two types of discourse challenge suggestions of theme within each other.

THE CASE OF LEVITICUS 10:1–20

Lev 10:1–20 begins with Aaron's sons Nadab and Abihu offering incense to God. The offering is an unsolicited act and God responds with grave consequences for Aaron's sons: they are incinerated. Aaron remains silent in the face of tragedy as Moses instructs Aaron's two nephews to remove the dead. A series of instructions follow with Moses forbidding Aaron and his two remaining sons from performing mourning rites or leaving the tent of meeting. God intercedes by addressing Aaron directly; the consumption of alchoholic beverages prior to entering the tent of meeting is prohibited. Moses proceeds with further instructions for the priestly consumption of various sacrificial portions. Subsequently, Moses discovers that the goat of the purification offering on behalf of the people which should have been consumed has been burnt. He interrogates Eleazer and Ithamar, Aaron's two remaining sons. Aaron responds on their behalf with the statement that the tragic events of the day make it inappropriate for the priests of his family to partake of the flesh of the sacrificial beast. Moses is satisfied with Aaron's response, and relents.

The Wider Literary Significance of Leviticus 10:1–20

The passage is part of a larger complex of narratives dealing with the ordination of priests (Lev 8) and the inauguration of the sacrificial cult with a series of sacrifices on behalf of the priest and the people (Lev 9). The successful initiation of the sacrificial cult under the guidance of Moses (Lev 8–9) is marred by Nadab and Abihu's deviation from authorized procedure (Lev 10:1–3). The ordination of priests is the fulfillment of commands issued in Exod 29:1–37. The gap between command and fulfillment is bridged by the construction of the tabernacle and its accoutrements (Exod 35–40), and the provision of instructions concerning the sacrificial procedures for the operation of the cult (Lev 1–7). Thus, all requisite information and provision for the commencement of sacrifice is set in place prior to Leviticus 8–10. A concern of the narrative of Lev 10:1–20 is the issue of illicit mixtures: the sacred and the profane, and, within the latter category, the clean and the unclean are to be kept apart. The legal prescriptions, in one way or another, have to do with the maintenance of these boundaries. This overarching concern of the passage continues into the legislation of chapters 11–5 which have to do with ritual purity; the literary corpus culminates with the regulations for the Day of Atonement, the most solemn ritual of purification in the cultic calendar. The reference to the death of Nadab and Abihu in Lev 16:1 provides a distant bracket enclosing the laws regarding ritual purity (chs. 11–15); thus, the subject of ritual impurity initiated in chapter 10 receives ample detail concerning possible pollutants prior to the outline of the annual procedure for their removal. The connections mentioned here are obvious, and have been noted by numerous interpreters over the years. The passage of Lev 10:1–20 has been integrated well with the surrounding material.

Commentators have spotted links of a more precise nature. Wenham describes the material of Leviticus 8–10 as a "literary tryptich": each chapter is a picture within a set of three (Wenham 1979, 133–4). The first two pictures in the series (chs. 8, 9) display a similar movement from command to fulfillment. Respectively, God and Moses issue the commands in the first and second cycles; their instructions are followed to the letter. The conclusion of the first two cycles witnesses divine fire consuming the sacrifices in Lev 9:22–4, a sign of God's approval. The last picture (ch. 10), in stark contrast, begins with a course of action without preceding command (v. 1bβ highlights this anomaly); the pattern is re-established from verse four onward with the instruction to clean up after the fearsome display of divine judgement. The result is a tightly-woven series of pictures where similarity between the first two panels draws out the difference in the third; the anomaly of Nadab and Abihu's initiative finds parallel in literary structure (Wenham 1979, 154).[1] Wenham's observation finds additional support in the fact that the divine judgement by fire (Lev 10: 2a) is an apt counterpart both for the transgression with fire (Lev 10:1) and the divine approval by fire in the previous chapter (Lev 9:24). The three-stop link establishes association through similarity inviting scrutiny; scrutiny yields the contrast of divine approval and disapproval by fire in Lev 9:24 and 10:2a respectively.[2]

---

[1] Additional correspondences and contrasts between the individual units are displayed in tabular form on p. 133 (Wenham 1979).

[2] The correspondence in the choice of the medium for communication (fire) between humans and divinity in chs. 9 and 10 has been noted by numerous commentators. Observations on the structure in part or whole include those of Hoffmann (1905, 293), Laughlin (1976, 562), Kiuchi (1987, 69), Levine (1989, 59), Hartley (1992, 133), and Douglas (1999, 201). Another factor contributing to the element of contrast is the obtrusive statement that the offering of Aaron's contravenes established procedure (Lev 10:1), especially in light of the recurring notice of adherence to protocol (Lev 8:4, 9, 13, 17, 21, 29, 36; 9:5, 7, 10, 21) in preceding cultic performances (Wenham 1979, 134). More recently, James Watts has expounded on the function of the repeated statements of conformity, and Nadab and Abihu's departure

David Damrosch sees two links involving the death of
Aaron's offspring: the passage looks backward to Israel's cultic
apostasy in Exodus 32, and forward to another errant episode also
involving a golden calf, the passage of 1 Kings 13–5 (Damrosch
1987, 70–2). The backward link is one of transgression leading to
punishment: Aaron's role in forging the abomination of the golden
calf meets the wrath of God in the death of his sons. Aaron's
comment on the death of his sons having a direct bearing upon his
person (Lev 10:19a) and the name Abihu (he, i.e. Aaron, is my
father) implicate Aaron as one bearing part of the responsibility for
their deaths.[3] Names also have to do with the second link: the
deaths of Nadab and Abijah, Jeroboam's sons, are reminiscent of
Nadab and Abihu. The passage of 1 Kings 13–5 also speaks of
retribution for deviation from cultic legitimacy: Jeroboam had
sponsored the creation of a cult involving a golden calf. Hence, it is
the case that similar elements point to a similar structure of
motivation in Exodus 32 and Leviticus 10, and 1 Kings 13–5.
Douglas agrees with the link between Leviticus 10 and Exodus 32.
However, she rejects the suggestion that the Nadab and Abihu
tragedy is a consequence of Aaron's role in the earlier incident in
Exodus (Douglas 1999, 201–2). Douglas prefers to view the
tragedy of Leviticus 10 as a parallel episode to that of Exodus 32.
Among other similarities, both episodes move from an illicit act
(Exod 32:1–14; Lev 10:1–2) to a clean-up operation (Exod 32:15–
20; Lev 10:3–20) involving elements of reproach and the removal
of the instruments of defilement and error. The point of the

---

from such conformity, as part of rhetoric supportive of priestly vocation,
privilege and authority within Leviticus (2007, 103–13). The point
Leviticus makes is that following correct procedure is vital, and the
priests, for the greater part, do a fine job.

   [3] Walter Houston too sees a connection between these episodes (2000,
36–7). Unlike Damrosch, however, he finds in Lev 10:1–20 a priestly
response to the negative portrayal of Aaron in the story of the golden calf.
The transgression of Aaron's sons casts obfuscation upon Aaron's role in
the earlier act of apostasy, by suggesting that the propensity to illegitimate
religious practice stems from other members of Aaron's family (Houston
2000, 39).

similarity is a reminder to the reader that the Leviticus episode is a continuation of the principles of covenant and grace governing the episode of the golden calf in Exodus (Douglas 1999, 202). In the absence of an explicit causal link between the two incidents, the reading by Douglas is the preferable option.[4]

The Internal Coherence of Leviticus 10:1–20

Difficulties arising in the search for thematic coherence in Lev 10:1–20 cluster around three main issues: premodern interpreters have struggled with defining the nature of Nadab and Abihu's crime, the contextual significance of the laws beginning at Lev 10:8 individually and as a group, and the substance of Aaron's explanation for abstinence from the consumption of the beast of the purification offering (Lev 10:19–20). The first and the third issues dominate the attention of Rabbinic exegesis; the second issue is less prominent for the Rabbis and, perhaps, only an incidental detail developing from their struggles with the first issue. By and large, modern interpreters struggle with the second and third issues, having settled on an interpretation of the crime of Aaron's sons.

Opinion about the cause of Nadab and Abihu's destruction may be divided into two general categories: those who think the duo committed a transgression, and those who see no error on their part. Of opinions in the former category, the compendia of Rabbinic exegesis *Midrash (Lev)* and *Pesiqta de Rab Kahana* are especially rich sources. While the interpretations vary, they share a common concern for specific components within Lev 10:1–20, or for other parts of the Pentateuch speaking of the incident. The

---

[4] Watts points to an element of contrast between the two episodes (2007, 127–9). Unlike Jeroboam, Aaron does not suffer the rage of YHWH. The Aaronide priesthood endures, whereas Jeroboam's dynasty wanes (1 Kgs 14–15). For Watts, the rhetorical effect of Lev 10:1–20, one to which the contrast contributes, is the elevation of the priesthood of Aaron. Despite the tragic circumstances of the day, Aaron perseveres in service to the cult with careful attention to correct procedure. Surely readers ought to conclude, in the estimation of Watts, that Aaron and his descendants are worthy of their appointment.

predominant interpretation in recent scholarship is among those voices of Rabbinic interpretation that find fault with Aaron's sons: the brothers ignited their incense from an illicit source (*Tg. Onq.*; *Tg. Ps.-J.*; *Midr. Lev* 20:8; *Sipra* Shemini 93:33; *Pesiq. Rab Kah.* 26:8; with reference to Lev 10:1b and 16:1). A second opinion takes the position that the two entered the adytum encroaching upon the divine presence (*Midr. Lev* 20:8; *Sipra* Shemini 93:33; *Pesiq. Rab Kah.* 26:8; presumably, with reference to בְּקֹרְבִי in Lev 10:3a, and to בְּקָרְבָתָם in Lev 16:1b). Taking אֲשֶׁר לֹא צִוָּה אֹתָם (Lev 10:1bβ) as criticism of the choice of the occasion for the offering, it has been suggested also that the offering of incense was superfluous and, thus, abusive of priestly privilege (Syr. to Lev 16:1; *Tg. Neof.* to Lev 16:1; *Midr. Lev* 20:8; *Sipra* Shemini 93:33; *Pesiq. Rab Kah.* 26:8). The proximity of the prohibition against the consumption of alchohol for priests while on duty (Lev 10:9) has led to the conjecture that the two priests were intoxicated (*b. 'Erub.* 63a; *Midr. Lev* 20:9; *Pesiq. Rab Kah.* 26:9). Furthermore, a list of Aaron's descendants mentions Nadab and Abihu in Num 3:4 with the comment that they had no offspring leading to some interpreters taking this comment as another possible explanation for divine retribution in Lev 10:2 (*Midr. Lev* 20:9; *Pesiq. Rab Kah.* 26:9–10); the crime is identified specifically as an undue amount of pride attached to their office and ancestry. Opinions of the second category—those finding no fault in the actions of the brothers—view the consumption of the brothers by divine fire as an act of glorification, a sanctification of the sanctuary through a sacrifice most holy (*Sipra* Shemini 93:23, 36; Philo *Somn.* 2:67; *Decal.* 2:57–8; *Fug.* 59; *Migr.* 169–70). This interpretation is based on a reading of the quotation of Moses concerning the sanctifying process in the presence of God in Lev 10:3 (בִּקְרֹבַי אֶקָּדֵשׁ).[5]

---

[5] Robert Kirschner (1983, 375–93) provides an assessment of Philo's interpretation within the currents of Hellenistic thought. Specifically, he draws a connection between the Philonic notion of the destruction of the body by fire in Lev 10:2 as sanctification and the Hellenistic dichotomy of the earthly body and the divine soul which constitute the person (1983, 387).

It is likely, however, that the use of fire from a profane source
is the sole factor of motivation behind the terrible pyrotechnic
display of divine force. The mention of this error lies in the heart
of the narrative (Lev 10:1b) leading up to the act of incineration.
As Kiuchi (1987, 68–9) and Milgrom (1991, 634) have pointed out,
the offering of incense itself is not flawed since the text designates
specifically the flames (coals) as the item out of place (זרה אש, and
not קְתרת זרה); this factor leaves out the possibility of any error
involving the offering as a whole as the source of divine
discontent.[6] The prohibition against alcohol consumption for
priests on duty (Lev 10:9) and the comment on the absence of
offspring to the brothers (Num 3:4) are located beyond the
immediate circumstances leading up to the incident, without clear
indication of having any bearing on the cause for the disaster. In
addition to the absence of any indication in the narrative that the
pair entered the most holy portion of the tabernacle, the fact that
the flames shot forth from before the divine presence
(מלפני יהוה) in the most holy portion of the tabernacle renders
such an interpretation of events unlikely.[7] Finally, Philo's reading of
the incident as an act of glorification for the brothers cannot be
substantiated; Segal (1989, 91–5) has demonstrated with examples
from the Hebrew Bible (Lev 22:32; Ezek 28:22; Num 20:13) that
the sanctification of God (Niphal of כבד) may take place within
the context of a retributive act of judgement. The consistent

---

[6] Bryan Bibb, however, finds this argument unconvincing for the fact
that direct reference to a profane source for the fire is lacking (2001, 87–
88). Furthermore, he points out that the biblical corpus lacks precise
legislation concerning proper procedure for incense offerings. According
to Bibb, the mistake of Nadab and Abihu is spontaneity leading to
unguarded improvisation in a novel situation. The story is an index to the
grave dangers in navigation beyond the boundaries of the established
system of cult, into areas inhabited by the awesome and terrifying
presence of Israel's god (Bibb 2001, 88–9, 95–6).

[7] The observation is Milgrom's (1991, 634). He adds, in strengthening
his argument, that the bodies were removed from the front of הקדש
(v. 4b; i.e. outside the tent of meeting), the place where they fell (1991,
605).

employment of the adjective זָר with negative connotations in reference to religious practice (*TDOT* 4:55–6; *TWOT* 1:238) works against a positive evaluation of Nadab and Abihu's initiative.

The laws pose another challenge for those seeking thematic coherence within the passage; this description is especially true for more recent commentators. Specifically, the prohibition against the consumption of alcohol for priests performing cultic duties (v. 9) is felt to be a contextual misfit, along with the rulings concerning the priestly consumption of various sacrificial portions in Lev 10:12–5 (Wenham 1979, 158; Milgrom 1991, 611; Hartley 1992, 158; Gerstenberger 1996, 114–6; Budd 1996, 149 and 154). Despite these reservations, thematic connections between the laws have been noted. Bertholet (1901, 31) points to the consequence of death in verse 9a as a point of similarity with preceding prescriptions forbidding mourning (v. 6a) and departure from the tent of meeting (v. 7a). Milgrom (1991, 614), following Elliger (1966, 137–8), and Budd (1996, 149) extend the grave consequence to cover the preceding narrative with its tragic conclusion (v. 2b). With regard to the latter portion of the prescriptions Budd also observes a connection: the persistent concern with distinctions between the sacred and the profane, and the clean and unclean in verses 12–5 marks a common point with the preceding prescriptions of verses 8–11 (1996, 154).

Building on the insights of Budd, it may be said that the concern with boundaries between such illicit mixtures is the concern of the entire passage, narrative and laws. This overarching theme extends to cover the prohibition concerning alcohol as well as to Nadab and Abihu's use of "strange fire" within the divine precinct. Even Aaron's decision to abstain from the flesh of the purification offering (vv. 16–20) may be conceived as abstention from an inappropriate mixture. The notation by Milgrom and others of the repeated mention of the consequence of death is more significant than they envision. The consequence of death due to the transgression of boundaries in cultic performance is shared by the laws of verses 9–11, the prescriptions of verses 6–8, and the narrative of the burning of Aaron's sons (vv. 1–3). The nexus between not just similar consequences, but similar forms of oversight is a causal construction that dominates the passage. That causal construct casts a shadow over the incident of verses 16–20, arousing expectations of punishment following the discovery of procedural deviation by Moses. It is only Aaron's explanation that averts the wrath of Moses (v. 19).

The nature of the dispute over the interpretation of Aaron's response to Moses in the incident involving the meat of the purification offering on behalf of the people (vv. 16–20) presents no problem for the thematic coherence of the passage. While opinion concerning the significance of the incineration of Aaron's sons (punishment or glorification) or its lack with concern to the laws may disturb the thematic unity of the passage, the conflicting interpretations of verses 16–20 are uniform in their concern for the preservation of the boundaries of the sacrificial cult. Two explanations for Aaron's response arise from Rabbinic exegesis: (1) the priests were in mourning (v. 19a) and thus, in light of the previous prohibition (vv. 6–7), disqualified as partakers of priestly portions (*b. Zebah* 101b; *Tg. Neof.*; *Tg. Ps.-J.*; *Midr. Lev* 13:1); (2) the meat had been defiled, presumably, from the presence of the two dead bodies (*b. Zebah* 101a). A number of recent commentators follow the first option (among others, Bush 1857, 90; Hartley 1992, 138; Budd 1996, 156). Kiuchi rejects both options preferring to find a cause in the notion of corporate responsibility in the unit of the family (1987, 72–7). By Kiuchi's reckoning, Aaron bears a degree of guilt for the crimes of Nadab and Abihu. Thus, the response to Moses entails reference (v. 17b) to a previous rite of purification on behalf of the priests which had become annulled by the deviant initiative of Aaron's sons (v. 19b). As Aaron's guilt remains without remission, he could not partake of the most holy portions of the sacrificial beast.[8] Milgrom's interpretation of the

---

[8] Roy Gane's perspective on this matter follows a similar tack (2005, 92). The events of the day had cast a shadow upon Aaron's house, rendering them unworthy of receiving a cultic prebend on that occasion. This perception of an extension of guilt to Aaron may be supported by recent observations made by Karen Eliasen. In departure from convention (see Lev 10:4 and 10:16), the narrator introduces Nadab and Abihu first as 'sons of Aaron' (Lev 10:1). Furthermore, it is Aaron that responds to Moses despite the fact that Moses is upset specifically with Eleazer and Ithamar (Lev 10:16–9). These factors, from Eliasen's

incident takes a different view (1991, 635–40). He proposes that the crimes and death of the sons of Aaron in close proximity to the divine seat had produced a dangerous level of contamination within the sanctuary. By this interpretation, the purification offering, after its blood has been applied to portions of the tabernacle, is thought to effect cleansing through the absorption of contaminants by the blood of the sacrificial beast and, by extension, the animal itself. Subsequently, through ingestion by the officiating priest, the contaminants are removed. The problem, as Milgrom observes, is that the level of contamination had risen to a point inappropriate for human consumption in the aftermath of the crimes of Aaron's sons. The degree of contamination approaches the level of pollution targeted by purification offerings performed for an error of the anointed priest endangering the people (Lev 4:1–21) and the annual rite of purgation for the sanctuary in Leviticus 16.[9] No portion of the purification offering

---

perspective, point to an identification of Aaron with his sons (Eliasen 2000, 85).

[9] Gane rejects Milgrom's suggestion that pollution arising from the wanton transgression of Aaron's sons could be transmitted across a distance to the sanctuary. While conceding that such modes for the transmission of impurity occur within the spatio-cultic constructs of ancient Israel's religious imagination, he limits their occurrence to specific acts of transgression: Molek worship (Lev 20:3); failure to comply with stipulated procedure for cleansing from certain physical impurities (Lev 15:31) and after contact with dead bodies (Num 19:13, 20; see Gane 2005, 151–7). The purification of the adytum on the Day of Atonement (Lev 16:11–9) is the means for the removal of contamination arising from such actions and failures. According to Gane (2005, 130–5, 163), the exclusive purification offerings functioning to cleanse the sanctuary are those of the Day of Atonement (Lev 16:11–9) and the inauguration of the sacrificial cult (Lev 8:14–7). The pollution in the purification offering for the congregation of interest in Lev 10:17–8 comes from the party making the offering (Gane 2005, 174–5). Gane's conclusion is based upon careful grammatical analysis (2005, 112–4, 136–9), that finds the preposition עַל to designate the object receiving purification (כִּפֶּר) within the formula עַל...כִּפֶּר. This is clear in cases where a result clause confirms the object

is to be consumed by priests within these procedures. The strength of Milgrom's argument, by his own description, lies in a couple of factors. It avoids the pitfall of the fact that no recrimination is leveled at Aaron, Eleazer, and Ithamar for ignoring the command of Moses to refrain from mourning rites (v. 6), an oversight of the proposal that the priests were engaged in mourning. Milgrom's proposal also explains the singular focus on the disposal of the purification offering by Moses in his inquiry (v. 17). Kiuchi's explanation with appeal to the concept of corporate responsibility, along with those who propose mourning as a factor of motivation, would disqualify the priests from partaking of any of the sacrificial portions advocated in the prescriptions of Lev 10:12–5. Why would Moses be concerned with the purification offering alone? As Milgrom correctly observes, it is only the offering devoted to the removal of impurity that absorbs the especially potent contaminants wrought by the events of the day; consequently, the

---

of purification (e.g., the subject that transits to a clean state in the clause טהרה ממקר), which corresponds with the party/object designated by the preposition in a preceding clause (וכפר עליה [Lev 12:7]; for a tabular compilation of data drawn from purification procedures for physical impurities, see p. 113). The application of such an interpretation of the formula to the procedure for the purification offering for the congregation (Lev 4:20) stands against Milgrom's interpretation of Aaron's response to Moses in Lev 10:19. Milgrom, however, counters with the argument that those offering a purification offering are purified prior to their entry into sacred precincts, as Lev 15:13 suggests regarding the individual making a purification offering because of uncleanness from genital emissions (Milgrom 2007, 162). By inference, the purification offering must effect cleansing for the sanctuary, not the one making the offering. With regard to the integrity of the argument in this study, either interpretation of the purification offering will do. Agreement with Gane's analysis does not disturb the conclusion here. For Gane, Aaron's consumption of the sacrificial portion is a post-requisite for the purification of the congregation (Gane 2005, 96, 99–105). The concern of Moses, by his assessment, still falls upon the expulsion of contaminants from the holy precinct or from those who would enter such places.

חטאת was the only sacrificial portion that was avoided by the priests.[10]

Each explanation for Aaron's response envisions an attempt to avoid a dangerous mixture of elements (the anointed state of the priests with defiled substances, or the defiled state of the priests with sacred portions of meat). A careful reading of the passage reveals that the other two problems in interpretation—the nature of the crime of Nadab and Abihu, and the thematic coherence of the laws and their relevance to the narrative—may be resolved by postulating such a common category of description. The broad thematic classification of an effort to deal with (the possibility of) an illicit mixture is applicable also to the incident of verses 16–20. In accordance with the nature of the content in the rest of the narrative sequence and the laws, Aaron's motivation in abstaining from the sacred portion is the maintenance of an appropriate distance between entities set apart by the antithetical categories of holiness and profanity, clean and unclean. Hence, the classification of Lev 10:1–20 as a 'complicated text' does not stem from the apparent thematic inconsistencies which the aforementioned problems in interpretation produce. The classification, as the following analysis will show, is a recognition of a conflict between a

---

[10] Hartley, with reference to Lev 4:12 and 6:17–24, disputes the suggestion that flesh infected with uncleanness may be eaten in a holy place or disposed of in a clean place (1992, 136). David P. Wright has pointed to clear indications (Lev 6:21–2; 16:27–8; Num 19:7–10) that the purification offering becomes unclean (1987, 129–32); procedures for the cleansing of persons and instruments coming in contact with the sacrificial portion are necessary. Yet, the designated place for the disposal of the ashes from the purification offering, as noted by Wright (1987, 134), is a clean place (Lev 4:11–2). In light of these observations, Wright argues for different levels of pollution in purification offerings (between those eaten and those burnt). Those offerings designated for consumption by the priest possess a lesser degree of impurity (Wright 1987, 131–2). Thus, the levels of contamination affect the placement of the sacrificial portion in the appropriate category in the graded scale of holiness reflected by the compartmentalization of Israel's tabernacle. Hartley's observation need not signal the demise of Milgrom's proposal.

formulation of theme in mid-stream and that which occurs at the conclusion of the narrative sequence: the expectation of a punitive measure aroused by the discovery of deviation from cultic regulations is dashed by the revelation of circumstances justifying exception. The analysis will show how thematic formulations in preceding narrative and laws contribute to the (mis-)reading.

Apart from thematic unity, literary patterning also lends a measure of coherence to the unit. Hartley has identified chiasmus as a structural device within Lev 10:1–20.[11] The laws are encased by two bodies of narrative with contrasting results (vv. 1–3 and 16–20). One step closer to the center finds two bodies of prescription concerned with procedures with regard to various specific circumstances (burial of the dead [vv. 4–7] and the consumption of sacrificial meat [vv. 12–5]). At the center of the passage is a series of prescriptions concerned with priestly conduct in general: in contrast to verses 4–7 and 12–5, no reference to any specific aspect of procedure occurs. Thus, part and parcel of the focus in the pattern of the passage is the explicit statement of the unifying theme of the passage: ‏ולהבדיל בין הקדש ובין החל ובין הטמא ובין הטהור‎.

The Narrative Sequence

The narrative sequence of Lev 10:1–20 consists of 24 clauses. Of the 24 clauses, 21 are consecutive imperfect clauses (wayyiqtol), the backbone of Biblical Hebrew narrative. The remaining three clauses (Lev 10:5b, 16a; 1–20 [14, 19, 20] by the designated numerical scheme for clauses) comprise of a subordinate (comparative) clause and two conjunctive clauses employing perfect verbal forms with another component of the clause standing between the conjunction and the verb (waw-X-qatal).

1 ‏ויקחו בני־אהרן נדב‎	1 Now Aaron's sons, Nadab
‏ואביהוא‎	and Abihu, each took his
‏איש מחתתו‎	censer, 2 put fire in it, 3 and
2 ‏ויתנו בהן אש‎	laid incense on it; 4 and they

[11] A tabular presentation of the following summary of Hartley's observation of structure may be found on p. 129 of his commentary (1992).

3 וישימו עליה קטרת 4 ויקרבו לפני יהוה אש זרה אשר לא צוה אתם 5 ותצא אש מלפני יהוה 6 ותאכל אותם 7 וימתו לפני יהוה 8 ויאמר משה אל־אהרן	offered unholy fire before the Lord, such as he had not commanded them. 5 And fire came out from the presence of the Lord 6 and consumed them, 7 and they died before the Lord. 8 Then Moses said to Aaron,
9 וידם אהרן 10 ויקרא משה אל־מישאל ואל אלצפן בני אזיאל דד אהרן 11 ויאמר אלהם	9 And Aaron was silent. 10 Moses summoned Mishael and Elzaphan, sons of Uzziel, the uncle of Aaron, 11 and said to them,
12 ויקרבו 13 וישאם בכתנתם אל־מחוץ למחנה 14 כאשר דבר משה 15 ויאמר משה אל־אהרן ולאלעזר ולאיתמר בניו	12 They came forward 13 and carried them by their tunics out of the camp, 14 as Moses had ordered. 15 And Moses said to Aaron and his sons Eleazer and Ithamar,
16 ויעשו כדבר משה 17 וידבר יהוה אל־אהרן לאמר	16 And they did as Moses had ordered. 17 And the Lord spoke to Aaron:
18 וידבר משה אל־אהרן ואל אלעזר ואל־איתמר בניו הנותרים	18 Moses spoke to Aaron and to his remaining sons, Eleazer and Ithamar:
19 ואת שעיר החטאת דרש דרש משה 20 והנה שרף 21 ויקצף על־אלעזר ועל־איתמר בני אהרן הנותרם לאמר	19 Then Moses made inquiry about the goat of the sin-offering, 20 and—it had already been burned! 21 He was angry with Eleazer and Ithamar, Aaron's remaining sons, and said,
22 וידבר אהרן אל־משה הן	22 And Aaron spoke to Moses,

23 וישמע משה   23 And when Moses heard
24 וייטב בעיניו   that, 24 he agreed. (vv. 1–20)

The first departure from the series of consecutive clauses describing the sequence of events is 1–20 (14). The clause is a subordinate clause declaring the fact that Aaron's nephews Mishael and Elzaphan had acted in accordance with the instructions of Moses; thus, 1–20 (14) is subordinate to the two preceding clauses (1–20 [12 and 13]) providing clarification of their exact compliance with the wishes of Moses. It should be noted that a similar report of an act of compliance in 1–20 (16) occurs without employing a subordinate clause of comparison, disrupting the flow of consecutive clauses. An analysis of the semantic structures underlying the narrative sequence in material to follow will reveal a reason for the distinction in form.

The clause 1–20 (19) places the direct object at the front of the clause. The direct object (שעיר החטאת) is the subject matter of all subsequent clauses; the clauses 1–20 (19–24) are concerned with the location of the remains of the sacrificial portion, and its mode of disposal. The departure from the series of consecutive clauses with the displacement of the verb from the initial position may be considered a case of contextualization.[12] The prominence

---

[12] In Buth's terminology, the contextualizing constituent (topic) is set in a position of prominence in order to signal the basis upon which the following clauses are grouped together (1995, 84–5). In Biblical Hebrew prose (specifically, that of the books of Genesis through Kings), this prominence is the result of the disruption of the normative verb-subject-object sequence in the clause with the placement of a clausal component (other than the verb or the conjunction) at the beginning (Buth 1995, 80–83), the operation of fronting. The opinion of *BHRG* (§46.2) excludes subordinate conjunctions and discourse markers (e.g. הנה) from inclusion within the function of prominence through fronting, by virtue of the observation that such particles govern the entire clause by occupying the right-hand margin. While this position with regard to the phenomenon of fronting is well-documented, it remains a fact that the choice to employ a subordinating conjunction or the particle הנה necessitates a formal departure from a series of consecutive clauses; it remains a worthwhile

of 'the goat of the purification offering' in 1–20 (19) marks the initiation of a sub-unit within the larger episode, establishing the basis for the inauguration of this sub-section in the narrative sequence. Furthermore, Milgrom points to a degree of elevation in gravity endemic to the placement of the direct object at the front of the clause (1991, 622); the fact that 1–20 (19) represents an elevation of the discussion to concern a holier sacrifice suggests that antithesis may be the intention behind the inversion of the clausal components in 1–20 (19). The latter portion of the speech introduced by 1–20 (18) concerns a sacrificial portion to be consumed in a clean place (במקום טחור); in contrast, the requirement is that the portion from the purification offering must be eaten במקום קדש. Further support for Milgrom's reading may be sought in the fact that 1–20 (19) employs the infinitive absolute prior to the finite verbal form. That the widespread use of the grammatical construction to enhance the intensity, certainty or grave significance of an action is well-attested (GKC §113.3; Joüon §§123i-k; Muraoka 1985, 86–7; *BHRG* §20.2.1) lends credibility to the proposal that an issue of grave importance—hence, the focused intensity of the search by Moses—has surfaced in 1–20 (19).

The departure from the series of consecutive clauses carrying the narrative sequence persists in 1–20 (20). The result of the quest by Moses (דָּרֹשׁ דָּרַשׁ) comes to the forefront with the particle הנה introducing the fact that the purification offering has been burnt in its entirety. Muraoka's study of the particle (1985, 137–40) uncovers a primary function of deixis in its use: the particle points out an event with emphasis upon its novelty, gravity, or quality of surprise. An accompanying function of the particle is the designation of the immediate presence of the speaker or of another character in the narrative; hence, הנה often signals a change of perspective within the narrative (*BHRG* §44.3.4; Berlin 1983, 62–63). In 1–20 (20), the narrator's employment of the particle highlights the perception of Moses as he encounters the object of his search. The occurrence of the particle in its regular position at the front of the clause necessitates departure from the series of

---

endeavour to investigate the significance of such formal distinctions from a semantic-pragmatic perspective.

consecutive clauses. The construction poses a disruptive force in Biblical Hebrew narrative inherent to the function of the particle. In 1–20 (20), the force of the disruption collaborates with the deictic function of the particle to lend prominence to a positive result of an effort initiated in the previous clause. Together, the two clauses 1–20 (19, 20) mark the occurrence of a significant deviation from cultic procedure, the beginning of a sub-section within the episode, for which Moses must seek redress.

Wenham's analysis of the structures of plot governing Lev 10:1–20 has determined that the pattern of command leading to fulfillment through obedience in chapters eight and nine bear heavily upon the passage at hand (1979, 154). Against the backdrop of the previous chapters, Nadab and Abihu's unsolicited initiative in 1–20 (1–4) portends ill consequences; the divine response with fire approximates the earlier response to a favourable offering (Lev 9:24) with the exception that its consuming flames now engulf those making the offering. The use of fire in judgement (1–20 [5]) also mirrors the offering with illicit fire (1–20 [2–4]) producing an element of balance in the act of retribution. Consecutive motifs enacting the path from transgression to punishment are afforded corresponding elements that highlight the causal connection; but in the case of Lev 9:24, the corresponding image of fire works to draw attention to a contrasting series of motifs, that of command leading to fulfillment. As observed by Wenham, the previous motivational pattern is quickly re-established (1–20 [10–4]) after the interruption posed by the tragedy involving Aaron's sons; order returns as swiftly as it was lost.[13] The return to events reflecting obedience to commands issued in 1–20 (10–4) may be seen in corresponding elements between the commands of Moses (as introduced by 1–20 [11]) and the narrator's report of their fulfillment (1–20 [12–3]):

---

[13] The return to 'order' in these clauses prompts Watts (2007, 111) to postulate thematic continuity across Leviticus 8–10. The incineration of Nadab and Abihu is a timely reminder of the importance of following instructions: this is the theme of Leviticus 8–10 as a whole according to Watts. The theme underscores the gravity of the priestly task, and the legitimacy of the Jerusalem temple (Watts 2007, 110–1).

קרבו שאו את־אחיכם מאת פני־הקדש אל־מחוץ למחנה

ויקרבו וישאם בכתנתם אל־מחוץ למחנה

That subordinate clause 1–20 (14) brings a halt to the series of consecutive clauses in the narrative sequence in order to establish the fact that Mishael and Elzaphan had carried out the orders of Moses has been noted. From the illustration above, it may be seen that corresponding lexical units between command and report back-up the content of 1–20 (14) by emphasizing the connection. The pronounced restoration of the pattern of obedience persists with a second cycle in 1–20 (15–6): once again, Moses issues a series of commands (1–20 [15]), and the narrative reports the fact that these are carried out (1–20 [16]). However, as previously mentioned in the syntactical notes to 1–20 (14), the language of 1–20 (16) is less obtrusive by virtue of the fact that 1–20 (16) does not sever the series of consecutive clauses. Moreover, the lexical correspondence between the prescriptive content and the report of compliance in 1–20 (10–4) is not present in 1–20 (15–6). While maintaining the fact that compliance is forthcoming, certain lexical and syntactical discrepancies between 1–20 (10–4) and 1–20 (15–6) would seem to suggest that the degree of compliance is flagging. Readerly suspicions are exarcebated, although not confirmed, when 1–20 (17–8) introduce two groups of commands without corresponding reports of compliance. The prescriptions by God (1–20 [17]) and Moses (1–20 [18]) concerning various issues relating to the cult receive no confirmation in the narrative sequence that they have been accepted and implemented. Is this omission indication of further movement toward a state of disorder among the priestly ranks so prominently demonstrated in the recent transgression of Nadab and Abihu? The syntactically disruptive conjunctive clauses 1–20 (19–20)—Moses discovers an infraction of religious procedure in the fact that the goat of the purification offering had been burnt—provide apparent confirmation for a projected sequence of motifs brewing in the mind of the reader. The reprimand of Moses introduced by the following clause of the narrative sequence (1–20 [21]) specifically reveals a departure from cultic norms promulgated in Lev 6:18–23; the sacrificial portion from the purification offering should have been eaten because its blood was not brought inside the sanctuary.

In the shadow of the death of Nadab and Abihu, readerly expectation of retribution is immediately aroused.[14] However, the conclusion of the narrative sequence with Aaron's explanation for abstention from the consumption of the sacrificial meat (1–20 [22]) and the acceptance of his response (1–20 [23–4]) quells projections of a progression from crime to punishment in the sequence of 1–20 (19–24). Upon conclusion, 1–20 (19–24) provides one more act of compliance with divine will: the displeasure of God over Aaron's consumption of a portion from the purification offering is averted.

In considering the structures of plot governing the narrative sequence of Lev 10:1–20, it has been informative to envision the narrative as a series of cyles alternating between transgression leading to punishment, and command leading to fulfillment (compliance). Specifically, these formulations afford focus upon the gradual decay in the nexus between command and fulfillment prior to the orchestrated mis-reading of 1–20 (19–21), the discovery of the burnt carcass. However, a thematic formulation closer to the substance of the narrative sequence and the laws is that which envisions a movement from defilement to a restoration of order in the cult. At the heart of this formulation lies the necessity of maintaining the boundary between the holy and the profane, and the clean and the unclean (within the category of the profane). Defilement occurs when a boundary is transgressed and an illicit mixture occurs; restoration entails the (re-)establishment of that boundary. This establishment of division between mutually repulsive substances involves the removal or annihilation of one

---

[14] Gerstenberger's comments on the passage (1996, 116) are a fine example of one reader's expectation of punishment for the cultic infraction of 1–20 (19–21). He writes, "On the one hand, what seems to us a tiny violation suffices to deliver the cultic officeholders over to Yahweh's annihilating fire (vv. 1f.); on the other, an (equally serious?) deviation from the sacrificial prescriptions is treated as a venial transgression prompting no further consequences at all (vv. 16–20)." The magnitude of the apparent infringement by refusal to partake of the purification offering is amplified in light of the severity of the punishment meted out to Nadab and Abihu.

substance in the presence of the other. The transgression of Nadab and Abihu (1–20 [1–4]) may be considered an act of defilement through their introduction of a profane substance (אֵשׁ זָרָה) into the realm of the holy. All subsequent acts in the narrative sequence are initiatives at the re-establishment and maintenance of purity in cultic procedure. These actions include the removal of the corpses (1–20 [10–4]), the instructions prohibiting mourning for priests on duty (1–20 [15–6]), the prohibition against the consumption of strong drink for priests on duty (1–20 [17]), instructions for the proper disposal and consumption of various sacrificial portions (1–20 [18]), and even Aaron's abstention from the meat of the purification offering (1–20 [19–24]).[15] While all these events in isolation need not assume a preceding incident of defilement endemic to the appellation 'restoration', their location within this specific narrative sequence constitutes a counter-movement to the error of Nadab and Abihu through their expressed interest in maintaining boundaries between dangerous mixtures.

In the case of 1–20 (19–24), the fact that the alleged error of Aaron, Eleazer, and Ithamar has to do with illicit mixtures is

---

[15] The prohibition against drinking wine (יַיִן) for priests on duty is echoed in Ezek 44:21. Nazirites are also commanded to abstain from alchoholic beverages (Num 6:2–4); even mothers bearing a child designated as a future Nazirite are to observe the restriction (Judg 13:4–5). The beverage should, however, not be considered an unclean substance; drink-offerings of שֵׁכָר to be poured out in the sanctuary are commanded by Num 28:7–8. More likely, it is the effect of the substance upon the individual's state that is repulsive in the holy precinct (Isa 28:7–13; Hos 4:11). Here and throughout the analysis of the passage, the term 'illicit mixtures' goes beyond the dichotomous categories of clean and unclean, and profane and holy in Israel's cultic terminology; deeds deemed morally repulsive to God also are under consideration. This extension is in keeping with the tenor of Lev 17–27 which extends the notion of holiness into the ethical realm. For example, Lev 19 combines ethical and cultic issues in its exhortation to Israel to be holy (19:2). Although cultic boundaries pertaining to notions of impurity dominate Lev 10:1–20, human shortcomings with or without connection to the maintenance of those boundaries are not far from the concern of the passage.

confirmed by the statement (by Moses) of a reason behind the priestly consumption of the purification offering: ואתה נתן לכם לשאת את־עון העדה   לכפר עליהם לפני יהוה (Lev 10:17b). The statement suggests that the process of atonement is rendered incomplete without the final stipulated component: the consumption of designated sacrificial portions by the priests.[16] The עון of the people remains in the midst of God's people and serves as an affront to the holy divine presence; the incompatibility of these two entities lies at the heart of the annual purgation of the sanctuary (Lev 16:1–34). The response of Aaron may be understood as an argument that in fact an act of defilement had been averted, and the safe removal of impurity effected by the

---

[16] The interpretation adopted for Lev 10:17b understands the two infinitive construct forms of the clause (לשאת and לכפר) as conveying the purpose for the consignment of the portions to the priests (*b. Pesaḥ* 59b; *b. Yoma* 68b; Hoffmann 1905, 298; Levine 1989, 63; Gane 2005, 99–100; Sklar 2005, 93–5; for the most frequent use of ל followed by the infinitive construct as a construction denoting purpose or result, see GKC §114f-k; *IBHS* §§36.2.3d; *BHRG* §20.1.3[iv], [vi]). The reception of the sacrificial beast (ואתה נתן לכם) and the accomplishment of the purpose of the offering require the consumption of a portion by the officiating priest. A contrary position in the minority understands the clause as depicting the consignment solely as the conferral of a reward for duties performed (Milgrom 1976, 333; Janowski 1982, 238–9); the infinitive construct forms do not denote purpose, and consumption by the priest has nothing to do with the process of purification and atonement. Milgrom since has backed away from this position to come in line with the view of the majority of interpreters (1991, 622–3). By the insertion of the infinitive φαγεῖν and the rendition of MT's לשאת with a purpose clause (ἵνα followed by the subjunctive), LXX makes it clear that the removal of עון is dependent upon the consumption of part of the sacrificial portion by the priest: τοῦτο ἔδωκεν ὑμῖν φαγεῖν, ἵνα ἀφέλητε τὴν ἁμαρτίαν τῆς συναγωγῆς καὶ ἐξιλάσησθε περὶ αὐτων ἔναντι Κυρίου (cf. Wevers 1997, 140). The designation of purpose is the predominant function of ἵνα introducing a clause employing the subjunctive verbal form (Smyth 1920, §§2193, 2196–7; Nunn 1938, §§184–5, 199; Blass and Debrunner 1961, §369). In the absence of any compelling reason to reject the witness of LXX, this interpretation of the majority seems probable.

initiative of the priests. Even if it be the case that readers subscribe to the understanding that Aaron and his remaining sons had entered a state of mourning, it would be incumbent upon them to understand that the priests had become unclean and disqualified from partaking of a sacred offering.[17] The alternative understanding—almost certainly the correct interpretation—that the offering had become overly contaminated through the overt act of cultic deviation by Nadab and Abihu, and their death would postulate that the mixture of unclean meat and anointed priests is one to be avoided. Both interpretations espouse an aversion for illicit mixtures in the cultic realm as a fundamental motivation.

Therefore, a thematic formulation designating the bi-polar series of motifs underlying the constitution of the narrative sequence may be stated at this point as follows: Defilement-Restoration. This thematic formulation may be understood as coming to apply to the narrative sequence of Lev 10:1–20 upon its conclusion. However, within the narrative sequence the restoration of order in the cultic realm appears to lose momentum. Representation for the fulfillment of command wanes in the course of the series of statements marking the movement from command to compliance. With the on-set of 1–20 (19–20), the disruption of the chain of consecutive clauses seems to signal, not just the beginning of a sub-unit within narrative, but a second cycle of defilement through cultic deviation in need of rectification. The lives of Aaron, Eleazer, and Ithamar hang in the balance at this point within the narrative sequence where a conjecture of theme for following events takes place. The conclusion will re-cast the brief sequence of clauses (1–20 [19–24]) as a query on the part of Moses, revealing another measure of restoration in the wake of the day's tragic events. Within such a final act of interpretation, the unique divine address to Aaron without the intervention of Moses

___

[17] Moses qualifies the portion as קֹדֶשׁ קֳדָשִׁים, to be consumed בְּמָקוֹם הַקֹּדֶשׁ in his rebuke introduced by 1–20 (21). Kiuchi's proposal (1987, 72–7) that the family had become tainted by Nadab and Abihu's deed falls under a similar category as the understanding that the priests had entered a state of mourning; the events of the day had rendered them unfit to partake of a most holy sacrificial portion.

(1–20 [17]) finds an explanation: the explicit warning to avoid illicit mixtures preempts the problem facing Aaron about the consumption of the purification offering. In the light of this revelation, Aaron's deed which comes to light in 1–20 (19–20) becomes an act of compliance following a command, an act allowing for the process of purification to move on. In fact, that which was considered an infraction against divine prescription becomes the act of compliance for which a reader may have been searching from 1–20 (17) onward.

The Legal Prescriptions

The legal material in Lev 10:1–20 is confined to the portions of direct speech introduced by 1–20 (17) and 1–20 (18) of the clauses in the narrative sequence. In the first block of material, God speaks to Aaron; in the second block of legal material, Moses addresses Aaron and his remaining sons. Hence, a distinct break from the narrative sequence occurs with the intercession of 1–20 (18). The commands of Moses to Aaron and his nephews (introduced by 1–20 [15]) are excluded by the definition of a legal prescription in this study; these commands address the immediate situation with their concern for the removal of the corpses and the restriction of impending mourning rites. In contrast, the prescriptions of Lev 10:9–11 and 10:12aβ–15 show concern for contingencies not immediately present in the narrative; the orientation toward circumstances arising in the future is also clearly mentioned within these prescriptive passages (Lev 10:9b, 15b). However, the commands of Lev 10:6–7 will be included in the analysis for the reason that they offer an abstraction—this term is to be understood in the manner it is employed in relation to narrative sequences in this study—of the thematic progression of the narrative sequence in such a manner as to influence the perception of the direction the narrative may take. Moreover, as it will be seen, these prescriptions also participate in the literary structures that bind the three blocks of prescriptive material.

רָאשֵׁיכֶם אַל־תִּפְרָעוּ 1	1 Do not dishevel your hair,
וּבִגְדֵיכֶם לֹא־תִפְרֹמוּ 2	2 and do not tear your
וְלֹא תָמֻתוּ 3	vestments, 3 or you will die
וְעַל כָּל־הָעֵדָה יִקְצֹף 4	4 and death will strike all the
וַאֲחֵיכֶם כָּל־בֵּית יִשְׂרָאֵל 5	congregation; 5 but your

יבכו
את־השרפה אשר שרף יהוה
6 ומפתח אהל מועד לא
תצאו
7 פן־תמתו
8 כי־שמן משחת יהוה עליכם

kindred, the whole house of Israel may mourn the burning that the Lord has sent. 6 You shall not go outside the entrance of the tent of meeting, 7 or you will die; 8 for the anointing oil of the Lord is on you. (vv. 6–7)

1 יין ושכר אל־תשת אתה
ובניך אתך
בבאכם אל־אהל מועד
2 ולא תמתו
3 חקת עולם לדרתיכם
ולהבדיל בין הקדש ובין
החל
ובין הטמא ובין הטהור
ולהורת את־בני ישראל את
כל־החקים
אשר דבר יהוה אליהם
ביד־משה

1 Drink no wine or strong drink, neither you nor your sons, when you enter the tent of meeting, 2 that you may not die; 3 it is a statute forever throughout your generations. You are to distinguish between the holy and the common, and between the unclean and the clean; and you are to teach the people of Israel all the statutes that the Lord has spoken through Moses.
(vv. 9–11)

1 קחו את־המנחה הנותרת
מאשי יהוה
2 ואכלוה מצות אצל המזבח
3 כי קדש קדשים הוא
4 ואכלתם אתה במקום קדש
5 כי חקך וחק־בניך הוא
מאשי יהוה
6 כי־כן צויתי
7 ואת חזה תנופה ואת שוק
התרומה
תאכלו במקום טהור אתה
ובניך
ובנתיך אתך
8 כי־חקך וחק־בניך נתנו
מזבחי שלמי בני ישראל
9 שוק התרומה וחזה התנופה
על אשי החלבים יביאו
להניף תנופה לפני יהוה
10 והיה לך ולבניך אתך

1 Take the grain-offering that is left from the Lord's offering by fire, 2 and eat it unleavened beside the altar, 3 for it is most holy; 4 you shall eat it in a holy place, 5 because it is your due and your sons' due, from the offerings by fire to the Lord; 6 for so I am commanded. 7 But the breast that is elevated and the thigh that is raised, you and your sons and daughters as well may eat in any clean place; 8 for they have been assigned to you and your children from the sacrifices of the offerings of well-being of the people of Israel. 9 The thigh that is raised and the breast that is elevated they shall bring,

לְחׇק־עוֹלָם together with the offerings by
11 כַּאֲשֶׁר צִוָּה יהוה fire of fat, to raise for an elevation offering before the Lord; 10 they are to be your due and that of your children for ever, 11 as the Lord has commanded. (vv. 12–5)

Verses 6–7

The series of prescriptions in verses 6–7 display a high degree of syntactical unity. Upon initiation with the asyndetic clause 6–7 (1), conjunctive clauses (6–7 [2–6]) proceed effecting the construction of a series of connected prescriptions. Two subordinate clauses (6–7 [7, 8]) disrupt the syntactical continuity of the series of conjunctive clauses at the end of the command set. The first of the two subordinate clauses (6–7 [7]) is introduced by the subordinating conjunction פֶּן; a negative purpose is introduced in order to discourage deviation from the preceding command. Notice the contrast in form with a preceding clause which accomplishes the same purpose without resorting to syntactical subordination (6–7 [3]): וְלֹא תָמֻתוּ. The difference in 6–7 (7) is the accomplishment of syntactical disjuncture; the use of a subordinate clause lends a measure of prominence to the avoidance of the consequence (פֶּן־תָּמֻתוּ).[18] The other subordinate clause of the command set is a verbless motive clause. The clause 6–7 (8) provides the reason for the command beginning with 6–7 (6): the anointing oil (שֶׁמֶן מִשְׁחַת יהוה) upon the priests precludes their departure from the holy precinct (וּמִפֶּתַח אֹהֶל מוֹעֵד לֹא תֵצְאוּ).[19]

---

[18] The full significance of the difference between 6–7 (3) and 6–7 (7) may be perceived only by considering the structure of meaning within the command set of vv. 6–7, in relation to those of the following command sets. The exposition of this interaction must be delayed.

[19] The prohibition of mourning and departure from the tent of meeting for the high priest because of the presence of holy oil upon his person is stated also in Lev 21:10–3. Both Exod 29:29 and Lev 21:10–3 limit anointing, with the accompanying restrictions, to the office of the

The topical unity of the command set is reflected in its concern over the possibility of defilement through the process of mourning. The subject of mourning is inherent to the verbs of 6–7 (1–5).[20] The clauses 6–7 (6–8) are included under the stated subject by virtue of their proximity to 6–7 (1–5), and the ease with which their content may be placed within the larger context of mourning: the priests must leave the tent of meeting in order to participate in rites of mourning. The command set is structured as two series of prescriptions enacting prohibitions (6–7 [1–4]; 6–7 [6–8]), encasing a single clause (6–7 [5]); the clause at the center, 6–7 (5), makes allowance for the performance of mourning rites by the larger community. As to the identified sequence of motifs governing the narrative sequence (Defilement-Restoration), the prescriptions offer a concise depiction twice. The two series of prohibitions with consequence (6–7 [1–3]; 6–7 [6–7]) within the command set

---

high priest. However, the unique circumstances of the inauguration of the sacrificial cult include Aaron's sons in the procedure of consecration with holy oil (Lev 8:30).

[20] The rending of garments is commonly associated with the display of grief and outrage (Gen 37:29–30; 44:13; Lev 13:45). The prescription of Lev 13:45 suggests that torn garments also designate a state of separation from the community. The maintenace of an unruly head of hair (6–7 [1]) in connection with mourning is only attested elsewhere in Lev 21:10. The meaning of the verb פָּרַע itself is in dispute. An alternative to the meaning adopted here is "to uncover" (LXX and *Tg. Neof.* to Lev 10:6). The exhortation to refrain from mourning by keeping one's turban (פְּאֵר) on the head in Ezek 24:23 suggests the possibility that 6–7 (1) prohibits the uncovering of the head as a sign of mourning; but Ezek 24:23 does not clearly associate the act of uncovering with the verb (פָּרַע) in question. In contrast, Num 6:5 and Ezek 44:20 employ the noun פֶּרַע in an antithetical statement to the shaving of the head; the reference to a full head of hair, the opposite of a shaved head, is certain. Therefore, with *Tg. Onq.* and *Tg. Ps.-J.*, the understanding of the verb as designating the maintenance of a long and unkempt head of hair is to be preferred. The prohibition of torn clothing and unkempt hair for anointed priests is repeated in Lev 21:10. The text of Deut 26:14 further specifies the incompatibility of mourning with the consumption of sacred portions.

portray clearly a movement from acts resulting in illicit mixtures
within the cultic realm (defilement) to measures tantamount to the
(partial) restoration of order (the removal of the perpetrators of the
illicit mixtures). The syntactical units portraying these thematic
abstractions of the narrative sequence grow smaller in the course of
the command set: beginning with a series of three conjunctive
clauses (6–7 [1–3]), the bi-polar structure shifts to reside within two
conjunctive clauses (6–7 [6–7]). The common thematic portrayal of
the narrative sequence in the two series of prescriptions is rendered
all the more prominent by the fact that they share an identical
event representing the commencement of restoration: the penalty
of death. In addition to the increasing compactness of the thematic
abstraction in the command set, a second mode of escalation may
be observed: the clauses (6–7 [6–7]) place greater stress upon the
final motif (Restoration) by effecting syntactical disruption through
the employment of a subordinate clause (6–7 [7]). This escalation
represents a shift from the earlier portrayal of the thematic
abstraction of the narrative sequence (6–7 [1–3]). The following
legal prescriptions of verses 9–11 and 12–5 will demonstrate a
similar shift of focus toward restoration, the elimination of
prohibited combinations.

Verses 9–11

The command set verses 9–11 is separated from the preceding
prescriptions with greater concern for the immediate situation of
the narrative by two clauses of the narrative sequence (1–20 [16,
17]). The second of the two clauses (1–20 [17]) introduces the
command set verses 9–11. The initial prohibition takes the form of
an asyndetic verbal clause (9–11 [1]). A conjunctive verbal clause
(9–11 [2]) proceeds with the command set introducing a similar
consequence to those of preceding prescriptions (6–7 [3, 7]): the
avoidance of the death penalty. The syntactical entity designated by
9–11 (3) is not a clause; the sequence חקת עולם לדרתיכם fails to
meet the criterion of predication for the identification of a clause.
If חקת עולם is to be considered the subject of a verbless clause,
the phrase ought to be definite in view of the fact that it designates
and qualifies the preceding ruling (9–11 [1–2]). The Aramaic
Targums correspond with the Masoretic Text in the omission of
the definite article at the conclusion of the construct chain; the
omission of the copula is attested in the Septuagint along with the

absence of the definite article.[21] Thus, 9–11 (3) should be considered an independent nominal grouping beneath the level of the clause (an independent syntactical constituent). The infinitive construct forms with the prefixed preposition ל (ולהבדיל and ולהורת) expand upon the initial nominal formation of 9–11 (3) by expressing the purpose of the perpetual statute; this construction often denotes purpose, result, obligation, or manner as part of the predicate in a verbal or verbless clause (GKC §114g-o; *IBHS* §§36.2.3c-f; *BHRG* §20.1.3).[22] The prefixed conjunction in the first of the two infinitives (ולהבדיל) should not lead to the conclusion that the form has assumed the role of a finite verb in a verbal clause, whose upper boundary is marked by the conjunction ו. It is probable that the conjunction in the first infinitive construct lends weight to the first in a series of two phrases introduced by infinitives; such use of the conjunction with items in a series within a clause has been documented in other places in the Hebrew Bible (*BHRG* §40.8.1b).[23] While the Aramaic Targums mimic the

---

[21] Although the copula may be omitted in certain types of clauses in Greek (proverbial sayings, impersonal constructions, questions and exclamations), ἔσται, the expected form in this case, is seldom omitted (Smyth 1920, §944–5; Blass and Debrunner 1961, §127–8). Hence, in agreement with Wevers (1997, 134), the rendition of LXX should be considered a nominal structure beyond the parameters of the preceding clause.

[22] The sense of obligation is equally viable in the context of 9–11 (1–3). Used in such a way, the infinitive constructs exhibit the force of an imperative.

[23] The insertion of the conjunction separating the phrase introduced by the infinitive construct from the rest of the predicate was identified as having the force of emphasis in GKC (§114p). The infinitive construct introduced by the preposition ל usually is dependent upon a preceding finite verb (Driver 1998, §204–7; GKC §114f-p), and it may not stand in the stead of a finite verb effecting predication without the presence of a nominal form standing as subject (*BHRG* §20.1.1). This restriction of the infinitive construct in view of its nominal character is confirmed, perhaps, by its negation with בלתי (GKC §114s; Joüon §124e; *GBH* §49.3.6; *BHRG* §20.1.1[3]). In contrast, *IBHS* (§36.3.2) allows the understanding

grammatical structure of the Hebrew text, the Septuagint omits the conjunction prior to the first infinitive construct of 9–11 (3), understanding the infinitive forms to constitute part of the syntactical unit beginning with חקת עולם לדרתיכם. In agreement with the Masoretic Text, the infinitives are understood as part of the independent syntactical constituent designated as 9–11 (3) in this presentation of the Hebrew text.[24] The nominal formation which is 9–11 (3) constitutes an especially obtrusive syntactical feature in the command set, by virtue of its existence outside the structure of inter-clausal syntax. As such, 9–11 (3) attains a degree of syntactical disruption surpassing even the force of asyndeton or of clauses employing an extraposed element at the front of the clause. Consequently, the content of 9–11 (3) achieves an elevated degree of prominence.

As a command set, verses 9–11 departs from the topic of mourning in the previous set of prescriptions (vv. 6–7). However, a degree of similarity remains: the prohibition (9–11 [1–2]) depicts a movement from an illicit mixture (the consumption of alcohol just prior to service within the holy precinct) to an act of restoration in the order of the cult (the removal of the errant party through

---

that the infinitive construct—in cases such as that of Lev 10:10–1 where the conjunction ו is prefixed to the initial infinitive construct, appearing to mark the initiation of a new clause apart from the clause governed by the finite verb—has the function of a finite verb, continuing the line of action from a preceding verbal clause. In light of the verifiable function of emphatic inclusion for the first item in a series of entities joint by conjunction (double conjunction) identified for the conjunction ו within the clause (GKC §114p; *IBHS* §39.2.1b[#6]; *BHRG* §§40.8.1[i]b), it is not necessary to depart from the statistically dominant role of ל + infinitive construct as an adjunct to the predicate within the clause. In the absence of a finite verb, it may be expected that the presence of an independent subject (not one in a construct relationship to the infinitive construct) be essential for the formation of a verbless clause.

[24] The rendition of the text in Syr. is the sole detractor. The expression of purpose captured by the infinitive constructs in MT is replaced (at the point of the first infinitive construct להבדיל) with a purpose clause employing a finite verb and introduced by the particle ה.

execution). The initial statement of purpose in 9–11 (3) clarifies this thematic commonality by clearly representing the activity of restoration in the cultic order: the creation of appropriate boundaries.[25] The projected death of the culpable party is the response to the projected circumstance of a neglect for the stipulated boundaries in cultic practice. Thus, it is the case that the command set verses 9–11 presents the series of motifs sustaining the narrative sequence in two clauses (9–11 [1–2]). While the prominence of the second motif (Restoration), witnessed through the syntactical intrusion of a subordinate clause, in the syntactical structure of 6–7 (6–7) is absent in 9–11 (1–2), the obtrusive nature of an independent syntactical constituent standing outside the confines of a clause (9–11 [3]) in the command set compensates for the lack. The statement of 9–11 (3) that the legislation purports to instruct Israel on the divine statutes, the designation of appropriate boundaries, encompasses the structural import of the cult; the statement designates the substance of restoration, the preservation of the sacred realm. The emphasis on the latter of the two designated motifs of the narrative sequence in verses 6–7 finds a counterpart in the pragmatic-semantic structure of verses 9–11.

Verses 12–5

The command set verses 12–5 is separated from the previous set by a single clause from the narrative sequence (1–20 [18]). The command set begins with an asyndetic clause, 12–5 (1), employing an imperative verbal form. A second imperative (but conjunctive) clause follows depicting a second act in the series of commands (12–5 [2]). Three statements of motivation for the commands

---

[25] Noteworthy is the similar collocation of the prohibition of strong drink for priests while serving in the holy precincts, and the exhortation to teach the people to observe the appropriate boundaries in Ezek 44:21–3. The language of the instructions for the nazirite (Num 6:1–21) evokes the sense of an illicit mixture in its prohibition of יין and שׁכר. The Nazirites are instructed to set themselves apart from wine and strong drink: מִיַּיִן וְשֵׁכָר יַזִּיר (Num 6:3aα). A clear boundary is set between the state of the individual after the consumption of an alcoholic beverage and the degree of sanctification inherent to the status of the Nazirite.

follow; these statements consist of subordinate clauses introduced by the conjunction כִּי (12–5 [3, 5, 6]). The first subordinate clause of three leads into a consecutive perfect clause (12–5 [4]). Although 12–5 (4) in theory may be considered a consecutive clause linking up with 12–5 (2) after the interceding motive clause 12–5 (3), the complementary nature of the content of 12–5 (3, 4) is a strong argument for the syntactical unity of the two clauses as a two-member statement of motivation: since the offering is most holy (12–5 [3]), it must be eaten in a holy place.[26] The clauses 12–5 (3–4) are set apart by the syntactical disjuncture of 12–5 (3), and the elevated degree of syntactical continuity between the two clauses (consecution). The return to the use of a conjunctive clause in 12–5 (7) adds another prescription to the command set with similar concerns, but with regard to a different sacrificial portion. The prescription is accompanied by a subordinate (motive) clause (12–5 (8) stating the legitimacy of the claim of the priests to portions of the peace offering.

The syntactical disjuncture of an asyndetic clause seems to signal the initiation of a new command set in 12–5 (9). A consecutive perfect clause (12–5 [10]) proceeds from 12–5 (9), and a subordinate (comparative) clause concludes by noting that the commands are in accordance with divine proclamation (12–5 [11]). The syntax of 12–5 (9–11) appears to designate a self-contained unit standing apart from the rest of the command set. However, the continued focus of 12–5 (9–11) on the disposal of

---

[26] Moreover, the repetition of the content of the command of 12–5 (2) in 12–5 (4) makes it less likely that the latter is a second command couched in a consecutive clause following the first. The corresponding use of the root קדשׁ in 12–5 (3, 4) strengthens the proposal that 12–5 (4) is a logical progression from the statement of 12–5 (3): *holy* items must be eaten in *holy* places. The repetition of the command to eat in the consecutive clause of 12–5 (4) functions to tie the motive statement of 12–5 (3–4) even more closely to the very command for which the statement seeks to underscore: ואכלוה מצות אצל המזבח. Together, the explanatory statement of 12–5 (3–4) with its emphasis on holiness clarifies the significance of the stipulation מצות אצל המזבח in 12–5 (2) for the cultic order of Israelite religion.

the peace offering, the subject matter of 12–5 (7–8), works against the interpretation of these clauses as a separate command set. Further examination reveals that the content of 12–5 (9–11) is reiteration of the substance borne by the explanatory statements of 12–5 (1–8). The content of 12–5 (10, 11) is similar to that of the motive clauses 12–5 (5, 6). The command of 12–5 (9) to bring parts of the peace offering in order to elevate (לְהָנִיף תְּנוּפָה) them before God (לִפְנֵי יהוה) is a command to transfer the items into the domain of the divine; the procedure constitutes a process of sanctification.[27] The result of the command of 12–5 (9) echoes the

---

[27] Through a thorough examination of passages denoting the act of elevation (הֵנִיף) or substances described as תְּנוּפָה, Milgrom has identified the procedure as the act of consigning objects held in the possession of individual human worshippers to divine possession (1991, 461–73). Such acts of dedication involve, among other entities, metals used in the construction of the tent of meeting (Exod 35:22; 38:24–9), the oil for the Menorah (Lev 14:12, 21), and the Levites for work in the tent of meeting (Num 8:11–21). Implicit to God's assumption of possession is the process of sanctification, the setting apart of material for the exclusive use of God. The collocation of the act of elevation and that of sanctification occurs in the passage of Exod 29:1–46, which contains the instructions for the ordination of Aaron and his sons, and specifically for the treatment of the sacred portions from the ram of ordination (אֵיל הַמִּלֻּאִים). Verses 26–8 contain much of the content of the statements of motivation in the command set vv. 12–5: the elevation of a part of the sacrificial portion before God (וְהֵנַפְתָּ אֹתוֹ תְּנוּפָה לִפְנֵי יהוה); the consignment of said portion to the priests (וְהָיָה לְךָ לְמָנָה); sanctification of the sacrificial portion (וְקִדַּשְׁתָּ אֵת חֲזֵה הַתְּנוּפָה). Clearly, the sanctification of the sacrificial portions is closely associated with the concept of elevating the items before God (see also the case of Israel's offering of first fruits in Lev 23:20). The divine assumption of possession forms the basis of the consignment of the items to the ordinands: the objects belong to God to share with his representatives among the people (see also Lev 7:34–5 and Num 6:20; the same principles underlie the consignment of the Levites to Aaron and his sons in Num 18–9). In the passage from Exod 29:1–46, the instructions for the sanctification of the sacrificial portions and their consignment to Aaron and his sons are the precursor to the requirement that the priests boil the meat in a holy place and eat it (vv. 31–3). From

import of the motive clause 12–5 (3) justifying the stipulations concerning the disposal of the grain offering: the sacrificial portion is holy. As a group of clauses, 12–5 (9–11) issues prescriptions that undergird the stipulation of 12–5 (7); the series of clauses are a functional counterpart in the laws regarding the peace offering (12–15 [7–11]) to the motivational statements supporting legislation for the proper consumption of the grain offering (12–5 [1–6]). The same principles that precipitate the requirements stipulated for the grain offering produce a similar requirement for the elevated portions of the peace offering. The distinct relationship between 12–5 (9–11) and 12–5 (7–8) provides a motive for the feature of asyndeton which sets the former grouping apart as a sub-unit within the command set; the clauses 12–5 (9–11) must be shown to belong together by being set apart from the rest of the command set, before their relationship as a motivational statement to 12–5 (7–8) may be determined.

The topical unity of the command set is clear; the prescriptions concern the proper procedure for the consumption of various sacrificial portions by the priests (the grain offering and the peace offering). The stipulations concerning the place of consumption reveal different levels of holiness in the sacrifices. The grain offering must be consumed in a holy place (within the courtyard of the tabernacle), whereas the only requirement for the consumption of the portions from the peace offerings is that they be eaten in a clean place (במקום טהור). Representation of the complete sequence of motifs comprising the narrative sequence (Defilement-Restoration) is absent in this command set; the prohibitions focus solely on the establishment of order within the cultic realm. The prescriptions 12–5 (1–2) and 12–5 (7) represent acts of placing sanctified substances within their proper sphere: the avoidance of illicit mixtures in the maintenance of the cultic

---

this fact, the reiteration of parts of the content of Exod 29:26–8 in 12–5 (9–11) may be seen as an extended statement of motivation for the prescription of 12–5 (7), with the added reminder that the stipulations come from a divine source (12–5 [11]).

order.[28] The initial statement of motivation for 12–5 (1–2) comprising of two clauses joined by consecution (12–5 [3–4]) makes explicit the overarching concern for the containment of sacred portions within sacred space.[29] Thus, the command set verses 12–5 displays a marked shift in focus to the act of restoration within the narrative sequence; this shift is the culmination of initial tendencies recognizable in certain syntactical features of the last two command sets. As a series of commands representing the motif of restoration within the thematic structure of the narrative sequence, the command set verses 12–5 performs the function in increasingly compact syntactical units. This process of compaction is evident in the change from two clauses (12–5 [1–2]) to one (12–5 [7]) in the representation of the motif.

Interaction of Narrative and Law in Leviticus 10:1–20

The three command sets of Lev 10:1–20 portray the sequence of motifs (or parts thereof) that sustain the narrative sequence when it attains its final form. These statements contain thematic abstractions of the narrative sequence; the laws extract the bound motifs of the narrative sequence and express these motifs within terse statements. The presence of more than one prescription bearing the thematic kernel of the narrative sequence is essential to the definition of the abstract sequence of motifs underlying the narrative sequence: the bi-polar series Defilement-Restoration emerges as the common semantic category encompassing the commands on a variety of topics dealing with more concrete circumstances. The multiple prescriptions bearing the thematic essence of the narrative performs a second function: in the command sets of verses 6–7 and 12–5, the thematic components

---

[28] Gerstenberger (1996, 126–7) has remarked that the series of prescriptions in Lev 10:12–5 is not mere repetition of statements already made in Lev 6:9 and 7:32–6. Within the context of Lev 10, the issue of eating the portions in the appropriate place occupies a more prominent place in expression.

[29] The other two statements of motive behind the legal prescriptions (12a–14 [5, 6, 8]) concern the designation of the sacrificial portions and the force of divine will which stands behind the prescriptions.

of the narrative sequence appear in increasingly brief formulations. As the syntactical units grow smaller (the number of clauses decrease), the thematic paradigm entwining narrative sequence and law emerges with greater clarity. The mechanics behind the thematic abstraction of narrative in command sets are familiar from the observations of previous passages under examination.

However, the command sets of Lev 10:1–20 display a unique feature. The first command set (vv. 6–7), through manipulation of the syntactical flow between clauses, lends prominence to the motif of restoration in the sequence of motifs comprising the narrative. The final command set (vv. 12–5) altogether dispenses with the motif of defilement; the shift of focus to the second of the two motifs is complete. The interceding command set (vv. 9–11) witnesses the transition: the prohibition of the command set represents the bi-polar thematic formulation for the narrative sequence, while the following nominal formulation portrays sole concern for the substance of restoration in the order of the cult. The protruding prominence of a grammatical feature (9–11 [3]) independent of a clause renders the shift in focus much more noticeable. As a medium of transition between the first and the third command sets, verses 9–11 constitutes the hinge within the prescriptive material of the passage.[30]

---

[30] The significance of the prominence of 9–11 (3) goes beyond designation of the shift in focus to the motif of restoration. By giving the motif its place of prominence, 9–11 (3) also sets the common thematic denominator of all the command sets at the center of the passage, the pivotal point of the chiastic structure in Lev 10:1–20 as noted by Hartley (1992, 129). While the laws of verses 12–5 dispense with the motif of defilement, it continues to hold the motif of restoration in common with the preceding command sets. The stated purpose of the statute in 9–11 (3) is also the only explicit statement of the abstract semantic category that comprises all the various means of restoration in the prescriptions and the narrative. In the narrative sequence, the crime of Nadab and Abihu is the failure to observe the exhortation of 9–11 (3); the failure generates the bulk of the narrative which is the assiduous application of the principle contained within 9–11 (3). The central position and prominence of 9–11 (3) is deserved.

As thematic abstractions of the narrative sequence or parts of it, the aforementioned thematic shift in the prescriptive material has an impact upon the reader's prognosis for events of the narrative sequence at the point of 1–20 (20–1) in the clauses of the narrative sequence. At this point, the discovery of the burnt carcass of the purification offering takes place. Is the shift of focus to the motif of restoration, a measure that brought death to Nadab and Abihu, further indication of impending doom for Aaron and his remaining sons? Is the perceived cultic infraction of 1–20 (20) an act of defilement standing at the head of an inevitable chain of events ending with a (possibly lethal) act of restoration of order in the cult? The apparent weakening of the people's resolution to execute the commanded acts for the establishment of order in the narrative sequence seems to suggest that disaster is around the corner. Is the exclusive focus on the motif of restoration in the latter portion of the laws a signal of impending retaliation, an address of the apparent weakening of the people's resolution to restore and maintain order in religious practice? Narrative and prescription work hand in hand to play on the reader's worst fears. The conclusion dismantles the reader's forecast of plot in mid-stream; the prescriptions, upon conclusion of the narrative sequence, merely become a composite thematic representation of a single cycle of defilement leading to restoration. There is no second act of defilement requiring an additional measure of restitution; the pronounced shift of focus to the motif of restoration in the latter part of the laws does not, after all, offer a forecast of a much needed measure of counteraction to priestly malpractice. The decisive actions of the priests, as it turns out, are not an abrogation of cultic procedure leaving a residue of pollutants, but part of the on-going act of restoration so aptly represented in the thematic shift in the latter portion of the laws. Thus, it is the case that ambiguities in the significance of emphases in the laws for the narrative prey upon discrepancies in theme between readerly projection and conclusion in the narrative sequence.

THE CASE OF NUMBERS 15:1–41

The passage of Num 15:1–41 begins with God speaking to Moses concerning cultic procedures in the country to which the people are journeying; according to divine promulgation, offerings of grain, oil, and wine are to accompany the whole offering, the peace offering, and the sacrifice for the fulfillment of a vow (Num 15:2–16). A second speech follows with the prescription that the Israelites are to offer a loaf from each first batch of dough in their new country (Num 15:17–21). Procedures for atonement follow in anticipation of the unintentional failure of the congregation or the individual in following the commandments issued through Moses (Num 15:22–31). The discovery of a man gathering wood on the Sabbath follows the speeches by God (Num 15:32–6). Those discovering the crime bring the culprit before the whole congregation, and they place him under arrest until a course of action may be determined. God pronounces death as the penalty, and the whole congregation carries out the order by hurling stones upon the culprit. A final speech by God prescribes the creation of tassels with blue strings at the corners of the garments of the Israelites (Num 15:37–41); this feature is to serve the people as a mnemonic device for keeping the commandments.

The Wider Literary Significance of Numbers 15:1–41

Some commentators on the passage feel that Num 15:1–41 has little connection with the surrounding material. For Gray (1906, 168) and Noth (1968, 114), the placement of the passage between the episode of reconnaissance by stealth (Num 13–4) and the rebellion of Korah's faction (Num 16) is arbitrary; more recently, Davies has expressed the same sentiment (1995, 149–50). Against this position, the majority of commentators finds a note of hope and assurance in the passage following upon the disastrous events of the previous chapter; the dispossession of the generation of the exodus from the promise of the land finds a measure of balance in the confirmation of the promise for a new generation as implied by the divine speeches of Num 15:1–41 (Keil and Delitzsch 1865, 100; Segal 1967, 63; de Vaulx 1972, 179; Wenham 1981, 127; Budd 1984, 167; Olson 1985, 170–4; 1996, 90, 97–9; Milgrom 1990, 117; Harrison 1992, 221; Ashley 1993, 277, 281–2). Olson (1985, 172–3; 1996, 97–9) underscores this shift of focus to the new generation by noting the repeated statement in the laws of the passage that stipulates the relevance of the prescribed measures for posterity (Num 15:14, 15, 21, 23, 38). Further indication of an orientation toward the future may be seen in the effort to apply an old law in a new context (Num 15:32–6), and in the prescription of a method for future generations to remember the commandments (Num 15:37–41).

While the passage of Num 15:1–41 moves to affirm divine ambitions for the future in the face of recent human failure, the laws also maintain an allusion to the preceding events. Snaith (1969, 156) and Wenham (1981, 133) observe that the warning against straying (תור) from the commandments and playing the part of the whore (זנה) in Num 15:39, is reminiscent of the recent crime of Numbers 13–4. The verb תור also characterizes the action of the spies (Num 14:34aα), which is summarily condemned in the divine speech of Num 14:26–35.[31] Olson (1996, 98) and Milgrom (1990, 127) add that the use of the root זנה in Num 15:39 forms a second lexical link (Num 14:33a) with the repudiated initiative of the spies. Therefore, it may be said in agreement with Budd (1984, 178), that the establishment of a mnemonic tool to guard against the abandonment of divine initiative in Num 15:37–41 is a fitting conclusion to the events of Numbers 11–4. Milgrom has made the remark that the emphatic statement of inclusion of the sojourner in the laws of Num 15:1–41 (vv. 14–6, 26, 29) establishes yet another link with the episode of the spies (1990, 117). In Num 13:1–14:45, it is Caleb, a sojourner, who stands out as the single stalwart soul in the face of a grave challenge (Num 14:24). In light of the narrative's celebration of Caleb's courage, the inclusive nature of the laws of Num 15:1–41 is one more affirmative gesture for the presence of the sojourner amidst the elected nation of Israel.

Thematic connections with material following the passage of Num 15:1–41 also exist. The paradigm of blatant disregard for divine authority exemplified in the violation of the Sabbath (Num 15:32–6) persists in the rebellion of Korah and his supporters in chapter 16 (Olson 1985, 173–4; 1996, 99–101). The impetus for the revolt, as stated by Olson (contra *Tg. Onq.* to Num 16:1–2) and demonstrated in Numbers 15 (vv. 1, 17, 22–3, 35–7), is the communication of instruction for the people through Moses. That the substance of Korah's accusation is an attack on the chosen

---

[31] The correspondence of the lexical choice תור with that of Num 14:34aα has also been noted more recently by Ashley (1993, 395) and Davies (1995, 162).

medium of divine communication is confirmed by the response of Moses in Num 16:5: the proposed object of inquiry of divine preference is the designated party to approach God on behalf of the people. As in Num 15:32–6, God visits the affront to divine initiative with severe measures resulting in death for the culpable party (Num 16: 31–5). Despite the stiff penalty meted out for the incident of Sabbath violation and the reminder to cling to the commandments (Num 15:37–41), the pattern of rebellion persists spreading to infect the larger community with grave consequences (Num 16:41–50).

The Internal Coherence of Numbers 15:1–41

Gray (1906, 168), Noth (1968, 114), and Davies (1995, 150) are equally doubtful that the units of Num 15:1–41 display any significant thematic continuity. In the view of Davies, any perceivable connection between the laws is tenuous, and the motive for their collocation in the present position is a mystery.

Among those who see some unity in the collection of laws, Olson puts forth the strongest argument (1996, 91–6). For him, the laws possess a framework of interlocking themes expressed in certain keywords and phrases: repeated references to future generations (vv. 15, 21, 23, 38), settlement in the land (vv. 2, 18), and the inclusion of the sojourner (14, 15, 16, 26, 29, 30) bind the various prescriptions together. Furthermore—as it has been illustrated by Olson—the arrangement of the legal and narrative units within the passage reveal a logical progression, despite its treatment of a variety of seemingly disparate topics. The sequence of laws begins with the prescription of additional offerings to accompany certain animal sacrifices (vv. 1–16) and an offering from each first batch of dough (vv. 17–21). These prescriptions are bound by their common focus upon settlement in the land (vv. 2, 18) and the future generations of Israel (vv. 15, 21): these two features have been shown to effect a significant thematic connection with the previous episode of Numbers 13–4. The prescriptions for atonement in the case of inadvertent error or omission with regard to the prescribed procedures (vv. 22–9) is a logical contingency flowing out of the degree of complexity in the preceding procedures. The prescription of verses 30–1 covers the contrasting circumstance where the error is not inadvertent, but an act of willful impiety in the face of divine authority. The transition to the illustration of a crime belonging to the category anticipated in the prescription of verses 30–1 in the narrative of verses 32–6 has been recognized by many (Keil and Delitzsch 1865, 103; Dillmann 1886, 85; Holzinger 1903, 61; de Vaulx 1972, 187; Budd 1985, 127; Harrison 1982, 228; Ashley 1993, 282; Olson 1996, 96). The thematic connection between prescription and narrative in verses 30–6 is unmistakable, and even recognized by some of those who see little thematic coherence within the chapter as a whole (Gray 1906, 182; Davies 1995, 158). To Olson's outline of a logical continuum binding the material of Num 15:1–41 may be added one more link: the existence of a suitable conclusion to Israel's misadventures of Numbers 13–4 in the reminder to keep the commandments (Num 15:37–41) is equally applicable to the transgression against the Sabbath in Num 15:32–6 (Keil and Delitzsch 1865, 104; Budd 1984, 177–8; Davies 1995, 161). The conglomeration of laws and narrative on a variety of topics in Num 15:1–41 is not, after all, without features expressing a unified corpus. Subsequent analysis will reveal even stronger thematic links abetted by certain syntactical features in the passage.

Despite the bonds holding the passage together, the present study classifies Num 15:1–41 as a complicated case. The classification is a response to the unusually high degree of imagination required of the reader in searching for a thematic basis for the coherence of the passage. Mutually exclusive thematic formulations for the narrative sequence exists; Olson's reading of the passage is one alternative in a set of possibilities. Subsequent analysis reveals the fact that the interpretation of the passage must remain indeterminate. Even beyond the conclusion of the passage, the reader's imagination through the act of interpretation cannot rest.

The Narrative Sequence

The narrative sequence of Num 15:1–41 consists of 13 clauses; four of the 13 clauses constitute acts of speech. The only exceptions to the consecutive imperfect clause (wayyiqtol), which characteristically dominates narrative texts in the Hebrew Bible, are two subordinate clauses. The first of the two subordinate clauses (Num 15:34b) is introduced by the subordinating conjunction כִּי; the second clause (Num 15:36b) has the subordinating conjunction כַּאֲשֶׁר at the front of the clause. Respectively, the functional designations causal/motivational and comparative may be applied to the two clauses departing from the consecutive series of the narrative sequence.

1 וידבר יהוה אל־משה לאמר	1 The Lord spoke to Moses saying:
2 וידבר יהוה אל־משה לאמר	2 The Lord spoke to Moses saying:
3 ויהיו בני־ישראל במדבר	3 When the Israelites were in
4 וימצאו איש מקשש עצים	the wilderness, 4 they found a
ביום השבת	man gathering sticks on the
5 ויקריבו אתו המצאים	sabbath day. 5 Those who
אתו מקשש	found him gathering sticks
עצים אל־משה ואל־אהרן	brought him to Moses, Aaron,
ואל כל־העדה	and to the whole congregation.
6 ויניחו אתו במשמר	6 They put him in custody,
7 כי לא פרש מה־יעשה לו	7 because it was not clear what
8 ויאמר יהוה אל־משה	should be done to him. 8 Then the Lord said to Moses,
9 ויציאו אתו כל־העדה	9 The whole congregation
אל־מחוץ למחנה	brought him outside the camp
10 וירגמו אתו באבנים	10 and stoned him 11 to death,
11 וימת	12 just as the Lord had
12 כאשר צוה יהוה את־משה	commanded Moses. 13 The
13 ויאמר יהוה אל־משה	Lord said to Moses:
לאמר	(vv. 1–41)

The syntactical disruption posed by the subordinate clause is endemic to its hypotactical nature. As the first disruption to the syntactical flow of the narrative sequence, the clause 1–41 (7) offers explanation for the preceding act of the group in placing the culprit under arrest (1–41 [6]): a course of action befitting the crime must be sought in consultation with God.

A second disruption to the series of consecutive clauses occurs with 1–41 (12). The clause 1–41 (12) is subordinate to the preceding three clauses (1–41 [9–11]), providing the detail of correspondence between the community's actions (1–41 [9–11]) and the specific demands of God (introduced by 1–41 [8]). It is noteworthy that the portion of narrative (1–41 [9–11]) offering description for the implementation of the divine imperative (1–41 [8]) inverts the sequence of certain lexical units (מחוץ למחנה→רגום→מות יומת) established within the substance of the command. The inversion witnessed by the corresponding lexical entities in the narrative clauses 1–41 (9–11) emphasizes fulfillment in every detail of the commandment; hence, the comparative clause 1–41 (12) underscores that which is already apparent within the preceding clauses 1–41 (9–11).

The bulk of the narrative sequence is devoted to the incident of the woodgatherer caught in violation of the Sabbath. The action flows swiftly from the discovery of the crime (1–41 [4]) to the imposition and execution of a penalty (1–41 [10–2]). Within this structure of plot, the departure of 1–41 (7, 12) from the series of consecutive clauses is eminent. The clause 1–41 (7) represents a barrier to the completion of the narrative sequence by virtue of the ignorance of the community concerning the correct course of action.[32] The problem is rectified through the inquiry of divine will on the matter. The pronouncement of the death penalty is a significant movement toward conclusion. The action of the community in accordance with the pronouncement represents the conclusion of the narrative sequence. The second departure from the series of consecutive clauses (1–41 [12]) marks this conclusion with reference to the fact that it is consequent upon the divine pronouncement, the act removing the single barrier to the conclusion. Hence, syntactical disruption designates points in the narrative sequence where significant movements or barriers occur in the process of reading and interpretation.

Notwithstanding the aforementioned interpretation of the narrative sequence, unresolved matters of interpretation persist in

---

[32] The passive form פֹּרַשׁ conceals the seat of indecision regarding the course of action (God or the עֵדָה). The postulation of the party behind the lack of determination becomes the issue of contention between competing interpretations for the narrative sequence. Hence, the syntactical prominence of 1–41 (7) is also significant as an indication of indeterminacy within the text regarding its interpretation.

the passage. Biblical scholars have not reached a consensus in establishing the nature of the problem in legal interpretation that requires an inquiry of God. The search for an explanation becomes the trigger for a radical and alternative interpretation of the events. A long-standing proposal for the crux of the matter finds a reason for the inquiry in the absence of a stipulated mode of execution for the violation of the Sabbath in legal prescriptions prior to Num 15:1–41. The Rabbis thought that Moses knew that the death penalty was required (Exod 31:14–5; 35:2), but that the method of execution had to be ascertained (*b. Sanh.* 78b; *Tg. Ps.-J.*; *Sipre Num* 114).[33] Several interpreters of the modern period have maintained this proposition as the most probable solution to the problem at hand (Keil and Delitzsch 1865, 104; Gray 1906, 183; Fishbane 1985, 100). Others depart from this traditional reading of the text and propose that the outstanding issue is the question of the culpability of the individual with reference to the prohibition of all work on the Sabbath. This solution may be divided among two types. There are those who think the inquiry raises the definition of 'work', with the specific issue as whether the gathering of sticks falls under the ban (Holzinger 1903, 64; Noth 1968, 117; Phillips 1969, 127–8; Budd 1984, 175–6). Weingreen's solution, located within the Rabbinic principle of סְיָג לַתּוֹרָה (a fence around the Torah), constitutes the second sub-category; by this principle, the intention to transgress the law may be deemed culpable. Consequently, the inquiry seeks clarification as to whether the gathering of sticks on the Sabbath constitutes the intention to kindle a fire (the specific act prohibited in Exod 35:3), and whether the penalty for the intention warrants the severity of that for the violation of the Sabbath (Weingreen 1966, 362–4). Weingreen's proposal has found some support among subsequent commentators on the text (Wenham 1981, 132; Ashley 1993, 291). Dissatisfaction with all the above solutions leads Gnana Robinson (1978, 301–17) to propose a misunderstanding of the original intent of the legislation in Exod 35:3 by a redactor as the cause of

---

[33] This view is accepted by Rashi (Rosenbaum and Silbermann 1965, 176), Ibn Ezra (Strickman and Silver 1999, 123) and Rashbam (Lockshin 2001, 223).

the present predicament. By Robinson's estimation, both the law in
Exodus and the crime of the woodgatherer have to do with
idolatry, the gathering of fuel and the kindling of 'strange fire'.
With reference to the procedure in the case of idolatry in Deut
17:2–6, an inquiry concerning the veracity of the crime must
precede the judgement. The case of Num 15:32–6, which is a case
of idolatry from the perspective of Robinson, is a reflection of this
procedure (1978, 314–5). A redactor misunderstands the nature of
the crime envisioned in the laws, and adds בְּיוֹם הַשַּׁבָּת in both
cases (Exod 35:3; Num 15:32b); in such manner, the substitution
of Sabbath violation as the crime in view takes place. Finally,
Milgrom (1990, 408–10) considers the case of the blasphemer in
Lev 24:10–23 as parallel to the case at hand. As in Lev 24:10–23, it
is the absence of a prescribed penalty that motivates the inquiry.
For Milgrom, the existence of the prescribed penalty in Exod
31:14–5 and 35:2–3 need not trouble interpreters because of the
imprecision of the narrator's designation for the temporal location
of   the   episode   within   the   wider   narrative:
וַיִּהְיוּ בְנֵי־יִשְׂרָאֵל בַמִּדְבָּר (1–41 [3]). In fact, the case of the
woodgatherer forms the precedent for the legislation of a penalty in
Exod 31:14–5 and 35:2–3 (Milgrom 1990, 409–10). According to
Milgrom, the temporal dislocation of the passage is to facilitate an
escalation of the penalty for sin with a 'high hand' from
excommunication to execution in conjunction with the preceding
prescription in its present location (Num 15:31b).

The lack of any explicit indication of regression to a prior
moment in the sequence of events coupled with the sheer volume
of narrative material between Exod 31:14–5 and the passage at
hand arranged in a perceivable general chronological progression,
renders Milgrom's suggestion improbable. The absence of any
explicit indication of temporal disjuncture or compelling deductive
criteria for such readerly postulation, leaves the assumption that the
flow of the narrative, on the whole, depicts a movement from the
past to the present in the world of the story in operation. In other
words, the availability of other interpretations which do not disturb
the temporal sequence of the events of the narrative compels
readers to suspend the implementation of Milgrom's suggestion.
The existence of a prescribed penalty for Sabbath violation in Exod
31:14–5 and 35:2–3 remains a salient piece of information going
into the events of Num 15:1–41. Robinson's proposal, as noted by

Olson (1985, 166–7) and Davies (1995, 160), is conjectural in its understanding of the original intent of Exod 35:3 and 1–41 (4) as the implication of idolatry. Even if the proposition be granted, the explanation for the inquiry of the people with reference to the procedure in Deut 17:2–6 cannot stand. The procedure in Deuteronomy stipulates that the inquiry is for establishing the certainty that the crime has taken place (Deut 17:4); from the stipulation that the penalty for a capital crime may only proceed on the declaration of more than one witness (Deut 17:6), it is clear that the law is concerned with the trustworthiness of the witnesses. Furthermore, the process does not make allowance for consultation with divinity in the process of verification; consequently, it may be assumed that the inquiry is to be directed at those witnessing the crime (Deut 17:6). The case of Num 15:32–6 displays inconsistencies with the procedure of Deut 17:2–6; noteworthy in the passage from Numbers are the lack of reference to the crime of idolatry and the interrogation of the witnesses. Even if the proposal that the familiarity of the form allows for the omission of certain details in the narrative of Num 15:32–6 be admitted, the intervention of God in the passing of sentence would remain a glaring inconsistency with the procedure of Deut 17:2–6. As for the proposal that the purpose of the inquiry was for ascertaining the culpability of intent with regard to the violation of the Sabbath, the charge of anachronism (Phillips 1969, 125–8; Robinson 1978, 302; Davies 1995, 159) has not been averted. Weingreen's attempts to find similar cases in the Hebrew Bible have been rebuffed. Phillips (1969, 126–7), with reference to Exod 20:16, points to the fact that perjury is an offense in itself; consequently, the crime of Deut 19:19 cannot be considered, as Weingreen proposes (1966, 363–4), one of the intention to commit murder through judicial process. According to Phillips (1969, 125–6), the use of the prohibition against the construction of idols in Exod 20:4a as evidence of culpability in the intention to commit idolatry is equally untenable; it is not clear that the prohibition is to be taken apart from the primary injunction against the worship of foreign deities (vv. 3–6). Torn from its context, Exod 20:4a can hardly be presented as depicting the manufacture of idols as bearing a degree of culpability commensurate with the worship of idols. Furthermore, Milgrom has argued convincingly against Weingreen's position with the observation that the gathering of food for a legitimate activity (eating) on the Sabbath is not permitted (Exod 16:22–30); surely, the gathering of material for the illegitimate activity of kindling of a fire (Exod 35:3) would be that much more obvious as an offense (Milgrom 1990, 408). Equally applicable is Milgrom's citation of the prohibition of a domestic chore in Exod 16:22–30 for the negation of the proposal that doubt existed concerning the applicability of the prohibition of work on the Sabbath to the domestic realm. Hence, it is clear that the blanket prohibition against work must cover the task of gathering sticks, and that the application of that law (Exod 20:8–11; 23:12; 31:14–5; 34:21; 35:2) in Num 15:32–6 should have been clear to the congregation (Robinson 1978, 302; Davies 1995, 160). Finally, the abundant testimony of other laws prescribing stoning as the customary mode of execution renders it unlikely that the method of execution should have been an issue (Weingreen 1966, 362; Milgrom 1990, 408; Davies 1995, 159). Stoning is the prescribed form of punishment for Molech worship (Lev 20:2), sorcery (Lev 20:27), blasphemy (Lev 24:16) the promotion of apostasy (Deut 13:11), idolatry (Deut 17:5), rebellion against parental authority (Deut 21:21), and fornication (Deut 22:21). It has been considered likely that the widespread occurrence of this mode of execution throughout the laws of the Pentateuch allowed for its omission in numerous prescriptions advocating the penalty of death (Weingreen 1966, 362; Davies 1995, 159).

Yet, the Rabbis are not without justification in proposing the mode of execution as the outstanding issue of the inquiry in Num 15:32–6. While the substance of the inquiry is omitted from the content of speech within the narrative sequence, the divine speech of intervention introduced by 1–41 (8) supplies death by stoning as the sole subject of elaboration in purview: מוֹת יוּמַת הָאִישׁ רָגוֹם אֹתוֹ בָאֲבָנִים כָּל־הָעֵדָה מִחוּץ לַמַּחֲנֶה. As noted previously, the narrative sequence picks up on the substance of the preceding divine speech by the reiteration and inversion of select lexical components in the report of compliance with divine will (see 1–41 [9–11]). In view of the specified increment spelt out in command and report, the traditional explanation has the strongest foothold within the context of the narrative sequence; consequently, the expectation that a reader would adopt this explanation in the course of the narrative sequence is reasonable. However, the suggestion of such an interpretation through the novelty of the prescribed mode of execution in judicial procedure does not eradicate its difficulties as a solution in the minds of readers. The degree of uneasiness expressed by Davies in accepting the traditional interpretation of the Rabbis as the least objectionable option in a series of unsatisfactory proposals (1995, 160), may be shared by other readers. The stream of alternative suggestions among recent commentators seems to reflect a degree of residual indeterminacy in the text despite the availability of this interpretation. Is there an alternative interpretation with foundation within the narrative sequence or its immediate vicinity?

Let us consider one more possible interpretation for the events of the narrative sequence. The barrier to the completion of the series of events ending with the penalty of death may not be ignorance on the part of the people in a matter of legal interpretation; instead, it may be reluctance to comply with a law requiring the most severe penalty that brings the judicial process to a halt. By this interpretation, the inquiry is an effort to accommodate the reticence of the people in initiating an act with horrific consequences, by transferring this responsibility to God on the pretense of legal clarification. Standing in sharp contrast is the initiative of Phinehas in defending the honour of God in the face of cultic apostasy (Num 25:1–15). The pleasure of God is enacted through the endowment of a perpetual priesthood upon his descendants as a reward for the zealous fervour of Eleazer's son. The alternative interpretation for Num 15:32–6 has been suggested as a possibility by R.K. Harrison (1992, 228–9).

Indeed, there are mitigating factors within and beyond the passage for such an interpretation. One factor arises from the common concern for the inclusion of the sojourner and posterity in the legal material introduced by 1–41 (1, 2) of the narrative sequence. The applicability of the laws for subsequent generations is mentioned throughout the body of prescriptions (Num 15:15b, 21b, 23, 38a). The concern for the sojourner is equally widespread. The supplementary cultic procedures (Num 15:1b–16; see vv. 14–6) and those outlining procedures for atonement (Num 15:22–31; see vv. 26a, 30a), both of which precede the episode of Sabbath violation, include the sojourner. Thus, two common features in the laws express inclusion for different groups across time. This concept of inclusion established through repetition is amenable with the suggested interpretation for the narrative sequence. As the text stands, the narrative sequence collaborates with the common concept established in the laws, by depicting the application of a penalty—a movement from crime to punishment—for the violation of a prescription applicable to the entire community (Exod 20:10). Within such a thematic progression, it is fitting that a barrier in the plot of the narrative sequence should be an affront to the concept of inclusion through the suggestion of exception, a case where the rule does not apply. By this interpretation, the clauses of the narrative sequence posing a degree of prominence through syntactical disruption—the representation of the congregation's reluctance to act (1–41 [7]), and the initiative of God in addressing that reluctance (1–41 [12])—depict a movement from problem to resolution in the narrative sequence. The movement entails the elimination of the suggestion of exception. With the influence of the content of two common features in the preceding laws, 1–41 (12) employs the concept of inclusion as a response to forces hostile to itself (latent in the content of 1–41 [7]) that would impede the completion of the narrative sequence.[34] The spirit of inclusion within the laws introduced by 1–41 (1, 2) fits the progression of the plot in the proposed interpretation for the narrative sequence.

A second factor of mitigation for the proposed interpretation for the narrative sequence is to be found in the laws introduced by 1–41 (13) of the narrative sequence. The thematic essence of this prescriptive material is equally adaptable to the proposed interpretation for the narrative sequence. The narrative sequence,

---

[34] The comparative clause 1–41 (12) reports compliance with the letter of divine commandment introduced by 1–41 (8). As it turns out, the commandment begins with a restatement of previous legislation for the penalty for the violation of the Sabbath (Exod 31:14–5; 25:2–3); according to the ruling in the narrative at hand, no exception to previous ruling on a prohibition applicable to every member of the household (Exod 20:10)—including servants, animals and sojourners—is to be admitted in the present case. Thus, the body of legislation invoked by the commandment introduced by 1–41 (8) advocates already the widespread applicability of the prohibition and the consequence for transgression, a concomitant feature of the concept of inclusion.

by the proposed reading, constitutes an occasion for a reminder to the congregation of the penalty spelt out in Exod 31:14–5 and 35:2–3. The sequence of events moves from a situation of judicial neglect to an act of judicial redress following a timely reminder. Correspondingly, the expressed purpose of the prescriptive discourse introduced by 1–41 (13) is that the people pass from a state of forgetfulness to one of remembering the commandments with the assistance of a visual aid. In expressing the consequence to be avoided (Num 15:39b; the people following their own judgement), the prescription gives expression to the specific event constituting the barrier to the proposed thematic progression for the narrative sequence. The pursuit of an exception to the prescribed penalty for the violation of the Sabbath is born of the people's affinity for independence from divine prescription. Once again, a component of the legal prescriptions addresses a feature of the plot in the proposed interpretation for the narrative sequence. The analysis of the legal prescriptions will draw out the contribution of Num 15:38–41 with greater detail.

There are more features within the text assimilable with the proposed reading for the narrative sequence. A third factor of support for the proposed understanding of the narrative sequence is the omission of the priest (כֹּהֵן) and the leader (נָשִׂיא) from the additional procedures of atonement (introduced by 1–41 [1]). The omission may be perceived through comparison with the procedures of Lev 4:13–21 on the same subject. The selective focus on the priest and the individual in Num 15:22–31 stands without satisfactory explanation up to the present moment.[35] The adoption

---

[35] Earlier commentators had posited a difference in the law in Num in that it envisions the failure to perform a requirement of the law, an act of omission (see Num 15:22aβ in comparison with Lev 4:2, 13, 22, 27, and 5:17). However, Gray argues that the phraseology of Num 15: 24, 29, 30 clearly envisions acts of commission as well; this distinction between the laws cannot be maintained. Instead, Gray sees divergent traditions behind the differences in detail between the bodies of prescription. However, he offers no description of a strategy in the combinations of these traditions in the present text (1906, 179). More recently, Milgrom's critique of Toeg's (1973, 1–20) proposal of a reworking of the Lev passage in Num

of the proposed interpretation provides an explanation. The proclamation of prescriptive procedures for atonement pertaining to the congregation (עדה) and the individual (נפש אחת) to the exclusion of the other parties covered by the parallel legislation in Leviticus (כב, נשיא) is in keeping with the specific focus of the narrative sequence: the error of the individual in breaking the Sabbath, and that of the congregation in its reluctance to apply the stipulated penalty. Milgrom's speculative suggestion that the Numbers passage is simply disinterested in the plight of the priest and the leader (1990, 404) finds clarification in the subject matter of the adjacent narrative. The guilty parties of interest to the laws of Num 15:22–9 are those of the narrative sequence: the individual and the עדה.

Beyond the confines of Num 15:1–41, the indictment of the congregation in the proposed interpretation finds a parallel in the episode of the spies. The relationship with that episode is a fourth factor standing in support of the proposed reading for the narrative sequence of Num 15:1–41. In the episode of the spies, it is the congregation (כל־העדה) that weeps and complains in reaction to the unfavourable report (Num 14:1); consequently, the ire of God is directed at the congregation (העדה הרעה הזאת) in the divine address through Moses (Num 14:27, 35). The charge issuing from divine lips is the refusal to stand steadfast upon the premise of divine promise witnessed by signs (Num 14:11). Thus, the theme of an errant congregation failing to bring the memory of past enactments to bear upon present circumstances in the episode of

---

15 criticises Toeg's argument for a similar oversight. Milgrom's solution is, like that of Gray, to understand the divergence to be the result of separate traditions (Milgrom 1990, 404–5). Milgrom suggests, in response to one of the differences between the bodies of prescription, that the tradition in Num is simply disinterested in the plight of the priest and the leader. The interpretation for the narrative sequence of Num 15:1–41 offered in the present analysis explains the narrowed focus (where the guilty parties are concerned) of the laws for atonement and purification in the variant passage from Num 15. Editorial selection from texts of variant traditions of cult finds function in a redactor's purpose as seen in the shape of the final form.

the spies finds an echo in the case of the violation of the Sabbath according to the proposed interpretation.

A fifth mitigating factor for the argument of the present analysis may be sought in the material following Num 15:1–41. The verses of Num 17:6–15 bear witness to an act of rebellion involving the entire congregation. The charge the congregation brings against Moses and Aaron for the demise of Korah's faction (Num 17:6b) stands in direct contradiction to the preceding rejection by God of Korah's group as possessing a degree of holiness equivalent to that of Moses and Aaron (Num 16:31–17:5; cf. Num 16:3, 7). The divine proclamation concerning the defiant gesture receives commemoration in the instalment of the bronze censers of the rebels around the altar (Num 17:4–5). Specifically, the narrative describes the censers as a memorial (זִכָּרוֹן), lest anyone else should be tempted to subvert the office of the priesthood and suffer the fate of Korah. Yet, the congregation fails to take stock of the tangible witness to divine proclamation in the events immediately following the act of commemoration. Evidently, it is the case that in events preceding and following the narrative sequence of Num 15:1–41, the congregation receives blame for the failure to remember the proclamations of God. As the brief overview of Num 15:1–41 has suggested, there are components of the legal material within Num 15:1–41 that suggest the incident of the violation of the Sabbath is one more case along similar lines. The interpretation proposed for the narrative sequence of Num 15:1–41 would strike a note of harmony with the surrounding material.

Notwithstanding the factors supporting the newly uncovered interpretation for the narrative sequence, the interpretation does not pass from the realm of plausibility to that of certainty. The interpretation arises because of a logical gap in the traditional interpretation that the proper means of execution is the object of the inquiry; suspecting fallibility in this interpretation, the reader searches surrounding material in order to uncover thematic structures adaptable to the events of the narrative sequence. The foregoing analysis has produced one more interpretation; but despite the mitigating factors for the adoption of the new interpretation, the narrative sequence itself does not resolve the issue in favour of one interpretation with clarity. The novel interpretation suggested is the substance of innuendo. The thematic ambiguity of the narrative sequence is clear when the thematic structures of the competing interpretations are formulated through the postulation of sequences of motifs. The traditional interpretation envisions the narrative sequence as a quest for an appropriate penalty for the crime of Sabbath violation, which was omitted in previous legislation; the congregation receives direction from God, and they comply with the sentence meted out. The series of motifs Crime-Sentence-Punishment is an apt description for such an understanding of the sequence of events. The competing interpretation in contention with the first understands the inquiry as an attempt to retard the judicial process because of the reluctance of the congregation to enforce such a grave penalty. The hiatus in the judicial process forces divine pronouncement on the matter. Thus, the intervention of God is not an act of disclosure, but one of encouragement or even coercion. The formulation Crime-Remand-Redress reflects the need for divine initiative (judicial remand) to set the congregation on the correct path. The replacement of the concluding motif in the initial formulation (Punishment) with Redress qualifies the act of retribution as the enactment of the corrective measure flowing from divine intervention. Even as Redress stands in binary opposition to Crime, it reflects the path of the narrative sequence through Remand. The former interpretation is a simple judgement sequence; in the case of the latter, the qualifying term 'judicial redirection' for the series of motifs would be more appropriate. The substance of the legal material is supportive of both interpretations. For the traditional interpretation, the inclusive element of the laws is depicted in the application of the penalty for Sabbath violation without exception; the inquiry merely provokes clarification of this principle without challenging it. The exhortation to remember the commandments is solely an additional indictment of the violation of the Sabbath. The proposed interpretation posits a challenge to the concept of inclusion in the inquiry of the elders, and includes the congregation under the reprimand endemic to the exhortation to remember the commandments. In terms of the sequence of application in the course of reading, it is certain that the mode of execution would arise as the initial solution to the quest for an explanation for the inquiry. The narrative sequence does not suggest an explicit link with the principle of inclusion or the connection between the inquiry; nor does the text indicate that the reminder to keep the commandments is reprimand for the preceding act of inquiry.

Indeed, the tentative postulation of reluctance in complying with prior divine prescription for the violation of the Sabbath is predicated upon the perception of a flaw in the traditional interpretation for the narrative sequence. It is the absence of a satisfactory explanation for the inquiry that drives the reader to explore other possibilities further removed from the immediate vicinity of the event. A plausible alternative interpretation is found; but the possibility remains unconfirmed. Thus, the process of reading moves from a hint of doubt to utter thematic obscurity. In this respect, the thematic interpretation of the narrative sequence remains indeterminate.

The Legal Prescriptions

Clauses of the narrative sequence (1–41 [2, 3–13]) stand between portions of legal prescription in Num 15:1–41. These separations of the legal material in the passage coincide with almost all boundaries between the command sets; the boundary between the command sets verses 17b–21 and verses 22–31 is the sole exception. Syntactical features of disjuncture accompany distinct semantic categories in the definition of the various command sets within the prescriptive text of Num 15:1–41. The command set verses 2b–16 prescribes additional offerings to accompany certain animal sacrifices. The command set verses 17b–21 concern an offering of an initial portion from the material for baking in every kitchen (ראשית ערסתכם חלה). Verses 22–31 prescribe procedures for transgressions of any commandment communicated through Moses. The final command set (vv. 38–41) issues instructions for the implementation of a method for Israel to remember the commandments. Within each command set, various syntactical features also mark boundaries between identifiable parts within the whole.

1 כִּי תָבֹאוּ אֶל־אֶרֶץ
מוֹשְׁבֹתֵיכֶם
אֲשֶׁר אֲנִי נֹתֵן לָכֶם
2 וַעֲשִׂיתֶם אִשֶּׁה לַיהוָה
עֹלָה אוֹ־זֶבַח
לְפַלֵּא־נֶדֶר אוֹ בִנְדָבָה אוֹ
בְּמֹעֲדֵיכֶם
לַעֲשׂוֹת רֵיחַ נִיחֹחַ לַיהוָה
מִן־הַבָּקָר
אוֹ מִן־הַצֹּאן
3 וְהִקְרִיב הַמַּקְרִיב קָרְבָּנוֹ
לַיהוָה
מִנְחָה סֹלֶת עִשָּׂרוֹן בָּלוּל
בִּרְבִעִית הַהִין
שָׁמֶן
4 וְיַיִן לַנֶּסֶךְ רְבִיעִית הַהִין
תַּעֲשֶׂה
עַל־הָעֹלָה אוֹ לַזָּבַח לַכֶּבֶשׂ
הָאֶחָד
5 אוֹ לָאַיִל תַּעֲשֶׂה מִנְחָה
סֹלֶת
שְׁנֵי עֶשְׂרֹנִים בְּלוּלָה בַשֶּׁמֶן
שְׁלִשִׁית הַהִין
6 וְיַיִן לַנֶּסֶךְ שְׁלִשִׁית הַהִין
תַּקְרִיב
רֵיחַ־נִיחֹחַ לַיהוָה
7 וְכִי־תַעֲשֶׂה בֶן־בָּקָר עֹלָה
אוֹ־זֶבַח
לְפַלֵּא־נֶדֶר אוֹ־שְׁלָמִים
לַיהוָה
8 וְהִקְרִיב עַל־בֶּן־הַבָּקָר
מִנְחָה סֹלֶת שְׁלֹשָׁה עֶשְׂרֹנִים
בָּלוּל בַּשֶּׁמֶן חֲצִי הַהִין
9 וְיַיִן תַּקְרִיב לַנֶּסֶךְ חֲצִי
הַהִין
אִשֵּׁה רֵיחַ־נִיחֹחַ לַיהוָה

1 When you come into the land you are to inhabit, which I am giving to you, 2 and you make an offering by fire to the Lord from the herd or from the flock— whether a burnt-offering or a sacrifice, to fulfil a vow or as a freewill-offering   or   at   your appointed festivals—to make a pleasing odour for the Lord, 3 then whoever presents such an offering to the Lord shall present also a grain-offering, one-tenth of an ephah of choice flour, mixed with one-fourth   of   a   hin   of   oil. 4 Moreover, you shall offer one-fourth of a hin of wine as a drink-offering with the burnt-offering or the sacrifice, for each lamb. 5 For a ram, you shall offer a grain-offering, two-tenths of an ephah of choice flour mixed with one-third of a hin of oil; 6 and as a drink-offering you shall offer one-third of a hin of wine, a pleasing odour to the Lord. 7 When you offer a bull as a burnt-offering or a sacrifice, to fulfil a vow or as an offering of well-being to the Lord, 8 then you shall present with the bull a grain-offering, three-tenths of an ephah of choice flour, mixed with half a hin of oil, 9 and you shall present as a drink-offering half a hin of wine, as an offering by fire, a pleasing odour to the Lord.

---

[36] The translation of the NRSV has inverted the order of the clauses

10 Thus it shall be done for each ox or ram, or for each of the male lambs or the kids. 11 According to the number that you offer, so you shall do with each and every one. 12 Every native Israelite shall do these things in this way, in presenting an offering by fire, a pleasing odour to the Lord. 13 An alien who lives with you, or who takes up permanent residence among you, 14 and wishes to offer an offering by fire, a pleasing odour to the Lord, 15–6 shall do as you do. 17 As for the assembly, there shall be for both you and the resident alien a single statute, a perpetual statute throughout your generations; 18 you and the alien shall be alike before the Lord. 19 You and the alien who resides with you shall have the same law and the same ordinance.
(vv. 2b–16)

1 After you come into the land to which I am bringing you, 2 whenever you eat of the bread of the land, 3 you shall present a donation to the Lord. 4 From your first batch of dough you shall present a loaf as a donation; 5 you shall present it just as you present a

10 כָּכָה יֵעָשֶׂה לַשּׁוֹר הָאֶחָד אוֹ לָאַיִל הָאֶחָד אוֹ־לַשֶּׂה בַכְּבָשִׂים אוֹ בָעִזִּים
11 כַּמִּסְפָּר אֲשֶׁר תַּעֲשׂוּ כָּכָה תַּעֲשׂוּ לָאֶחָד כְּמִסְפָּרָם
12 כָּל־הָאֶזְרָח יַעֲשֶׂה־כָּכָה אֶת־אֵלֶּה לְהַקְרִיב אִשֵּׁה רֵיחַ־נִיחֹחַ לַיהוָה
13 כִּי־יָגוּר אִתְּכֶם גֵּר אוֹ אֲשֶׁר־בְּתוֹכְכֶם לְדֹרֹתֵיכֶם
14 וְעָשָׂה אִשֵּׁה רֵיחַ־נִיחֹחַ לַיהוָה
15 כַּאֲשֶׁר תַּעֲשׂוּ
36כֵּן יַעֲשֶׂה 16
17 הַקָּהָל חֻקָּה אַחַת לָכֶם וְלַגֵּר הַגָּר חֻקַּת עוֹלָם לְדֹרֹתֵיכֶם
18 כָּכֶם כַּגֵּר יִהְיֶה לִפְנֵי יְהוָה
19 תּוֹרָה אַחַת וּמִשְׁפָּט אֶחָד יִהְיֶה לָכֶם וְלַגֵּר הַגָּר אִתְּכֶם

1 בְּבֹאֲכֶם אֶל־הָאָרֶץ אֲשֶׁר אֲנִי מֵבִיא אֶתְכֶם שָׁמָּה
2 וְהָיָה בַּאֲכָלְכֶם מִלֶּחֶם הָאָרֶץ
3 תָּרִימוּ תְרוּמָה לַיהוָה
4 רֵאשִׁית עֲרִסֹתֵכֶם חַלָּה תָּרִימוּ תְרוּמָה

2b–16 (15, 16) in its rendition of the Hebrew text. The nature of the numerical designation for this material in the translation (15–6) stems from the impossibility of separating the material to accord with the syntax of the Hebrew text.

5 בתרומת גרן כן תרימו
אתה
6 מראשית ערסתיכם תתנו
ליהוה
תרומה לדרתיכם

donation from the threshing-floor.
6 Throughout your generations
you shall give to the Lord a
donation from the first of your
batch of dough. (vv. 17b–21)

1 וכי תשגו
2 ולא תעשו את
כל־המצות האלה
אשר־דבר יהוה אל־משה
את כל־אשר צוה יהוה
אליכם
ביד־משה אשר צוה יהוה
והלאה
לדרתיכם
3 והיה אם מעיני העדה
נעשתה לשגגה
4 ועשו כל־העדה פר
בן־בקר אחד
לעלה לריח ניחח ליהוה
ומנחתו ונסכו
כמשפט ושעיר־עזים אחד
לחטת
5 וכפר הכהן על־כל־עדת
בני ישראל
6 ונסלח להם
7 כי־שגגה הוא
8 והם הביאו את־קרבנם
אשה ליהוה
וחטאתם לפני יהוה
על־שגגתם
9 ונסלח לכל־עדת בני
ישראל
ולגר הגר בתוכם
10 כי לכל־העם בשגגה
11 ואם־נפש אחת תחטא
בשגגה
12 והקריבה עז בת־שנתה
לחטאת
13 וכפר הכהן על־הנפש

1 But if you unintentionally 2 fail
to observe all these commandments that the Lord has spoken
to Moses—everything that the
Lord has commanded you by
Moses, from the day the Lord gave
commandment and thereafter,
throughout your generations—
3 then if it was done
unintentionally without the
knowledge of the congregation,
4 the whole congregation shall
offer one young bull for a burnt-
offering, a pleasing odour to the
Lord, together with its grain-
offering and its drink-offering,
according to the ordinance, and
one male goat for a sin-offering.
5 The priest shall make atonement
for all the congregation of the
Israelites, 6 and they shall be
forgiven; 7 it was unintentional,
8 and they have brought their
offering, an offering by fire to the
Lord, and their sin-offering before
the Lord, for their error. 9 All the
congregation of the Israelites shall
be forgiven, as well as the aliens
residing among them, 10 because
the whole people was involved in
the error. 11 An individual who
sins unintentionally 12 shall
present a female goat a year old for
a sin-offering. 13 And the priest

השגגת
בחטאה בשגגה לפני יהוה
לכפר עליו
14 ונסלח לו
15 האזרח בבני ישראל
ולגר הגר
בתוכם
תורה אחת יהיה לכם
לעשה בשגגה
16 והנפש אשר־תעשה
ביד רמה
מן־האזרח ומן־הגר
את־יהוה הוא מגדף
17 ונכרתה הנפש ההוא
מקרב עמה
18 כי דבר־יהוה בזה
19 ואת־מצותו הפר
20 הכרת תכרת הנפש
ההוא
21 ועונה בה

shall make atonement before the Lord for the one who commits an error, when it is unintentional, to make atonement for the person, 14 who then shall be forgiven. 15 For both the native among the Israelites and the alien residing among them—you shall have the same law for anyone who acts in error. 16 But whoever acts high-handedly, whether a native or an alien, affronts the Lord, 17 and shall be cut off from among the people. 18 Because of having despised the word of the Lord 19 and broken his commandment, 20 such a person shall be utterly cut off 21 and bear the guilt.
(vv. 22–31)

1 דבר אל־בני ישראל
2 ואמרת אלהם
3 ועשו להם ציצת
על־כנפי בגדיהם
לדרתם
4 ונתנו על־ציצת הכנף
פתיל תכלת
5 והיה לכם לציצת
6 וראיתם אתו
7 וזכרתם את־כל־מצות
יהוה
8 ועשיתם אתם
9 ולא־תתרו אחרי לבבכם
ואחרי עיניכם אשר־אתם
זנים אחריהם
10 למען תזכרו
11 ועשיתם את־כל־מצותי
12 והייתם קדשים
לאלהיכם

1 Speak to the Israelites, 2 and tell them 3 to make their garments throughout their generations 4 and to put a blue cord at each corner. 5 You have the fringe so that, 6 when you see it, 7 you will remember all the commandments of the Lord 8 and do them, 9 and not follow the lust of your own heart and your own eyes. 10 So you shall remember 11 and do all my commandments, 12 and you shall be holy to your God. 13 I am the Lord your God who brought you out of the land of Egypt, to be your God: 14 I am the Lord your God.
(vv. 38–41)

13 אני יהוה אלהיכם אשר
הוצאתי
אתכם מארץ מצרים
להיות לכם
לאלהים
14 אני יהוה אלהיכם

Verses 2b–16

The command set verses 2b–16 consists of laws prescribing additional sacrificial procedures. As prescriptions of a procedural nature, the laws, by and large, begin with an initial subordinate (conditional) clause, and proceed with consecutive perfect clauses (weqatal). The clause 2b–16 (1) is subordinate: it specifies Israel's entry into the land promised as the initial circumstance for the following prescriptive procedure. A consecutive perfect clause (2b–16 [2]) further specifies the occasion of a meat offering (עלה או־זבח) as an additional circumstance. The apodosis begins with the consecutive perfect clause 2b–16 (3); but the next clause (2b–16 [4]) breaks the series of two consecutive clauses by employing a conjunctive clause: the verb is separated from the conjunction ו through the intercession of another clausal component (the direct object). The syntactical disjuncture afforded by the change to a conjunctive clause in 2b–16 (4) may be explained best as an effort to indicate a break in the sequence of events in the procedure in order to indicate that 2b–16 (4) is not the next step to follow in the procedure, but the second member of a pair of actions to be implemented (2b–16 [3–4]).[37] The content of

---

[37] A similar explanation has been offered for the disruption of a series of consecutive imperfect (wayyiqtol) clauses with a conjunctive clause (waw-X-qatal) in narrative. Niccacci's analysis (1994, 164) of Gen 3:14–7 is a case in point. The series of three verbal clauses, each introducing a segment of direct speech, witnesses the transition from a consecutive clause, to an asyndetic clause, and then to conjunction as the mode of linkage: ולאדם אמר ← אל־האשה אמר ← ויאמר יהוה אלהים אל־הנחש. The transition (by our analysis, a shift to a greater degree of syntactical disjunction) is explained, according to Niccacci, as a transition to a secondary line in narrative. The three clauses do not convey independent

the clauses support such an interpretation for the syntax. The drink offering (2b–16 [3]) and the grain offering (2b–16 [4]) together constitute the addition to the animal sacrifice to be performed upon arrival in the new country; they are the offerings of a settled, agricultural society in contrast to those of a nomadic society. In other words, 2b–16 (3–4) constitutes the significant legislative increment conditioned by the circumstance spelt out in the initial statement of the protasis (2b–16 [1]): settlement in the new country. As a prescriptive pair of clauses occurring as a novel feature in cultic procedure, 2b–16 (4) designates the increment by the expression על־העלה או לזבח לכבש האחד: for every animal of the meat sacrifice, the offerings of grain and drink are the additional requirement. The fact that the expression covers both clauses (2b–16 [3–4]), despite occurring only in the latter of the two, is attested by 2b–16 (8) and 2b–16 (10–1). The former clause, 2b–16 (8), places the expression of increment (על־בן־הבקר) in the first additional offering (the specification for a grain offering) of a similar pair of prescriptions (the provision of grain and drink offerings). The clauses 2b–16 (10–1) specify the distribution of both items as additional offerings in accordance with the number of animals offered.[38] From a perusal of the command set, it may be seen that the bi-partite offering of grain and drink occurs also as the additional component in two other sub-sections of the

---

actions in succession; the acts of the second and third clauses are, on the contrary, actions closely related to that of the first clause (Niccacci 1994, 194). Commenting on a similar syntactical phenomenon in 2 Sam 13:19, *BHRG* (§47.2[ii]d) also describes the transition from a consecutive imperfect clause to a conjunctive clause (waw-X-qatal) as the shift to comment on a related action in a similar type of situation. The syntactical shift signals the transition in the situation of communication, the move from the elements of a sequence of action in a narrative, to the elements of a catalogue.

[38] A later prescription for a combination of meat, drink and grain offerings in Num 28 clearly establishes a grain offering for each animal sacrificed. See, specifically, the notice concerning the distribution of the grain offering in the case concerning burnt offerings for the beginning of the month (Num 28:11–3).

command set (2b–16 [5–6, 7–9]), prescribing supplementary offerings for two other animal offerings (אִיל, בֶּן־בָּקָר). Noteworthy is the uniform choice of conjunction—as opposed to consecution as the dominant mode of inter-clausal linkage in the command set—as the mode of inter-clausal linkage within the pair in all three cases. This consistent syntactical deviation from the mode of inter-clausal linkage (consecution) established in 2b–16 (2–3) supports the perception of the two additional offerings as a pair, a single two-member entity, within the flow of events comprising the procedure.

The occurrence of the conjunction אוֹ in 2b–16 (5) introduces a new sub-section for additional offerings to accompany the sacrifice of a ram as a burnt offering or a peace offering. By virtue of the conjunction אוֹ, the clause is conjunctive.[39] The persistence of conjunction (as opposed to reversion to the use of a consecutive clause) as the form of linkage in 2b–16 (5) functions to maintain a degree of separation from the previous procedure which is, with the inception of 2b–16 (5), a recognizably different sub-section within the command set.[40] The new sub-section deals with a

---

[39] The absence of the conjunction וְ renders the consecutive perfect form (weqatal) an impossibility.

[40] The use of a relatively lesser degree of syntactical disjuncture to mark the initiation of this sub-section (the clauses 2b–16 [1, 7, 13] are subordinate clauses introducing conditions) likely has to do with the fact that the ram (אִיל) is omitted as an option in the initial prescriptive procedures for the burnt offering (Lev 1:1–17) and the peace offering (Lev 3:1–17). In the procedures of Lev 1 and 3, only animals from the herd (Lev 1:3; 3:1) and flock (Lev 1:10; 3:6) are mentioned among quadrupeds: categories of domesticated beasts in keeping with those of two sub-sections introduced by subordinate clauses (2b–16 [1, 7]). The final sub-section deals with a different sub-category within the command set: the place of the non-native Israelite. As the text stands, the conjunctive clause 2b–16 (5) introduces an alternative to the smaller class of animal, those from the flock. Possibly, the lesser degree of syntactical disjuncture in the clause in relation to other clauses introducing sub-categories indicates a closer relationship between 2b–16 (5–6) and 2b–16 (1–4). Perhaps, one might argue that the former is a sub-category within

different animal being offered as a sacrifice: a ram as opposed to a beast of the flock. As with 2b–16 (4), 2b–16 (6) employs a conjunctive clause (instead of a consecutive clause as one might expect upon the initiation of a new procedure) to represent the second member of the bi-partite supplementary offering. The phrase ריח־ניחח ליהוה occurs within the clause 2b–16 (6), standing in apposition to ויין לנסך שלשית ההין. The qualification of the offering as being acceptable to God stands at the conclusion of the sub-section establishing the legitimacy of the prescription.[41]

---

the latter. However, the different proportions required in the supplementary offerings to accompany the sacrifice of a ram work against the combination of 2b–16 (5–6) with 2b–16 (1–4) as a single sub-category in the command set.

[41] The phrase ריח־ניחח ליהוה evokes the image of a sacrifice involving burnt portions; hence, Rashi (Rosenbaum and Silbermann 1965, 72) rejects the notion that the similar phrase (with the additional term אשה) occurring later in 2b–16 (9) as applying to the drink offering. But Milgrom (1990, 124) has argued for אשה as possessing the more restricted meaning of 'gift', based on the separation of the חתאת, a sacrificial offering with the distinct purpose of purification, from the category אשה later in v. 25. In light of Milgrom's observations, it is likely that the phrase ריח־ניחח ליהוה similarly denotes the more abstract notion of being acceptable to God (as witnessed by *Tg. Onq.* and Syr.) without the semantic restrictions of the concrete image. The possibility that the phrase and its variant (אשה ריח־ניחח ליהוה) stands as a concluding qualification for each entire preceding prescribed procedure in 2b–16 (6, 9), renders the interpretive option that the phrase is an independent nominal formation (not a clausal component standing in apposition to another within a clause) standing in apposition to all the clauses constituting each procedure an attractive proposition. However, the ancient witnesses stand against such an interpretation of the syntax in 2b–16 (6) by employing constructions that clearly bind the expression to the individual clause. The targums employ the dependent infinitival construction לאתקבלא ברעוא קדם יוי, and LXX ties the expression to the clause with the prepositional phrase εἰς ὀσμὴν εὐωδίας Κυρίῳ. Only Syr., like MT, renders the expression as a nominal formation without explicit indication of its syntactical relationship to the clause: ܪܝܚܐ ܒܣܝܡܐ ܠܡܪܝܐ.

The syntax of the following sub-section is familiar. The subordinate clause 2b–16 (7) expresses a new condition, and a consecutive perfect clause (2b–16 [8]) proceeds with the prescribed procedure. A conjunctive clause (2b–16 [9]) intercedes, departing from consecution as the form of linkage, to express the second member of the bi-partite supplementary offering to accompany the offering of a bull. The following clauses, 2b–16 (10–2), are prominent within the command set by virtue of the high degree of syntactical disjuncture they possess: the clauses are a series of three asyndetic verbal clauses. The fact that the clauses express detail pertinent for all the prescribed procedures up to this point accounts for the degree of prominence through syntactical disjuncture; the clauses are, in effect, a summary of the preceding prescriptions. The first two clauses 2b–16 (10–1) state the applicability of the preceding additional offerings for every one of the designated animals in accordance with its kind; the final asyndetic clause (2b–16 [12]) applies the cultic requirements to every native Israelite (כל־האזרח). Exceptions to the rule regarding offering and offerer are negated in the statement of summary for procedures up to this point in the legal discourse.

The next sub-section applies the procedural guidelines outlined so far to the sojourner. The sub-section begins with a subordinate (conditional) clause (2b–16 [13]), and a consecutive perfect clause (2b–16 [14]) proceeds with a second clausal component to the condition. The apodosis consists of two clauses: a subordinate (comparative) clause (2b–16 [15]) and an asyndetic clause (2b–16 [16]). The degree of prominence in the syntactical configuration of the two clauses of the apodosis ensures that the equal application of the prescribed procedural guidelines, the prescriptive content of 2b–16 (15–6), is not missed. Three more asyndetic clauses belabour the content of 2b–16 (15–6). The especially high degree of syntactical disjuncture coupled with the nature of the content elevates the prominence of these clauses to achieve a force of summary for the sub-section—and beyond that, for the entire command set—akin to that of 2b–16 (10–2). The complementary tenor of 2b–16 (17–9) in relation to 2b–16 (10–2) strengthens the argument for 2b–16 (17–9) as a set of clauses encapsulating a common element in the laws of the entire command set: all six asyndetic clauses (2b–16 [10–2, 17–9]) express the extensive application of the laws, the product of inclusion. In

relation to this function in the asyndetic clauses 2b–16 (10–2, 17–
9), 2b–16 (17) is especially effective in its use of syntax for the
conveyance of its message. The noun הקהל lends a greater degree
of syntactical disjuncture to 2b–16 (17) as an extraposed element
standing before the clause; but the function of the extraposed
component goes beyond this task.[42] The syntactical role of הקהל
within the verbless clause is assumed by לכם ולגר הגר. As a
single nominal formation in a position of prominence before the
clause, הקהל lends grammatical and semantic unity to its multi-
member counterpart (לכם ולגר הגר) within the clause. The
unification of the two prepositional phrases within the single
concept of the extraposed element matches the pronounced
singularity of the other nominal formation within the clause,
חקה אחת. Subject and predicate stand as unified entities before the
reader: one law for one people. Thus, it is the case that the process
of grammatical and conceptual unification witnessed in the
formation of the extraposed element of 2b–16 (17) imitates the
message of the clause; the native and the sojourner stand as a single
entity under the requirements of a single law before God. The
inclusion of the sojourner with the native Israelite within the

---

[42] The rendition of the verse in Syr. omits MT's הקהל; in contrast,
LXX and *Sam. Tg.* take the term with the preceding clause. Following
LXX in his translation, Milgrom (1990, 120–1) goes against the division of
clauses in MT with the argument that הקהל specifically omits the
sojourner (cf. Josh 8:35). In the presentation of an alternative
interpretation, Milgrom includes הקהל with 2b–16 (17), but limits the
term to designate only the native Israelite (the solution is based on the
analogy of Num 15:29a, which, according to Milgrom, equates הקהל with
האזרה. Such a specific definition of the term need not be the case (see
TWOT §1991). The term may designate a gathering of various sorts for
various purposes (compare Gen 28:3; 35:11; 49:6; Prov 21:16). Within the
context of 2b–16 (17), the term designates the larger community in the
wilderness including the alien. Such is the opinion of Holzinger, who in
considering the term a gloss to bring the clause in conformity with the
inclusive statement of v. 26 (with reference to the function of
כי לכל־העם בשגגה) denies that the narrow definition for the term in
Lev 4:13 is applicable in this case (1903, 63).

specific context of this legal passage is the explicit statement of the
following prescription (2b–16 [18]): כֶּכֶם כַּגֵּר יִהְיֶה לִפְנֵי יְהוָה.
Within 2b–16 (17), the movement toward inclusion receives one
more instalment: the nominal formation חֻקַּת עוֹלָם לְדֹרֹתֵיכֶם,
by standing in apposition to חֻקָּה אַחַת, extends the promulgation
to cover subsequent generations.[43]

As a command set, verses 2b–16 attain topical unity by virtue
of the fact that the laws are concerned with the singular issue of
prescribing additional bloodless offerings to accompany designated
animal sacrifices upon entry into the promised land. This singular
purpose is the basis for the designation of verses 2b–16 as a single
command set separate from the others. Within the command set,
semantic boundaries accompanied by various forms of syntactical
disjuncture between groups of laws have been noted for the
formation of the various sub-sections: the parts that combine to
form a recognizable topical unit. Commentators have noted a
second common feature in the laws of verses 2b–16: the laws
constitute procedural extensions (or combinations) which express a
widened applicability of the cult in various respects. Milgrom, for
example, considers the legislation to depict "a merger between two
ways of life, that of the shepherd and that of the farmer" (1990,
118). Olson's observations on the subject are more extensive (1996,

---

[43] That the phrase חֻקַּת עוֹלָם לְדֹרֹתֵיכֶם does not constitute a verbless
clause is certain from the absence of determination in חֻקַּת עוֹלָם; one
would expect determination in the noun phrase should it be the case that
it constitutes the subject while designating a law only just prescribed.
Notice how, in contrast, the subject of the verbless clause 2b–16 (17)
חֻקָּה אַחַת exhibits determination by the presence of the accompanying
numeral. The Aramaic versions *Tg. Onq., Tg. Neof.* and Syr. omit the
definite article in their rendition of MT's חֻקַּת עוֹלָם; the first two
translations also, in contrast, include the definite article for MT's
חֻקָּה אַחַת despite the presence of the numeral. The rendition of the
clause in LXX secures predication for חֻקָּה אַחַת יִהְיֶה לָכֶם וְלַגֵּר הַגָּר in MT by
invoking the copula in ἔσται. The copula is noticeably missing for the
following phrase: νόμος αἰώνιος εἰς γενεὰς ὑμῶν. The contrast strongly
suggests that the latter phrase in LXX too is not a clause, but a
construction in apposition to νόμος εἰς (חֻקָּה אַחַת).

92–4). In addition to a widening of the types of produce included with a burnt offering or a peace offering, the legislation of verses 2b–16 extends the prescription of accompanying sacrifices previously confined to specific occasions (Lev 23:12–4, 18; Num 6:14–7) to apply whenever the specified meat offerings are made. The alien also receives a role in the operation of the sacrificial cult. The observations of both scholars are confirmed in the preceding syntactical analysis of verses 2b–16. The principle of inclusion, which undergirds all the procedures of the various sub-sections, is visible in the statements of the syntactically prominent (asyndetic) clauses previously identified as having the force of summary in the command set. Every designated meat offering is to be accompanied by the appropriate supplementary offerings (2b–16 [10–1]). Every native must comply with the prescribed procedures (2b–16 [12]); moreover, the prescribed procedures are to apply to all sojourners as well (2b–16 [17–9]). To follow the sequence of the laws is to follow the expansion of the principle of inclusion, from every sacrificial offering to every potential human participant in the sacrificial cult.

Verses 17b–21

The syntax of the command set verses 17b–21 exhibits unique features. Based on previous cases, one might expect the temporal/circumstantial framework for the command set to be cast as a subordinate clause; the command set at hand employs an independent infinitival phrase (17b–21 [1]) standing before the consecutive perfect clause 17b–21 (2). Together, 17b–21 (1–2) establish the temporal/circumstantial setting for the following prescriptions. The occurrence of an infinitive construct governed by the preposition בְּ (with or without וַיְהִי or וְהָיָה preceding) with a consecutive verbal clause (wayyiqtol or weqatal) following, has been considered by many grammarians the functional equivalent of a temporal clause employing a subordinating conjunction with a finite verbal form (GKC §114r; *IBHS* §36.2.2; Joüon §124k). However, the syntactical distinction of *BHRG* is preferable. Unlike the conditional clause employing a finite verbal form, the infinitive construct may not replace the finite verb as the independent predicate (i.e. without independent nominal or pronominal construction to stand as subject) in a verbal clause (*BHRG* §20.1.1). Hence, as a temporal statement, the infinitive construct often is governed by a preposition (often בְּ or כְּ), and placed as part of the predicate in relation to the finite verb within a clause (*IBHS* §36.2.2 [# 2, 3, 5, 6]; *BHRG* §20.1.5). In 17b–21 (1–2), the infinitival construction governed by the preposition בְּ (thus making the entity a prepositional phrase) fails to attain predication without the presence of a governing finite verb; the phrase (17b–21 [1]) stands beyond the parameters of the following clause, being excluded by the presence of the consecutive perfect form וְהָיָה (17b–21 [2]). Thus, 17b–21 (2) stands as the initial clause of the command set, with the characteristic syntactical disjuncture in prescriptive discourse being expressed by the independent syntactical constituent of 17b–21 (1).[44] In contrast to the extraposed infinitival construction 17b–21 (1), the infinitive construct of 17b–21 (2), בַּאֲכָלְכֶם, is governed by the consecutive perfect verbal form וְהָיָה, the primary constituent of the predicate in the clause. In terms of function, 17b–21 (2) provides a second circumstantial component for the following prescriptions. Thus, the circumstantial and temporal framework for the command set is expressed by the pair of infinitival constructions. The following procedure is to take place when the Israelites enter the promised land and consume its produce. The stark transition to the use of asyndeton for the rest of the command set (17b–21 [3–6]) is odd. Such a high degree of syntactical disjuncture, apart from the purpose of signaling a change in topic, is usually reserved for prescriptions displaying a higher level of urgency or gravity, or for statements expressing the thematic essence or principle of the command set as a whole. In previous cases, the presence of grammatical constructions or particles with the function of emphasis occurred with the identification of such function for a clause. No such feature may be found in the clauses 17b–9 (3–6). The effect of asyndeton in 17b–9 (3–6) is the creation of a distinct separation of the prescriptive

---

[44] Similar to the foregoing analysis, *BHRG* (§46.2[i][4]) considers the formation to be a "type of dislocated construction." The location of the temporal adjunct prior to the clause renders the form similar to that of extraposition; the difference is the lack of a component within the clause sharing a common referent with the dislocated member. However, the elements of syntactical disjuncture and prominence remain.

clauses from the foregoing statement providing the circumstantial framework for the laws (material constituting the protasis in a conditional sentence); the syntactical relation by consecution between 17b–9 (1) and 17b–9 (2) is severed by asyndeton in 17b–9 (3). The on-set of 17b–9 (3) signals the initiation of the apodosis. The actual prescriptive content of the command set is carried by a choppy texture of four asyndetic clauses portraying various aspects of a single command. The first command establishes the fact that an offering is to take place (תרימו תרומה ליהוה), whereas the second adds the notation that it shall be a portion of the dough offered as a loaf (ערסתכם חלה ראשית). The third command establishes the offering as equivalent to that of grain from the threshing floor (כתרומת גרן). Finally, the last command adds the fact that the requirement extends to subsequent generations (תרומת לדרתיכם). Each clause of 17b–21 (3, 4, 6) takes up the content of the last, while offering an increment; in contrast, 17b–21 (5) is concerned solely with establishing the equivalence of the offering from dough, with that from the raw material (grain).

As a command set, verses 17b–21 portray a distinct focus on the requirement for an offering from the baking of each Israelite household. Despite the ambiguity of the term ערסה in 17b–21 (4), the association with חלה and the contrast with תרומת גרן (17b–9 [5]) clearly establish the offering as the prepared product of grain from the oven.[45] That the command set constitutes an extension of

---

[45] The occurrences of the term in Ezek 44:30 and Neh 10:37 do not clarify the meaning of the term. The ancient witnesses attest to the uncertainty. The term φυράματος (dough) is the rendition of LXX; the term אצותא (a cooking utensil) is the equivalent in *Tg. Onq.*, and Syr. concurs with the phrase ܚ ܓ ܘ ܪ ܐ ܩ ܘ ܡ ܚ. Budd follows the lead of LXX and accepts 'dough' as the appropriate translation (1984, 170). Gray, with reference to the term עַרְסָן (and its cognate in Syriac) in the Hebrew of the Talmud, thinks the term in 17b–9 (4) to designate a type of barley porridge (1906, 177). Levine (1993, 394) favours the interpretation of the term as a utensil derived from the term for its usual content (עַרְסָן); the interpretation is based on the analogy of מִשְׁאֶרֶת (a kneading trough), a derivative from שְׂאֹר (dough with leaven). This last suggestion, as

the requirement of an offering from the first portion of Israel's produce from the farm (Lev 19:24–5; 23:10–1) to the household has been noted (de Vaulx 1972, 184; Milgrom 1990, 121; Olson 1996, 94). Despite the absence of any clause standing out from the rest of the prescriptive passage in order to express the principle of inclusion, the content of the command set persists with the application of the principle with regard to the offering of first fruits. The presence of the principle may be seen in the portrayal of the present procedure as an extension of one directed at the farming community (17b–21 [5]); the extension of the law to include subsequent generations propagates the same principle (17b–21 [6]).

Verses 22–31

The command set verses 22–31 is the sole command set in the legal prescriptions of Num 15:1–41 without the barrier of material from the narrative sequence standing between the command set and the last one. The syntactical format of verses 22–31 is typical of prescriptive procedure: sequences of consecutive clauses carry the bulk of the prescription. Three sub-sections dealing with cases of different circumstance are attested.

A subordinate clause (22–31 [1]) carrying the initial component of a conditional statement marks the beginning of the command set and the first sub-section. Prior to the initiation of the series of consecutive clauses, the presence of the negative particle of 22–31 (2) necessitates the imposition of a conjunctive clause. An immediate transition to the consecutive chain of clauses (22–31 [3–6]) is forestalled, as an expression through negation for the initial component of the conditional statement (22–31 [1]) is represented in 22–31 (2). Syntactical disjuncture—as it is perceived in relation to the greater degree of syntactical continuity in the following clauses (22–31 [3–6])—marks a break in the series of events in the procedure (22–31 [2]) in order to offer clarification for the preceding clause (22–31 [1]). The negative statement of 22–

mentioned by Milgrom (1990, 122), may be the best option for the reason that אמסה later, in Rabbinic Hebrew, comes to designate a cradle.

31 (2) is even more significant when viewed in relation to the narrative sequence. The clause implies the fault of the congregation—the precondition for the procedure of atonement outlined in 22–31 (1–10)—in neglecting a requirement of divine commandment; the previously discussed alternative interpretation for the narrative sequence, in explaining the purpose for the people's inquiry of God, finds fault with the congregation. The clause 22–31 (2), in placing one more syntactical barrier to the initiation of the series of consecutive clauses, raises the prominence of one more hint that the alternative interpretation for the narrative sequence may be the correct one. A series of four consecutive perfect clauses proceed with the prescription; the transition from the protasis to the apodosis occurs with the on-set of 22–31 (4). The consecutive clause 22–31 (6) represents the terminus of the prescribed procedure for the atonement of the congregation. The subordinate clause 22–31 (7) severs the series of consecutive clauses in order to initiate a paragraph explaining the final component of the procedure: וְנִסְלַח לָהֶם (22–31 [6]). The initial statement (22–31 [7]) restates the inadvertence of the offending party. The imposition of the pronoun הֵם between the conjunction וְ and the verb in 22–31 (8) blocks immediate transition to a consecutive clause (a transition that does occur with the next clause) from the initial syntactical disjuncture marking the beginning of the statement of motivation (22–31 [7]). Given the significance of inadvertence as a mitigating factor in the initial clause of the statement of motivation, it is almost certain that the position of the pronoun fulfills the function of fronting for the purpose of focus; the willingness of the עֵדָה (the referent of הֵם) in making an offering upon becoming aware of the error (cf. 22–31 [3–4]) contitutes confirmation for the inadvertence of the act of transgression.[46] The consecutive perfect clause 22–31 (9) repeats

---

[46] Buth makes a functional distinction between the imposition of a clausal component between the conjunction וְ and the finite verb of a clause for the purpose of disrupting a consecutive series of clauses (e.g. weqatal→waw-X-yiqtol), and the case where the choice of the interceding clausal component is significant. While the latter function entails the former, the occurrence of the former function need not include the latter

the final component of the prescribed procedure (22–31 [6]), presenting it as the consequence of the preceding factors of mitigation (22–31 [7–8]). The final clause of the first sub-section in the command set disrupts the syntactical flow of the clauses (with a subordinate clause) in order to restate the inadvertence of the error (22–31 [10]).[47] Thus, the explanatory paragraph (22–31 [7–10])

(1995, 77–102). The element of emphasis has been understood as a definitive feature of the latter category by Niccacci (1994, 122–6). The term 'fronting' is a descriptive term used in the analysis of 22–31 (8) to denote specifically the placement of a clausal component before the finite verb, in order for that component to occupy a prominent position before the reader. Within the operation of fronting, Buth identifies the sub-categories 'contextualization' and 'focus'; the former employs a fronted element in order to denote the topic of the following clauses, whereas the latter does the same in order to present the most salient item of information within the clause (Buth 1995, 84–5). Prior to the article by Buth, van der Merwe had made similar functional distinctions between focus and topicalization/contextualization (with a wider range of sub-categories) in his own analysis of the phenomenon in Biblical Hebrew (1991, 129–44).

[47] The absence of a noun phrase functioning as the subject in 22–31 (10) precludes predication for the sequence of phrases; 22–31 (10) appears not to fulfill the fundamental criterion for the definition of a clause. Yet, the presence of the subordinating conjunction כִּי suggests that the following words constitute a clause (*BHRG* §11.5.2, 40.1). An alternative interpretation of the syntax of 22–31 (9–10) is to take כִּי as the asseverative particle standing before a prepositional phrase in order to affirm the unity of sojourner and native as a single entity (לְכָל־הָעָם) in error (בִּשְׁגָגָה). This interpretation understands לְכָל־הָעָם to be in apposition to the two-member prepositional adjunct לְכָל־עֲדַת בְּנֵי יִשְׂרָאֵל וְלַגֵּר הַגָּר בְּתוֹכָם in 22–31 (9). Similar syntactical operations reflecting a trend toward inclusion were observed in 2b–16 (17) and 22–31 (15). Against this interpretation of 22–31 (9–10) as a single clause is the observation that the asseverative particle כִּי usually stands before the entire clause, or directly before the predicate (Muraoka 1985, 158–64). The example of Isa 32:13b seems to present an exception to the rule; there, the particle stands after the finite verb (the imperative form וַחֲגֹרָה), directly before a prepositional phrase governed by the verbal

comes to an end with the repetition of the content of the clause at its inception.[48]

---

predicate. However, the possibility that the predicate is absent within the sequence כִּי עַל־כָּל־בָּתֵּי מָשׂוֹשׁ קִרְיָה עַלִּיזָה by reason of ellipsis—an absence which leads to the postulation that the prepositional phrase is governed by וְהָגּוֹרָה in v. 11b—would cancel Isa 32:13b as an exception to the placement of the asseverative particle כִּי within a clause. Also against the proposed interpretation of the syntax in 22–31 (9–10) stand the ancient witnesses to the text. In accordance with MT, *Tg. Onq.* seems to understand the prepositional phrases of 22–31 (10) as a clause through its employment of the subordinating conjunction אֲרֵי to match MT's כִּי. The renditions of 22–31 (10) by *Tg. Neof.* (אֲרוּם לְעַמָּא אִירַע בְּשָׁלוּתָא) and Syr. (ܒܛܠܘܬܐ ܗܘ ܕܓܕܫ, ܗ ܓܝܪ ܠܟܠܗ ܥܡܐ) also supply the subordinating conjunction, with the additional feature of explicit indication for predication in the sequence of words. Similarly, LXX allows for predication with the omission of the preposition from MT's בִּשְׁגָגָה (a move in line with the suggestion in *BHS* for emendation to הַשְׁגָגָה) providing the abstract value 'involuntary (act)' as subject for the clause: ὅτι παντὶ τῷ λαῷ ἀκούσιον. In light of the grammatical rarity endemic to the suggested interpretation and the textual witnesses standing against it, Gray's suggestion that the case represents an example of "violent ellipsis" seems to be the best option (Gray 1906, 181; insertions in italics in the following quotation are Gray's). By this interpretation, כִּי is the subordinating (causal) conjunction introducing a clause where the predicate is present virtually: "*for to all the people* belongs what was committed *in error*."

[48] The repetition of the declaration of inadvertence in a motive clause constitutes the formation of inclusio; the group of clauses 22–31 (7–10) receives formal confirmation as a distinct paragraph constituting a statement of motivation for the sub-section as a whole. That the consecutive clause 22–31 (9) should not be considered a return to the prescription of the procedure for atonement after a brief statement of motivation (22–31 [7–8]) may be seen in the fact that 22–31 (9) repeats the content of 22–31 (6), the final component of the procedure. The repetition cannot be considered a return to a previously stated point in the procedure in order to carry on with the prescription of the procedure: the clause 22–31 (6) is the end of the line. For a similar interpretation of the

The subordinate (conditional) clause 22–31 (11) begins a new procedure for the inadvertent error of an individual. The syntactical structure of this sub-section in the command set is similar, with minor variation, to that of the last. No negative statement follows the initial subordinate clause; three consecutive perfect clauses immediately proceed with the apodosis of the conditional sentence. The sequence of prescribed actions ends, as with the last sub-section, with the forgiveness of the culpable party (22–31 [14]). A single asyndetic clause employing an extraposed element (לבני ישראל ולגר הגר בתוכם האזרח) ends the sub-section on the procedure of atonement for the individual. As a clause posing such a high degree of syntactical disruption, 22–31 (15) affords prominence for the inclusion of the sojourner in the command set; the content of 22–31 (9, 16) clarifies that the statement of inclusion in 22–31 (15) is applicable for all the procedures of the command set. As was the case of 2b–16 (17), the internal syntax of 22–31 (15) is especially adept at communicating the statement of inclusion. The extraposed component places before the reader, prior to the commencement of the clause, the separate constituents (one noun phrase and one prepositional phrase) of the community to come under the jurisdiction of the legislation; the pronoun that assumes the role of the extraposed component within the clause (לכם) combines both parties as a single entity, the recipient of legal address. The grammatical movement between plurality and singularity mimics the function of inclusion: the law views the two groups within the community as a single entity.[49] The asyndetic clause 22–31 (15) also gives prominence to the notion of inadvertence (לעשה בשגגה), a significant component of the laws

---

relationship between 22–31 (7–10) and 22–31 (1–6), see Kellermann's reading of these verses (1973, 109–10).

[49] A similar grammatical operation accomplishing a similar effect was observed in 2b–16 (17). While the opposite movement from a singular entity in the extraposed component to multiple entities within the clause was the case in 2b–16 (17), the interchange had the same effect of a visible illustration of unity within diversity: two parties under one requirement.

espoused by two motive (subordinate) clauses of the last sub-section (22–31 [7, 10]).

The clause 22–31 (16) is the beginning of a new sub-section in the command set; 22–31 (16–21) prescribes action to be taken in the case of a transgression against the law with 'high hand' (בְּיָד רָמָה). The syntactical disjuncture afforded by a conjunctive clause employing an extraposed element (וְהַנֶּפֶשׁ אֲשֶׁר־תַּעֲשֶׂה בְּיָד רָמָה מִן־הָאֶזְרָח וּמִן־הַגֵּר) marks the transition to a new case with a different circumstance within the command set. Since the conjunction in וְהַנֶּפֶשׁ is attached to the extraposed element, it occurs beyond the parameters of the clause (אֶת־יְהוָה הוּא מְגַדֵּף). Occurring at the beginning of a new sub-section, the conjunction governs the entire sub-unit introducing it as the third member in a tripartite command set; the conjunction ו performs a similar function in 22–31 (11). In 22–31 (16), the extraposed element is resumed within the clause by the independent pronoun הוּא, the subject of the participial clause. The prescription ensues with 22–31 (17); a consecutive perfect clause spells out the consequence for the crime envisaged in 22–31 (16). The following four clauses (22–31 [18–21]) may be regarded as an extended statement of motivation beginning with the subordinate clause 22–31 (18). The content of the clauses are a repetition of events covered in 22–31 (16–7). The clauses 22–31 (18–9) restate the culprit's disdain for divine authority (the import of 22–31 [16]) in order to highlight the deliberate nature of the transgression as the motivating factor for the harsh judgement. The clauses of 22–31 (20–1) repeat the substance of that judgement. All the clauses of 22–31 (18–21) express a higher degree of disjuncture in comparison to the syntactical bond (consecution) between the clauses of the main prescriptive body (22–31 [16–7]). After the initial subordinate clause (22–31 [18]) initiating the extended statement of motivation, a conjunctive clause (22–31 [19]) repeats the initial statement of rebellion in the motive clause 22–31 (18) with the added specification that divine commandment (וְאֶת־מִצְוָתוֹ) was the object of disdain.[50] A higher degree of

---

[50] That 22–31 (18, 19) denote different aspects of a single act probably accounts for the absence of a shift to a consecutive perfect clause in the

syntactical disjuncture appears with the last two clauses (22–31 [20–1]). The emphatic presence of the infinitive absolute preceding the finite verb (GKC §113n; Joüon §123e-k; BHRG §20.2.1) in 22–31 (20) suggests that a degree of forcefulness in keeping with the severity of the penalty (excommunication) is the reason for the additional measure of prominence afforded by asyndeton. The second clause (22–31 [21]) maintains the syntactical disjuncture of asyndeton in placing the full weight of the horrific penalty squarely upon the shoulders of the culprit.

As a command set, verses 22–31 display topical unity with its singular focus on procedures to follow in the case of transgression (inadvertent or otherwise) against divine promulgation. Clauses exhibiting a high degree of syntactical disjuncture (22–31 [11, 16]) mark boundaries between the various sub-sections dealing with different cases. Within each sub-section, clauses displaying a greater degree of prominence through syntactical disjuncture (asyndeton and subordination) either offer justification for the prescriptions as part of a statement of motivation (22–31 [7, 10, 15, 19, 20, 21]), or express the inclusion of the sojourner within the purview of the command set (22–31 [10, 15]). Those clauses displaying syntactical prominence as part of statements of motivation go beyond expressing justification and explanation for the laws. The contrasting categories of inadvertence (22–31 [7, 10]) and deliberate rebellion (22–31 [18]) germane to the import of the causal clauses (those introduced by כִּי) underscore the element of antithesis produced by the appearance of the final sub-section (22–31 [16–21]): the transition to the opposite category of a deliberate attack upon divine authority. Within the statement of motivation initiated by the causal clause 22–31 (18), the prominence of the penalty of excommunication (כָּרַת) established by asyndeton (22–31 [20–1]) stands in contrast to the end result of the procedures for inadvertent transgression: forgiveness (נִסְלַח). One final observation regarding the syntactical and semantic structures of the command set verses 22–31 must be mentioned. As a portrayal of

second of the two clauses. Such a transition within the confines of a paragraph offering explanation/justification within a sub-section occurred in the case of 22–31 (7–10).

one of the bi-polar sequences of motifs applicable to the interpretation of the narrative sequence, the final sub-section of the command set presents the sole candidate up to this point in the legal material of Num 15:1–41. The clauses 22–31 (16–7) exhibit a distinct movement from crime to punishment, a definitive structure undergirding the story of the violation of the Sabbath.

Verses 38–41

The verses 38–41 are a command set consisting largely of consecutive perfect clauses; by and large, the command set acts to outline a procedure for the creation of tassels on the edge of the garments of the Israelites to function as a reminder to keep the commandments. The syntax of verses 38–41 is unique in that the prescriptions (38–41 [3–14]) are not separated from the commission of Moses to present the law before the people (38–41 [1–2]). Elsewhere in the passage, the laws are designated as the content of the command to speak (see Num 15:2, 18). An asyndetic clause (38–41 [1]) employing the imperative form דַּבֵּר initiates the act of speech, and consecutive perfect clauses proceed with the instruction (38–41 [2–8]). The prescribed actions for the people begin with 38–41 (3); a sequence of consecutive perfect clauses traces a line from the first step in the creation of the mnemonic device (צִיצִת) to the envisaged performance of the commandments (38–41 [3–8]). The conjunctive clause 38–41 (9) marks the end to the prescribed procedure with a prohibition; the transition from consecution to conjunction reflects the semantic transition with the shift to a higher degree of syntactical disjuncture in 38–41 (9). The following clause is subordinate (38–41 [10]). This clause introduced by the conjunction לְמַעַן declares the purpose of the preceding prohibition (as well as the foregoing procedure) with the opposite consequence of the one negated by the prohibition: Israel must remember the commandments. That the following consecutive perfect clauses (38–41 [11–2]) are not to be considered a resumption of the procedural sequence of 38–41 (3–8) after a momentary disruption (38–41 [9–10]), is confirmed by the fact that 38–41 (11) repeats the content of 38–41 (8). More likely is the explanation that 38–41 (11–2) are the continuation of the subordinate (purpose) clause 38–41 (10)—the clause being in itself a repetition of part of the procedural sequence (38–41 [7]). The clauses 38–41 (10–2) may be considered a statement of purpose for the prohibition (38–41 [9]) by repeating part of the foregoing procedure (38–41 [10–1] repeat the substance of 38–41 [7–8]), and adding the requirement of holiness before God as the ultimate purpose for the prescription. Two final asyndetic verbless clauses conclude the command set (38–41 [13, 14]). Both clauses provide prominence for the identity of the law-giver (אני יהוה אלהיכם); an attached relative clause (subordinate to the phrase יהוה אלהיכם) within 38–41 (13) declares the status of being Israel's national deity as the motive behind the divine act of redemption. A glance at Lev 19:2 reveals the holy divine identity as the motivating factor behind the demand for Israel to be holy. Thus, the blunt statement אני יהוה אלהיכם may be perceived as the declaration of a state of being (holy) that motivates fidelity in keeping the commandments. This exhortation is the function of the command set as a whole.

The topical distinction of the command set within the body of legislation is clear. The prescription for the construction of a mnemonic device to secure the observation of divine commandment stands out from the subject matter of surrounding legislation. Within the command set, the most prominent clauses— measured by the degree of syntactical disjuncture they impose— either establish the ontological foundation, the divine personality, for the command set (the verbless asyndetic clauses 38–41 [13–4]), or designate purpose for the prescription (the subordinate clause 38–41 [10]). Where the structure of motifs sustaining the narrative sequence is concerned, the command set designates the final two motifs in the alternative interpretation proposed for the narrative sequence (Remand and Redress). The exhortation to the people to look upon the device in aid of memory (38–41 [6]) and to remember the commandments (38–41 [7, 10]) captures the essence of the motif of judicial remand: the act of divine legal intercession in the narrative sequence is the act of spurring the people's memory of past prescription. The consequence of remembering divine commandment in the command set is the act of compliance (38–41 [8, 11]). This following component in the procedure of the command set is an apt description for the motif of judicial redress in the narrative sequence; compliance with the memory of past legislation constitutes the return to the legitimate course of action under the given circumstance. Of course, remembering and complying with divine legislation, as prescribed in the command set, need not assume momentary hesitance on the part of the congregation inherent to the make-up of the sequence of motifs Crime-Remand-Redress. On this point, the command set gives voice to the element of desistance from the grave possibility of error in legal procedure through the sole prohibition within the command set: the people must refrain from following their own judgement to the detriment of legitimate legal praxis (38–41 [9]).[51] Thus, within the mutual interaction of the content in the clauses of the command set, two motifs in the proposed alternative interpretation for the narrative sequence receive representation. One of the two motifs in particular receives amplification through the syntactical prominence of a subordinate clause in 38–41 (10): the rekindling of the people's memory which is essential to the motif of judicial redirection (Remand). The principle of inclusion so forcefully represented in previous command sets (vv. 2b–16, 17b–21, 22–31), while not receiving representation with syntactical prominence, remains present in the laws of verses 38–41: the clause 38–41 [3] mentions that the ruling applies to subsequent generations, and 38–41 (7, 11) designate all commandments as deserving of attention. As a complement to the understanding of the narrative sequence as a case of judicial redirection, the principle of inclusion challenges and overturns the initiative of the congregation in seeking an alternative to the wholistic application of divine instruction.

---

[51] The prohibition of 38–41 (9) clarifies the culpable element within the act of 'forgetting' the commandments. The references to the eyes and the heart are references to instruments of deception leading to religious apostasy and foolish behaviour (Num 16:28; Deut 29:17; Judg 21:25; Job 31:7, 24–8; Prov 12:15). The established association of the reliance upon one's own eyes and heart with the way of culpable error is the factor behind the perception of a subversive tone behind the recommendation for an individual to follow those very instruments of estimation in Eccl 11:9a (Murphy 1992, 116–7; Fox 1999, 317–8). Culpability inherent to the failure to recall divine commandment is strengthened further by equation with the activity expressed by the verbal root זנה in 38–41 (9). That the import of this act (זנה) is closely linked with illicit religious practice and worthy of retribution is attested throughout the biblical corpus (Exod 34:15; Lev 17:7; 20:5; Deut 31:16; Judg 2:17; Hos 2:7).

The Interaction of Narrative and Law in Num 15:1–41

In contributing to the thematic coherence of the legal prescriptions, syntax has two functions: syntactical disjuncture demarcates boundaries between command sets, and promotes prominence for concepts binding the command sets as a corpus. The former function promotes awareness of the plurality within the corpus, leading to the quest for connections between the parts. The latter function makes the network of ideas constituting the bonds an obtrusive presence to the reader. The emerging principle of inclusion in the command sets verses 2b–16, 17b–21, and 22–31 is the product of a process of abstraction from numerous prescriptions applying the principle within cases of specific circumstance. Syntactical prominence in the first (vv. 2b–16) and last (vv. 22–31) command sets of those just mentioned bring the common feature of the principle of prominence to the forefront (2b–16 [10, 11, 12, 17, 18, 19]; 22–31 [10, 15]). All these clauses of syntactical prominence offer summary or motivation at the conclusion of command sets or their various sub-sections.

The point of intersection between the first three command sets and the narrative sequence, with reference to the radical and secondary interpretation for the narrative sequence, occurs by way of a hint. The suggestion that the narrative sequence constitutes a reminder to the congregation to observe *all* the commandments of God (the contribution of the final command set, vv. 38–41)—and thus, that the pivotal point of the narrative sequence (Remand) constitutes the defeat of the initiative in seeking exception from the principle of inclusion—is without explicit indication in the narrative sequence. That place of prominence in the narrative sequence is reserved for the series of motifs so clearly alluded to in the final sub-section of the third command set (22–31 [16–7]).; thus, the traditional formulation Crime-Sentence-Punishment is the most recognizable interpretation going into the bulk of the narrative sequence (1–41 [3–13]). The thematic hint afforded by prominence for the principle of inclusion emerges with force only with the expressed purpose for the procedure of the final command set. The subordinate (purpose) clause 38–41 (10) raises the issue of the congregation's faithfulness in remembering the commandments to the surface; in collaboration with the preceding prohibition (38–41 [9]), 38–41 (10) ignites an alternative interpretation for the narrative sequence upon the foundation of readerly discontent with the earlier interpretive option. Divine pronouncement of the culprit's fate is not judicial clarification, but divine intervention in the face of judicial inertia: the initial interpretation of Crime-Sentence-Punishment for the series of actions is replaced by the alternative of Crime-Remand-Redress.

The process of reading through Num 15:1–41 is an illustration of a clash between the 'hermeneutical' and 'proairetic' codes of Barthes. A projected course of action in the early stages of the narrative sequence forecasts that the narrative sequence will be a simple story of crime leading to retribution. In fact, this forecast of theme is sustained as far as 1–41 (12) in the clauses of the narrative sequence. The prompt for the alternative interpretation of events upon conclusion of the narrative sequence clashes with readerly forecast and perceptions throughout the narrative sequence. However, without explicit confirmation within the text for the secondary interpretation—bearing in mind also the difficulty of the initial (and traditional) reading—for the narrative sequence, the reader remains suspended in speculation.

SUMMARY: THE INTERACTION OF NARRATIVE AND LAW IN THE COMPLICATED CASES

The process of the thematic abstraction of narrative sequences in adjacent bodies of legal prescription has not changed among the cases deemed complicated. Series of pivotal motifs are removed from extensive chains of clauses depicting the sequence of actions. This stage in the process of abstraction can occur with laws naming components of the series of motifs (often the members at the poles), or evoking terms representative of the series of motifs within the context of the narrative sequence. Some groups of command sets may proceed then with a second stage in the process of abstraction, creating a general category of theme (names governing a series of motifs or names for specific motifs) capable of accommodating the variety of cases through juxtaposition. It is often the case that concepts common to a variety of laws, and complementary to the series of motifs sustaining the adjacent narrative sequence (e.g. the concept of inclusion in Num 15:1–41), emerge with the discernment of common and general themes among the laws.

Similarities between the simple and complicated cases cease at this point. Where the simple cases offer thematic prominence through abstraction for the sake of clarification, the complicated cases do so to produce a degree of obfuscation in the process of reading. Shifts to emphasis upon particular motifs in a series (Lev 10:1–20) and conflicting interpretations from different sets of motifs (Num 15:1–41), play up tensions between projections of theme in the course of a narrative sequence and thematic formulations that occur upon conclusion. The laws are well-placed at select points in the narrative sequence to exploit these tensions between competing interpretations. The laws provoke readerly projections at the initiation of, or in the course of, narrative sequences, and challenge such forecasts at the terminus.

In both passages, Lev 10:1–20 and Num 15:1–41, the effect is the provision of an occasion for introspection on the part of the reader. In Lev 10:1–20, the forecast of retribution for the restoration of order in the cult, based on a hasty reading of circumstances dubbed as a case of cultic infringement, is arrested by Aaron's explanation for the actions of the priests. With Moses, the reader is relieved from the anxiety of the perception of error, and prompted to examine the details of sacrificial procedure with greater care. In the case of Num 15:1–41, an unresolved conflict of alternative interpretations forces the examination of the boundary between innocence and culpability. The reader is alarmed by the ease with which the initial interpretation of the inquiry of the people as a quest for clarification in judicial procedure takes place. The alternative interpretation suggested by the laws at the end of the narrative sequence, through the progression of thoughts evoked in the course of the narrative sequence, implicates the reader as a party to the possible error of the congregation.[52] Was it all simply a case of neglect for the commandments of God? The degree of readerly participation in the act of interpretation determines the degree to which the process of self-examination occurs for the reader.

---

[52] It may be recalled that the laws of Num 15:22–31 examine the boundary between inadvertent infractions of divine commandment, and crimes committed in depraved indifference to divine authority.

CHAPTER FOUR
SYNTAX AND LAW
IN LEVITICUS AND NUMBERS:
METHOD AND CASES

The preceding chapter concludes the description of abstraction as a strategy of interpretation working to bring together specific passages of law and narrative in Leviticus and Numbers. The fifth chapter—following the one at hand—continues the discussion about abstraction as a literary feature of the Hebrew Bible. Beginning with a summary of the obervations made about abstraction thus far, the fifth chapter proceeds to explore in brief the relevance of abstraction for the act of interpretation beyond the combination of narrative and law, and even beyond the act of reading. The discussion about abstraction comes to pause in the fourth chapter. The present chapter exists to explore further one aspect of the preceding analysis: the qualities of continuity and discontinuity in the system of syntax within the passages of law. Specifically, the present chapter seeks to ascertain whether the system of graded levels of syntactical discontinuity (or continuity) between the components of the text (the types of clauses and other syntactical constituents) adopted in the present study is applicable throughout the legal material of Leviticus and Numbers.

Endemic to the preceding discussion on the thematic abstraction of narrative sequences within legal prescriptive texts, is the observation of the role of syntax in facilitating interpretation. Crucial to the role of syntactical structure in the legal texts of Leviticus and Numbers is the ability of certain types of clauses to pose a degree of syntactical disruption. The identification of topical boundaries and statements of thematic significance for the larger literary unit takes its cue from a reader's ability to perceive such structures which lend prominence to the boundaries within the

197

text, and its points of thematic and emphatic interjection. In considering the syntactical contours of the text, readers become aware of the process of abstraction through observation of the multiple facets—the various command sets—which comprise a thematically distinct passage of law. Also displaying syntactical prominence within command sets are clauses that vie for additional attention for a variety of reasons; this latter function of syntactical disjuncture is, as demonstrated in the readings from portions of Leviticus and Numbers, especially important in identifying the dominant concepts that qualify bodies of law and narrative. Discussion concerning the ability of syntax to effect an awareness of the role of clauses within the larger context of the text comes within the purview of textlinguistics or discourse analysis. The discourse analysis of Biblical Hebrew regularly proceeds with reference to the fact that texts are a form of communication. The assumption of this approach is that syntactical structure in written and oral texts encodes the functional features of the communicative context. Such emphases in the study of texts are pursued often within the discussion of pragmatics. Thus, the discussion of inter-clausal syntax in Biblical Hebrew legal texts must begin with an understanding of the communicative context of all discourse, the realm of pragmatics.

PRAGMATICS AND SYNTACTICAL STRUCTURE BEYOND THE CLAUSE

The term 'pragmatics' has been applied to the description of a plethora of linguistic phenomena; the term often occurs where grammatical features are found to encode information beyond that of a semantic nature. At the most basic level, as it may already be perceived by the reader, pragmatics may be deemed to be any feature of language designating the function of communication, as distinct from the simple act of performing the function of communication. Words and sentences refer to concepts and events. In contrast, pragmatics concerns the attitude or posture of the communicator with regard to the content of those words and sentences as that attitude comes to be registered in the grammar of a language. This distinct interest of pragmatics is evident in the description of the context of communication, the focus of pragmatics, in the work of Jean-Marc Heimerdinger. In describing the use of language, Heimerdinger begins with the observation that the system of a language, its internal organization, is determined by factors in operation beyond the system of language, within the socio-cultural matrix of human society which forms the context of communication (1999, 30–1).[1] Function within the context of communication selects one grammatical form over another within a given situation of communication. Communication, therefore, is a process between two or more parties sharing a network of socio-cultural norms that determine the grammar of a language (Heimerdinger 1999, 31). The effectiveness of communication is predicated upon a high degree of agreement with regard to the grammar effected by the socio-cultural norms of the society. A central point of interaction between grammar and the surrounding determinative framework of communication, according to Heimerdinger, is the manner in which the parties in communication perceive and conceptualize subject matter. One of the ways such shared acts of conceptualization enter a grammar is through the organization of information according to the abstract categories of 'foreground' and 'background' (Heimerdinger 1999, 31). A primary line of information emerges from which items that detract from its purview are set aside as information constituting a secondary line of communication. The secondary line is usually perceived as performing a support role for the primary line. These cognitive categories by concept extend beyond the clause, working

---

[1] Heimerdinger's intention in these pages is to explain the unique contribution of Functional Grammar. But the fact that pragmatics is of prime concern in his exposition is underscored by the following opinion from a footnote: "Syntactic features are explained by semantic and pragmatic facts. Semantics deals with the relation between forms and the use made by these forms by the speaker in communication, at the propositional or illocutionary level. Pragmatics deals with the two previous levels of linguistic form and the communicative functions these forms fulfil within the larger framework of the context in which the forms occur" (Heimerdinger 1999, 30–1). It is evident that Heimerdinger considers pragmatics to be the larger framework under which syntax and semantics are subordinate in the evaluation of any given act of communication.

their way into the grammatical structure of paragraphs, episodes, and even whole stories.

As a rule, recent studies of inter-clausal syntax in Biblical Hebrew adhere to the separation of the pragmatic component of language as a distinct entity from the referential world of the text. Along with this awareness comes the focus on the role of individual clauses in the formation of the larger unit, the text. This elevated interest of pragmatics in the larger unit of the text is a natural by-product of its expansive search for the horizons of the communicative framework for all discourse. The work of Talstra, for example, considers the organizational categories 'domain' and 'perspective' to be operational at the level of the text (1997, 83–6). These categories are recognizable as pragmatic in orientation by their focus on the systemic network of values within the function of communication. 'Domain' concerns the linguistic attitude of the speaker: discourse reflects an awareness of the proximate presence of the audience, whereas narrative does not.[2] 'Perspective' indicates whether an event is seen as being anterior (backward perspective) or posterior (forward perspective) from the temporal location of the perspective of an identified clause-type (incorporating a specific verbal form) functioning as the main line clausal form (zero perspective) in a given text. By monitoring perspective within a given domain (narrative or discourse), one may determine detractions (backward and forward perspective) from the main line (zero perspective) of a text (Talstra 1997, 97).[3] In evaluating

---

[2] By the term 'discourse' Talstra designates both the component of direct speech and the places in a text where an author's direct address of a reader becomes apparent. Talstra's division between narrative and discourse within the category 'domain' follows the position of Schneider (GBH §48.1.3.1). Schneider's categorization is an adaptation of principles propounded by Harald Weinrich (1971) regarding the use of the various tenses in several European languages.

[3] Talstra refers to the distinction between the main line and secondary line within the text as functions indicated by the parameter 'relief' (1997, 83). The idea of 'perspective' as indication of departure from the foreground in Biblical Hebrew grammar was raised by Schneider (GBH §§48.1.3, 48.2, 48.3). Schneider considered the imperfect (yiqtol) and

syntactical organization at the level of the text, Talstra insists on the identification of these determinative categories which assign each clause its place within the text before considering the relationship of the text to the events it portrays (1978, 169). Thus, the constitution of syntax as a component within the context of communication is allowed recognition, in order that the definitive features of the system may emerge without interference from a reader's understanding of the nature of events in the world described by the text. It is only through this strict separation that syntactical organization at the level of the text may be studied as a pragmatic function depicting an author's or speaker's perception of the events portrayed. Without the isolation of pragmatics as a distinct category of organization in the text, the ability to mark the main body of information in a text apart from that of a subsidiary nature is lost. The system of organization in the context of communication must be an independent system before it can function as a way of commenting on the information borne by the text.

The concepts of 'foreground' or 'main line' and their corresponding converse values are, as seen in the work of Talstra, essential to the discussion of syntactical continuity and discontinuity in the two previous chapters. These postulations of structure within texts all assume a reader's ability to perceive departures from an established continuum within a given stretch of clauses. That such concepts influence attempts to describe the syntactical structure of Biblical Hebrew beyond the sentence becomes obvious in considering a few examples of such endeavours.[4]

---

consecutive imperfect (wayyiqtol) forms "die Haupt-Tempora" in direct speech and narrative respectively. In narrative for example, the occurrence of the perfect form (qatal) indicates backward perspective; in direct speech, the use of the perfect form indicates backward perspective, and the consecutive perfect (weqatal) indicates forward perspective.

[4] What follows is a brief and selective review of recent scholarship on inter-clausal syntax in Biblical Hebrew in order to locate the method of the present study within the wider background of theory. The review is not intended to be exhaustive, but only a representative selection to

BIBLICAL HEBREW SYNTAX
AND THE CONCEPT OF 'MAIN LINE'

A proposition which has gained some prominence in current discussion of Biblical Hebrew syntax comes from the hand of Robert E. Longacre. Longacre's proposition begins with the observation that texts display a hierarchy: clauses constitute paragraphs which, in turn, make up a discourse.[5] The type of discourse determines the choice of the main line clause-type, the smallest unit in the constitution of a discourse. For example, the discourse category 'narrative' contains the assumptions that the discourse is agent-oriented and action-oriented (Longacre 1992, 178). The latter assumption determines that the main line consists of clauses of a sequential and punctiliar nature.[6] At the heart of Longacre's definition of narrative as action-oriented lies the conception that the dynamic components of a narrative stand in contrast to those of a static nature in defining the main sequence of action by which the story proceeds (Longacre 1989, 82). On the basis of this definition, Longacre identifies a hierarchy of clause-types displaying an increasing degree of departure from the main

---

highlight useful concepts as well as inadequacies within current theoretical formulations in dealing with legal prescriptive texts in Leviticus and Numbers. The review and the ensuing study are, like the previous syntactical analyses of the last two chapters, primarily concerned with the relationship of clause-types (form) to the accomplishment of syntactical continuity and discontinuity within the structure of texts. Comprehensive and critical surveys of recent developments in the study of Biblical Hebrew syntax concentrating on structures beyond the sentence have been written by van der Merwe (1994) and Lowery (1995). Both essays begin with the exposition of the currents of linguistic theory that inform present methods of approach to Biblical Hebrew syntax; descriptions of current problems and suggestions for new directions in research follow.

  [5] In narrative, by Longacre's use of the term, 'discourse' roughly corresponds to the concept of a story.

  [6] Both qualifications designating the sequentiality and punctiliar nature of narrative refer to the temporal aspect of the events described within narrative.

line of a narrative.[7] The consecutive imperfect clause (wayyiqtol) is the main line clause-type, whereas the use of the perfect[8] denotes a secondary line of action; the latter clause-type is deemed to be weakly sequential and not always punctiliar (1992, 178). The use of the imperfect or the participle is one step further from the main line of narrative discourse; the durative nature of these clause-types represents a greater degree of departure from the punctiliar requirement of the main line, than the clause deploying the perfect verbal form. Longacre considers imperfect and participial clauses as constituents of background clauses. One step further from the main line are clauses which constitute setting; these consist of verbless clauses, existential clauses (clauses employing the particle יֵשׁ), and any verbal clause employing the root היה.[9] The outermost margins of this scheme (furthest from the main line) consists of negative clauses (irrealis) and clauses employing ויהי followed by a temporal phrase (back reference).

On the temporal axis of the future is a discourse category closer to the character of the legal prescriptions clauses in Leviticus and Numbers. Predictive discourse, another of Longacre's categories of text-types, displays much the same emphasis on sequentiality and the punctual aspect; the difference lies in the temporal orientation of predictive discourse which consists of projection toward the future. Consecutive perfect (weqatal) clauses carry the main line of predictive discourse, and clauses employing imperfect forms (secondary line of action), participles (background), the verb היה, and verbless clauses (setting) strike a trail marking increasing distance from the main line of predictive discourse.[10]

---

[7] Longacre uses the terms 'on-the-line' and 'off-the-line' in his scheme of classification.

[8] This does not include the consecutive perfect form (weqatal), which is further removed from the main line on the account of its frequentative aspect.

[9] All this information is represented in the form of a diagram (Longacre 1989, 81; 1992, 180).

[10] This information is available also in the form of a diagram (Longacre 1989, 107; 1992, 181).

Longacre provides a comprehensive scheme by which departures from the main line of a narrative indicated by formal deviation from the consecutive imperfect clause create an outline of the contours in the text. Detractions from the main line at the beginning or through the course of a literary unit may be classified as background, setting, or flashback. These elements stand in support of main line clauses which advance the movement of the story. However, it may be said that Longacre's definition of foreground or main line is essentially flawed because of its inability to function as an adequate description for the material. Recently, the incisive criticism of Heimerdinger has exposed, among other things, the inadequacy of temporal sequentiality as a defining criterion for the occurrence of the consecutive imperfect (wayyiqtol) clause in narrative. Heimerdinger cites examples where consecutive imperfect clauses introduce a flashback, express actions overlapping with those of previous consecutive imperfect clauses, and even perform summary and evaluation of foregoing material (1999, 85–93). Heimerdinger proceeds with his criticism by showing examples of clauses employing the perfect form (clauses fulfilling the function of a secondary line in Longacre's evaluation) that fulfill Longacre's criteria for main line clause-types in narrative discourse (1999, 93–8). According to Heimerdinger's criticism, the proposition that the consecutive imperfect clause is the main line clause-type in narrative discourse is rendered untenable in accordance with Longacre's definition for the main line. The consecutive perfect clause (weqatal) as the main line clause-type in predictive discourse, by analogy, would seem equally unlikely. However, this criticism is true only when elements of the referential world (in this case, temporal sequence) are brought to bear upon the definition of the main line in narrative or other types of discourse.

In contrast, Niccacci pursues a description of Biblical Hebrew syntax by recognizing the ability of syntactical structure to determine the contours of the text apart from semantics. Although semantic considerations are brought in to determine the significance of syntactical disjuncture, Niccacci defends the view that syntactical disjuncture is the accomplishment of syntax itself (1994b, 179). Niccacci adopts Weinrich's dictum that a text consists of a sequence of logical linguistic signs between two significant breaks in communication (Niccacci 1994b, 177). The linguistic signs are of two types: signs of connection and signs of interruption. Inherent to the system of syntax is a network of independent and dependent clauses signalling connection and interruption respectively. Independent clauses are those consisting of a verbal predicate in the initial position of the clause following the conjunction (if one exists) that is not of a subordinating variety. Furthermore, the clause must be of a type that may stand as an independent clause (in accordance with criteria just mentioned) at the beginning of a unit of text. According to this definition, the common notion of syntactical dependence is extended to cover other types of clauses beyond those employing a subordinating conjunction. Dependent clauses depict a secondary line of information; as such, they constitute signs of interruption indicating departure from the main line of communication which consists of independent clauses (Niccacci 1994a, 127–8; 1997, 198–200).[11] Niccacci's proposition of hypotaxis as indicative of the syntactical interruption of the main line of communication offers an account for the distribution of the various types of clauses in the text. The classification of clauses according to formal criteria begins first—as with Talstra and Schneider—with the distinction between narrative and direct speech (Niccacci 1994a, 119).[12] Within

---

[11] The preceding definition of independent clauses as main line clause-types admits exceptions. Weqatal clauses, which do not occur at the beginning of passages of direct speech, are, nevertheless, considered main line clauses in direct speech on the temporal axis of the future. The same applies to waw-X-yiqtol clauses and X-qatal clauses, cases where the verb does not stand at the front of the clause, occurring at the beginning of direct speech on the temporal axes of the future and the past respectively. On the temporal axis of the present, the verbless clause occurring at the beginning of a passage of direct speech or in mid-stream may be on the main line (Niccacci 1997, 189–90). Where formal criteria for the definition of independent clauses as main line clauses do not concur, according to Niccacci the definition of main line is to take precedence over form (1997, 199).

[12] Thus, Niccacci's book-length study of Biblical Hebrew syntax (1990) conducts its investigation treating narrative and direct speech (Niccacci uses the term 'discourse') within separate chapters.

narrative, the transition from independent consecutive imperfect clauses (wayyiqtol) to dependent waw-X-qatal clauses signals the transition to a secondary line of communication. The function of the latter type of clause with respect to the main line wayyiqtol clause is of a variety: among other functions, Niccacci prescribes the establishment of antecedent information, circumstantial information, and contrast (1997, 172–5). Within direct speech, main line clauses are classified in accordance with the temporal axes of the past, present, and future (Niccacci 1990, 73; 1994a, 131). Most pertinent to the syntactical analysis of prescriptive texts is the temporal axis of the future. Within this category, the transition from main to secondary line may be seen in the shift from consecutive perfect clauses (weqatal) to waw-X-yiqtol clauses. Niccacci's categories also account for other forms deemed to produce syntactical disjuncture in the preceding analysis of passages from Leviticus and Numbers. Not only are subordinate clauses classified as forms of syntactical interruption, but extraposed components are considered the functional equivalent of clauses performing the role of a protasis, a dependent clause in a conditional formulation (Niccacci 1990, 145–50; 1996, 435–7). While this study follows a stricter definition of the clause, it is nonetheless noteworthy that extraposition is recognized as a disruptive component within Niccacci's description of Biblical Hebrew syntax.

Niccacci's analysis of Biblical Hebrew syntax with attention to the pragmatic features of main line and secondary line is an improvement over the work of Longacre. Essentially, this improvement finds its source in the foundational commitment to separate syntax from semantic detail emerging from the evaluation of the nature of events in the world depicted by texts. Longacre's postulation of a variety of discourse categories finds its motivation in such semantic categories. These putative categories, as shown by Heimerdinger, misrepresent the formal distinctions between clauses; they also obscure the innate ability of syntax to function as a self-contained system of structure prior to its interaction with semantics. One example of an innapropriate infiltration of semantic considerations into syntactical analysis in Longacre's method has been pointed out by Niccacci. The description of any clause employing the root היה as departure from the main line in narrative may ignore a formal classification (that which ויהי shares with any other consecutive imperfect clause) in preference for a semantic distinction (Niccacci 1995, 547–8).[13] Such a distinction indeed may be worthy of consideration; however, its adoption from the on-set of analysis overlooks the possibility of a reason behind a formal syntactical category (the wayyiqtol clause).

Randall Buth's approach to Biblical Hebrew syntax, like that of Niccacci, avoids the pitfalls of Longacre's method. While admitting that a series of consecutive imperfect clauses in narrative often depict an order of events in temporal sequence, Buth demonstrates that this cannot be the assumption in all cases.[14] Instead, Buth explains a series of consecutive imperfect forms as the product of "the pragmatic constraints of organizational sequentiality and the author's desire to recount these specific events as structurally equal without any narrative pause or distraction" (1995, 86–7). Implicit to this definition of the consecutive imperfect (wayyiqtol) clause is the perception of foreground or main line depicted by syntactical form as a construction that does not designate values within the world of the text on its own (Buth 1995, 88).[15] The primary function of main line clauses is to stand in opposition to clauses outside the main line in order to specify texture within the text. As with Niccacci, syntax provides a means of defining the 'bumps in the road' before semantics interprets the multifarious significance of those 'bumps' for the meaning of the text. Buth envisions a system of continuity and discontinuity of the main line within two general categories represented by distinctions in the form of the verb. Within the two categories denoting oppositions in tense (past or non-past), aspect (perfective or imperfective), and mood (realis or irrealis), the absence of the verb from the initial position of the clause (with allowance for the precedence of the conjunction) marks the

---

[13] In this case, D.A. Dawson's application of Longacre's insights (1994) is the direct recipient of Niccacci's criticism.

[14] The demonstration is forged with reference to the clauses of Judg 11:1 and Jon 1:16–21 (Buth 1995, 86–7).

[15] Buth suggests that the term "mainline event" be used in preference to 'foreground' in order to place emphasis upon the pragmatic structural nature of the concept (1995, 88).

disruption of the main line.[16] The consecutive imperfect clause indicates main line in past time, and consecutive perfect clauses do the same for passages not depicting events in the past.[17] Thus, for example, the transition to a waw-X-yiqtol clause would signal departure from the main line of prescriptive texts (non-past, imperfective, realis) by disrupting the dominant verb-subject-object (VSO) order common in consecutive perfect clauses (weqatal). By similar means, a movement away from the main line in narrative texts (past time, perfective, realis) is effected by the transition to a waw-X-qatal clause from a series of consecutive imperfect clauses. In speaking of such transitions within the text, Buth prefers to offer description with reference to the binary concepts of continuity and discontinuity (1995, 97–9). These concepts depict the reader's immediate perception of stop and flow in the process of reading. Furthermore, such syntactical guidelines are easily transferred into the semantic realm. Semantic continuities within the text may be topical or actional; episode boundaries enforced by syntactical discontinuity may be easily identified as topical boundaries, whereas disjuncture between individual actions may indicate dramatic pause in climactic sequences.[18] The effect,

---

[16] The formulations of Gentry for the pragmatic categories of inter-clausal syntax on the whole follow the lead of Buth's guidelines (Gentry 1998; see table on p. 13). For Gentry, the distinction between statements of affirmation and negation forms another criterion—in addition to the order of constituents within the clause—for determining the disruption of the main line (Gentry employs the terms 'sequential' and 'non-sequential' to represent the dichotomy of main line and secondary line). Clauses of negation signal non-events; such clauses represent disruptions to the main sequence of clauses (Gentry 1998, 14).

[17] Refer to p. 99 in Buth's article (1995) for a tabular presentation of this information. Buth, in contrast with Niccacci, finds the separate treatment of the various clause-types under the dichotomy of narrative and direct speech misplaced. In his view, this distinction obscures the similar opposing functions of tense and aspect in both categories (1995, 85).

[18] Buth demonstrates the function of dramatic pause with reference to Esth 7:6–10 (1995, 91).

according to him, is similar to the experience generated by the retardation of motion in film. Actions in sequence are afforded a broken texture with each component receiving an added measure of prominence. The advantage of recognizing continuity and discontinuity as pragmatic features of syntactical structure is the ability to identify a common class of signals in communication that accomplishes a host of functions pertinent to the semantic realm. Discontinuities in the system of language introduce "parallel actions, out-of-sequence actions, new topics, new units and even mark dramatic pause in a grammatical inversion" (Buth 1995, 99–100). A multitude of functions come to expression within the grammar of a language through a single medium: syntactical continuity and discontinuity.

As it has been mentioned, Niccacci also espouses the concept of discontinuity through his description of interruption to the main line; but the articulation of discontinuity as transition from independent clauses to dependent ones may obscure other syntactical features less assimilative to a system of parataxis and hypotaxis. A second weakness in Niccacci's system is shared with Buth's analysis of Biblical Hebrew syntax. Both descriptions concern themselves with discontinuity as departure from formal syntactical categories identified as the main line of a text; but the concept of discontinuity as expressed by syntax may designate an entity of varying strength in accordance with the type of clause in question. In this aspect, Longacre's system is more concise in that it recognizes various degrees of departure from the main line. A system recognizing different grades of discontinuity in syntax is able to recognize boundaries within textual selections not displaying the main line clause-types identified by Niccacci and Buth. The concern of this study is syntactical structure in the legal prescriptions of Leviticus and Numbers; a single example from previous analysis of selections from this corpus will suffice in illustrating the aforementioned weaknesses in method. It was observed that asyndeton within series of commands often divided the prescriptions into sets comprising distinct topical units, or raised to prominence specific clauses of greater thematic significance. It was often the case that asyndeton intervened in the midst of conjunctive clauses (e.g. waw-X-yiqtol clauses). Buth's focus on the formal properties of the verb (or its absence) and word order within the clause overlooks the omission of the coordinating conjunction ו in the segmentation of texts: no escalation in the degree of syntactical disjuncture occurs in the transition from a waw-X-yiqtol clause to an X-yiqtol clause.[19] Niccacci specifically denies the relevance of ו (being present or absent) when considering the relationship of (waw)-X-yiqtol and (waw)-X-qatal clauses to the discourse structure of the wider syntactical context; the syntactical subordination of these clauses to the main line clauses is secured solely on the fact that the verbs do not occur in the initial position of the clause (Niccacci 1994a, 128). While this analytical stance works well in defining interruptions to series of clauses designated as the main line in a text (on the temporal axis of the future, weqatal clauses), it is evidently inadequate in texts not displaying the designated clause-types of the main line, as well as in those texts containing copious amounts of material apart from the main line.[20] Even Longacre's graded scheme of departure from an established main line flounders in analyzing legal prescriptions. The criteria of sequential and punctual actions defining the main line of the various identified types of discourse oriented toward the future (predictive discourse, hortatory discourse, instructional discourse, procedural discourse) fails to capture the definition of the main line in legal prescriptions where consecutive perfect clauses often do not occur (Longacre

---

[19] In this respect, Gentry's proposal of the presence or absence of ו as a mitigating factor in tandem with the order of the constituents in the clause for the determination of the pragmatic qualities of continuity and discontinuity in a text is an improvement over the work of Niccacci and Buth (Gentry 1998, 9–10).

[20] For example, the entire series of commands in the previously encountered analysis of Lev 24:15b–22 would fall outside the main line in Niccacci's scheme. Many clauses have the verb apart from the initial position in the clause (following the coordinating conjunction where one exists); other clauses are governed by subordinating conjunctions. Similarly, Buth's scheme which has the consecutive perfect clause representing the main line in texts not designating past action sweeps all the clauses of Lev 24:15b–22 off the main line. Without reference to the main line, little can be said with regard to the syntactic boundaries of the passage.

applies the term 'juridical discourse'). Without a categorical description of the nature of the events or states defining the main line, the postulation of a hierarchy of clause-types depicting an incremental order of departure from the main line becomes impossible. Consequently, Longacre refrains from the proposition of such a hierarchy for the legal prescriptions of the Hebrew Bible (1992, 189; 1994, 91).

Notwithstanding the complexities of the problems within the various theoretical propositions, a solution is at hand. The recognition of a graded system of continuity (or discontinuity) inherent to the morpho-syntactic systemic structure of Biblical Hebrew grammar provides a variable measuring device for the identification of disruptions to the syntactical flow of clauses in any given text. Such a system measuring syntactical continuity and discontinuity must move beyond a narrow focus upon verbal form (as well as the absence of the verb in verbless clauses), word order, and the presence of subordinating conjunctions. These measures would address the identified difficulties in the proposals of Niccacci and Buth by creating a paradigm within which any text may find its niche. Within such a system, the identification of the main line becomes immaterial; what matters is the degree of syntactical continuity or discontinuity in relation to the clauses in its vicinity. The system must be rigorously pragmatic in its outlook: it must consider the quality of a syntactical link as a component within the hierarchy of continuity and disjuncture inherent to syntactical form without being defined by semantic categories. This additional stipulation addresses the nebulous connection between the definitive categories of the referential world and morpho-syntactic categories dealing with structures beyond the clause: form takes precedence over content. Consequently, Longacre's difficulty in locating the place of each clause within the legal prescriptions may find resolution in a hierarchy of order.

A MODIFIED APPROACH TO INTER-CLAUSAL SYNTAX IN LEGAL PRESCRIPTIONS

It must be stated from the beginning that the task at hand is not to present a complete system of syntax for all types of texts in the Hebrew Bible. While care is taken to ensure that no statement contradicts the nature of material from other types of texts, the purpose of the following survey is limited in the scope of its investigation to the prescriptive material of a legal nature in Leviticus and Numbers.[21] The confinement of the investigation to the aforementioned books occurs to define a manageable task within the space alloted to this chapter. The more specific aim of the study in verifying the specific statements made concerning the nature of Biblical Hebrew syntax in the preceding analysis of selected texts from Leviticus and Numbers with reference to a larger textual corpus, imposes further restriction in scope.

At the epitomy of the hierarchy of clauses displaying a descending degree of syntactical continuity stands the consecutive perfect clause. From the survey of various works on inter-clausal syntax in Biblical Hebrew, it may be seen that the clause deploying the consecutive perfect verb is regarded widely as constituting the main line in texts displaying an orientation toward the future. Within this study, the classification 'consecutive clause' refers to clauses employing the consecutive perfect form (weqatal) in view of the fact that prescriptive texts are the object under surveillance. The rationale behind the classification stands upon the recognition of the form as a distinct morpho-syntactic entity: the weqatal form cannot be reduced to a simple case of the perfect form (qatal) following the conjunction ׳. This fact has received widespread recognition among works of grammar (Driver 1998, §104; GKC §112a; *GBH* §27.4; Joüon §43a). More recent studies on the structure of syntax beyond the level of the clause continue to view the clause deploying the consecutive perfect form as a distinct category within the relationship of clauses constituting the text (Niccacci 1990, 159–60; 1994a, 128). The unique quality of the consecutive perfect form is indicated by the transition, wherever negation occurs, to a clause employing the imperfect form (yiqtol); if it was the case that weqatal is simply the coordinating conjunction preceding the perfect verbal form, it might be expected that the perfect form (qatal) would occur in the clause of negation (Polotsky 1985, 158; Longacre 1992, 181). While the consecutive clause often depicts events in temporal or logical

---

[21] The criteria for the recognition of material as legal prescriptions follows the guidelines laid down prior to the preceding syntactical analysis of the selections from Leviticus and Numbers.

succession (hence, its dominance in procedural texts), its primary function is, as Buth has shown, pragmatic: the designation of the highest degree of syntactical continuity within the system of inter-clausal connection.

One degree of departure from the highest level of syntactical continuity in legal prescriptive texts is expressed by the conjunctive clause, which consists of any clause introduced by a coordinating conjunction (ו or או) not part of a consecutive verbal construction (in legal prescriptions, weqatal). Whether the transition from a consecutive perfect clause is accomplished by the use of another type of conjunction apart from the ו of the verbal morpheme weqatal, the absence of the finite verb immediately after the conjunction (waw-X-yiqtol, as emphasized by Niccacci, Buth, and Gentry), or the absence of a finite verb altogether, the result exhibits one common constitutive characteristic which defines the conjunctive clause: the presence of a coordinating conjunction not part of the construction of the consecutive verbal form. The conjunctive clause represents a formal departure from the specific morpho-syntactic category denoted by the consecutive perfect clause with its specifically fluid brand of syntactical continuity. The transition to waw-X-qatal (or waw-X-yiqtol in future-oriented texts) probably is—as evidenced by the survey of studies in Biblical Hebrew syntax—the most documented type of syntactical transition in recent studies on Biblical Hebrew syntax. The system of classification adopted here includes verbless clauses with a coordinating conjunction. This decision is not intended to diminish any functional distinction between verbal clauses, and those clauses not employing a finite verb as predicate. The definition of the classification 'conjunctive clause' is adopted in recognition of the fact that, within legal prescriptions, the presence of the coordinating conjunction is the most significant factor in the definition of an intermediate degree of syntactical disjuncture between consecutive clauses, and those of the highest degree of discontinuity.

With Gentry (1998, 10) and against Niccacci (1994a, 128), it may be affirmed that the absence or presence of the conjunction ו is a significant contingency in evaluating the formal representation of the degree of syntactical continuity from one clause to another. The asyndetic clause (with or without finite verb) is one member of a variety of clause-types representative of a greater degree of syntactical disjuncture within the hierarchy. In the analysis of selected legal passages from Leviticus and Numbers, asyndetic clauses mark divisions between command sets, and raise the profile of prescriptions or statements of urgency or thematic significance for the wider context.

A subordinate clause is a clause (with or without finite verb) governed by a subordinating conjunction (e.g. כִּי, אִם, לְמַעַן). Along with asyndetic clauses, subordinate clauses offer a greater measure of syntactical disjuncture in comparison with consecutive clauses and conjunctive clauses. While the concomitant feature of the transition to the use of an imperfect form (yiqtol) as a force of disruption to a series of consecutive perfect clauses has received much attention, the presence of a subordinating conjunction as a feature of syntactical disjuncture in itself has often been overlooked. The identification of the significance of subordinate clauses in the syntactical arrangement of legal prescriptive texts identifies a distinction with regard to waw-X-yiqtol clauses—a distinction that may be overlooked by studies in Biblical Hebrew inter-clausal syntax exclusively focused on the formal properties of verb-form and word order within the clause—with consequences for the demarcation of structure in texts with few or no consecutive clauses. Recently, an article by Benigni (1999) on the function of the particle כִּי as a significant feature in Biblical Hebrew text-syntax sheds light on the role of subordinate clauses in delimiting the syntactical boundaries in texts. Benigni understands the particle to perform the role of a 'text deictic' in the same vein as other particles such as הִנֵּה, הֵן, and עַתָּה, or the phrase בְּיוֹם אֲדֹנָי.[22] The presence of a text deictic such as כִּי marks a break in the text (whether narrative or direct speech), shifting the clause governed by the particle to a different level from that of a

---

[22] Following Schneider, Benigni deems that text deictics, "whose primary role is to be found in the spoken language, articulate a sequence of clauses, drawing the listener's attention to the beginning, the transition, the climax and the end of the narration" (Benigni 1999, 131). Along with Schneider and Talstra, Benigni accepts Harald Weinrich's parameters of 'linguistic attitude' (Talstra uses the term 'domain'), the division of the text into the domains of narrative and comment (including direct speech).

main (i.e. independent) clause. Thus, the particle כִּי, in the view of Benigni, performs the role of a "macrosyntactic sign" working in conjunction with changes in verbal form. Perhaps further indication of a pragmatic function in the syntactical feature of subordination may be seen in the fact that statements of condition or cause, common semantic correlates of syntactical subordination, come to expression apart from formal indications of syntactical subordination. It is not uncommon for consecutive and conjunctive clauses to express conditions or to make statements pertaining to motivation. This flexibility expressed in the departure from the use of formal indicators of grammatical hypotaxis in cases where its deployment seems appropriate raises the possibility of another function for syntactical subordination: a function grounded in the formal properties of the pragmatic structures of discourse in the text.

Causing a similar degree of syntactical disjuncture as asyndetic and subordinate clauses is a clause deploying an extraposed constituent standing before the clause. The criteria followed for the identification of extraposition in this study is similar to, among others, those of the more focused analysis of the feature in Ecclesiastes by Backhaus (1995). The extraposed member may be a nominal construction (including infinitives, participles, and prepositional phrases) or a pronominal entity standing before the clause.[23] Within the clause, a syntactical constituent sharing ties to a referent with the entirety, or part, of the extraposed constituent expresses the syntactical role of the extraposed entity. The existence of the extraposed member beyond the confines of the clause is marked often by the intercession of a conjunction (subordinate or coordinate, including the conjunction forming part of the consecutive verbal morpheme) governing the clause or an interrogative pronoun (Backhaus 1995, 1–2). However, the guidelines laid down by Backhaus allow for the definition of extraposition wherever a constituent of the clause assumes the syntactical role of the extraposed constituent within the clause, even without such

---

[23] Such formations may include relative clauses expanding upon the concept of the extraposed entity.

intercession of a conjunction or interrogative pronoun. In contrast, the approach of this study deems it prudent to observe more stringently the requirement that the extraposed entity and its corresponding member within the clause be separated by the imposition of another constituent of the clause in cases where no conjunction or interrogative pronoun exists to express the upper boundary of the clause. This additional measure of caution would distinguish extraposition from cases where it may be argued that mere apposition within the confines of the clause occurs between the so-called extraposed constituent and its co-referent clausal constituent standing in the initial position of the clause. However, exceptions to the rule may occur in cases where a pronoun (independent or suffixed) constitutes the extraposed entity or its resumptive constituent within the clause.[24] In such cases the high

---

[24] The proposal of such a requirement flows from the effort to offer an adequate description of Biblical Hebrew syntax. It has been observed from the exhaustive study of clauses in Leviticus and Numbers that the problem envisioned—the absence of syntactical separation between the extraposed entity and its co-referent within the clause—occurs in clauses employing a finite verbal form as predicate as well as verbless clauses. However, the statistical dominance of the separation of the extraposed consituent from its co-referent within the clause makes it plausible that a grammatical convention is being observed where such separation occurs. The exceptions to the rule occur in cases where a pronoun is involved in the identification of extraposition. Typically, verbless clauses of the type where an independent pronoun standing as subject in the clause shares reference with an adjacent nominal formation at the front of the clause (e.g. דוד הוא המלך) constitute exceptions to the rule. Arguably, such cases have been considered examples of extraposition (*casus pendens*) on the grounds that in rare cases where the particle הלא occurs, the insertion is made so as to separate the alleged extraposed constituent at the front of the clause from the other components of the clause (Geller 1991, 18). However, the imposition of the particle may in itself be a distinguishing mark of syntactical variation, the genesis of extraposition. More compelling is Revell's observation that the resumptive pronoun often does not agree in number or gender with the co-referent nominal formation in verbless clauses of this type (1989, n. 9). The observation

degree of semantic overlap, with the use of a pronoun, renders it improbable that apposition between nominals is occurring within the boundaries of the clause. A further refinement of the guidelines of Backhaus is the stipulation that in cases where resumption is performed by the subject inherent to a verbal morpheme, the intercession of the conjunction or the interrogative pronoun is necessary so as to clarify the distinction between extraposition and the X-yiqtol clause (where X is the subject of the clause).[25] Apart from Niccacci's brief treatment of extraposition as a form of syntactical subordination, major studies of this syntactical feature have been undertaken by Gross (1987) and Khan (1988). The work of Gross is exhaustive in its structural definition of the various clauses employing extraposition. For

---

which Revell makes as an argument against the understanding of the pronoun as copula—compare with Goldenberg's description of the so-called 'imperfectly-transformed cleft sentence' (1998, 116–22)—is equally applicable to defining the degree of syntactical independence of the resumptive pronoun from its co-referent constituent in defining extraposition. Ultimately, the case for exception may lie in the fact that the pronoun performs the role of deixis: it points to the presence of a proximate element in the vicinity of the clause. The element of reference—with the exception of pronouns functioning as adjectives (הַמֶּלֶךְ הַהוּא)—betrays the degree of syntactical independence. Thus, the requirement that the co-referent syntactical constituents be separated for the identification of extraposition may be waived in cases where either of, or both, the constituents are pronouns.

[25] As the point has been made in the course of ch. 2, the interceding presence of the particle separating the extraposed constituent from the clause does not occur without exception. As a satellite of the clause with a syntactical role within the clause, the extraposed member comes under the jurisdiction of the particle governing the clause. Such a particle may stand prior to the extraposed constituent (see vv. 17 and 19a in Lev 24 where וֹ precedes the extraposed constituent even as כִּי separates the extraposed member from the clause). Presumably, the choice to employ the particle governing the clause as a marker of division between the extraposed member and the morpheme bearing its resumptive constituent is determined with reference to the need for such separation as indicative of extraposition.

example, a large section of his book examines cases where the extraposed entity functions as the direct object within the clause (1987, 6–28); another section deals with cases where pronominal constructions assume the syntactical role of extraposed entities within the clause, performing an adverbial function (1987, 78–85). Throughout the study, Gross distinguishes between cases where the syntactical relationship between extraposed constituents and clauses—the syntactical role of the extraposed constituent within the clause—are marked (e.g. the presence of the particle אֵת or a preposition at the beginning of the extraposed member) and unmarked. Similarly, Khan's more compact treatment of the topic pays attention to the formal features of extraposition with a section on the form of juncture between the extraposed element and the clause (1988, 69–70), and another section on the form of resumption (e.g. prepositional phrase, subject of verbal morpheme) within the clause (1988, 71–9). Khan's identification of the functions of extraposition is particularly rich. Extraposition marks the beginning and end of segments of speech (1988, 78–86). Within such spans of speech, extraposition often occurs at the initiation of a new topic (1988, 79–81), or at the beginning of sub-topics within the larger topical unit (1988, 81–2). In narrative, extraposition stands at the initiation of an episode, and at moments of transition in theme (1988, 82–3). Extraposition also accompanies the shift to information of a background nature (1988, 83) and the designation of an episode of climax (1988, 85). Khan's conclusions include several of the shifts in the level of communication marked by the intrusion of syntactical features of disjuncture witnessed in the preceding analysis of legal prescriptions.

The greatest degree of syntactical discontinuity is expressed by words and phrases occurring as independent syntactical constituents. Such entities project a degree of syntactical prominence by virtue of the fact that they stand outside the system of inter-clausal syntax. The qualification of the independent syntactical constituent as a grammatical feature 'outside' the system of inter-clausal syntax refers to its exclusion as a constituent of a clause. As phrases without mooring in a syntactical construction with predication as a feature (i.e. the phrases are not members of the subject, object, or modifier in a clause), independent syntactical constituents are grammatical 'islands' in bodies of propositions (segments of texts) composed of clauses in connection. While an independent syntactical constituent often qualifies clauses or groups of clauses (being syntactical constituents of the text, but not the clause), its disembodied existence (outside the parameters of a clause) draws attention to itself as a syntactical anomaly in the lexical flow between clauses in the text. Two consequences of significance for the following study flow from the definition of the independent syntactical constituent. Firstly, the exclusion of independent syntactical constituents from a system of syntax identifying connections between clauses renders their degree of syntactical disjuncture exceptional. Independent syntactical constituents stand at the pinnacle of the hierarchy of syntactical constituents displaying increasing degrees of syntactical disjuncture. Secondly, the absence of a syntactical connection with a constituent within a clause (in contrast with extraposed constituents) limits the quality of syntactical disjuncture in an independent syntactical constituent to itself: the measure of syntactical disjuncture does not apply to the following clause. The degree of syntactical disruption inherent to the function of the independent syntactical constituent has been noted. In contrast with the procedures of Backhaus, Gross (1987, 150–2) and Khan (1988, 74) include independent syntactical constituents as examples of extraposition (noted as cases where the resumption of the alleged component of extraposition does not occur within the clause). Indeed, it is often the case that such independent constituents establish the subject matter for the following clauses. The transitions in the pragmatic landscape applicable to extraposition apply also to independent syntactical constituents. The following analysis of material in Leviticus and Numbers will confirm the instincts of Gross and Khan with respect to independent syntactical constituents.

The existence of a hierarchy of disjuncture and continuity in the syntax of the text entails the understanding that the quality of continuity or discontinuity inherent to one type of clause or feature is relative to the presence of alternative forms present in the text. The perception of change in the fluidity of movement from clause to clause is felt only when fluctuations within the hierarchy take place. Thus, explanations by appeal to the pragmatic landscape, the organization of information in the text, need take place only where movements within the hierarchy—

pertinent distinctions of contrast in the form of inter-clausal syntax—occur within the text.

Where syntactical disjuncture occurs in a clause or other syntactical constituent, it must be determined with recourse to the content of the clauses of the passage whether a boundary of the text (transitions between sections or sub-sections of topical distinction in the text) bears marking, or whether a single clause or syntactical constituent is being elevated to prominence. While the pragmatic component must be distinguished from the semantic component of the text, it is often semantic content that provides clues for determining variations in the communicative context of discourse. Such considerations stand behind the use of the qualification 'semantic-pragmatic' to describe this approach to syntax at various points in the work at hand.

The explanations accorded to the syntactical structures of the text, both in preceding and subsequent analysis of the clauses of legal prescription, appeal to current notions of pragmatics operative in the structures of discourse. The points of transition (in their various degrees) in the situation of communication—the shift from the main sequence of action to events perceived as constituting setting or a catalogue of parallel acts in narrative texts, the elevation of a dominant principle in the midst of a series of prescriptions—would be shown to correspond with the identified formal features of inter-clausal discontinuity in syntax. Such a procedure for verification could be open to the charge that the anchor for the proposed theory of syntax, the alleged pragmatic categories of discourse endemic to the structure of texts, is an arbitrary modern imposition upon ancient texts. In response to this challenge it may be said, in agreement with Lowery (1995, 118–9), that consistency is the measure of the feasibility of the theory. The degree to which the formal properties of the text display correspondence with the proposed categories for the organization of the communicative constraints within the text establishes the strength of both poles in the theory: the consistency of interaction fosters the mutual verification of form (the formal categories of inter-clausal syntax) and function (the pragmatic categories of discourse). Indeed, it is the effort to seek verification through consistency that informs the decision to survey the larger corpus of legal material in Leviticus and Numbers.

THE INTERACTION BETWEEN CONSECUTIVE, CONJUNCTIVE, SUBORDINATE AND ASYNDETIC CLAUSES IN THE LEGAL PRESCRIPTIONS OF LEVITICUS AND NUMBERS

The format of the presentation will follow that of the analyses of the legal prescriptions in previous chapters. Beside the Hebrew text will be the English translation of the NRSV. The scheme of enumeration will mark each clause of the Hebrew text in accordance with criteria previously outlined. The column within which the English translation occurs will designate the verse numbers in accordance with the Hebrew text; the heading preceding each passage will also designate the book and the chapter from which the example is drawn. The sole exception to the numerical scheme in the legal prescriptions examined in previous chapters is that the verse numbers only serve to designate the portion of text under examination: no divisions into individual command sets—a series of prescriptions bound by a distinct topical unity—are designated.

Lev 1:2aβ–4

The first prescribed procedure in Leviticus outlines the steps to be followed in offering an animal from the herd as a burnt offering (Lev 1:3–9).

אָדָם כִּי־יַקְרִיב מִכֶּם 1	1 When any of you bring an
קָרְבָּן לַיהוָה	offering of livestock[26] to the Lord,
מִן־הַבְּהֵמָה מִן־הַבָּקָר 2	2 you shall bring your offering
וּמִן־הַצֹּאן	from the herd or from the flock. 3
תַּקְרִיבוּ אֶת־קָרְבַּנְכֶם	If the offering is a burnt-offering
אִם־עֹלָה קָרְבָּנוֹ 3	from the herd, 4 you shall offer a
מִן־הַבָּקָר	male without blemish; 5 you shall
זָכָר תָּמִים יַקְרִיבֶנּוּ 4	bring it to the entrance of the tent
אֶל־פֶּתַח אֹהֶל מוֹעֵד 5	of meeting, for acceptance in your

---

[26] Contrary to the translation of the NRSV, the system of accents in MT places מִן־הַבְּהֵמָה with the material of 2aβ–4 (2).

יקריב אתו   behalf before the Lord. 6 You shall
לרצנו לפני יהוה   lay your hand on the head of the
6 וסמך ידו על ראש העלה   burnt-offering, 7 and it shall be
7 ונרצה לו לכפר עליו   acceptable in your behalf as
atonement for you (vv. 2aβ–4).

The series of clauses begins with a subordinate clause (2aβ–4 [1]) employing an extraposed subject (אדם); a high degree of syntactical disjuncture stands at the beginning of the prescriptive passage. The second clause 2aβ–4 (2) maintains a high degree of syntactical disjuncture (asyndeton) in its statement of the two classes from which the sacrificial beast is to come: מן־הבקר ומן־הצאן. A second conditional statement ensues with the subordinate clause 2aβ–4 (3); this clause introduces the procedure for the first candidate, a beast from the herd. Two asyndetic clauses (2aβ–4 [4, 5]) stipulate that the animal must be a male without defect, and that the procedure is to take place before the tent of meeting. Consecutive clauses then proceed with the prescribed series of events (2aβ–4 [6, 7]). It may be seen that clauses bearing a high degree of syntactical disjuncture function to mark topical boundaries—including the initiation of sub-categories within the prescriptive passage (the subordinate clauses 2aβ–4 [1, 3]). The persistence of syntactical disjuncture within series of commands on a distinct topic raises the prominence of specific essential characteristics of the offering (2aβ–4 [2, 4, 5]) prior to clauses of a greater degree of syntactical continuity prescribing the course of action to follow (2aβ–4 [5, 6]). These details pertaining to elements within the prescribed procedure (qualities of the sacrificial beast and location) stand outside the series of clauses (2aβ–4 [6, 7]) concerned with the course of events constituting the sacrificial procedure extending beyond 2aβ–4 (7).

Lev 2:1–3

The second chapter of Leviticus outlines the procedure for offerings of grain. Verses 1–3 outline the general procedure before variations in the preparation of the grain are spelt out in following verses.

1 ונפש כי־תקריב קרבן   1 When anyone presents a grain
מנחה ליהוה   offering to the Lord, 2 the offering

2 סלת יהיה קרבנו
3 ויצק עליה שמן
4 ונתן עליה לבנה
5 והביאה אל־בני אהרן
הכהנים
6 וקמץ משם מלא קמצו
ומשמנה על כל־לבנתה
7 והקטיר הכהן
את־אזכרתה המזבחה
אשה ריח ניחח ליהוה
8 והנותרת מן־המנחה
לאהרן ולבניו
קדש קדשים מאשי יהוה

shall be of choice flour; 3 the worshipper shall pour oil on it, 4 and put frankincense on it, 5 and bring it to Aaron's sons the priests. 6 After taking from it a handful of the choice flour and oil, with all its frankincense, 7 the priest shall turn this token portion into smoke on the altar, an offering by fire of pleasing odour to the Lord. 8 And what is left of the grain-offering shall be for Aaron and his sons, a most holy part of the offerings by fire to the Lord (vv. 1–3).

The consecutive perfect clauses of 1–3 (3–7), which represent the highest degree of syntactical continuity in the passage, carry the prescribed events of the procedure. The passage begins with a subordinate clause with an extraposed subject (ונפש) introducing the circumstance for the procedure (1–3 [1]). The second clause (1–3 [2]), is asyndetic, setting itself apart from the series of consecutive clauses (1–3 [3–7]) flowing from the initial conditional clause (1–3 [1]). The prescription of 1–3 (2) specifies the essential ingredient in the offering (סלֶת): a descriptive statement clearly outside the parameters of the series of actions in the following procedure. The conjunctive clause 1–3 (8) breaks the sequence of consecutive perfect clauses. The syntactical disjuncture of 1–3 (8) marks the specification that the remainder of the offering belongs to the priests as being outside the series of prescribed events for the sacrificial procedure; the preceding consecutive clause (1–3 [7]) is the fiery culmination of the sacrifice.[27]

Lev 5:15–6b, 23–6

The clauses of Lev 5:15–6b form part of a procedure for atonement in the case of a breach of trust.

---

[27] The transition from a series of consecutive clauses to a conjunctive clause in v. 10 in the same chapter occurs for the same reason.

1 נֶפֶשׁ כִּי־תִמְעַל מַעַל	1 When any of you commit a
2 וְחָטְאָה בִּשְׁגָגָה מִקָּדְשֵׁי	trespass 2 and sin unintentionally in
יְהוָה	any of the holy things of the Lord,
3 וְהֵבִיא אֶת־אֲשָׁמוֹ	3 you shall bring, as your guilt
לַיהוָה אַיִל תָּמִים	offering to the Lord, a ram without
מִן־הַצֹּאן בְּעֶרְכְּךָ	blemish from the flock, convertible
כֶּסֶף־שְׁקָלִים	into silver by the sanctuary shekel; it
בְּשֶׁקֶל־הַקֹּדֶשׁ לְאָשָׁם	is a guilt-offering.[28] 4 And you shall
4 וְאֵת אֲשֶׁר חָטָא	make restitution for the holy thing in
מִן־הַקֹּדֶשׁ יְשַׁלֵּם	which you were remiss, 5 and shall
5 וְאֶת־חֲמִישִׁתוֹ יוֹסֵף	add one-fifth to it 6 and give it to the
עָלָיו	priest
6 וְנָתַן אֹתוֹ לַכֹּהֵן	(vv. 15–6b).

An initial subordinate clause with extraposed subject (15–6b [1]) presents the condition that precipitates the procedure; a high degree of syntactical disjuncture stands at the head of the passage. Consecutive perfect clauses carry the sequence of events that lead into the procedure (15–6b [2, 3, 6]). Although 15–6b (4–5) may be considered events within the temporal sequence of succession, the clauses are set apart from the series of consecutive perfect clauses by conjunction. A glance at the wider context reveals that the requirements portrayed by 15–6b (4–5) are additional requirements for reparation beyond the offering of a sacrifice in the cases of the previous passage (5:1–13), where no misappropriation of property occurs. Thus, it may be understood that conjunctive clauses (15–6b [4, 5]) in the present text set apart elements of the procedure forming part of the act of restoration inherent to the commission of the beast (15–6b [3]) in the process of atonement. The element of disruption in 15–6b (4–5) represents a shift from the presentation of events as components of a process, to a catalogue of actions constituting different aspects of one component in the process: the act of reparation beginning with 15–6b (3).

---

[28] Unlike the translation of the NRSV, MT has לְאָשָׁם as a prepositional phrase forming a part of the clause 15–6b (3).

A similar procedure of atonement with reparation later on in the same chapter (vv. 23–6) confirms the assessment of the semantic-pragmatic concerns behind the syntax of verses 15–6b.

1 וְהָיָה כִּי־יֶחֱטָא	1 When you have sinned 2 and
2 וְאָשֵׁם	realize your guilt, 3 and would
3 וְהֵשִׁיב אֶת־הַגְּזֵלָה ...	restore what you took by robbery
4 וְשִׁלַּם אֹתוֹ בְּרֹאשׁוֹ	..., 4 you shall repay the principal
5 וַחֲמִשִׁתָיו יֹסֵף עָלָיו	amount 5 and shall add one-fifth to
לַאֲשֶׁר הוּא לוֹ יִתְּנֶנּוּ בְּיוֹם	it. You shall pay it to its owner
אַשְׁמָתוֹ	when you realize your guilt. 6 And
6 וְאֶת־אֲשָׁמוֹ יָבִיא לַיהוָה	you shall bring to the priest, as
אַיִל תָּמִים	your guilt-offering to the Lord, a
מִן־הַצֹּאן בְּעֶרְכְּךָ לְאָשָׁם	ram without blemish from the
אֶל־הַכֹּהֵן	flock, or its equivalent, for a guilt-
7 וְכִפֶּר עָלָיו הַכֹּהֵן לִפְנֵי	offering. 7 The priest shall make
יְהוָה	atonement on your behalf before
8 וְנִסְלַח לוֹ עַל־אַחַת	the Lord, 8 and you shall be
מִכֹּל אֲשֶׁר־יַעֲשֶׂה לְאַשְׁמָה	forgiven for any of the things that
בָהּ	one may do and incur guilt thereby
	(vv. 23–6).

The procedure proceeds with consecutive perfect clauses up to the point where the act of reparation begins: the surrender of the misappropriated item (23–6 [5]). Although the order within the catalogue of events constituting the restoration of equity differs from that of verses 15–6b, the same three elements (restoration of principal, an additional amount and the offering of a sacrifice) are attested. The first component occurs within the series of consecutive clauses (23–6 [4]), and the other two are conjunctive clauses forming a list of acts within the same class of action (23–6 [5, 6])—multiple facets of a single event.

Lev 6:2aβ–3

The clauses of Lev 6: 2aβ–3 are part of the prescribed procedure for the disposal of the charred remnants from the burnt offering.

1 זֹאת תּוֹרַת הָעֹלָה	1 This is the ritual of the burnt-
2 הִוא הָעֹלָה עַל מוֹקְדָה	offering. 2 The burnt-offering itself
עַל־הַמִּזְבֵּחַ	shall remain on the hearth upon

כל־הלילה עד־הבקר the altar all night until the morning,
3 ואש המזבח תוקד בו 3 while the fire on the altar shall be
4 ולבש הכהן מדו בד kept burning. 4 The priest shall put
5 ומכנסי־בד ילבש on his linen vestments 5 after
על־בשרו putting on his linen undergarments
6 והרים את־הדשן אשר next to his body; 6 and he shall
תאכל האש take up the ashes to which the fire
את־העלה על־המזבח has reduced the burnt-offering on
7 ושמו אצל המזבח the altar, 7 and place them beside
the altar (vv. 2aβ–3).

The prescriptive passage begins with the asyndetic verbless clause 2aβ–3 (1), and the formal category persists in the second clause (2aβ–3 [2]). A higher degree of syntactical continuity occurs with the conjunctive clause (waw-X-yiqtol) 2aβ–3 (3). The functional significance of the syntactical disjuncture in 2aβ–3 (1–3) in relative contrast with the consecutive clauses of the procedure itself is familiar. The clauses qualify the entire procedure by name (2aβ–3 [1]), or offer prescriptive details pertaining to objects (the sacrificial portion and the flame on the altar) within the ritual outside the strict procedural concerns of the process of disposal (2aβ–3 [2, 3]).[29] Within the series of clauses prior to the first consecutive perfect clause, 2aβ–3 (3) employs the conjunction ו in order to link the two clauses within that series sharing a similar concern: the consumption of the sacrificial portion by fire. The procedure of disposal begins with the consecutive perfect clause 2aβ–3 (4); but it is quickly cut off by the following conjunctive clause (2aβ–3 [5]) offering additional detail closely related to the investment of the priest in the appropriate attire (2aβ–3 [4]) by returning to a prior event: the wearing of the linen undergarments by the priest. As previously seen, a conjunctive clause represents a following act closely associated to that of a previous clause in a series of consecutive clauses. Consecutive perfect clauses (2aβ–3 [6, 7]) carry on with the procedure.

---

[29] Of course, 2aβ–3 (1) is an asyndetic clause also functioning to mark the initiation of the legal passage as a whole.

Lev 6:19–21a

The clauses of Lev 6:19–21a provide another example of the use of conjunctive clauses in the midst of asyndetic clauses in order to link commands in a series more closely connected by topic. These clauses occur in a passage of laws loosely connected beginning at verse 18aβ concerning the disposal of a purification offering; asyndeton is the dominant form of syntactical sequence among the clauses.

1 הכהן המחטא אתה	1 The priest who offers it as a sin-
יאכלנה	offering shall eat of it; 2 it shall be
2 במקום קדש תאכל	eaten in a holy place, in the court
בחצר אהל מועד	of the tent of meeting. 3 Whatever
3 כל אשר־יגע בבשרה	touches its flesh shall become holy;
יקדש	4 and when any of its blood is
4 ואשר יזה מדמה	spattered on a garment, you shall
על־הבגד אשר יזה	wash the bespattered part in a holy
עליה תכבס במקום קדש	place. 5 An earthen vessel in which
5 וכלי־חרש אשר	it was boiled shall be broken
תבשל־בו ישבר	(vv. 19–21a).

The use of the conjunction ו links the three clauses of 19–21a (3–5) as a series of commands all dealing with people or items which have come in contact with the flesh or the blood of the sacrificial beast.

Lev 13:9–11

The clauses of Lev 13:9–11 concern a procedure for the identification of a contaminating disorder of the skin. The passage displays all the four types of clauses according to the scheme of classification.

1 נגע צרעת כי תהיה באדם	1 When a person contracts a
2 והובא אל־הכהן	leprous disease, 2 he shall be
3 וראה הכהן	brought to the priest. 3 The
4 והנה שאת־לבנה בעור	priest shall make an examination,
5 והיא הפכה שער לבן	4 and if there is a white swelling
6 ומחית בשר חי בשאת	in the skin 5 that has turned the
7 צרעת נושנת הוא בעור	hair white, 6 and there is quick
בשרו	raw flesh in the swelling, 7 it is a

וטמאו הכהן 8   chronic leprous disease in the
לא יסגרנו 9   skin of his body. 8 The priest
כי טמא הוא 10   shall pronounce him unclean; 9
he shall not confine him, 10 for
he is unclean (vv. 9–11).

A subordinate clause with extraposed subject marks the
beginning of the case with a hypothetical circumstance (9–11 [1]).
The consecutive perfect clauses 9–11 (2, 3) proceed with the first
steps of the procedure to be followed. The three conjunctive clauses
9–11 (4, 5, 6) break the series of consecutive perfect clauses in order
to present a catalogue of the observations pertaining to the
examination (depicted by 9–11 [3]). Once again, conjunctive clauses
stand apart from consecutive clauses depicting a series of related
statements to one component in the series of events prescribed. An
even higher degree of syntactical disjuncture (asyndeton)
accompanies the declaration of the significance of the list of
observations: צרעת נושנת הוא בעור בשרו (9–11 [7]). The next
appropriate step in the procedure follows with the consecutive
perfect clause 9–11 (8). An asyndetic clause of negation forbids an
alternative course of action (9–11 [9]) to that of the last step in the
procedure (9–11 [8]). Hitherto, the function of asyndeton in relation
to clauses displaying a higher degree of syntactical continuity has
been to draw attention to topical boundaries, or to give prominence
to qualifying statements regarding entire series of laws or specific
elements within a series of commands. The case of 9–11 (9) shows
that the clause-type may also be emphatic for the reason of contrast
(in this case, negation).[30] A subordinate verbless clause (9–11 [10])
outlines the reason for the prohibition of 9–11 (9).

---

[30] The representation of syntactical disruption through asyndeton for
the sake of pointing out unifying principles behind a group of
prescriptions or providing additional detail to parts of prescriptive clauses
may be classified under the general category of epexegesis: such clauses
make statements about other clauses. Gentry has identified the use of
asyndeton (with qatal in initial position) in narrative with the function of
epexegesis in relation to the previous clause or clauses (1998, 19). The
case of emphasis for the sake of contrast in 9–11 (9), on the other hand,

Lev 16:3–4

The clauses of Lev 16:3–4 stand at the beginning of the prescribed procedure for Israel's annual ritual of atonement.

1 בְּזֹאת יָבֹא אַהֲרֹן אֶל־הַקֹּדֶשׁ	1 Thus shall Aaron come into
בְּפַר בֶּן־בָּקָר לְחַטָּאת וְאַיִל	the holy place: with a young bull
לְעֹלָה	for a sin-offering and a ram for a
2 כְּתֹנֶת־בַּד קֹדֶשׁ יִלְבָּשׁ	burnt-offering. 2 He shall put on
3 וּמִכְנְסֵי־בַד יִהְיוּ עַל־בְּשָׂרוּ	the holy linen tunic, 3 and shall
4 וּבְאַבְנֵט בַּד יַחְגֹּר	have the linen undergarments
5 וּבְמִצְנֶפֶת בַּד יִצְנֹף	next to his body, 4 fasten the
6 בִּגְדֵי־קֹדֶשׁ הֵם	linen sash, 5 and wear the linen
7 וְרָחַץ בַּמַּיִם אֶת־בְּשָׂרוּ	turban; 6 these are the holy
8 וּלְבֵשָׁם	vestments. 7 He shall bathe his
	body in water, 8 and then put
	them on (vv. 3–4).

The series of acts constituting the procedure begins and proceeds with consecutive perfect clauses (3–4 [7, 8]). Asyndetic clauses and conjunctive clauses make qualifying statements concerning the entire procedure, or provide more specific details beforehand concerning objects having a part in the procedure. The non-consecutive clauses of 3–4 (1–6) may be conceived as an introductory passage to the procedure proper. The asyndetic clause 3–4 (1) designates the following procedure as the proper way to approach the holy presence of God for the annual ritual. A second asyndetic clause (3–4 [2]) stands at the head of a series of clauses connected by conjunction (3–4 [3–5]). The prescriptions of 3–4 (2–5) all involve elements of Aaron's attire; it is appropriate that the clauses should form a series linked by conjunction. One final asyndetic (verbless) clause breaks the series of conjunctive clauses in order to qualify all the items of clothing of the previous clauses as holy (3–4 [6]). As a group of clauses providing more specific

---

simply seeks to draw attention to the contradistinctive content of the clause itself.

detail concerning a single component within the procedure, 3–4 (2–6) support the consecutive perfect clause 3–4 (8).[31]

Lev 17:3–4

The clauses of Lev 17:3–4 form part of a passage of laws requiring the slaughter of an animal to take place within the context of the cult.

1 איש איש מבית ישראל אשר
ישחט
שור או־כשב או־עז במחנה או
אשר
ישחט מחוץ למחנה ואל־פתח
אהל מועד לא הביאו להקריב
קרבן
ליהוה לפני משכן יהוה
2 דם יחשב לאיש ההוא
3 דם שפך
4 ונכרת האיש ההוא מקרב
עמו

1 If anyone of the house of Israel slaughters an ox or a lamb or a goat in the camp or slaughters it outside the camp, and does not bring it to the entrance of the tent of meeting, to present it as an offering to the Lord before the tabernacle of the Lord, 2 he shall be held guilty of bloodshed; 3 he has shed blood, 4 and he shall be cut off from the people (vv. 3–4).

The initial clause 3–4 (1) which introduces the law is a conjunctive clause with extraposed subject standing before the clause: איש איש מבית ישראל אשר ישחט שור או־כשב או־עז במחנה או אשר ישחט מחוץ למחנה. The coordinating conjunction, part of the lexeme ואל־פתח, governing the clause 3–4 (1) excludes the extended extraposed subject with its two embedded clauses (all material prior to ואל־פתח) from the domain of the

---

[31] Compare 2aβ–3 (4–5) of Lev 6:2aβ–3. A similar relationship of a non-consecutive clause to a consecutive perfect clause expresses a complementary relationship with the former (2aβ–3 [5]) providing additional detail on a related subject to the latter (2aβ–3 [4]). As in the case of the passage at hand, the subject matter pertains to the attire of the priest. The difference in Lev 6:2aβ–3 is that the additional detail occurs as a conjunctive clause disrupting the flow of the consecutive clauses of the procedure.

clause. Here, as elsewhere in legal discourse, the occurrence of extraposition effects a high degree of syntactical disjuncture at the beginning of a set of commands. The maintenance of a high degree of syntactical disjuncture (asyndeton) in the next two clauses prior to the consecutive perfect clause depicting the consequence of excommunication (3–4 [4]) renders 3–4 (2, 3) prominent in the eyes of the reader. The repeated statement that the (illegitimate) shedding of blood has taken place forms the basis for the following judgement couched in the consecutive clause 3–4 (4): the foundational principle motivating the law receives prominence within the syntactical structure of the series of clauses.

Lev. 18:3–4

Where consecutive clauses are absent from a body of law, the interchange between asyndeton and conjunction remains to determine the syntactical landscape of the text. A series of commands prohibiting acquiescence to Canaanite and Egyptian custom and law constitute Lev 18:3–4.

1 כמעשה ארץ־מצרים אשר	1 You shall not do as they do
ישבתם־בה	in the land of Egypt, where
לא תעשו	you lived, 2 and you shall not
2 וכמעשה ארץ־כנען אשר אני	do as they do in the land of
מביא	Canaan, to which I am
אתכם שמה לא תעשו	bringing you. 3 You shall not
3 ובחקתיהם לא תלכו	follow their statutes. 4 My
4 את־משפטי תעשו	ordinances you shall observe 5
5 ואת־חקתי תשמרו ללכת	and my statutes you shall keep,
בהם	follow them: 6 I am the Lord
6 אני יהוה אלהיכם	your God (vv. 3–4).

An asyndetic clause (3–4 [1]) initiates a series of clauses on the subject. Conjunction links the following two commands (3–4 [2, 3]) together with 3–4 (1) to form the first group of laws enacting the statement of prohibition. The asyndetic clause 3–4 (4) breaks the preceding series of conjunctive clauses to mark a new beginning. The conjunctive clause 3–4 (5) forms a second member in the new group of laws propounding a positive statement on the subject of fidelity to Israel's God. The final asyndetic verbless clause (3–4 [6]) stands apart as the principal rationale behind the two complementary sets of prescriptions expressing prohibition and exhortation.

Lev 19:2aβ–4

That the syntactical disjuncture of subordination is a significant factor in the portrayal of reasons for prescriptions or motives for compliance is attested by the interchangeability of subordination and asyndeton in the communication of such information. The laws of Lev 19:2aβ–4 demonstrate the disruptive force of a subordinate clause within a set of prescriptions related by subject matter.

קְדֹשִׁים תִּהְיוּ 1	1 You shall be holy, 2 for I the
כִּי קָדוֹשׁ אֲנִי יְהוָה אֱלֹהֵיכֶם 2	Lord your God am holy.
אִישׁ אִמּוֹ וְאָבִיו תִּירָאוּ 3	3 You shall revere your mother
וְאֶת־שַׁבְּתֹתַי תִּשְׁמֹרוּ 4	and father, 4 and you shall
אֲנִי יְהוָה אֱלֹהֵיכֶם 5	keep my sabbaths: 5 I am the
אַל־תִּפְנוּ אֶל־הָאֱלִילִים 6	Lord your God. 6 Do not turn
וֵאלֹהֵי מַסֵּכָה לֹא תַעֲשׂוּ לָכֶם 7	to idols 7 or make cast images
אֲנִי יְהוָה אֱלֹהֵיכֶם 8	for yourselves: 8 I am the Lord
	your God (vv. 2aβ–4).

An asyndetic clause (2aβ–4 [1]) begins the series of laws with a general call to holy living. The subordinate clause 2aβ–4 (2) provides a statement of motivation rooted in the holy character of God. Beyond the first two clauses containing the exhortation to holiness, asyndetic clauses (2aβ–4 [3, 6]) introduce sets of related commands bound by conjunction (2aβ–4 [3–4, 6–7]). The first set (2aβ–4 [3–4]) occurs in sequence in the Decalogue (Exod 20:10–2), and the second set (2aβ–4 [6–7]) concerns idolatry. Within each set of commands, the syntactical disjuncture of asyndetic verbless clauses (2aβ–4 [5, 8]) raises the profile of the principle of holiness standing behind the commands by interrupting the syntactical continuity of the commands just established by preceding conjunctive clauses (2aβ–4 [4, 7]). That these abstract statements of principle are partial restatements of 2aβ–4 (2) reveals the similarity of subordinate clauses as disruptive syntactical elements, compelling attention to foundational concepts within sets of commands.

Lev 19:13

There are numerous examples of asyndetic clauses amidst clauses bearing greater syntactical continuity raising the visibility of the qualification of surrounding prescriptions with expressions of a more abstract nature. These qualifications function by including the surrounding prescriptions under a larger statement capable of application within numerous concrete situations. In contrast, the following example from Leviticus 19 demonstrates the use of asyndeton within series of prescriptions on a distinct topic in order to express a shift to more concrete expressions of the preceding prescriptions. The series of commands in Lev 19:13 forbid extortion and robbery.

1 לא־תעשק את־רעך	1 You shall not defraud your
2 ולא תגזל	neighbour; 2 you shall not steal;
3 לא־תלין פעלת שכיר	3 you shall not keep for yourself
אתך עד־בקר	the wages of a labourer until morning (v. 13).

The series of commands begins with the asyndetic clause 13 (1) setting verse 13 apart from the previous series of commands in verse 12 connected by conjunction. As expected, the series of commands on a distinct topic proceeds with a conjunctive clause (13 [2]). The reversion to asyndeton in 13 (3) occurs in order to mark the transition to a statement of specification. The final command (13 [3]) prohibits a specific type of extortion and illegal seizure: the witholding of a hireling's wages.

Lev 19:15

The four clauses of Lev 19:15 exhort just judgement. A single conjunctive clause is the sole exception to the series of asyndetic clauses.

1 לא־תעשו עול במשפט	1 You shall not render an unjust
2 לא־תשא פני־דל	judgement; 2 you shall not be
3 ולא תהדר פני גדול	partial to the poor 3 or defer to the
4 בצדק תשפט עמיתך	great: 4 with justice you shall judge your neighbour (v. 15).

The shift to a higher degree of syntactical continuity with the conjunctive clause 15 (3) draws 15 (2, 3) into a tighter relationship within the series of commands. The two clauses depict two opposing parties judges may deem worthy of preferential treatment to the detriment of equity in the application of the law.

Lev 19:17

The series of commands in Lev 19:17 concern the proper handling of a grievance. The passage provides an example of asyndeton among clauses with greater syntactical continuity functioning as a marker of emphasis for the sake of contrast.

1 לא־תשנא את־אחיך בלבבך	1 You shall not hate in your
2 הוכח תוכיח את־עמיתך	heart anyone of your kin;
3 ולא־תשא עליו חטא	2 you shall reprove your neighbour, 3 or you will incur guilt yourself (v. 17).

Asyndeton marks the beginning of the series of commands on the issue (17 [1]). The second clause 17 (2) is also asyndetic; it resists the transition to a conjunctive clause to represent syntactical continuity between the three clauses, so as to express an emphatic note of contrast from the previous prohibition (17 [1]). Direct confrontation with the aim of resolving the grievance is to be preferred to the harbouring of a grudge in silence. Subsequent to 17 (2), the conjunctive clause 17 (3) represents the natural shift to a higher degree of syntactical continuity within a series of commands on the same topic.

Lev 19:27–8, 21:5

The clauses of Lev 19:27–8 are a series of commands prohibiting the use of certain body-markings. The interchange between asyndeton and conjunction communicates continuity and discontinuity between clauses.

1 לא תקפו פאת ראשכם	1 You shall not round off the
2 ולא תשחית את פאת זקנך	hair on your temples 2 or mar
3 ושרט לנפש לא תתנו	the edges of your beard. 3 You
בבשרכם	shall not make any gashes in
4 וכתבת קעקע לא תתנו	your flesh for the dead 4 or
בכם	tattoo any marks upon you:
5 אני יהוה	5 I am the Lord (vv. 27–8).

Asyndeton marks the beginning of the series of prohibitions (27–8 [1]). Conjunctive clauses follow with other prohibitions concerning other parts of the body or other types of markings (27–8 [2–4]). An asyndetic verbless clause (27–8 [5]) establishes, once again, the guiding principle of the divine identity behind the promulgations. The clause following 27–8 (5)—not shown in the presentation of the text—is an asyndetic clause beginning a new topic on the consumption of blood.

The same syntactical pattern reflecting topical unity on the same subject occurs in Lev 21:5.

1 לֹא־יִקְרְחֻה קָרְחָה בְּרֹאשָׁם	1 They shall not make bald spots upon their heads, 2 or shave off the edges of their beards, 3 or make any gashes on their flesh (v. 5).
2 וּפְאַת זְקָנָם לֹא יְגַלֵּחוּ	
3 וּבִבְשָׂרָם לֹא יִשְׂרְטוּ שָׂרָטֶת	

The clauses of Lev 21:5 are part of a series of commands regarding the issue of mourning (Lev 21:1bβ–6). The laws are a loosely connected series of commands: asyndeton is the dominant form of sequence between clauses. Within this loose syntactical formation, the three clauses of Lev 21:5 exhibit a higher degree of connection among themselves with conjunction linking 5 (2–3) with 5 (1). A sub-group of commands on self-mutilation in connection with mourning becomes distinct.

Lev 20:7–8

The following clauses reveal the similar interchangeability between subordination and asyndeton in setting forth the foundational principle behind a series of laws. The clauses of Lev 20:7–8 come at the end of a procedure prescribing excommunication for the one consulting a medium or a wizard.

1 וְהִתְקַדִּשְׁתֶּם	1 Consecrate yourselves therefore, 2 and be holy; 3 for I am the Lord your God. 4 Keep my statutes, 5 and observe them; 6 I am the Lord; I sanctify you (vv. 7–8).
2 וִהְיִיתֶם קְדֹשִׁים	
3 כִּי אֲנִי יְהוָה אֱלֹהֵיכֶם	
4 וּשְׁמַרְתֶּם אֶת־חֻקֹּתַי	
5 וַעֲשִׂיתֶם אֹתָם	
6 אֲנִי יְהוָה מְקַדִּשְׁכֶם	

Consecutive perfect clauses convey the prescription of a process of sanctification and obedience. Twice, the series of consecutive perfect clauses are punctuated by clauses of a higher degree of syntactical disjuncture in order to express the foundational tenet of the call to holiness and obedience: the identity of God. This statement, which is expressed by an asyndetic verbless clause in 7–8 (6), is carried first by a subordinate verbless clause in 7–8 (3).

Lev 20:18

The clauses of Lev 20:18 deal with the case of a man having sexual relations with a woman during the period of her menstrual flow.

1 וְאִישׁ אֲשֶׁר־יִשְׁכַּב אֶת־אִשָּׁה	1 If a man lies with a woman
דָּוָה	having her sickness and uncovers
וְגִלָּה אֶת־עֶרְוָתָהּ אֶת־מְקֹרָהּ	her nakedness, he has laid bare
הֶעֱרָה	her flow 2 and she has laid bare
2 וְהִיא גִּלְּתָה אֶת־מְקוֹר דָּמֶיהָ	her flow of blood; 3 both of
3 וְנִכְרְתוּ שְׁנֵיהֶם מִקֶּרֶב עַמָּם	them shall be cut off from their
	people (v. 18).

Although the initial clause of the law is consecutive, the presence of the extraposed member וְאִישׁ with an attached relative clause produces a high degree of syntactical disjuncture appropriate to the beginning of a new unit. Instead of immediate transition to a consecutive perfect clause, the second clause 18 (2) is conjunctive (waw-X-qatal), maintaining one degree of syntactical disjuncture greater than the following consecutive perfect clause (18 [3]). Conjunction in 18 (2) sets the clause apart, from what would proceed otherwise as a series of consecutive clauses following 18 (1), in order to distinguish 18 (2) as a correlated fact of 18 (1) within the prescribed procedure. The man and the woman are guilty for having acted in concert.

Lev 23:10aβ–11

The clauses of Lev 10aβ–11 are part of a prescribed procedure for the offering of a sheaf from the first fruits of Israel's harvest.

1 כִּי־תָבֹאוּ אֶל־הָאָרֶץ אֲשֶׁר	1 When you enter the land that I
אֲנִי נֹתֵן	am giving you 2 and you reap its

לכם
2 וקצרתם את־קצירה
3 והבאתם את־עמר ראשית
קצירכם
אל־הכהן
4 והניף את־העמר לפני
יהוה לרצנכם
5 ממחרת השבת יניפנו הכהן

harvest, 3 you shall bring the
sheaf of the first fruits of your
harvest to the priest. 4 He shall
raise the sheaf before the Lord,
so that you may find acceptance;
5 on the day after the sabbath
the priest shall raise it
(vv. 10aβ–11).

The syntax of these clauses bring no surprise. A subordinate
(temporal) clause (10aβ–11 [1]) stands at the head of the
procedure, and consecutive perfect clauses proceed with the
prescribed course of action (10aβ–11 [2–4]). The asyndetic clause
10aβ–11 (5) disrupts the syntactical flow of the previous clauses in
order to offer more specific detail (regarding the timing of the
offering) to the preceding prescription (10aβ–11 [4]).

Lev 26:1–2

The subject matter in these clauses may be divided into two
categories: prohibition against the worship of idols and exhortation
for the worship of Israel's God. Asyndeton and conjunction
conspire to mark the boundaries between the two groups of
commands.

1 לא־תעשו לכם אלילם
2 ופצל ומצבה לא־תקימו לכם
3 ואבן משכית לא תתנו
בארצכם
להשתחות עליה
4 כי אני יהוה אלהיכם
5 את־שבתתי תשמרו
6 ומקדשי תיראו
7 אני יהוה

1 You shall make for
yourselves no idols 2 and erect
no carved images or pillars,
3 and you shall not place
figured stones in your land, to
worship at them; 4 for I am
the Lord your God. 5 You
shall keep my sabbaths 6 and
reverence my sanctuary: 7 I am
the Lord (vv. 1–2).

The asyndetic clause 1–2 (1) initiates the series of commands
on illicit worship with the use of inanimate objects; conjunctive
clauses (1–2 [2, 3]) link the commands to form a set. The
subordinate verbless clause 1–2 (4) brings syntactical disjuncture in
order to express the motivating rationale behind the previous

prescriptions: the identity of Israel's God. The asyndetic clause 1–2 (5) stands at the head of the next series of commands exhorting, in contrast, legitimate devotion to God through reverence for ordained holy days and the designated place of divine presence. Conjunction in 1–2 (6) proceeds with a measure of syntactical continuity following the commencement of a series of commands on the new subject matter in 1–2 (5). The governing principle of holiness standing behind the prescriptions is repeated in an asyndetic verbless clause (1–2 [7]); once again, the syntax of the laws reveals the interchangeability of asyndeton and subordination in posing syntactical disruption for the purpose of expressing a qualifying concept pertinent to the body of prescription. The topical dissection of the series of clauses in Lev 26:1–2 produces two complementary halves expressing prohibition and positive exhortation on the issue of religious devotion.

Lev 19:29

A similar transition from prohibition to exhortation may be seen in Lev 19:29; there, it is the prohibition of selling one's daughter into prostitution that stands in contrast to the proper devotion to Israel's venerable religious institutions. The separation of the commands into two topical groupings by the imposition of asyndeton, however, remains the same.

1 אַל־תְּחַלֵּל אֶת־בִּתְּךָ	1 Do not profane your daughter by
לְהַזְנוֹתָהּ	making her a prostitute, 2 so that
2 וְלֹא־תִזְנֶה הָאָרֶץ	the land may not become
3 וּמָלְאָה הָאָרֶץ זִמָּה	prostituted 3 and full of depravity.
4 אֶת־שַׁבְּתֹתַי תִּשְׁמֹרוּ	4 You shall keep my sabbaths 5
5 וּמִקְדָּשִׁי תִּירָאוּ	and reverence my sanctuary: 6 I am
6 אֲנִי יְהוָה	the Lord (v. 29).

The asyndetic clauses 29 (1) begins the command set on the polluting effects of prostitution. A second statement (29 [2]) cautioning against the spread of the defilement to the land is appended to the first clause by conjunction. The consecutive clause 29 (3), which binds together 29 (2–3) more tightly within the set of commands involving the detrimental effects of prostitution (29 [1–3]), extends the statement of caution in 29 (2) by envisioning the ultimate consequence of the defilement filling the entire country.[32] Asyndeton intercedes in 29 (4) to begin the series of exhortation to religious fervour connected by conjunction (29 [5]). The asyndetic clause 29 (6) closes the series of commands with the overarchinging presence of the holy and jealous divine identity standing behind the laws.

Num 10:2–3

The prescriptive procedure of which Num 10:2–3 is a part details instructions for assembly and mobilization in the wilderness.

1 עשה לך שתי חצוצרת כסף	1 Make two silver trumpets;
2 מקשה תעשה אתם	2 you shall make them of
3 והיו לך למקרא העדה	hammered work; 3 and you
ולמסע	shall use them for summoning
את־המחנות	the congregation, and for
4 ותקעו בהן	breaking camp. 4 When both
5 ונועדו אליך כל־העדה	are blown, 5 the whole
אל־פתח	congregation shall assemble
אהל מועד	before you at the entrance of
	the tent of meeting (vv. 2–3).

The asyndetic clause employing an imperative form 2–3 (1) begins with the order to construct two trumpets of silver. Asyndeton in 2–3 (2) persists with the syntactical disjuncture of asyndeton in order to add a specific detail pertaining to the construction of the trumpets (2–3 [1]) prior to the continuation of the procedure with details regarding the use of the trumpets (2–3

---

[32] Contrary to the translation by the NRSV and despite the fact that the envisioned events of 29 (2, 3) may be conceived as being in logical succession, 29 (2) is taken to be a second prohibition linked by conjunction to 29 (1), not a negative consequence following the initial prohibition (29 [1]). Notice how the latter function of a consequence following the transgression of a prohibition in the series of clauses is expressed by the consecutive perfect clause 29 (3).

[3–5]). Consecutive perfect clauses carry the main body of the procedure.

Num 10:5–8

The clauses of Num 10:5–8 are part of a procedure outlining the various signals afforded by trumpet blasts beginning with Num 10:4.

1 וּתְקַעְתֶּם תְּרוּעָה	1 When you blow an alarm, 2 the
2 וְנָסְעוּ הַמַּחֲנוֹת הַחֹנִים	camps on the east side shall set
קֵדְמָה	out; 3 when you blow a second
3 וּתְקַעְתֶּם תְּרוּעָה שֵׁנִית	alarm, 4 the camps on the south
4 וְנָסְעוּ הַמַּחֲנוֹת הַחֹנִים	side shall set out. 5 An alarm is to
תֵּימָנָה	be blown whenever they are to set
5 תְּרוּעָה יִתְקְעוּ לְמַסְעֵיהֶם	out. 6 But when the assembly is to
6 וּבְהַקְהִיל אֶת־הַקָּהָל	be gathered, you shall blow, 7 but
תִּתְקְעוּ	you shall not sound an alarm.
7 וְלֹא תָרִיעוּ	8 The sons of Aaron, the priests,
8 וּבְנֵי אַהֲרֹן הַכֹּהֲנִים	shall blow the trumpets; 9 this shall
יִתְקְעוּ בַּחֲצֹצְרוֹת	be a perpetual institution for you
9 וְהָיוּ לָכֶם לְחֻקַּת עוֹלָם	throughout your generations
לְדֹרֹתֵיכֶם	(vv. 5–8).

The consecutive perfect clauses 5–8 (1–4) proceed from the clauses of verse four in portraying the method of effecting mobilization for the various parts of the camp. The asyndetic clause 5–8 (5) breaks the preceding series of consecutive clauses in order to clarify an essential detail of the preceding procedure by emphasizing the common element in the prescribed actions of 5–8 (1–4): an alarm (תְּרוּעָה) must be raised for the mobilization of any sector of the camp. The discursive statement of 5–8 (5) stands at the head of a group of clauses (5–8 [5–8]) providing auxiliary detail in relation to the procedure of mobilization ensconced in consecutive clauses (5–8 [1–4, 9]). Following the break from the series of consecutive clauses in 5–8 (5), conjunction sets in (5–8 [6, 7, 8]) to hold the clauses of auxiliary detail together as a group (5–8 [5–8]). The clauses 5–8 (6–7) proceed with the exposition of extraneous detail (albeit of relation to the issue of mobilization), by dealing with the contrasting circumstance where only the assembly of the community is required; no alarm is to be raised for this purpose. One last clause deviating from the series of consecutive clauses, the conjunctive clause 5–8 (8), restricts the privilege of blowing the trumpet to the sons of Aaron. The non-consecutive clauses of 5–8 (5–8) bound by conjunction may be taken to be an expository paragraph clarifying various components in, and denoting additional elements external to, the procedure of mobilization. A return to the series of consecutive clauses ensues with 5–8 (9).

Num 18:20aβ–20b

The commands of Num 18:20aβ–20b deal with Aaron's portion in inheritance; subsequent material reveals that the allotment is directed at the priesthood in general throughout the period of Israelite nationhood (see Num 18:21–5).

1 בארצם לא תנחל	1 You shall have no allotment in
2 וחלק לא־יהיה לך	their land, 2 nor shall you have any
בתוכם	share among them; 3 I am your
3 אני חלקך ונחלתך בתוך	share and your possession among
בני ישראל	the Israelites (vv. 20aβ–20b).

The asyndetic clause 20aβ–20b (1) initiates the series of commands with the prohibition of inheritance from the land for Aaron. The conjunctive clause 20aβ–20b (2) proceeds from the beginning of the unit with a second prohibition on the same subject. The asyndetic verbless clause 20aβ–20b (3) makes an emphatic statement of contrast declaring God himself to be Aaron's portion.

Num 19:4–5

The clauses of Num 19:4–5 form part of the procedure of cleansing after contact with a corpse.

1 ולקח אלעזר הכהן מדמה	1 The priest shall take some of
באצבעו	its blood with his finger 2 and
2 והזה אל־נכח פני אהל־מועד	sprinkle it seven times towards
מדמה שבע פעמים	the front of the tent of
3 ושרף את־הפרה לעיניו	meeting. 3 Then the heifer
4 את־ערה ואת־בשרה	shall be burned in his sight; 4
ואת־דמה	its skin, its flesh, and its blood,

עַל־פִּרְשָׁה יִשָּׂרֵף   with its dung, shall be burned (vv. 4–5).

The consecutive perfect clauses 4–5 (1–3) form part of a chain of consecutive clauses following an initial asyndetic clause (Num 19:2b), which marks the beginning of the prescribed procedure. The asyndetic clause 4–5 (4) breaks the sequence of consecutive clauses in order to set apart from the body of the procedure a note of specification: the burning of the beast set forth in 4–5 (3) is to include the skin, flesh, blood, and dung of the animal. Thus, syntactical disjuncture in 4–5 (4) occurs to mark the shift to epexegesis as the mode of discourse.

Num 30:4–5

The law in Num 30:4–5 forms part of a larger body concerning vows; these verses deal with the particular situation of a woman who has uttered a vow while being part of her father's household.

1 וְאִשָּׁה כִּי־תִדֹּר נֶדֶר לַיהוָה	1 When a woman makes a vow
2 וְאָסְרָה אִסָּר בְּבֵית אָבִיהָ	to the Lord, 2 or binds herself by
בִּנְעֻרֶיהָ	a pledge, while within her
3 וְשָׁמַע אָבִיהָ אֶת־נִדְרָהּ	father's house, in her youth, 3
וֶאֱסָרָהּ	and her father hears of her vow
אֲשֶׁר אָסְרָה עַל־נַפְשָׁהּ	or her pledge by which she has
4 וְהֶחֱרִישׁ לָהּ אָבִיהָ	bound herself, 4 and says
5 וְקָמוּ כָּל־נְדָרֶיהָ	nothing to her; 5 then all her
6 וְכָל־אִסָּר אֲשֶׁר־אָסְרָה	vows shall stand, 6 and any
עַל־נַפְשָׁהּ יָקוּם	pledge by which she has bound
	herself shall stand (vv. 4–5).

The series of clauses begins with the subordinate clause with extraposed subject 4–5 (1), laying down the initial circumstance for the following judgement. Consecutive perfect clauses (4–5 [2–4]) proceed with the series of actions leading to the judgement that the vow is to remain valid (4–5 [5]). The conjunctive clause 4–5 (6), which departs from the series of consecutive clauses, expresses a related aspect of the judgement handed down in the previous consecutive perfect clause (4–5 [5]): pledges (אסר) and vows (נדר) are equally binding in this case.[33] Identical syntactical transitions in verses eight and 12b of the same chapter convey similar organization of information regarding the same events.

Num 35:20–1

The clauses of Num 35:20–1 envision a case of pre-meditated murder where the cities of refuge will offer no protection from the avenging relative of the deceased.

1 ואם־בשנאה יהדפנו	1 Likewise, if someone pushes
2 או־השליך עליו בצדיה	another from hatred, 2 or hurls
3 וימת	something at another, lying in wait,
4 או באיבה הכהו בידו	3 and death ensues, 4 or in enmity
5 וימת	strikes another with the hand, 5
6 מות־יומת המכה	and death ensues, 6 then the one
7 רצח הוא	who struck the blow shall be put to
8 גאל הדם ימית	death; 7 that person is a murderer;
את־הרצח בפגעו־בו	8 the avenger of blood shall put the murderer to death when they meet (vv. 20–1).

The syntactical structure of the law in this case divides the statement into protasis and apodosis. The subordinate clause 20–1 (1) introduces the initial condition of the law at its beginning. The use of the coordinating conjunction או excludes 20–1 (2, 4) from membership within a series of consecutive clauses. Thus, the

---

[33] The fact, in contrast, that the actions denoted by the verbal conjugations of נדר and אסר are bound by consecutive sequence in 4–5 (1–2) is evidence of the effectiveness of syntax in reflecting the context of communication; the events are placed as a series of clauses forming the protasis in 4–5 (1–4). The placement of the validity of the two events in the alternative syntactical relationship of conjunction in 4–5 (5–6) means to affirm the equality of the promissory debt in both events by virtue of the fact that they are related acts. The syntactical disjuncture of conjunction in 4–5 (6) brings out this semantic relationship within 4–5 (1–2) in the pronouncement of divine judgement.

statements introducing alternative circumstances stand out from the consecutive clauses (20–1 [3, 5]) that form part of the protasis for each circumstance. This departure is effected by the clauses introduced by אוֹ standing apart from the series of consecutive clauses proceeding from an initial subordinate clause (as 20–1 [2] does from 20–1 [1, 3]), or marking disjuncture from the preceding consecutive clause (20–1 [4]). The transition to, and sustenance of, an even higher degree of syntactical disjuncture (than conjunction) separates the apodosis from the protasis. The three asyndetic clauses 20–1 (6, 7, 8) make a forceful presentation of the prescribed judgement following the conditional statement (20–1 [1–5]).

THE FUNCTIONS OF EXTRAPOSITION
AND INDEPENDENT SYNTACTICAL CONSTITUENTS
IN THE LEGAL PRESCRIPTIONS
OF LEVITICUS AND NUMBERS

In what follows the same presentational format and system of numerical designation will be used as in the previous segment surveying the clauses of Leviticus and Numbers. As in previous chapters offering analysis of Hebrew texts, independent syntactical constituents will receive separate numerical designation from the surrounding clauses.

Lev 3:1–2

The portion of Leviticus under examination here comes from a larger section dealing with procedures for the peace offering.

1 וְאִם־זֶבַח שְׁלָמִים קָרְבָּנוֹ	1 If the offering is a sacrifice of
2 אִם מִן־הַבָּקָר הוּא מַקְרִיב	well-being, 2 if you offer an
3 אִם־זָכָר אִם־נְקֵבָה תָּמִים	animal of the herd, 3 whether
יַקְרִיבֶנּוּ	male or female, you shall offer
לִפְנֵי יְהוָה	one without blemish before the
4 וְסָמַךְ יָדוֹ עַל־רֹאשׁ קָרְבָּנוֹ	Lord. 4 You shall lay your hand
5 וְשָׁחַטוֹ פֶּתַח אֹהֶל מוֹעֵד	upon the head of the animal 5
6 וְזָרְקוּ בְּנֵי אַהֲרֹן הַכֹּהֲנִים	and slaughter it at the entrance
אֶת־הַדָּם	of the tent of meeting; 6 and
עַל־הַמִּזְבֵּחַ סָבִיב	Aaron's sons the priests shall
	dash the blood against all sides
	of the altar (vv. 1–2).

Two subordinate clauses (1–2 [1, 2]) stand at the head of this section offering instruction on the procedure for the sacrifice of an animal from the herd as a peace offering. The asyndetic clause with extraposed subject (אִם־זָכָר אִם־נְקֵבָה)—the object suffix on the verbal formation יַקְרִיבֶנּוּ refers to, and assumes the syntactical role of each extraposed member within the clause—draws attention to the fact that the following procedure applies without regard to the gender of the beast. Thus, 1–2 (3), in maintaining a high degree of syntactical disjuncture, stands apart from the following sequence of consecutive clauses (1–2 [4–6]) flowing out of the two initial conditional clauses (1–2 [1, 2]). The clause remains distinct in order to offer specification (the very function of the extraposed member) concerning a component of the ritual carried by the consecutive clauses: the procedure applies without regard to the gender of the beast. Prior analysis has identified such an epexegetical function for asyndetic clauses without an extraposed member.[34]

Lev 3:3–5

The procedure for the peace offering initiated in Lev 3:1–2 continues in the clauses of Lev 3:3–5.

1 וְהִקְרִיב מִזֶּבַח הַשְּׁלָמִים אִשֶּׁה לַיהוָה 2 אֶת־הַחֵלֶב הַמְכַסֶּה אֶת־הַקֶּרֶב וְאֵת כָּל־הַחֵלֶב אֲשֶׁר עַל־הַקֶּרֶב וְאֵת שְׁתֵּי הַכְּלָיֹת וְאֶת־הַחֵלֶב אֲשֶׁר עֲלֵהֶן אֲשֶׁר עַל־הַכְּסָלִים וְאֶת־הַיֹּתֶרֶת עַל־הַכָּבֵד עַל־הַכְּלָיוֹת יְסִירֶנָּה 3 וְהִקְטִירוּ אֹתוֹ בְנֵי־אַהֲרֹן	1 You shall offer from the sacrifice of well-being, as an offering by fire to The Lord, 2 the fat that covers the entrails and all the fat that is around the entrails; the two kidneys with the fat that is on them at the loins, and the appendage on the liver, which he shall remove with the

---

[34] The two occurrences of אֵם in 1–2 (3) are taken to be coordinating conjunctions binding the various entities in a chain of words. As a coordinating conjunction performing a similar function to אוֹ, אֵם may govern syntactical constituents beneath the level of the clause (*GBH*, §53.5.2.2; *BHRG*, §31.1.3).

המזבחה kidneys. 3 Then Aaron's sons
על־העלה אשר על־העצים shall turn these into smoke on
על־האש אשה ריח ניחח ליהוה the altar, with the burnt-offering that is on the wood on the fire, as an offering by fire of pleasing odour to the Lord (vv. 3–5).

The asyndetic clause 3–5 (2) has a lengthy extraposed member standing before the clause; the object suffix on יסירנה collectively designates the role of the various extraposed entities (all material leading up to the final verb) within the clause. The clause 3–5 (2) disrupts the series of consecutive perfect clauses carrying the events of the prescribed procedure, in order to offer specific detail concerning the portion of the peace offering that is to be offered to the deity. The clarification of 3–5 (1), with the precise details in the extraposed elements of the clause, is the purpose of 3–5 (2). The offering culminates with a return to the sequence of consecutive clauses; the burning of the items offered upon the altar is the last component (3–5 [3]). The practice of disrupting consecutive clauses with clauses employing extraposition is repeated in the procedures for animals from the flock at the same point in each following procedure for the same identifiable cause (Lev 3:9, 14–5). The repetition of the specification to remove the fat of the animal with syntactical prominence throughout the chapter, and its reiteration in an asyndetic clause (Lev 3:17b) at the end of the final procedure (offering from a goat of the flock) suggest the importance of this specific aspect of the peace offering.

Lev 6:8–11

The series of clauses in Lev 6:8–11 come at the end of a procedure of prescription concerning an offering of grain.

והרים ממנו בקמצו 1 1 They shall take from it a handful
מסלת המנחה of the choice flour and oil of the
ומשמנה ואת כל־הלבנה grain-offering, with all the
אשר frankincense that is on the
על־המנחה offering, 2 and they shall turn its
והקטיר המזבח ריח 2 memorial portion into smoke on
ניחח the altar as a pleasing odour to the

אזכרתה ליהוה

3 והנותרת ממנה יאכלו

אהרן ובניו

4 מצות תאכל במקום קדש

5 בחצר אהל־מועד

יאכלוה

6 לא תאפה חמץ

7 חלקם נתתי אתה מאשי

8 קדש קדשים הוא כחטאת

כאשם

9 כל־זכר בבני אהרן

יאכלנה

10 חק־עולם לדרתיכם

מאשי יהוה

11 כל אשר־יגע בהם יקדש

Lord. 3 Aaron and his sons shall eat what is left of it; 4 it shall be eaten as unleaven cakes in a holy place; 5 in the court of the tent of meeting they shall eat it. 6 It shall not be baked with leaven. 7 I have given it as their portion of my offerings by fire; 8 it is most holy, like the sin-offering and the guilt-offering. 9 Every male among the descendants of Aaron shall eat of it, 10 as their perpetual due throughout your generations, from the Lord's offerings by fire; 11 anything that touches them shall become holy (vv. 8–11).

The consecutive clauses 8–11 (1, 2) convey part of the series of events constituting the procedure. The end of the procedure, the conjunctive clause 8–11 (3), sets apart the provision for priests to consume a portion of the offering from the series of events constituting the enactment of the offering. From this point in the legislation, asyndetic clauses expand upon components of the procedure with specific detail (8–11 [5, 6, 9, 11]), qualify items mentioned within the procedure (8–11 [8]), or make mention of a deed extraneous to the temporal progression of the procedure with an effect to its outcome (8–11 [7]). The series of phrases constituting 8–11 (10) is a syntactical entity independent of a clause. The absence of the definite article in חק־עולם—the term designates legislation just mentioned—makes it unlikely that the phrase constitutes the subject with the following material, לדרתיכם מאשי יהוה, as predicate.[35] The prominence of 8–11 (10)

---

[35] In agreement with LXX (νόμιμον αἰώνιον) and against the rendition of the NRSV ("perpetual due"), the present reading understands חק to refer to a legal decree in 8–11 (10). This understanding of the term is dominant throughout the book of Leviticus (Lev 3:17; 7:36; 10:9; 16:29, 31, 34; 17:7; 23:14, 41). Furthermore, Hartley points to the similar

as an independent syntactical constituent among a sequence of clauses raises the visibility of the perpetuity of the allotment for Aaron's descendants, and the regulations governing its consumption and preparation. Thus, an additional measure of syntactical disjuncture (the independent constituent of 8–11 [10]) elevates a qualifying statement standing over the asyndetic clauses 8–11 (4–9, 11), which expand upon the procedure (8–11 [1–3]) with the addition of more precise details.

Lev 7:31–2

The clauses of Lev 7:31–2 are part of a series of prescriptions governing the manner in which the peace offering is presented to the priests before God. The precise clauses from this portion of the text concern the portions of the animal the priests are to receive for their own consumption.

1 וְהִקְטִיר הַכֹּהֵן אֶת־הַחֵלֶב הַמִּזְבֵּחָה 2 וְהָיָה הֶחָזֶה לְאַהֲרֹן וּלְבָנָיו 3 וְאֵת שׁוֹק הַיָּמִין תִּתְּנוּ תְרוּמָה לַכֹּהֵן מִזִּבְחֵי שַׁלְמֵיכֶם 4 הַמַּקְרִיב אֶת־דַּם הַשְּׁלָמִים וְאֶת־הַחֵלֶב מִבְּנֵי אַהֲרֹן לוֹ תִהְיֶה שׁוֹק הַיָּמִין לְמָנָה	1 The priest shall turn the fat into smoke on the altar, 2 but the breast shall belong to Aaron and his sons. 3 And the right thigh from your sacrifices of well-being you shall give to the priest as an offering; 4 the one among the sons of Aaron who offers the blood and fat of the offering of well-being shall have the right thigh for a portion (vv. 31–2).

The process of transfer in the commission of parts of the animal to God and the priests proceeds with consecutive clauses (31–2 [1–2]). The conjunctive clause 31–2 (3) breaks the sequence of events in order to append a related action to a clause (31–2 [2]) serving as a member within the chain of consecutive clauses; the

---

qualification of perpetuity (עוֹלָם) that occurs with the term bearing the meaning of a decree in Lev 3:17, 7:36 and 17:7 (1992, 89). There is no reason to postulate for 8–11 (10) a departure from the normative interpretation of the term.

right thigh is to be offered to the priesthood along with the breast (31–2 [3]). The asyndetic clause with extraposition (the pronominal suffix in לֹו assumes the syntactical role of the extraposed member within the clause) 31–2 (4) ushers in an even higher degree of syntactical disjuncture (than that of conjunction) in offering specification for 31–2 (3): specifically, it is the priest presiding over the offering of the blood and the fat who is to receive the right thigh (31–2 [4]).

Lev 11:2b–8, 20–3

Both passages from verses 2b–8 and 20–3 are portions from a larger body of laws in Leviticus 11 concerning dietary restrictions for Israel.

1 זֹאת הַחַיָּה אֲשֶׁר תֹּאכְלוּ מִכָּל־הַבְּהֵמָה אֲשֶׁר עַל־הָאָרֶץ	1 From all the land animals, these are the creatures you may eat.
2 כֹּל מַפְרֶסֶת פַּרְסָה וְשֹׁסַעַת שֶׁסַע פְּרָסֹת מַעֲלַת גֵּרָה בַּבְּהֵמָה אֹתָהּ תֹּאכֵלוּ	2 Any animal that has divided hoofs and is cloven-footed and chews the cud—such you may eat.
3 אַךְ אֶת־זֶה לֹא תֹאכְלוּ מִמַּעֲלֵי הַגֵּרָה וּמִמַּפְרִיסֵי הַפַּרְסָה	3 But among those that chew the cud or have divided hoofs, you shall not eat the following:
4 אֶת־הַגָּמָל	4 the camel,
5 כִּי־מַעֲלֵה גֵרָה הוּא	5 for even though it chews the cud,
6 וּמַפְרִסָה אֵינֶנּוּ מַפְרִיס	6 it does not have divided hoofs;
7 טָמֵא הוּא לָכֶם	7 it is unclean for you.
8 וְאֶת־הַשָּׁפָן	8 The rock-badger,
9 כִּי־מַעֲלֵה גֵרָה הוּא	9 for even though it chews the cud,
10 וּפַרְסָה לֹא יַפְרִיס	10 it does not have divided hoofs;
11 טָמֵא הוּא לָכֶם	11 it is unclean for you.
12 וְאֶת־הָאַרְנֶבֶת	12 The hare,
13 כִּי־מַעֲלֵה גֵרָה הִוא	13 for even though it chews the cud,
14 וּפַרְסָה לֹא הִפְרִיסָה	14 it does not have divided hoofs;
15 טְמֵאָה הִוא לָכֶם	15 it is unclean for you.
16 וְאֶת־הַחֲזִיר	16 The pig,
17 כִּי־מַפְרִיס פַּרְסָה הוּא	17 for even though it has divided hoofs
18 וְשֹׁסַע שֶׁסַע פַּרְסָה	18 and is cloven-footed,
19 וְהוּא גֵּרָה לֹא־יִגָּר	19 it does not chew the cud; 20 it is unclean for you. 21 Of their flesh you shall not eat, 22

טמא הוא לכם 20   and their carcasses you shall
מבשרם לא תאכלו 21   not touch; 23 they are unclean
ובנבלתם לא תגעו 22   for you (vv. 2b–8).
טמאים הם לכם 23

The dietary regulations concerning animals on the land proceed in a loose formation of asyndetic clauses (2b–8 [1, 3, 7, 11, 15, 20, 21, 23]). A shift to a higher degree of syntactical continuity (in this case, conjunctive clauses) signals the grouping together of clauses more closely related in subject matter. On the other hand, the additional feature (to asyndeton) of extraposition, or the occurrence of independent syntactical constituents accompany information of a specific nature in relation to the surrounding material: the designation of the specific class of animal or individual animal permitted for consumption, or under ban. The system of graded levels of syntactical discontinuity places clauses deploying extraposition (in any type of clause) at the same level as asyndetic and subordinate clauses. However, it is the case that among clauses of the same type (asyndetic, subordinate, conjunctive, consecutive), the additional feature of extraposition may indicate an added degree of prominence. The first departure from the asyndetic series of clauses is the asyndetic clause with extraposition, 2b–8 (2); the clause specifies the class of animal permitted for consumption, a drastic expansion of information from the pronominal reference זאת in 2b–8 (1). Returning to the series of asyndetic clauses without extraposition, 2b–8 (3) introduces a list of animals not permitted for consumption; each animal on the list is an independent syntactical constituent without connection to a clause (2b–8 [4, 8, 12, 16]) enacting a prominent statement of specification (with relation to 2b–8 [3]) with the elevated degree of syntactical disjuncture.[36] Thus, the shift to a

---

[36] This syntactical independence occurs despite the fact that each member is preceded by the direct object marker, suggesting that the entities are the collective direct object designated by the pronoun in את־זה (2b–8 [3]). However, the suggestion that each member of the list is really an extraposed entity (right-dislocation) meets with the problem that

higher degree of syntactical disjuncture in the use of independent syntactical constituents represents the transition to statements of specification for a preceding clause (2b–8 [3]). Following each independent syntactical constituent, a subordinate clause (2b–8 [5, 9, 13, 17]) expresses a reason for the ban; conjunctive clauses (2b–8 [6, 10, 14, 18–9]) follow with additional clauses to the statement of explanation. The abiding significance of each explanatory statement (that the animal is unclean; 2b–8 [7, 11, 15, 20]), the summary clause for the series of clauses beginning with a subordinate clause, represents a return to the series of asyndetic clauses in the body of legislation. The final three clauses of the passage of laws are statements applicable to all the prohibited items of food in the preceding list (2b–8 [21, 22, 23]). Among these three clauses the asyndetic clauses (2b–8 [21, 23]) are representative of the dominant mode of linkage between clauses in the passage. The sole exception, the conjunctive clause 2b–8 (22), forges a greater degree of syntactical continuity between two prohibitions against contamination through some form of contact with the unclean beasts. The prohibitions stand out from the surrounding clauses declaring the unclean state of the animals just named (2b–8 [20, 23]). In keeping with the pattern of syntax in the passage, conjunction in 2b–8 (22) occurs to link those clauses closer in subject matter.

The epexegetical function of the independent syntactical constituent just seen is repeated in the dietary restrictions regarding insects.

1 כל שרץ העוף ההלך על־ארבע שקץ הוא לכם 2 אך את־זה תאכלו מכל שרץ העוף ההלך על־ארבע אשר לא כרעים ממעל לרגליו לנתר בהן	1 All winged insects that walk upon all fours are detestable to you. 2 But among the winged insects that walk on all fours you may eat those that have jointed legs above their feet, with which to leap on the ground. 3 Of them you may eat: 4 the locust

groups of clauses (2b–8 [5–7, 9–11, 13–5]) stand between each supposedly extraposed member.

עַל־הָאָרֶץ — according to its kind, the bald
3 אֶת־אֵלֶּה מֵהֶם תֹּאכֵלוּ — locust according to its kind, the
4 אֶת־הָאַרְבֶּה לְמִינוֹ — cricket according to its kind, and
וְאֶת־הַסָּלְעָם לְמִינֵהוּ — the grasshopper according to its
וְאֶת־הֶחָגָב לְמִינֵהוּ — kind. 5 But all other winged
5 וְכֹל שֶׁרֶץ הָעוֹף אֲשֶׁר־לוֹ — insects that have four feet are
אַרְבַּע רַגְלַיִם — detestable to you (vv. 20–3).
שֶׁקֶץ הוּא לָכֶם

The passage is part of the same system of laws as that of Lev 11:2b–8; asyndeton is the dominant mode of relation between clauses. The asyndetic clause with extraposition, 20–3 (1), prohibits all crawling insects with four legs for consumption. The salience of this information set within an extraposed component standing before the clause sets up the information for the contrast that is to come with the notice of exception (20–3 [2–4]). The asyndetic clause 20–3 (2) introduces the statement of exception for those insects with jointed legs. The following asyndetic clause introduces a list of examples of such exceptions (20–3 [4]). Four items in succession constitute a series of phrases independent of a clause; the departure from the established syntactical order of inter-clausal sequence is salient. The syntactical disjuncture of 20–3 (4) serves to mark the influx of specific detail with regard to 20–3 (2–3), as well as to complement the elevated syntactical platform (extraposition) for the element of contrast in 20–3 (1): the creatures of 20–3 (4) are those permitted for consumption in contradistinction to the winged insects of 20–3 (1). The conjunctive clause with extraposition 20–3 (5)—a degree of syntactical continuity in keeping with the asyndetic clauses of the passage—repeats the general prohibition of insects with four feet walking upon the earth in the diet of the community. The repetition forms a ring of contrast (20–3 [1, 5]) around the list of exceptions (20–3 [4]); the elements of antithesis (20–3 [1] over against 20–3 [4]) receive a measure of syntactical prominence. As in Lev 11:2b–8, independent syntactical constituents elevate the prominence of information providing specific detail in relation to previous clauses. Novel is the function of contrast for both the features of extraposition and independent syntactical constituents in verses 20–3.

Lev 12:2aβ–8

The chapter from which Lev 12: 2aβ–8 comes concerns matters pertaining to defilement from the process of childbirth.

1 אשה כי תזריע	1 If a woman conceives 2 and
2 וילדה זכר	bears a male child,
3 ואם־נקבה תלד	3 If she bears a female child,
4 וטמאה שבעים כנדתה	4 she shall be unclean for two weeks, as in her menstruation;
5 אם־לא תמצא ידה די שה	5 If she cannot afford a sheep,
6 ולקחה שתי־תרים או שני	6 she shall take two turtle-doves
בני יונה	or two pigeons, one for a burnt
אחד לעלה ואחד לחטאת	offering and the other for a sin-
7 וכפר עליה הכהן	offering; 7 and the priest shall
8 וטהרה	make atonement on her behalf, 8 and she shall be clean (vv. 2aβ–8).

The combination of extraposition and subordination standing at the head of a passage of laws has been witnessed in several previous examples (Lev 1:2aβ–4; 2:1–3; 5:15–6b). As in the last two cases from Leviticus 11, the extra feature of extraposition within clauses of the same type (e.g. asyndetic, conjunctive) may indicate a higher degree of syntactical disjuncture. Here in Lev 12:2aβ–8, the distinction marks the absolute beginning of a set of commands from those clauses standing at the head of its various sub-sections. In the example at hand, the subordinating conjunction כי marks the conditional statement for the main case (2aβ–8 [1]), whereas אם introduces each sub-section dealing with variations of the previous case (2aβ–8 [3, 5]).[37] Furthermore, the absolute beginning

---

[37] The subordinate clause 2aβ–8 (3) begins a set of commands including a procedure for the purification of the mother with the offering of a burnt offering and a purification offering (Lev 12:6–7). The subordinate clause 2aβ–8 (5) anticipates the situation where the sacrificial animals are beyond the means of the new mother. The combination of כי

of the passage of law, 2aβ–8 (1), has the additional feature of the extraposed subject אֵשׁה. The element of disjuncture marking the beginning of each section may be perceived with the elevated degree of syntactical continuity (the on-set of consecutive clauses) proceeding from each subordinate clause.

Lev 14:5–6

The clauses of Lev 14:5–6 are part of a passage dealing with procedures of purification for one suffering from a skin disorder.

1 וצוה הכהן	1 The priest shall command
2 ושחט את־הצפור האחת	2 that one of the birds be
אל־כלי־חרש על־מים חיים	slaughtered over fresh water in
3 את־הצפר החיה יקח אתה	an earthen vessel. 3 He shall
ואת־עץ	take the living bird with the
ארז ואת־שני התולעת	cedar wood and the crimson
ואת־האזב	yarn and the hyssop, 4 and dip
4 וטבל אותם ואת הצפר החיה	them and the living bird in the
בדם הצפר השחטה על המים	blood of the bird that was
חיים	slaughtered over fresh water
	(vv. 5–6).

This portion of the procedure moves along with consecutive perfect clauses bearing each component in the series of events (5–6 [1, 2, 4]). The asyndetic clause with extraposition 5–6 (3) is the sole detractor from the series of consecutive clauses; the syntactical role of the extraposed element את־הצפר החיה is assumed within the clause by the pronominal suffix on אתה. The function of the syntactical disjuncture at this point is to mark the element of contrast borne by the extraposed entity את־הצפר החיה; the previous clause had dealt with the slaughter of the other bird (5–6 [2]).

---

and אם with the former introducing the primary conditional statement followed by sub-conditions (introduced by the latter) has been documented well; among others, see Jöuon (§167e), *IBHS* (§38.2d, fn. 20) and *BHRG* (§40.9I [1]).

Lev 17:8aβ–10

The commands of Lev 17:8aβ–10 are part of a segment of speech dealing with a series of issues from the prohibition of the offering of burnt offerings away from the tabernacle (Lev 17: 8aβ–9), to the cleansing procedure for one consuming the flesh of an animal found dead (Lev 17:15–6).

1 אִישׁ אִישׁ מִבֵּית יִשְׂרָאֵל
וּמִן־הַגֵּר
אֲשֶׁר־יָגוּר בְּתוֹכָם אֲשֶׁר־יַעֲלֶה
עֹלָה
אוֹ־זֶבַח
וְאֶל־פֶּתַח אֹהֶל מוֹעֵד לֹא
יְבִיאֶנּוּ
לַעֲשׂוֹת אֹתוֹ לַיהוה
2 וְנִכְרַת הָאִישׁ הַהוּא מֵעַמָּיו
3 אִישׁ אִישׁ מִבֵּית יִשְׂרָאֵל
וּמִן־הַגֵּר הַגָּר
בְּתוֹכָם אֲשֶׁר יֹאכַל כָּל־דָּם
וְנָתַתִּי פָנַי בַּנֶּפֶשׁ הָאֹכֶלֶת
אֶת־הַדָּם
4 וְהִכְרַתִּי אֹתָהּ מִקֶּרֶב עַמָּהּ

1 Anyone of the house of Israel or of the aliens who reside among them who offers a burnt offering or sacrifice, and does not bring it to the entrance of the tent of meeting, to sacrifice it to the Lord, 2 shall be cut off from the people. 3 If anyone of the house of Israel or of the aliens who reside among them eats any blood, I will set my face against that person who eats blood, 4 and will cut that person off from the people (vv. 8aβ–10).

Thus far, the syntactical feature of extraposition has been shown to pose syntactical disruption in order to sustain a topical boundary only as part of a clause already bearing a high degree of syntactical discontinuity (subordinate and asyndetic clauses). Here in Lev 17: 8aβ–10, the extraposed member אִישׁ אִישׁ מִבֵּית יִשְׂרָאֵל וּמִן־הַגֵּר with its subordinate elements stands before a conjunctive clause (8aβ–9 [1]): the material prior to וְאֶל־פֶּתַח אֹהֶל form the extraposed member whose syntactical role within the clause is borne by the subject endemic to the verbal form לֹא יְבִיאֶנּוּ. Without extraposition in 8aβ–9 (1), the series of commands (preceded by the introduction to speech וַאֲלֵהֶם תֹּאמַר) would begin with a conjunctive clause. The consecutive clause 8aβ–9 (2) proceeds with the rest of the command set dealing with the issue of sacrifice away from the established cultic locus. The consecutive clause with extraposition 8aβ–9 (3) brings syntactical disjuncture in order to mark the beginning of a new topic: the consequence for the consumption of blood. The phrase

הָאֲכִלַת אֶת־חָדָם takes the place of אִישׁ אִישׁ מִבֵּית יִשְׂרָאֵל וּמִן־הַגֵּר הַגָּר בְּתוֹכָם, with its embedded clause אֲשֶׁר יֹאכַל כָּל־דָּם, within the clause beginning at וְנָתַתִּי. Without the element of extraposition, it would be a consecutive clause initiating the new topic. Thus, it is evident that extraposition, by virtue of its nature, attains a degree of syntactical disjuncture capable of declaring a topical boundary. As with the previous topic, a consecutive clause (8aβ–9 [4]) proceeds with the rest of the command set.

Lev 23:2aβ–3

The series of prescriptions regarding the Sabbath in Lev 23: 2aβ–3 are part of a chapter concerned with the festivals in Israel's annual cycle.

מוֹעֲדֵי יהוה אֲשֶׁר־תִּקְרְאוּ 1	1 These are the appointed
אֹתָם	festivals of the Lord that you
מִקְרָאֵי קֹדֶשׁ אֵלֶּה הֵם מוֹעֲדָי	shall proclaim as holy
שֵׁשֶׁת יָמִים תֵּעָשֶׂה מְלָאכָה 2	convocations, my appointed
וּבַיּוֹם הַשְּׁבִיעִי שַׁבַּת שַׁבָּתוֹן 3	festivals. 2 For six days shall
מִקְרָא־קֹדֶשׁ	work be done; 3 but the seventh
כָּל־מְלָאכָה לֹא תַעֲשׂוּ 4	day is a sabbath of complete rest,
שַׁבָּת הִוא לַיהוה בְּכֹל 5	a holy convocation; 4 you shall
מוֹשְׁבֹתֵיכֶם	do no work: 5 it is a sabbath to
	the Lord throughout your
	settlements (vv. 2aβ–3).

The clauses are a loosely bound series of commands concerning the weekly day of rest: asyndeton is the dominant form of linkage between the clauses (2aβ–3 [1, 2, 4, 5]). In the series of asyndetic clauses, the deployment of the additional feature of extraposition in 2aβ–3 (1) establishes the beginning of the series of commands with an additional measure of syntactical disjuncture. The independent pronoun הֵם is the subject of the verbless clause 2aβ–3 (1); the pronoun refers to the content of the preceding extraposed member, God's appointed festivals. Within the command set in a sea of asyndetic clauses, the coordinating conjunction ו binds two statements (2aβ–3 [2, 3]) of closer relation: the prescriptions of 2aβ–3 (2, 3) share a focus upon the temporal aspect of the boundary between the sacred and the profane.

Lev 23:13–4

Within the same chapter, the series of clauses in Lev 23:13–4 forms part of the procedure for offering a sheaf from the first fruits of the harvest.

1 וּמִנְחָתוֹ שְׁנֵי עֶשְׂרֹנִים סֹלֶת בְּלוּלָה בַשֶּׁמֶן אִשֶּׁה לַיהוָה רֵיחַ נִיחֹחַ 2 וְנִסְכֹּה יַיִן רְבִיעִת הַהִין 3 וְלֶחֶם וְקָלִי וְכַרְמֶל לֹא תֹאכְלוּ עַד־עֶצֶם הַיּוֹם הַזֶּה עַד הֲבִיאֲכֶם אֶת־קָרְבַּן אֱלֹהֵיכֶם 4 חֻקַּת עוֹלָם לְדֹרֹתֵיכֶם בְּכֹל מֹשְׁבֹתֵיכֶם	1 And the grain-offering with it shall be two-tenths of an ephah of choice flour mixed with oil, an offering by fire of pleasing odour to the Lord; 2 and the drink-offering with it shall be of wine, one-fourth of a hin. 3 You shall eat no bread or parched grain or fresh ears until that very day, until you have brought the offering of your God: 4 it is a statute for ever throughout your generations in all your settlements (vv. 13–4).

The conjunctive clauses 13–4 (1–2) sever the series of consecutive clauses (just preceding the passage at hand) carrying the bulk of the procedure. The transition to the use of conjunctive clauses sets apart from the sequence of events the accompanying offerings of grain and drink to the sacrifice of a lamb as a burnt offering. The requirement for abstinence from the consumption of the harvest before the offering—a statement clearly outside the temporal progression of the procedure—occurs as a third conjunctive clause (13–4 [3]). The qualification of the entire prescribed series of offerings as a perpetual statute occurs in the especially prominent construction of an independent syntactical constituent: predication does not occur within 13–4 (4). As with asyndetic clauses amidst clauses of a lower degree of syntactical disjuncture, independent syntactical constituents elevate the prominence of qualifying statements governing a series of prescriptions.[38]

---

[38] For the same function performed by independent syntactical constituents, see vv. 21b and 31b in Leviticus 23.

Num 4:25–7a

The prescriptions of Num 4:25–7a are the greater part of God's stipulation of the duties of the Gershonites in the wilderness.

1 זאת עבדת משפחת	1 This is the service of the clans of
הגרשני לעבד	the Gershonites, in serving and
ולמשא	bearing burdens: 2 They shall carry
2 ונשאו את־יריעת	the curtains of the tabernacle. . .
המשכן. . .	3–4 and they shall do all that needs
3 ואת כל־אשר יעשה להם	to be done with regard to them. 5
4 ועבדו³⁹	All the service of the Gershonites
5 על־פי אהרן ובניו תהיה	shall be at the command of Aaron
כל־עבדת	and his sons, in all that they are to
בני הגרשני לכל־משאם	carry, and in all that they have to
ולכל עבדתם	do (vv. 25–7a).

The asyndetic verbless clause 25–7a (1) initiates the subject matter of the duties of the Gershonites, and a consecutive clause proceeds with the definition of the duties (25–7a [2]). The content of 25–7a (3) is an independent syntactical constituent, even though the direct object marker designates it as the object of the verb ועבדו in 25–7 (4): the position of the consecutive perfect form excludes 25–7a (3) from the clause, and there is nothing to assume the role of the independent constituent within the clause 25–7a (4). As a construction posing syntactical disruption to the flow of the clauses in the passage, 25–7a (3) elevates the profile of the miscellaneous tasks related to the function of the items under the charge of the Gershonites as an additional component to bearing the items (25–7a [2]).⁴⁰ The consecutive clause 25–7 (2) is disrupted

---

³⁹ The numerical designation for 25–7a (3, 4) in the translation (the clauses occurring together as 3–4) reflects the irretrievable combination of this material in the translation of the NRSV. The sequence of the components in the Hebrew text has been reversed.

⁴⁰ The usual syntactical arrangement in the creation of an additional item closely related to an event on the series of consecutive clauses depicting a procedure, would place the content of 25–7a (3–4) within a conjunctive clause. Here in 25–7a (3), greater prominence is confined

with a measure of syntactical disjuncture in order to communicate a complementary component endemic to the commission of the prescribed action in 25–7 (2). The shift to an asyndetic clause in 25–7a (5) places the auxiliary statement that the Gershonites are to take their orders from Aaron and his sons apart from the consecutive clauses (2b5–7a [2, 4]) declaring the duties of the Gershonites. As a comment on the duties of the Gershonites, the asyndetic clause 25–7 (5) elevates the instructions of Aaron and his sons on the matter as a specific and important aspect of tending to the tasks.

Num 5:6aβ–10

The commands of Num 5:6aβ–10 designate the recipients of restitution and sacrificial portions in accordance with variant circumstances. As an example of the use of extraposition in legal prescriptions, the clauses demonstrate the versatility of the syntactical construction within a brief passage.

1 איש או־אשה כי יעשו	1 When a man or a woman wrongs
מכל־חטאת	another, breaking faith with the
האדם למעל מעל ביהוה	Lord, 2 that person incurs guilt
2 ואשמה הנפש ההוא	3 and shall confess the sin that has
3 והתודו את־חטאתם אשר	been committed. 4 The person
עשו	shall make full restitution for the
4 והשיב את־אשמו בראשו	wrong, 5 adding one-fifth to it,
5 וחמישתו יסף עליו	6 and giving it to the one who was
6 ונתן לאשר אשם לו	wronged. 7 If the injured party has
7 ואם־אין לאיש גאל להשיב	no next-of-kin to whom restitution
האשם	may be made for the wrong, 8 the
אליו	restitution shall go to the Lord for
8 האשם המושב ליהוה לכהן	the priest, in addition to the ram of

solely to the object of the labour. Levine (1993, 170) finds a statement of conclusion in the statement of 25–7a (3–4); but the probable distinction between carrying the designated items of the cult and the wider task of performing duties related to their transportation and function (כל־אשר יעשה להם) suggests an adjunction to, not summary of, the earlier statement (25–7a [2]).

מלבד איל הכפרים

אשר יכפר־בו עליו

9 וכל־תרומה לכל־קדשי

בני־ישראל

אשר־יקריבו לכהן לו יהיה

10 ואיש את־קדשיו לו יהיו

11 איש אשר־יתן לכהן לו

יהיה

atonement with which atonement is made for the guilty party. 9 Among all the sacred donations of the Israelites, every gift that they bring to the priest shall be his. 10 The sacred donations of all are their own; 11 whatever anyone gives to the priest shall be his (vv. 6aβ–10).

The primary circumstance underlying the prescriptive statement is introduced by the subordinate clause 6aβ–10 (1) with an extraposed subject (איש או־אשה) standing before the clause. Notice that the secondary circumstance introduced by the subordinate clause with אם, 6aβ–10 (7), is without extraposition: the initiation of a sub-section is the function of syntactical disjuncture in 6aβ–10 (7). Following the initial conditional statement of 6aβ–10 (1), consecutive clauses carry the series of events in the procedure (6aβ–10 [2, 3, 4, 6]). The sole exception, the conjunctive clause 6aβ–10 (5), sets aside an additional feature (the addition of a fifth of the designated value for restitution) to the act of recompense (6aβ–10 [4]) stated in the series of consecutive clauses. The subordinate clause 6aβ–10 (7) begins a new case with variation from the circumstances of the first case. The contrasting statement of the apodosis (an asyndetic clause, 6aβ–10 [8], and a conjunctive clause, 6aβ–10 [9]) to this secondary circumstantial development (6aβ–10 [7]) has a higher degree of syntactical discontinuity than the cluster of consecutive clauses in the first case (6aβ–10 [2–6]). The degree of syntactical prominence is motivated by the desire to magnify the contrasting judgement in view of the exceptional circumstance of 6aβ–10 (7). Within the series of clauses 6aβ–10 (8–9), conjunction in 6aβ–10 (9) binds the two related clauses (6aβ–10 [8, 9]) focused on transactions of reparation with the priest as the recipient. Syntactical disjuncture returns in the two final prescriptions of the passage (6aβ–10 [10, 11]) with the use of extraposition, breaking the series of two prescriptions joined by conjunction with their focus on the portion of the priest. The extraposed nominal entities ואיש את־קדשיו are respectively resumed within the clause of 6aβ–10 (10) by the prepositional suffix in לו and the subject within the verbal morpheme יהיו. In the case of 6aβ–10 (11), the extraposed element אִישׁ is the designated indirect object (לֹ) in the clause. Thus, clauses with extraposition (6aβ–10 [10, 11]) stand with an asyndetic clause (6aβ–10 [8]) and a conjunctive clause (6aβ–10 [9]) in forming a much more loose structure of syntax in the second case (6aβ–10 [7–11]) of two. As a sub-section of the main case (6aβ–10 [1–6]), the heightened degree of syntactical disjuncture in 6aβ–10 (7–11) underlines the element of contrast to the preceding main case (6aβ–10 [1–6]).

Num 10:9–10

The clauses of Num 10:9–10 are part of a section prescribing the construction of two silver trumpets for the purpose of raising a signal for various communal occasions.

1 וְכִי־תָבֹאוּ מִלְחָמָה בְּאַרְצְכֶם עַל־הַצַּר הַצֹּרֵר אֶתְכֶם	1 When you go to war in your land against the adversary who oppresses you, 2 you shall sound an alarm with
2 וַהֲרֵעֹתֶם בַּחֲצֹצְרוֹת	the trumpets, 3 so that you may be
3 וְנִזְכַּרְתֶּם לִפְנֵי יהוה אֱלֹהֵיכֶם	remembered before the Lord your God 4 and be saved from your
4 וְנוֹשַׁעְתֶּם מֵאֹיְבֵיכֶם	enemies. 5 Also on your days of
5 וּבְיוֹם שִׂמְחַתְכֶם וּבְמוֹעֲדֵיכֶם וּבְרָאשֵׁי חָדְשֵׁיכֶם	rejoicing, at your appointed festivals, and at the beginnings of your months, 6 you shall blow the
6 וּתְקַעְתֶּם בַּחֲצֹצְרֹת עַל עֹלֹתֵיכֶם וְעַל זִבְחֵי שַׁלְמֵיכֶם	trumpets over your burnt-offerings and over your sacrifices of well-being; 7 they shall serve as a
7 וְהָיוּ לָכֶם לְזִכָּרוֹן לִפְנֵי אֱלֹהֵיכֶם	reminder on your behalf before the Lord your God: 8 I am the Lord your
8 אֲנִי יהוה אֱלֹהֵיכֶם	God (vv. 9–10).

The subordinate clause 9–10 (1) begins the prescribed procedure for summoning the community to arms; consecutive clauses complete the envisioned sequence of events (9–10 [2–4]). The series of prepositional phrases constituting 9–10 (5) are a syntactical entity independent of a clause. With the similar effect of a subordinate (temporal) clause, the syntactical interruption stands to break the sequence of clauses in order to mark the beginning of a new subject: the function of the trumpets at a variety of festivals having nothing to do with war (the subject matter of the previous set of commands). The consecutive perfect clause 9–10 (7) proceeds with the command set, before asyndeton intercedes to establish the divine identity as the authority behind the legislation (9–10 [8]).

Num 18:12–5

The legal statements of Num 18:12–5 form part of a speech whereby God transfers various offerings to the priests for their consumption. The clauses from the larger passage are mostly strung together loosely with asyndeton as the dominant form of linkage between clauses. The additional feature of extraposition marks boundaries between the various offerings under concern just as it does so at the beginning of this passage (Num 18:12–5) on the offering of first fruits.

1 כל חלב יצהר וכל־חלב תירוש ודגן ראשיתם אשר־יתנו ליהוה לך נתתים	1 All the best of the oil and all the best of the wine and the grain, the choice produce that they give to the Lord, I have given to you.
2 בכורי כל־אשר בארצם אשר־יביאו ליהוה לך יהיה	2 The first fruits of all that is in their land, which they bring to the Lord, shall be yours;
3 כל־טהור בביתך יאכלנו	3 everyone who is clean in your house may eat of it.
4 כל־חרם בישראל לך יהיה	4 Every devoted thing in Israel shall be yours.
5 כל־פטר רחם לכל־בשר אשר יקריבו ליהוה באדם ובבהמה יהיה־לך	5 The first issue of the womb of all creatures, human and animal, which is offered to the Lord, shall be yours; 6 but the firstborn of human beings
6 אך פדה תפדה את בכור האדם	you shall redeem, 7 and the firstborn of unclean animals you shall redeem (vv. 12–5).
7 ואת בכור־הבהמה הטמאה תפדה	

The asyndetic clause with the additional feature of extraposition 12–5 (1)—the object suffix in נתתים refers to the string of phrases before לך constituting the extraposed element—sets the beginning of the series of commands concerning items offered as the first fruits from Israel's produce; the previous clauses deal with portions from all classes of animal and grain sacrifices. Asyndetic clauses without extraposition carry on with statements under the same topic of first fruit offerings (12–5 [2–6]). The clause 12–5 (7) is conjunctive for the sake of binding a second statement of a close relationship to the previous clause, 12–5 (6): both clauses deal with exceptional cases where the offerring is to be redeemed.

Num 18:21–3

The prescriptions in Num 18:21–3 are part of a speech whereby God declares the inheritance of Aaron and his sons, and the Levites. The portion under examination consists largely of clauses linked by conjunction.

1 וְלִבְנֵי לֵוִי הִנֵּה נָתַתִּי כָּל־מַעֲשֵׂר בְּיִשְׂרָאֵל לְנַחֲלָה חֵלֶף עֲבֹדָתָם אֲשֶׁר־הֵם אֶת־עֲבֹדַת אֹהֶל מוֹעֵד 2 וְלֹא־יִקְרְבוּ עוֹד בְּנֵי יִשְׂרָאֵל אֶל־אֹהֶל מוֹעֵד לָשֵׂאת חֵטְא לָמוּת 3 וְעָבַד הַלֵּוִי הוּא אֶת־עֲבֹדַת אֹהֶל מוֹעֵד 4 וְהֵם יִשְׂאוּ עֲוֹנָם 5 חֻקַּת עוֹלָם לְדֹרֹתֵיכֶם	1 To the Levites I have given every tithe in Israel for a possession in return for the service that they perform, the service in the tent of meeting. 2 From now on the Israelites shall no longer approach the tent of meeting, or else they will incur guilt and die. 3 But the Levites shall perform the service of the tent of meeting, 4 and they shall bear responsibility for their own offenses; 5 it shall be a perpetual statute throughout your generations (vv. 21–3).

The sequence of conjunctive clauses (21–3 [1–2]) is broken by the consecutive perfect clause 21–3 (3); the higher degree of syntactical continuity unites 21–3 (2, 3) as a series of clauses concerned with the act of offering sacrifices before the tent of meeting. The series of commands linked by conjunction carries on with 21–3 (4). Despite the translation of the NRSV, 21–3 (5) is not a clause, but an independent syntactical entity elevated as a general qualification for the entire series of commands.[41]

Num 18:30b–1

Further on in chapter 18 of Numbers, the text turns to the subject matter of agricultural produce set apart for the consumption of the Levites.

1 בהרימכם את־חלבו ממנו	1 When you have set apart the
2 ונחשב ללוים כתבואת גרן	best of it, 2 then the rest shall
וכתבואת יקב	be reckoned to the Levites as
3 ואכלתם אתו בכל־מקום	produce of the threshing-floor,
אתם	and as produce of the wine
וביתכם	press. 3 You may eat it in any
4 כי־שכר הוא לכם חלף	place, you and your
עבדתכם	households; 4 for it is payment
באהל מועד	for your service in the tent of
	meeting (vv. 30b–1).

The clauses of Num 18:30b–1 follow the designation of the address Moses is to deliver to the people: ואמרת אלהם (Num 18:30a). As asyndetic or subordinate clauses often do, the independent syntactical constituent 30b–1 (1), performing the same function as that of a temporal clause, stands at the beginning of the body of laws. Consecutive perfect clauses carry on with the series of acts constituting the transfer of goods, and their consumption by the Levites (30b–1 [2–3]). The subordinate verbless clause 30b–1 (4) justifies the transaction as payment for services rendered by the Levites.

---

[41] As in previous cases with similar wording, the absence of determination in חק עולם renders it unlikely that the phrase stands as the subject in a verbless clause (given that the ruling is the legislation only just passed). Of course, determination would not occur should the phrase be interpreted—as is the case in the preceding analysis—as a noun qualifying the preceding body of prescription.

Num 19:10–1a

The clauses of Num 19:11–3 cover the end of the procedure for the production of a cleansing agent, the ashes of a red heifer (10–1a [1–3]), and the beginning of a passage of laws prescribing the use of said substance (10–1a [4–6]).

1 וכבס האסף את־אפר	1 The one who gathers the ashes
הפרה	of the heifer shall wash his
את־בגדיו	clothes 2 and be unclean until
2 וטמא עד־הערב	evening. 3 This shall be a
3 והיתה לבני ישראל לגר	perpetual statute for the
הגר בתוכם	Israelites and for the alien
לחקת עולם	residing among them. 4 Those
4 הנגע במת לכל־נפש אדם	who touch the dead body of any
וטמא שבעת ימים	human being shall be unclean for
5 הוא יתחטא־בו ביום	seven days. 5 They shall purify
השלישי	themselves with the water on the
וביום השביעי	third day and on the seventh day,
6 יטהר	6 and so be clean (vv. 10–1a).

Consecutive perfect clauses carry the end of the procedure for de-contamination after collecting the cleansing agent (10–1a [1–3]). The consecutive clause with extraposed subject standing before the clause 10–1a (4) breaks the series of consecutive clauses, initiating a series of prescriptions dealing with the various cases where the cleansing agent is required. The new series of laws remains a loose syntactical formation with asyndetic clauses (10–1a [5, 6]) carrying on from the initial break from the series of consecutive clauses. The intercession of extraposition at the point of topical transition in the text demonstrates the syntactical disjuncture of the syntactical feature; its absence would leave a consecutive clause standing at this important transition.

Num 28:3aβ–8

The series of commands in Num 28: 3aβ–8 stipulate the daily offerings the community are to present to God.

1 זה האשה אשר תקריבו	1 This is the offering by fire that
ליהוה	you shall offer to the Lord: 2 two
2 כבשים בני־שנה תממים	male lambs a year old without

שנים ליום
עלה תמיד
3 את־הכבש אחד תעשה
בבקר
4 ואת הכבש השני תעשה
בין הערבים
5 ועשירית האיפה סלת
למנחה
בלולה בשמן כתית רביעת
ההין
עלת תמיד העשיה בהר סיני
לריח ניחח אשה ליהוה
ונסכו רביעת
ההין לכבש האחד
6 בקדש הסך נסך שכר
ליהוה
7 ואת הכבש השני תעשה
בין הערבים
8 כמנחת הבקר וכנסכו
תעשה
אשה ריח ניחח ליהוה

blemish, daily, as a regular offering. 3 One lamb you shall offer in the morning, 4 and the other lamb you shall offer at twilight; 5 also one-tenth of an ephah of choice flour for a grain-offering, mixed with one-fourth of a hin of beaten oil. It is a regular burnt-offering, ordained at Mount Sinai for a pleasing odour, an offering by fire to the Lord. Its drink-offering shall be one-fourth of a hin for each lamb; 6 in the sanctuary you shall pour out a drink-offering of strong drink for the Lord. 7 The other lamb you shall offer at twilight 8 with a grain-offering and a drink-offering like the one in the morning;[42] you shall offer it as a pleasing odour to the Lord (vv. 3aβ–8).

The asyndetic verbless clause 3aβ–8 (1) initiates the series of commands. The series of phrases 3aβ–8 (2) are an independent syntactical constituent specifying the exact offerings referred to in 3aβ–8 (1); the elevation in the degree of syntactical discontinuity signals the shift to epexegesis. Proceeding with the passage of commands, the asyndetic clause 3aβ–8 (3) offers instruction as to the designated time for the sacrifice of the first lamb. Conjunction in 3aβ–8 (4) binds the designated time for the sacrifice of the second lamb close to the instruction regarding the first lamb (3aβ–

---

[42] The NRSV, by its punctuation, understands כמנחת הבקר וכנסכו to be part of the clause stipulating the requirement for a second offering of a lamb at twilight (3aβ–8 [7]). However, the placement of a major disjunctive accent (*atnach*) on הערבים at the conclusion of 3aβ–8 (7) renders the division between clauses pursued here as the preferable option in accordance with MT.

8 [3]). The commands closer in subject matter—both statements have to do with the sacrifice of a lamb—are held together by a higher degree of syntactical continuity (conjunction). The series of phrases in 3aβ–8 (5) are independent of a clause; the independent syntactical constituent specifies the grain-offering and drink-offering as gifts to accompany the sacrifice of the animals (more specification with regard to 3aβ–8 [1] in the manner of 3aβ–8 [2]). The series of clauses beginning with the asyndetic clause 3aβ–8 (6) are bound together by conjunction in 3aβ–8 (7). The impetus for the higher degree of syntactical continuity between these last two clauses (3aβ–8 [6, 7]) is the combination of two precise acts of sacrificial offering (the offering of a sacrifice of meat with its accompanying offering of drink) that are viewed as a complementary pair. The combination of these acts as two movements of close relation is appropriate following the prominent statement of 3aβ–8 (5), which declares with specific detail the items to supplement the sacrifice of the lambs. The exhortation that all the components of the sacrifice at twilight be a pleasing offering to God is a return to the medial degree of syntactical continuity in the passage (asyndeton), from which the conjunctive clauses and the independent syntactical constituents are departures in opposing degrees of syntactical fluidity. The conjunctive clauses bind prescriptions of a closer relationship in subject matter, and independent syntactical constituents interrupt the series of clauses in order to provide specific details concerning items referred to in the prescriptive clauses. The hierarchy of continuity/discontinuity inherent to the system of inter-clausal syntax and its functional significance in legal prescriptions is evident.

Num 30:3–16

Chapter 30 of Numbers introduces legislation defining situations where pledges remain valid, and those in which the responsibility of the one taking the vow may be set aside.

1 אִישׁ כִּי־יִדֹּר נֶדֶר לַיהוָה	1 When a man makes a vow to the
אוֹ־הִשָּׁבַע	Lord, or swears an oath to bind
שְׁבֻעָה לֶאְסֹר אִסָּר	himself by a pledge, 2 he shall not
עַל־נַפְשׁוֹ	break his word; 3 he shall do
2 לֹא יַחֵל דְּבָרוֹ	according to all that proceeds out

3 בכל־היצא מפיו יעשה
4 ואשה כי־תדר נדר
ליהוה
5 ואסרה אסר בבית אביה
בנעריה
6 ושמע אביה את־נדרה
ואסרה
אשר אסרה על־נפשה
7 והחריש לה אביה

of his mouth. 4 When a woman makes a vow to the Lord, 5 or binds herself by a pledge, while within her father's house in her youth, 6 and her father hears of her vow or her pledge by which she has bound herself, 7 and says nothing to her;

8 אם־הניא אביה אתה
ביום שמעו
9 כל־נדריה ואסריה
אשר־אסרה
על־נפשה לא יקום

8 But if her father expresses disapproval to her at the time that he hears of it, 9 no vow of hers, and no pledge by which she has bound herself, shall stand;

10 ואם־היו תהיה לאיש
11 ונדריה עליה או מבטא
שפתיה
אשר אסרה על־נפשה
12 ושמע אישה ביום שמעו
13 והחריש לה

10 If she marries, 11 while obligated by her vows or any thoughtless utterance of her lips by which she has bound herself, 12 and her husband hears of it 13 and says nothing to her at the time that he hears,

14 ואם ביום שמע אישה אתה
יניא אותה
15 והפר את־נדרה אשר
עליה ואת
מבטא שפתיה אשר אסרה
על־נפשה
16 ויהוה יסלח־לה

14 But if, at the time that her husband hears of it, he expresses disapproval to her, 15 then he shall nullify the vow by which she was obligated, or the thoughtless utterance of her lips, by which she bound herself; 16 and the Lord shall forgive her (vv. 3–9)

The initial series of commands prescribing the keeping of a vow made by a man is introduced by the subordinate clause 3–9 (1); the subject (איש) of the clause is extraposed. This first section is a loose formation of commands proceeding with asyndetic clauses (3–9 [2–3]). Extraposition (ואשה) also accompanies the subordinate clause introducing the case of a woman making a vow while still a part of her father's household (3–9 [4]). In that case, of which 3–9 (4–7) are a part, consecutive perfect clauses (3–9 [5–7]) proceed from the initial subordinate clause initiating the series of commands on a distinct subject. The syntactical continuity in 3–9 (4–7) expresses the unity of these clauses. Proceeding beyond 3–9 (1–7), it becomes evident, with regard to the entire passage of laws, that subordinate clauses with the additional feature of extraposition stand to mark the major topical divisions within the text. The clauses 3–9 (1, 4) stand at the head of sections on vows taken by men and women. On the other hand, subordinate clauses without extraposition (3–9 [8, 10, 14]) introduce variant circumstances within the larger section concerning vows performed by women (beginning with 3–9 [4]]). The passage of Num 30:3–9 is one more example of extraposition within clauses of the same type (subordinate) working to establish the major divisions within a syntactical structure of disjuncture marking the topical boundaries within a passage of laws.[43]

THE SYNTACTICAL FEATURES
OF CONTINUITY AND DISCONTINUITY

The degree to which a clause poses continuity or disruption to a sequence of clauses is dependent upon the element of contrast within a given series of clauses. Asyndetic clauses in succession, for example, constitute a singular mode of syntactical transition from clause to clause. While the rhythmic cadence of a disjointed series of utterances is perceivable, no variation in the relationship between the clauses exists to require explanation from syntactical

---

[43] The number of sub-sections within the section concerning vows made by women goes on within the chapter. Subordinate clauses (without extraposition) introduced by אִם envision the case of a woman making a vow while within the household of her husband leading to the husband's approval (Num 30:11a), and also the case where he disapproves (Num 30:13aα). The same type of clause (Num 30:15aα, 16a) introduces two more sub-sections. The clauses of Num 30:15aα–5b repeat the statement that silence on the part of the husband concerning a vow uttered by his wife in his house is consent; verse 16a begins the prescription that the nullification of the wife's oath after a period following the oath bears penalty for the husband.

categories of structure pertaining to the communicative context of the clauses. It is within a text containing contrasting degrees of syntactical continuity that syntactical disjuncture is accentuated, and perceived as a departure from a series of clauses espousing a higher degree of syntactical continuity. It is the element of change that invites scrutiny of the content within clauses in seeking explanation for the transition in form. Within the hierarchy defining the degree of syntactical continuity or discontinuity inherent to each formal feature, each type of clause and feature of inter-clausal syntax displays its purpose.

While variation in form alerts readers to the elements of syntactical continuity and discontinuity in the text, the determination of the significance of such contours in the text must consider also the content of the clauses. This attention to the semantic component in the text is evident in the analysis where the outline of transitions in the communicative context—the attempt to describe the functions for syntactical discontinuity and continuity in the text—coincides with an evaluation of the meaning borne by each clause. Even as syntax maintains the independence of its system of marking discontinuities, the organization of the text into categories reflecting, among other transitions, shifts to epexegesis or a catalogue of actions closely related is an organization with significance for the meaning of the text as a whole, the relationship of one body of information with another. Perhaps, the clearest examples of the interaction between the pragmatic component in syntax and semantics are the cases where the determination as to whether syntactical discontinuity marks a topical boundary or prominence for a single clause must reckon with the content of all clauses involved.

The scrutiny of all clauses of legal prescription in Leviticus and Numbers has produced abundant testimony for the prevalence of the semantic-pragmatic categories prescribed for the account of Biblical Hebrew syntax in reading the legal prescriptions in the selected texts of the second and third chapters of this work. The following paragraphs are a taxonomic summary for the survey of the clauses of legal prescription in Leviticus and Numbers, relating the syntactical properties identified to their functions.

Asyndetic Clauses

Asyndetic clauses present a high degree of syntactical disjuncture in texts. This element of syntactical discontinuity is perceived wherever asyndetic clauses punctuate texts consisting largely of clauses displaying a higher degree of syntactical continuity (conjunctive and consecutive clauses). From the examples presented from Leviticus and Numbers, it may be seen that asyndetic clauses stand at the beginning of series of commands on distinct topics. The transition to asyndeton from a clause-type displaying a higher degree of syntactical continuity (a conjunctive or consecutive clause) marks the initiation of the new topic. The topical boundary enacted by the asyndetic clause is visible equally in the higher level of syntactical continuity of the clauses following the asyndetic clause.

Within series of clauses on a distinct topic, asyndetic clauses preceding or disrupting a chain of consecutive clauses specify and clarify elements participating in the procedural progression carried by the consecutive clauses. Clarity emerges with focus upon specific components inherent to or related with the prescribed procedure. In relation to conjunctive clauses and with regard to the function of specification, asyndetic clauses often mark transitions to more concrete statements of prescription. The opposite transition to a statement of greater generality is usually the case where asyndeton—amongst consecutive and conjunctive clauses—raises the visibility of statements expressing principles, foundational concepts or other significant general qualifications affecting a group of prescriptions. All the aforementioned functions of asyndetic clauses in relation to clauses of a greater degree of syntactical continuity may be broadly classified as being epexegetical; these clauses of prominence expand or comment on a single clause or group of clauses in their vicinity.

Elsewhere within sets of commands on a single topic, asyndetic clauses stand out in order to draw attention to themselves for the sake of contrast (sometimes in the form of negation following a positive prescription). Occasionally, the severity of a judgement (e.g. מות יומת) or the mere desire to distinguish an apodosis from the preceding protasis motivates the syntactical disruption of asyndeton. Other features of grammar related to the expression of emphasis—the occurrence of הנה or the infinitive absolute for example—often accompany such uses of the asyndetic clause.

Subordinate Clauses

Abundant are the examples of subordinate clauses standing at the beginning of sets of commands introducing the conditions (often the topic as well) under which the prescriptions apply.

Within sets of commands on a given subject, subordinate clauses disrupt clauses of greater syntactical continuity in order to motivate adherence to laws through statements of explanation or purpose. The identity of such statements with those portrayed elsewhere within the same series of commands by asyndetic clauses (e.g. אֲנִי יְהוָה אֱלֹהֵיכֶם) testifies to a corresponding degree of syntactical prominence for subordinate clauses. In the case of the statement אֲנִי יְהוָה אֱלֹהֵיכֶם, it emerges with clarity that the divine identity as a foundational precept for a collection of laws may easily be expressed as motivation and explanation for the promulgation of those laws.

Conjunctive Clauses

Several functions of asyndetic clauses in relation to those of greater syntactical fluidity are seen also to operate within the relationship between conjunctive clauses and consecutive clauses. Conjunctive clauses stand apart from consecutive clauses in order to provide additional information on objects, animals, or persons participating within prescribed procedures carried by consecutive clauses: the function of epexegesis for the sake of clarification and specification. Also attested are cases where contrast (including transition to a statement of negation) merits the change to a conjunctive clause from a series of consecutive clauses. The procedure is brought to a standstill in order to observe a different perspective on one component in the chain of events; the element of antithesis rises to prominence with the additional measure of syntactical disjuncture. A unique function of the conjunctive clause amidst consecutive clauses is the portrayal of events closely related to, or displaying a different aspect of, one existing in a sequence of consecutive clauses. In such cases, conjunctive clauses bring a halt to the series of events in a procedure in order to append one or more events of a similar type to a single component within the procedure. A related aspect of this function is the occurrence of alternative circumstances (introduced by אוֹ) among a series of consecutive clauses within a passage of prescription: the alternatives are set apart as members of a catalogue in relation to one clause in the series of clauses in a procedure.

In relation to other clauses displaying a greater degree of syntactical disjuncture (usually asyndetic clauses), conjunctive clauses, following upon such clauses standing at the beginning of a set of commands, link the prescriptions to form a topical unit distinct from surrounding material. Where such a group of commands on a single topic form a loose sequence of asyndetic clauses, conjunction works to band together those members of closer relation to form sub-groupings within the larger formation. Clauses of prescription bearing resemblance in subject matter emerge with distinction as a group with the added measure of syntactical continuity binding the clauses together. Similarly, consecutive clauses bring together statements of greater affinity within a group of clauses of greater syntactical discontinuity (asyndetic and conjunctive clauses) in an auxiliary role in relation to the consecutive clauses of a procedure.

Consecutive Clauses

Consecutive clauses display the highest degree of syntactical continuity. These clauses often bind the components of a sequence of events (usually in temporal and logical succession) forming a meaningful series: the elements of a process with a beginning and a conclusion. Within the laws of Leviticus and Numbers, such a series is often a procedure with an identifiable purpose at its conclusion. The consecutive clause represents one extreme in a continuum from which a series of increments in syntactical disjuncture provides a system of breaks within the text. The number of significant changes in the communicative stance at such junctures testifies to the elements of continuity and discontinuity inherent to the system of syntax in the legal prescriptions of Leviticus and Numbers.

Clauses with an Extraposed Constituent
Preceding the Clause

The deployment of extraposition is the representation of a degree of syntactical disjuncture similar to that of asyndetic and subordinate clauses. The functions associated with the use of extraposition approximate those of clauses displaying a higher degree of syntactical disjuncture, especially those of asyndetic clauses. Clauses displaying an extraposed constituent preceding the clause often stand at the head of a series of clauses on a distinct topic. Extraposition marks the commencement of a new topic by disrupting a series of clauses (or a single clause) displaying a greater degree of syntactical continuity (consecutive and conjunctive clauses); the boundary enacted by the deployment of extraposition may be felt equally in cases where it is followed by clauses displaying a higher degree of syntactical continuity. Within a passage of laws where a single type of clause exists (asyndetic, subordinate, conjunctive, or consecutive clauses), the additional feature of an extraposed constituent prior to the clause could express the elevated degree of syntactical disjuncture required for the demarcation of a topical boundary in the text.

The distinction of extraposition among clauses of the same type also functions to distinguish the beginnings of main sections of law from those of sub-sections. This distinction is visible from examples where subordinate clauses with extraposition stand at the initiation of a prescriptive procedure, whereas subordinate clauses without extraposition introduce cases with slight variations from the circumstances of the initial (main) case.

Within sections of law exhibiting a degree of unity in topic, clauses deploying an extraposed constituent prior to the commencement of the clause draw attention to themselves by standing apart from clauses with a higher degree of syntactical continuity. Clauses with extraposition are prominent amidst consecutive clauses and conjunctive clauses. Where clauses of the same type (consecutive, conjunctive, subordinate, or asyndetic clauses) permeate the unit of text, the additional feature of an extraposed member may express an additional measure of syntactical disjuncture. The dominant functions associated with extraposition in such cases are specification and clarification for a proximate clause or group of clauses. The shift to a higher degree of syntactical discontinuity in such cases raises to prominence a clause offering clarity by focus upon a concise aspect of proximate legislation, or providing concrete examples, usually, for a preceding statement. Such uses for extraposition may be classified within the category of epexegesis. A less common function for the use of extraposition is to provide prominence for a clause standing in opposition to another clause. The measure of increase in the level of visibility for the clause provided by the feature of extraposition heightens a reader's awareness of the element of contrast in prescriptive texts.

Independent Syntactical Constituents

By virtue of the fact that independent syntactical constituents stand outside the system of inter-clausal syntax, these constructions exact the highest degree of syntactical disjuncture among those surveyed. Independent syntactical constituents represent transition to a greater degree of syntactical discontinuity from any type of clause. The functions associated with the elevation of the degree of syntactical discontinuity with the use of independent syntactical constituents largely overlap with those of asyndetic clauses and extraposition in relation to clauses of a lower degree of syntactical discontinuity. As is the case with asyndetic clauses, subordinate clauses and clauses with extraposition, independent syntactical constituents stand to mark the transition to a new topic within a body of prescription. It is often the case that the independent constituent names the topic for the clauses that follow.

Within groups of prescriptions on a distinct topic, independent syntactical constituents stand to offer specific examples for preceding general statements or to provide auxiliary detail, accompanying events, for a proximate statement of prescription. Clarification and precision are the accomplishments of such independent syntactical constituents through their focus upon specific components within the surrounding prescriptions. A complementary function of the syntactical feature is the promulgation of a qualification encompassing the entire body of prescription (חק־עולם לדרתיכם). These functions are epexegetical in orientation; the independent syntactical constituents rise to prominence in order to comment or expand upon surrounding material through the magnification of specific components within prescriptions, or reference to qualifications governing an entire body of prescription. A rare function of the independent syntactical constituent is its use to sever a series of consecutive clauses bearing a sequence of prescribed actions in order to introduce an action closely associated with the last preceding prescribed act in the sequence of events (see analysis of

Num 4:25–7a). This function of setting a complementary act apart from the sequence of events in a procedure is usually associated with the intrusion of a conjunctive clause within a series of consecutive clauses; the heightened degree of syntactical disjuncture of the independent syntactical constituent works equally well in performing the function.

CHAPTER FIVE
READING AND LIVING:
THE RELEVANCE OF ABSTRACTION

The purpose of this chapter of conclusion is two-fold. Firstly, the intention is to provide a compact summary of the process of abstraction and its functions as these have been described in this study. A second intention for the chapter—by far the major component in terms of the allotment of space—is the modest advancement of the discussion by further exploring the implications of the phenomenon of abstraction (process and function) for the experience of readers, beyond the reading of law in conjunction with narrative. This secondary objective of extending the application of abstraction will encompass also the consideration of human thought beyond the activity of reading. Here, the posture is one of suggestion, rather than that of extensive analysis. This chapter in conclusion will begin with a summary of the process and function of the abstraction of narrative in law. In starting out, it is informative to consider the opinions of Michael Fishbane in his comments on many of the texts examined in this volume. The reason for such a choice of a beginning is the prominence of a subject essential to the operation of abstraction in Fishbane's study: the topical plurality of the laws.

In addressing the intertextual quality of biblical interpretation within the Hebrew Bible, Fishbane speaks of the filling out of lacunae in biblical legislation through consultation, within narrative, with divine opinion in cases beyond circumstances envisioned in previous legislation (Fishbane 1985, 91–7). The result is an interpretation addressing omissions and ambiguities in previous legal pronouncement that may indicate a process of growth in the body of law in the Hebrew Bible. In his analysis of legal texts included in the present work (Lev 24:10–23; Num 9:6–14; 15:32–6;

27:1–11), Fishbane finds clear indication of such a process of legal exegesis within the legal legislation of the Pentateuch. In three of the cases cited (Lev 24:10–23; Num 9:6–14; 27:1–11), he observes a proliferation of legal prescription on matters extending well beyond the circumstances of the legal conundrum born of the events of the narrative (Fishbane 1985, 102–3). For him, these conglomerations of laws on related matters—some more distant than others—show signs of literary and historical development. It appears that an initial act of legal exegesis couched in narrative constitutes the occasion for editorial insertion of laws on different topics of some relation to the situation in the story. Fishbane cites, for example, the legal prescriptions permitting the deferred celebration of the Passover in Num 9:6–14; divine pronouncement on the matter goes beyond the problem of certain victims of defilement on the occasion of the normative celebration, to concern the plight of those on a distant journey and the sojourner (Fishbane 1985, 103). Another example exists in the extension of legislation on the issue of inheritance in order to address the loss of tribal landholdings in the absence of sons to the deceased (Num 27:1–11); the circumstances of the case at hand are, once again, exceeded in order to include cases where more distant candidates for inheritance according to a hierarchy of succession are required (Fishbane 1985, 103–4). Inherent to the process of growth—with reference both to the legal ruling instigated by the events of the narrative and the group of laws of related interest surrounding that ruling—is the activity of a community of scribes seeking direction in the proliferation of circumstantial variation in the interpretation of biblical law. Circumstances arising in the experiences of the community require the consultation of established traditions.[1]

---

[1] A comprehensive survey of the voluminous literature on intertextuality and inner-biblical exegesis in the Hebrew Bible is beyond the scope of this chapter. For a concise treatment of the phenomenon by Fishbane, consult his essay "Inner Biblical Exegesis" (1986). Bernard Levinson's work (1998; 2005; 2008, 57–88) has shed much light on the role of lexical permutations that produce the illusion of correspondence with the pronouncements of older legal texts of prestige in the genesis of newer ones enacting legislation in novel situations. Levinson's historical

However, Fishbane's observation of the accretion of legal prescriptions on different topics within these texts of legal innovation has uncovered a feature of editorial genius, perhaps, just beyond the reach of his observation. This feature of interest regards the rhetorical role of the cluster of commandments on different topics in facilitating the exegetical extension of previous legislation to meet the demands of the novel situation arising in the narrative. It is not simply the case that legal augmentation through narrative and prescription furnishes the occasion for the insertion of other rulings of tenuous relationship to the issue at hand. Successive layers of editorial interpolation pick up upon the original initiative for change, and strengthen its argument by riding the principle and ethos of its innovation. How does this rhetoric for change occur?

THE PROCESS OF ABSTRACTION

The present work began with the affirmation of Iser's postulation of a natural affinity on the part of readers to seek connections between adjacent bodies of texts where no clear connections are offered; proximity is the invitation to comparison. Turning to the collocation of laws on different subject matter, it has been demonstrated in the cases of the present study that the readerly affinity for a connection between the laws, the discernment of a common denominator, finds satisfaction in the editorial selection of the individual laws within the collection. If it is the case that the process of editorial accretion in the formation of such a collection of laws is the proliferation of prescriptions containing the identifiable common denominator, then the composite literary product at the conclusion of the process only underlines the

---

survey of prominent sources on the phenomenon of 'rewriting' within the Hebrew Bible (2008, 95–181) affords a good point of entry into discussion about inner-biblical exegesis, tracing its development. For an overview of variety in intertextual reference with regard to the various agents of such reference (authors, editors, readers), see Kirsten Nielsen's essay "Intertextuality and Hebrew Bible" (2000). Studies in the phenomenon within specific texts and topics abound: among others, Levinson 1998, 53–97; Stackert 2007, 113–208; Schaper 2004, 125–44.

prominence of that common feature. Such common features in the collection of laws are the principles and themes that hold the group together. The isolation of this systematic structure of combination is the accomplishment of abstraction as demonstrated in the reading of narrative and law in Leviticus and Numbers.

Specific clauses within passages of law represent the thematic essence of adjacent narrative sequences by invoking a word, phrase, or clause capable of qualifying the sequence of events in the narrative sequence. Alternatively, individual prescriptions may designate the motifs standing at the poles of the narrative sequence. The thematic clarity achieved in this initial stage in the process of abstraction often receives the complementary measure of a second movement: the juxtaposition of laws on different topics invites the identification of common elements in the laws leading to their collocation. The emergence of a thematic category capable of absorbing each specific law as a sub-set within the category is the accomplishment of this second stage in the process of abstraction. The result is the emergence of a general thematic framework encompassing all the laws and the narrative sequence in the second stage of abstraction. It is not simply the case that each law comes to be perceived as a member of a larger common theme; the thematic import of the narrative sequence, by analogy through proximity, expands to reveal its typological qualities in relation to other narratives. Throughout the process, syntax assists with the compaction of the thematic representation of events in the narrative sequence in diminished units within the laws (from multiple clauses to two clauses, a clause, or a phrase), and in the demarcation of boundaries between groups of commands in order to underscore plurality in topic within the series of laws. The perceived disjuncture within passages of law often are countered by another function of syntax: syntactical disjuncture raises the prominence of clauses bearing the collective theme (a product of the second stage of abstraction) or complementary concepts to the theme standing behind all the laws in the passage. Similarities emerge in the face of plurality. These are the nuts and bolts of the procedure of abstraction.

The process of abstraction produces categories of theme capable of assimilating the series of events in a narrative sequence. Where such agreement in theme occurs within the laws and between narrative and law, the function of abstraction is to draw attention to specific themes in the narrative in order to underline those semantic structures that characterize the narrative (the cases designated 'simple'). In contrast, there are cases where no such agreement occurs (the cases designated 'complicated'). Contradiction or the semblance of contradiction in theme occurs between groups of laws adjacent to the narrative. Alternatively, the theme in a group of laws may stand in direct contrast to the thematic essence endemic to one possible interpretation of the narrative. In either scenario—contending formulations of theme in different groups of laws vying to influence the reading of the adjacent narrative, or contentions in theme between laws raising one plausible interpretation against another suggested within the narrative—the contradiction underlines alternative interpretations for a stretch of narrative. The contradictory interpretations may be assigned to differences between readerly projections in the course of the narrative and perspectives that come to light at the time readers reach, or move just beyond, the conclusion. A reader may be led to adopt one of the interpretations, or be left suspended without resolution in favour of one of the alternatives. Either way, the result is a degree of introspection as readers ponder the interpretive choices they make between the commencement and the conclusion of a stretch of narrative. These insights, the mechanics of abstraction and the functions of their application, constitute the heart of the argument for the dissertation.

ABSTRACTION AND RHETORIC

With the mechanics and functions of abstraction in mind, the stage is set for a thorough comprehension of editorial strategy behind the inclusion of legislation on issues beyond the measure of legal augmentation required by the situation in the narrative. The description of the process of abstraction lays bare the elements of the hermeneutical enterprise which is the process of redaction. Specifically the description supplies an answer to the question: What does the multiplication of legislation on different topics in the laws of Lev 24:10–23, Num 9:6–14 and 27:1–11 have to do with the acts of legal exegesis that these texts represent? From the preceding summary of the process of abstraction, it may be surmised that even as abstraction through law extracts the theme of narrative from a protracted series of events in chronological succession, the juxtaposition of laws on different topics forces attention to the common denominator within the passage of laws. The definitive theme of the legal passage and the narrative enlarges through the identification of the common denominator between the laws. Complementary concepts to the themes capable of application beyond the individual prescription and the specific circumstances of the narrative emerge also through the juxtaposition of the laws on different subject matter.

The prominence afforded over-arching themes and general concepts for narrative and law effects a subtle shift in the understanding of Lev 24:10–23: the narrative is not just a tale of crime and punishment, but one with a marked emphasis on judicial equity (measure for measure). The prescription of death for the abuse of the divine name finds membership in a series of prescribed retributions in keeping with the gravity of the crime. Similarly, the call for the enactment of a second Passover celebration for those defiled from contact with a corpse (Num 9:6–14) is shown to be an act of solidarity in concert with prescriptive measures allowing for the inclusion of those on a journey and the resident alien. By enacting legislation to supply an heir in a succession of situations where a different candidate for inheritance of varying distance from the deceased by relation is postulated, the agnatic principle seeking the closest member to the departed landholder comes to the forefront in Num 27:1–11. The ruling in favour of Zelophehad's daughters becomes an allotment of inheritance of familial resemblance to others displaying favour for the closest relative to the deceased according to an established hierarchy. The ruling is shown to be in line with the normative situation where the eldest son of the deceased inherits.

It may be seen in these cases that the expansion of the topical parameters in the narrative supports the expansion of the legal tradition to accommodate the novel circumstance. From this perspective, the cluster of legal prescriptions around the specific ruling addressing directly the situation in the narrative is not so much an act of topical deviation, as it is a tool for the integration of the novel ruling arising from the circumstances of the narrative. Through the contribution of the process of abstraction, the legal proclamation in response to the outstanding problem in the narrative acquires an air of legitimacy through the demonstration of its consistency in principle with the prescriptions on other matters within the group. By association with such principles, the rulings arising from the narrative profess their affinity with elements within the larger legal context of pentateuchal law.[2] Far from being legal excursions of dubious authenticity, the legal pronouncements arising from such crises expressed in narrative are portrayed as adhering to the tenor of the greater body of laws.[3] The function of abstraction is essential to the nature of the rhetoric in these combinations of narrative and law.

RHETORIC AND READING

In speaking of the rhetorical application of abstraction, the effect upon the reader in proceeding through a portion of narrative and law has come to attention. The discussion thus far has focused on the ability of laws adjacent to a portion of narrative to point to themes straddling the sequence of events, and complementary

---

[2] For Fishbane, the ability to identify the foundational patterns in older texts lies at the heart of the process of growth in the biblical corpus (1986, 34–6). The authority of the editorial expansion rests on its ability to perceive the message of an older passage, and to appropriate the essence of its content in addressing a novel situation. This strategy, according to Fishbane, is the movement between "tradition and the individual talent." Through the principle of talion in Lev 24:10–23, the pronouncement of death for the blasphemer (the contribution of P) is shown to be in accord with older legal traditions and narratives. Frymer-Kensky speaks of the law of talion as an explicit statement of equity between deed and recompense. However, the postulation of an adequate and appropriate response to a crime is fundamental to all systems of law (Frymer-Kensky, 1980, 230). Thus, the reference to the principle of talion is a reference to a foundational assumption in (older) legal discourse. On the law of talion as an integral feature of plot in biblical narratives, see studies by Bernard S. Jackson (2006, 189–91, 196–9), Philip J. Nel (1994) and T.A. Boogart (1985).

[3] Levinson, however, sees tension in acts of legal drafting that draw upon older laws. While there is a necessity to forge continuity with older legal corpora of prestige, there exists also propensity for finding new paths of legal reasoning in addressing novel circumstances (Levinson 1998, 3–6; 2008, 16). Such acts of legal innovation, therefore, subvert the very texts they cite to proclaim the legitimacy of their undertaking.

concepts within that portion of narrative. One effect of the process of abstraction is its ability to designate the kinship of the laws and the narrative in the given portion of the text to other laws in the Hebrew Bible. While the comprehension of this facet of abstraction cannot be divorced from the process of reading, it is another application of abstraction that, perhaps, more effectively illustrates the role of the reader as recipient of editorial and authorial rhetoric. The reference is to the contention between thematic formulations made prior to the conclusion of the narrative sequence (the quality of enigma essential to the 'hermeneutical code' of Barthes), and those that come into view at the conclusion (the 'proairetic code'). This element of contention is a feature of interpretation emerging from the analysis of cases designated to be complicated. The trait of reading that comes into play is the sequential or temporal aspect—the fact that readers move from right to left and down the page in absorbing the content of the Hebrew text—of the reading process.

The emphasis upon the sequential flow which is the process of reading stands against the notion that the meaning in a text resides solely as an object to be apprehended when the whole of the text, read and digested, may be viewed as a monolithic entity. This erroneous proposition ignores the reality of an unfolding consciousness of the referent—the object of the communicative content of the text—that movement through the text evokes. Stanley Fish (1980b, 83) regards this oversight as the misguided transformation of "a temporal experience into a spatial one," the apprehension of the text as "a whole (sentence, page, work) which the reader knows (if at all) only bit by bit, moment by moment." In actuality, as Fish quite correctly observes, the experience of the reader is a process, and the account of that process must reflect the reader's thoughts at significant points in progress (Fish 1980b, 73–4). Where narrative is concerned, ample regard must be accorded the readerly response to probabilities incited by elements through the course of events and their subsequent confirmation or negation in following events. In this respect, reading narrative is a diachronic procedure; the reader's progress through the text, by and large, follows the chronological sequence of events within the story. What matters in the experience of reading is not just the final outcome allowing for the assignment of a descriptive appellation to the sequence of events (where such final determination is possible), but also every misconception that the reader has along the way.

Such tensions between readerly projection and conclusion in the interpretation of the complicated passages of narrative and law have produced one case where one of the contending interpretations has prevailed, and another case where the meaning of the passage was left indeterminate. In either case, the proposed effect upon the reader was a degree of introspection regarding the reader's level of understanding with respect to the regulations of the sacrificial cult (Lev 10:1–20) and the boundary between innocence and inadvertent error (Num 15:1–41). But to speak of introspection on the part of the reader is to designate a connection between the rhetoric of the text and the process of reading, and the experience of the reader beyond the contemplation of events and propositions within the text. While the reader brings information gained from the experience of living in the world (knowledge of human structures of motivation, the laws of physics, etc.) to bear upon the act of reading, the element of introspection forged in the process of reading begs readers to bring the experience from reading back into their journey in the world. Nothing short of an exchange between worlds—that of the story and that of the reader's existence in the world—is the operative intention behind the generation of introspection. How (if at all) does the experience of reading narrative and law facilitate such a connection?

READING AND LIVING

In an essay exploring the relevance of narrative to human experience, Stephen Crites describes consciousness as the fulcrum between story and reality (Crites 1989, 72). The comment is predicated upon the observation that the life of the reader holds the quality of chronological succession in common with narrative: human experience may be seen as a succession of events through time. The memory of the past exists as a chronicle of events linked through time. While it remains possible to offer varying, even contradictory, interpretations of those events, the series of images constituting the chronicle may not be replaced or removed; any oral account of those events, perhaps as part of a conversation between friends, must offer a description or summary of the series of images if the account understands itself to be an honest representation of those events (Crites 1989, 72–6). As the subject turns to contemplate the future, the forecast of events based on current circumstances and the traits of the personalities involved, hopes and aspirations come to dominate the imagination of the subject in anticipation. Such acts of contemplation entail the postulation of sequences of events, narratives of prediction or aspiration, as the individual speculates about the future in conversation with another. Implicit to the realm of anticipation, of course, is the strong possibility of a significant departure in the nature of the events of the future from projections in the present.

The present is, as Crites remarks, the point of decision between the immutable past and the future of numerous possibilities (1989, 78–9). Within the moment of the present, individuals may take stock of events in their past and choose a course of action for the future. In doing so, the narrative sequences of the past may be combined with those of the unfolding future to produce a new and extended narrative sequence. An old story is taken up in the new: narratives of defeat become lessons leading to success, even as stories of malcontent become catalysts for a quest leading to self-discovery. The categories of interpretation and imagination involved in human experience are, after all, similar to the thematic formulation for narrative sequences in the act of reading; readers participate in conjecture within the course of a narrative sequence, and they offer interpretations at the conclusion of the narrative sequence. Even within the course of the narrative sequence, readerly acts of anticipation involve the postulation of motifs—recognizable groups of events within the longer series of events which is the narrative sequence—further on in the narrative sequence based upon motifs already encountered.[4] The location of the reader within the chronological sequence of events in narrative mimics that of the individual in the sequence of events in human experience; thus, the interpretation of narrative is inseparable from the quality of consciousness integral to human existence.

Continuities between the act of reading and human experience are not confined to the common location of the reader's perspective within the sequence of events in narrative and the

---

[4] Of course, the role of the individual in determining the outcome of the future is absent in the role of the reader of narrative.

world of human habitation. In fact, the primary operation of naming narrative sequences and their component parts (the component motifs essential to the descriptive word, phrase, or clause applied to the narrative sequence), whether in foresight or hindsight, involves the interface between human experience and written text. The nominations for sequences of events (both the descriptive statements for narrative sequences and their motifs) are, for Barthes, not arbitrary acts of readerly postulation. They are, on the contrary view, the characterization of states and actions in accordance with patterns of behaviour known from the arena of human experience (Barthes 1974, 19; 1988, 140–2). For example, the combination of the events of proposing, accepting, and honouring an agreement under the term 'appointment' finds its reflex in the practical norms of human society. It is the sum of information culled from events already witnessed, conversations (over)heard and books read that render the sequences of events in narrative recognizable to readers. Narrative texts, according to Barthes, abet the spontaneity of readers in subsuming series of actions under generic terms that distinguish one series of actions apart from another series. Narrative, like language, partakes of the process of signification; the reader's search for the generic term of description adheres to the guidelines of a code already in existence. In light of this fact, the observation by Barthes that readers bring a plurality of texts—including sets of actions intrinsic to collective human experience in social intercourse—to bear upon the reading of narrative is an accurate assessment of the act of reading (Barthes 1974, 10–1).[5]

---

[5] The degree to which the elements of the narrative correspond to elements within the repertoire of collective human experience has been called the degree of verisimilitude (*vraisemblance*) in the text. Culler states that the identification of the socio-literary conventions at work go a long way in determining the modes through which expressions of reality in the text intersect with the world of the reader; Culler identifies five levels of verisimilitude in works of literature (1975, 140–60). The first level— perhaps the one most pertinent to the analysis undertaken in the present work—covers constructions of action and character in the text directly derivative of those in the world of the reader. The second and third levels

In keeping with the observations of Barthes, Wilder writes of the innate affinity of the human mind for seeking out the beginning and the end to sequences of events and the movement between the poles, the elements of a story (Wilder 1991, 134–5). This probing for the definitive boundaries of a story—an essential element in the naming of a series of events—is born of a natural interest for seeking the contingent reflex down the line for specific components within chains of events. Readers are interested to know of the way problematic situations at the beginning of a story work themselves out at the end; states and actions within any given sequence of events incite yearning for a measure of closure. One of the reasons for this interest in the flow of narrative from the point of the incitement of expectation to closure is the reader's recognition of a lifelike quality in the cinematic progression of thought and deed, the marriage of consequence and strict temporal succession. This recognition forms the impulse for historiography: the orientation of a community in time through the establishment of foundational precedents with a view for direction in the future (Wilder 1991, 141). The past, in a sense, determines the future and all aspirations for the future must address the past. There is little doubt, according to Wilder, that the ability of narrative and story-telling to arouse recognition for the correspondence between art and life goes to the heart of the popular appeal of narrative texts.

It is not an overstatement to say that the conjunction of events in the formation of distinct sequences in the process of reading narrative is a constant feature of human consciousness. In quoting Julian Jaynes, Herbert Schneidau affirms that the human

---

respectively pertain to cultural stereotypes and patterns arising from specific literary genres; indices to types of character and coherent sequences of events may be perceived only with reference to the codes and norms of the relevant cultural group and genre. The third level of verisimilitude is assumed by the fourth and fifth levels. The fourth level acknowledges explicitly the conventions of a literary genre as it raises the possibility of deviation from those conventions. The fifth level of verisimilitude—the instrument of parody and literary irony—exposes the inadequacies of the genre, invoking the coded indices to character and plot as it orchestrates their subversion.

perception, in understanding its surroundings, is incessant in its quest to link individual states and actions to form chains of events subject to the dictates of the norms of cause and effect (Schneidau 1986, 134). This quest for a causal connection—an essential operation in the combination of linking motifs in the formation of narrative sequences—extends to encompass the smallest elements: the act of entering a room, the grasping of an outstretched hand, diving into a swimming pool. Through the consistent evaluation of the probable forces of motive in the various agents, every deed is brought to fit with another in the unfolding drama before the observing eye.[6] No element of action, as Schneidau notes, is left out in the interpretive scheme engaged in the on-going process of constructing a story from the mass of activity before an observer.

From the brief survey of opinions set forth by Crites, Barthes, Wilder, and Schneidau, it has become evident that the operations of reading narrative texts—such operations as those described in the function of abstraction in the confluence of narrative and law in the Hebrew Bible—find close correspondence in human experience. The operations of linking events through the perception of a causal nexus, naming those chains of events and seeking the location within the sequence from which a name is formulated are relevant also to the interpretation of events in the experience of life. With the degree of correspondence between reading and living, one might seek out within texts the indices, explicit and implicit, of such a relationship and their function.

---

[6] The basis for the stability of the nexus between cause and effect is the establishment of patterns of human response, in accordance with known modes of human motivation. When the perception of incongruence with established modes of motivation occurs, judgement is suspended until further events supply a coherent context for the reestablishment of the connection. Where such reinstatement is not forthcoming, the actions are deemed erratic. Such perceived deviations from established patterns of human behaviour betray the regulating presence of the norm.

READING, LIVING, AND ABSTRACTION

The close association between narrative and the experience of readers as they make their way through life has been exploited at numerous points in biblical narrative. Readers are enticed to adopt the stance of an audience as stories are told to multitudes gathering at the feet of prominent characters within biblical narrative. At such points in the unfolding narrative, according to Wilder, the storyteller bridges the distance between story and audience (both listeners within the narrative and readers) with invitations to evaluate the claims of truth within the stories, and to adapt those claims to the circumstances confronting the audience (Wilder 1991, 136–7). While such stories are really embedded narratives related by characters to other characters within biblical narrative, the narrator's passive or overt approval of the opinions of such storytellers and the often wide and indefinite nature of the intended audience conspire to allow readers to identify easily with the group of listeners. Wilder has in mind recitals of the gospel story by the apostles in Acts and the various parables of Jesus in the Gospels. In telling such stories, the storyteller's vocative exhortations for listeners to be attentive to the details of the story often invoke a connection between the story and the lives of the individuals listening to the story; an implicit (or even explicit) invitation to compare the events of the story and its claims to truth to those in the lives of the audience occurs.[7] The operative assumption on the part of the storyteller is, of course, that recognizable elements of reality exist within the framework of the story.

Wilder does not proceed to offer a specific example to demonstrate his proposition. However, a glance at the parable of the good Samaritan in Luke 10:30–7 would be helpful as an illustration. In response to the inquiry of a certain student of religious law (νομισκός τις), Jesus relates the story of a Samaritan

---

[7] Such exhortations to the audience, in the view of Wilder, are part and parcel of the formal devices for establishing the setting for the narration of a story (1991, 136). Such elements of performance lend a "heightened tenor" to the teachings of Jesus, invoking the attention and imagination of the audience.

who seeks to relieve the wounds of one beaten by robbers while on a journey (Luke 10:30–6). In the following exchange between Jesus and his interlocutor which clarifies the definition of a 'neighbour' (πλησίον) in Luke 10:36–7, the preceding narrative is characterized as an act of being a neighbour to the victim of robbers (Luke 10:36), and one of compassion (Ὁ ποιήσας τὸ ἔλεος). Familiar epithets capable of standing in summary for the story—'being a neighbour' and 'acting with compassion'—are invoked to offer clarification (a neighbour is compassionate, and being compassionate is the mark of a neighbour) for one another, and to characterize the adjacent narrative. Through the anonymity of the interlocutor (one from the multitude), readers are invited to bring their vocabulary to bear upon the consideration of the events in the story. Are the defining statements of nomination for the narrative of the parable appropriate in light of the way things are in the world?

The Hebrew Bible contains numerous examples of similar enticements for readers to evaluate defining statements in speech for stories related by the same character. The blessing of the community at large by Moses in the closing chapters of Deuteronomy includes an abridged rehearsal of the acts of God at Sinai (Deut 33:2–5). This event forms the context for the pronouncements of goodwill by Moses for the various tribes (Deut 33:6–25). In returning to describe the acts of God (Deut 33:26–9), Israel is designated by Moses as 'a people saved by God' (עַם נוֹשַׁע בַּיהוה) in verse 29. The recount of the divine possession of Israel (Deut 33:3) and the granting of divine direction through law (Deut 33:4) stand in collocation within the same speech with the characterization of Israel as the recipient of salvation (Deut 33:29). In light of the descriptive appellation of verse 29, the event at Sinai is seen less as the imposition of divine requirement, and more as an act of guidance and protection. As with the passage from Luke, the anonymity of the addressee—this time through the sheer magnitude of the designated audience—and the absence of contradiction through the voice of the narrator, pulls readers within the orbit of the designated audience. Readers are invited to revisit all cases in their repository of experience where instruction takes the function of protective guidance.

More direct means of initiating the link between nominations for narrative sequences in texts and those occurring in the world

inhabited by readers (statements by the narrator with implications
for the reader as addressee) occur in biblical literature. Such direct
intimations of a link include descriptive statements concerning
narratives issuing from the perspective of the omniscient narrator;
the reader, in this case, is the designated audience without doubt.
One way in which this connection is made is through the
suggestion that readers apply examplary courses of action forged
through the events of narrative within similar circumstances in
their own lives. The narrator's statement of summary in such cases
includes a note of exhortation for readers to act in accordance with
the example of a character. Theologians concerned with such
manoeuvres speak of the realm of possibility in narrative. For Paul
Fiddes, narrative does not only imitate life; narrative texts may also
generate experiences through exhortation. In this sense narrative
contains an element of eschatology; narrative texts envision a world
that might be (Fiddes 2000, 31–2). Fiddes refers to the end of
chapter 20 in the Gospel of John as an example. The events in the
narrative of the chapter (John 20:1–29) move from the discovery of
the empty tomb to the confession of belief in Jesus as the
resurrected Christ by the various companions of Jesus. The
purpose for the account is stated to be that readers may come to
make a similar confession (John 20:31). The insinuated appellation
of 'path to belief' for the preceding narrative (ἵνα πιστεύσητε ὅτι
Ἰησοῦς ἐστιν ὁ Χριστὸς ὁ υἱὸς τοῦ θεοῦ) becomes the designated
course of action for readers to follow. Even as the witness of the
empty tomb goads the disciples of Jesus on to the journey to faith,
the witness of the writer is to inspire a similar act in those who read
the text.

    The degree of exhortation in another passage is reduced
without departing from the practice of alluding to definitive labels
for stretches of narrative. The narrator's commendation for the
actions of Mordecai in the concluding words of Esther (Esth 10:3)
may be perceived in the glowing epithets employed in their
description. While the clauses of Esth 10:3b explain Mordecai's
popularity among the people, their content also is an apt
description for Mordecai's initiatives in a sizable portion of the
book (Esth 4:1–8:17): the elimination of the deadly plot against the
Jewish people. The actions of seeking the good of the people
(דרש טוב לעמו) and intercession (ודבר שלום לכל־זרעו) on

behalf of the oppressed are held up as patterns of behaviour for emulation.[8]

While the element of exhortation may not be applicable to the actions of God in Exodus 14, the narrator's appeal to a reader's standards of behaviour is still evident in the statement of approval applied to divine initiative. The awe-inspiring events of God's rescue of Israel from the Egyptians in Exodus 14 receive summary in the hands of the narrator at the conclusion of the passage (Exod 14:30–1). The statement proclaiming God's act of salvation for Israel on that day (ויושע יהוה ביום ההוא את־ישראל ביד מצרים) in verse 30 receives the further qualification that the act was a 'mighty hand' (היד הגדלה) at work upon Egypt (Exod 14:31). The narrator's statement evokes the reader's familiarity with acts of rescue and redemption, even as it invites the examination of the miraculous features in the exodus from Egypt that would qualify the experience as unsurpassed in grandeur in the estimation of the reader.

At numerous points in narrative, the appeal to a reader's perception of chains of events in life—whether the goal is simple recognition or didactic in scope—come to prominence. At the heart of the transaction between story and the world of the reader is the literary operation which stands as the subject matter of this work: the procedure of abstraction. The reader's ability to recognize sequences of events and their component parts and to

---

[8] John Barton points to similar statements of exhortation through praise for the actions of particular characters at the conclusion to narratives in Jonah and Daniel (2000, 57–8). Barton refrains from elaboration and explanation with reference to specific examples in Daniel. A glance at the concluding statements of the narrative of the final vision in the book produces an example. The plight of the faithful is portrayed with little detail (Dan 11:33–5; 12:1–3) in a narrative largely devoted to the acts of God's opponents. The faithful suffer persecution, and lose many from among their ranks. They are tested sorely by harsh conditions before Michael rises to deliver them. A statement of conclusion to the vision in Dan 12:12 names their story and their character as one of perseverance (המחכה), and lauds their example by the pronouncement that they are a happy lot (אשרי).

acknowledge that those definitions may change through the course
of encountering the series of events, applies both to reading and
living. The reality of the interface between life and art underlies the
dramatic urgency of reading narrative with attention to the
operation of abstraction. To indulge in abstraction is to walk the
narrow path between reading and living through stretches where
no clear boundary may exist between the two entities.

Inseparable from the operation of abstraction in all human
perception is the practice of interpretation. Crites is correct to
recognize that within the ability to abstract the essence of a story
lies the power to explain, to manipulate, and to control (Crites
1989, 85–6). Abstraction, according to Crites, allows for the
dissolution of "the sense of narrative time." The emergent value
for such a dissolution of narrative's temporal aspect is the "non-
narrative and atemporal coherence" that underlies narrative. The
ability to arrive at this value is, according to Crites, the strategy of
abstraction and the basis for the formation of consciousness.[9] The
abstracted value—the thematic formulation for a narrative
sequence—becomes the designated identity for the narrative that,
in turn, determines its ability to function in combination with other
narratives. The ability to explain the meaning of a narrative and to
incorporate it within the structure of a larger unit of narrative is, in
essence, the ability to sway the reader's perception of the narrative.
There is no understanding or explanation apart from the procedure
of abstraction. Every thematic formulation identified in this study
as finding a narrative sequence for its reference is an act of

---

[9] Of course, the definition of the 'abstraction' of narrative by Crites
lacks the descriptive detail of the decomposition of a name for a narrative
sequence into its component parts as practiced by, among others,
Tomashevsky and Barthes. However, the understanding by Crites of
abstraction as the detachment of "images and qualities" from experience
"for the formation of generalized principles and techniques" agrees with
the idea of abstraction in the present study. The extraction of the thematic
essence of a narrative sequence is the identification of a general principle
or concept (capable of generating a multitude of narratives with a variety
of circumstances) that comes to completion through the reader's
experience of passing through the course of the narrative sequence.

interpretation; consequently, they are attempts to manipulate the understanding of the reader. Furthermore, as the critical survey of Fishbane's analysis of certain combinations of narrative and law has demonstrated, such formulations of theme through abstraction have the ability to forge a resemblance through membership within a general category with other formulations of theme. Where the members of such a set (e.g. numerous laws depicting crimes leading to punishment) represent an eclectic collection from multiple sources and traditions, abstraction for interpretation and manipulation becomes an operation spanning the history of the text. Abstraction, beyond the bridging of art and life, becomes a link between authors, editors, and readers, throughout the genesis, combination, and comprehension of texts.

The widespread applicability of abstraction in thematic formulation beyond its use in the collocation of narrative and legal texts is evident from the variety of the examples cited from biblical literature. From the paranetic discourses of Deuteronomy to the parables in the Gospels, abstract statements of the essence of a narrative occur. Explicit and implicit references to the activity of prescribing names for sequences of events abound in the direct address of the reader in statements of summary and in the words of characters in narrative. The categories of genre cannot confine the practice of abstraction. In the manner of its rhetoric, deployment of abstraction encompasses the simple emphatic outline of an aspect of theme and the enhancement of the experience of reading through misdirection. Thus, the occurrence of abstraction occurs throughout the variety of perspectives in the text (narrators and characters within narrative), across categories of genre, and within the variety of rhetorical strategies in narrative. Spanning the breadth of the biblical text, reaching backward to its history and upward to the lives of its readers, the procedure of abstraction forges links between the message(s) of the text, the voices that gave it life, and the eyes and ears that receive it. Given the pervasiveness of abstraction in human thought and perception, it seems myopic to overlook the intricacies of its procedure and deployment.

REFERENCE LIST

Andersen, Francis I. 1994. Salience, implicature, ambiguity, and redundancy in clause-clause relationships in Biblical Hebrew. In *Biblical Hebrew and discourse linguistics*, ed. Robert D. Bergen, 99–116. Dallas: Summer Institute of Linguistics.

Ashley, Timothy R. 1993. *The book of Numbers*. NICOT. Grand Rapids: Eerdmans.

Backhaus, Franz Josef. 1995. Die Pendenskonstruktion im Buch Qohelet. *ZAH* 8: 1–30.

Bal, Mieke. 1997. *Narratology: Introduction to the theory of narrative*. 2d ed. Toronto: University of Toronto Press.

Barthes, Roland. 1974. *S/Z: An essay*. Translated by Richard Miller. New York: Hill and Wang.

_____. 1975. An introduction to the structural analysis of narrative. Translated by Lionel Duisit. *New Literary History* 6/2: 237–72.

_____. 1981. Theory of the text. Translated by Ian McLeod. In *Untying the text: A post-structuralist reader*, ed. Robert Young, 31–47. London: Routledge and Kegan Paul.

_____. 1986. *The rustle of language*. Translated by Richard Howard. New York: Hill and Wang.

_____. 1988. The sequences of actions. In *The semiotic challenge*, trans. Richard Howard. Los Angeles: University of California Press.

Barton, John. 2000. Disclosing human possibilities: Revelation and biblical stories. In *Revelation and story: Narrative theology and the centrality of story*, ed. Gerhard Sauter and John Barton, 53–60. Aldershot: Ashgate.

Benigni, Antonella. 1999. The Biblical Hebrew particle כִּי from a discourse analysis perspective. *ZAH* 12: 126–45.

Berlin, Adele. 1983. *Poetics and interpretation of biblical narrative.* Sheffield: Almond.

Bertholet, Alfred. 1901. *Leviticus.* KHC 3. Tübingen: J.C.B. Mohr.

Bingham, Charles William, trans. 1984. *Commentary on the four last books of Moses arranged in a harmony,* vol. 2/1. Grand Rapids: Baker.

Bibb, Bryan D. 2001. Nadab and Abihu attempt to fill a gap: Law and narrative in Leviticus 10.1–7. *JSOT* 96: 83–99.

Blake, Frank R. 1944. The Hebrew waw conversive. *JBL* 63: 271–95.

Blass, F., and A. Debrunner. 1961. *A Greek grammar of the New Testament and other early Christian literature.* Translated by Robert W. Funk. Chicago: University of Chicago Press.

Boogart, T.A. 1985. Stone for stone: Retribution in the story of Abimelech and Shechem. *JSOT* 32: 45–56.

Bremond, Claude. 1964. Le message narratif. *Communications* 4: 4–32.

————. 1966. La logique des possibles narratifs. *Communications* 8:60–75.

Brunner, Jerome. 2002. *Making stories: Law, literature, life.* New York: Farrar, Straus and Giroux.

Budd, Philip J. 1984. *Numbers.* WBC 5. Waco: Word.

————. 1996. *Leviticus.* Grand Rapids: Eerdmans.

Bush, George. 1857. *Notes, critical and practical on the book of Leviticus: Designed as a general help to biblical reading and instruction.* New York: Ivison & Phinney.

Buth, Randall. 1995. Functional grammar, Hebrew and Aramaic: An integrated textlinguistic approach to syntax. In *Discourse analysis of biblical literature: What it is and what it offers,* ed. Walter R. Bodine, 77–102. Atlanta: Scholars Press.

Calloud, Jean. 1976. *Structural analysis of narrative.* Translated by Daniel Patte. Philadelphia: Fortress.

Cambell, Gregor. 1993. Structuralism. In *Encyclopedia of contemporary literary theory: Approaches, scholars, terms,* ed. Irena R. Makaryk, 199–204. Toronto: University of Toronto Press.

Carmichael, Calum. 1996. *The spirit of biblical law.* Athens: University of Georgia Press.

Crites, Stephen. 1989. The narrative quality of experience. In *Why narrative?: Readings in narrative theology*, ed. Stanley Hauerwas and L. Gregory Jones, 65–88. Grand Rapids: Eerdmans.

Culler, Jonathan. 1975. *Structuralist poetics: Structuralism linguistics and the study of literature*. London: Routledge & Kegan Paul.

Culley, Robert C. 1985. Exploring new directions. In *The Hebrew Bible and its modern interpreters*, ed. Douglas A. Knight and Gene M. Tucker, 167–200. Philadelphia: Fortress.

_____. 1992. *Themes and variations: A study of action in biblical narrative*. Atlanta: Scholars Press.

Damrosch, David. 1987. Leviticus. In *The literary guide to the Bible,* ed. Robert Alter and Frank Kermode, 66–77. Cambridge: Harvard University Press.

Davies, Eryl W. 1981. Inheritance rights and the Hebrew levirate marriage, pt. 1. *VT* 31: 138–44.

Dawson, David Allan. 1994. *Text-linguistics and Biblical Hebrew.* JSOTSup 177. Sheffield: Sheffield Academic Press.

Dillmann, August. 1886. *Die Bücher Numeri, Deuteronomium und Josua.* 2d ed. Leipzig: S. Hirzel.

Douglas, Mary. 1993. The forbidden animals in Leviticus. *JSOT* 59: 3–23.

_____. 1999. *Leviticus as literature*. Oxford: Oxford University Press.

_____. 2004. *Jacob's tears: The priestly work of reconciliation*. Oxford: Oxford University Press.

Driver, Samuel Rolles. 1998. *A treatise on the use of the tenses in Hebrew and some other syntactical questions*. 4th ed. Grand Rapids: Eerdmans.

Eliasen, Karen C. 2000. Aaron's war within: Story and ritual in Leviticus 10. *Proceedings-Eastern Great Lakes and Mid-West Biblical Societies* 20: 81–98.

Elliger, Karl. 1966. *Leviticus*. Tübingen: J.C.B. Mohr.

Fiddes, Paul S. 2000. Story and possibility: Reflections on the last scenes of the Fourth Gospel and Shakespeare's *The Tempest*. In *Revelation and story: Narrative theology and the centrality of story*, ed. Gerhard Sauter and John Barton, 29–51. Aldershot: Ashgate.

Fish, Stanley E. 1980a. Interpreting the *variorum*. In *Reader-response criticism: From Formalism to Post-Structuralism*, ed. Jane P. Tompkins, 164–84. Baltimore: Johns Hopkins University Press.

_____. 1980b. Literature in the reader: Affective stylistics. In *Reader- response criticism: From Formalism to Post-Structuralism*, ed. Jane P. Tompkins, 70–100. Baltimore: Johns Hopkins University Press.

Fishbane, Michael. 1985. *Biblical interpretation in ancient Israel.* Oxford: Clarendon.

_____. 1986. Inner biblical exegesis. In *Midrash and literature*, ed. Geoffrey H. Hartman and Sanford Budick, 19–37. New Haven: Yale University Press.

Fisher, E.J. 1982. Lex talionis in the Bible and rabbinic tradition. *Journal of Ecumenical Studies* 19: 582–7.

Forbes, John. 1854. *Symmetrical structure of scripture.* Edinburgh: T & T Clark.

Fox, Michael V. 1999. *A time to tear down and a time to build up: A rereading of Ecclesiastes.* Grand Rapids: Eerdmans.

Frymer-Kensky, Tikva. 1980. Tit for tat: The principle of equal retribution in Near Eastern and biblical law. *BA* 43:230–4.

Geller, Stephen A. 1991. Cleft sentences with pleonastic pronoun: A syntactic construction of Biblical Hebrew and some of its literary uses. *JANESCU* 20:15–33.

Gentry, Peter J. 1998. The system of the finite verb in Classical Biblical Hebrew. *HS* 39:7–39.

Gerstenberger, Erhard S. 1996. *Leviticus: A commentary.* Translated by Douglas W. Stott. OTL. Louisville: Westminster.

Goldenberg, Gideon. 1998. Imperfectly formed cleft sentences. In *Sudies in Semitic linguistics: Selected writings by Gideon Goldenberg*, 116–22. Jerusalem: Magnes.

Gray, George Buchanan. 1906. *A critical and exegetical commentary on Numbers.* ICC. New York: Scribner.

Greimas, Algirdas Julien. 1983. *Structural semantics: An attempt at a method.* Translated by Daniele McDowell, Ronald Schleifer and Alan Velie. Lincoln: University of Nebraska Press.

Greimas, Algirdas Julien. 1987. *On meaning: Selected writings in semiotic theory.* Translated by Paul J. Perron and Frank H. Collins. Minneapolis: University of Minnesota Press.

Gross, Walter. 1987. *Die Pendenskonstruktion im Biblishen Hebräisch.* St. Ottilien: EOS.

Gunn, David M. 1987. New directions in the study of Hebrew narrative. *JSOT* 39: 65–75.

Harrison, R.K. 1980. *Leviticus: An introduction and commentary.* Downers Grove: Inter-Varsity.

_____. 1992. *Numbers: An exegetical commentary.* Grand Rapids: Eerdmans.

Hartley, John E. 1992. *Leviticus.* WBC 4. Dallas: Word.

Heimerdinger, Jean-Marc. 1999. *Topic, focus and foreground in ancient Hebrew narratives.* JSOTSup 295. Sheffield: Sheffield Academic Press.

Hoffmann, D. 1905. *Das Buch Leviticus.* Berlin: Poppelauer.

Holzinger, H. 1903. *Numeri.* Tübingen: J.C.B. Mohr.

Houston, Walter. 2000. Tragedy in the courts of the Lord: A socio-literary reading of the death of Nadab and Abihu. *JSOT* 90: 31–39.

Iser, Wolfgang. 1978. *The act of reading: A theory of aesthetic response.* Baltimore: Johns Hopkins University Press.

_____. 1980. The reading process: A phenomenological approach. Translated by Catherine Macksey and Richard Macksey. In *Reader- response criticism: From Formalism to Post-Structuralism,* ed. Jane P. Tompkins, 50–69. Baltimore: Johns Hopkins University Press.

Jackson, Bernard S. 1996. Talion and purity: Some glosses on Mary Douglas. In *Reading Leviticus,* ed. J.F.A. Sawyer, 107–23. Sheffield: Sheffield Academic Press.

_____. 2000. *Studies in the semiotics of biblical law.* JSOTSup 314. Sheffield: Sheffield Academic Press.

_____. 2006. *Wisdom-Laws: A study of the Mishpatim of Exodus 21:1–22:16.* Oxford: Oxford University Press.

Janowski, Bernd. *Sühne als Heilgeschehen: Studien zur Sühnetheologie der Priesterschrift und zur Wurzel KPR im Alten Orient und im Alten Testament.* WMANT 55. Neukirchen: Neukirchener Verlag.

Jobling, D. 1978. *The sense of biblical narrative: Three structural analyses in the Old Testament.* JSOTSup 7. Sheffield: Sheffield Academic Press.

Keil, C.F. and F. Delitzsch. 1865. *Biblical commentary on the Old Testament*, vol. 3. Translated by James Martin. Edinburgh: T. & T. Clark.

Kellermann, Diether. 1970. *Die Priesterschrift von Numeri 1:1 bis 10:10.* Berlin: Walter de Gruyter.

_____. 1973. Bemerkungen zum Sündopfergesetz in Num 15:22ff. In *Wort und Geschichte: Festschrift für Karl Elliger zum 70. Geburtstag,* ed. Hartmut Gese and Hans Peter Rüger, 107–13. Neukirchen: Neukirchener Verlag.

Kermode, Frank. 1983. *The art of telling: Essays on fiction.* Cambridge: Harvard University Press.

Khan, Geoffrey. 1988. *Studies in Semitic syntax.* Oxford: Oxford University Press.

Kirschner, Robert. 1983. The Rabbinic and Philonic exegeses of the Nadab and Abihu incident. *JQR* 73: 375–93.

Kiuchi, N. 1987. *The Purification Offering in the Priestly literature: Its meaning and function.* JSOTSup 56. Sheffield: Sheffield Academic Press.

Kotze, Robert J. 1989. The circumstantial sentence: A catch-them-all term. *JNSL* 15:109–26.

Lafont, Sophie. 1994. Ancient Near Estern laws: Continuity and pluralism. In *Theory and method in biblical and cuneiform law: Revision, interpolation and development,* ed. Bernard M. Levinson, 91–118. JSOTSup 181. Sheffield: Sheffield Academic Press.

Laughlin, John C.H. 1976. The "strange fire" of Nadab and Abihu. *JBL* 95: 559–65.

Lemaire, A. 1972. Le 'pays de Hepher' et les 'filles de Zelophehad' à la lumière des ostraca de Samarie. *Sem* 22:13–20.

Levine, Baruch A. 1989. *The JPS Torah commentary: Leviticus.* New York: Jewish Publication Society.

_____. 1993. *Numbers 1–20: A new translation with introduction and commentary.* AB 4. New York: Doubleday.

_____. 2000. *Numbers 21–36: A new translation with introduction and commentary.* AB 4a. New York: Doubleday.

Levinson, Bernard M. 1991. The right chorale: From the poetics to the hermeneutics of the Hebrew Bible. In *"Not in heaven": Coherence and complexity in biblical narrative*, ed. Jason P. Rosenblatt and Joseph C. Sitterson, Jr., 129–53. Bloomington: Indiana University Press.

_____. 1998. *Deuteronomy and the hermeneutics of legal innovation*. Oxford: Oxford University Press.

_____. 2005. The birth of the lemma: The restrictive reinterpretation of the Covenant Code's manumission law (Leviticus 25:44–46). *JBL* 124: 617–39.

_____. 2008. *Legal revision and religious renewal in ancient Israel*. Cambridge: Cambridge University Press.

Lévi-Strauss, Claude. 1967. The structural study of myth. In *Structural anthropology*, vol. 1, trans. C. Jacobson and B.G. Schoepf, 202–27. Garden City: Anchor.

_____. 1976. Structure and form: Reflections on a work by Vladimir Propp. In *Structural anthropology*, vol. 2, trans. Monique Layton, 115–43. New York: Basic.

Livingston, Dennis H. 1986. The crime of Leviticus 24:11. *VT* 36: 352–4.

Lockshin, Martin I., trans. 2001. *Rashbam's commentary on Leviticus and Numbers: An annotated translation*. BJS 330. Providence: Brown Judaic Studies.

Lowery, Kirk E. 1995. The theoretical foundations of Hebrew discourse Grammar. In *Discourse analysis of biblical literature: What it is and what it offers*, ed. Walter R. Bodine, 103–30. Atlanta: Scholars Press.

Longacre, Robert E. 1989. *Joseph: A story of divine providence. A text theoretical and textlinguistic analysis of Genesis 37 and 39–48*. Winona Lake: Eisenbrauns.

_____. 1992. Discourse analysis and the Hebrew Verb: Affirmation and restatement. In *Linguistics and Biblical Hebrew*, ed. Walter R. Bodine, 177–89. Winona Lake: Eisenbrauns.

_____. 1994. Weqatal forms in Biblical Hebrew prose. In *Biblical Hebrew and discourse linguistics*, ed. Robert D. Bergen, 50–98. Dallas: Summer Institute of Linguistics.

Merwe, Christo H.J. van der. 1991. The function of word order in Old Hebrew with special reference to cases

where a syntagmeme precedes a verb in Joshua. *JNSL*
17: 129–44.

Merwe, Christo H.J. van der. 1994. Discourse linguistics and
Biblical Hebrew grammar. In *Biblical Hebrew and discourse
linguistics*, ed. Robert D. Bergen, 13–49. Dallas: Summer
Institute of Linguistics.

Merwe, Christo H.J. van der, Jackie A. Naudé, and Jan H.
Kroeze. 1999. *A Biblical Hebrew reference grammar*.
Sheffield: Sheffield Academic Press.

Milgrom, Jacob. 1976. Two kinds of H@at[t[a"]t. *VT* 26:
333–337.

_____. 1990. *The JPS Torah commentary: Numbers*. New
York: Jewish Publication Society.

_____. 1991. *Leviticus 1–16: A new translation with
introduction and commentary*. AB 3. New York: Doubleday.

_____. 2000. *Leviticus 17–22: A new translation with
introduction and commentary*. AB 3a. New York: Doubleday.

_____. 2001. *Leviticus 23–27: A new translation with
introduction and commentary*. AB 3b. New York: Doubleday.

_____. 2007. The preposition מִן in the חטאת pericopes.
JBL 126: 161–3.

Mittwoch, H. 1965. The story of the blasphemer seen in a
wider context. *VT* 15: 386–89.

Muraoka, Takamitsu. 1985. *Emphatic words and structures in
Biblical Hebrew*. Jerusalem: Magnes.

Murphy, Roland E. 1992. *Ecclesiastes*. WBC 23a. Dallas: Word.

Nel, Philip J. 1994. The talion principle in Old Testament
narratives. *JNSL* 20: 21–9.

Niccacci, Alviero. 1990. *The syntax of the verb in Classical Hebrew
prose*. JSOTSup 86. Sheffield: Sheffield Academic Press.

_____. 1994a. On the Hebrew verbal system. In *Biblical
Hebrew and discourse linguistics*, ed. Robert D. Bergen, 117–
37. Dallas: Summer Institute of Linguistics.

_____. 1994b. Analysis of biblical narrative. In *Biblical
Hebrew and discourse linguistics*, ed. Robert D. Bergen, 175–
98. Dallas: Summer Institute of Linguistics.

_____. 1995. Review of David Allan Dawson's *Text-
linguistics and Biblical Hebrew*. *Liber Annuus* 45:543–80.

Niccacci, Alviero. 1996. Finite verb in the second position of the sentence: Coherence of the Hebrew verbal system. *ZAW* 108: 434–40.

————. 1997. Basic facts and theory of the Biblical Hebrew verb system in prose. In *Narrative syntax and the Hebrew Bible: Papers of the Tillburgh conference 1996,* ed. Ellen Van Wolde, 167–202. Leiden: Brill.

Nielsen, Kirsten. 2000. Intertextuality and Hebrew Bible. In *Congress volume: Oslo 1998,* eds. A. Lemaire and M. Sæbo, 17–31. VTSup 80. Leiden: Brill.

Noth, Martin. 1968. *Numbers: A commentary.* Translated by James D. Martin. Philadelphia: Westminster.

Nunn, H.P.V. 1938. *A short syntax of New Testament Greek.* 5th ed. Cambridge: Cambridge University Press.

Olson, Dennis T. 1985. *The death of the old and the birth of the new: The framework of the book of Numbers and the Pentateuch.* BJS 71. Chico: Scholars Press.

————. 1996. *Numbers.* Louisville: John Knox.

Polotsky, Hans Jacob. 1985. A note on the sequential verb-form in Ramesside Egyptian and in Biblical Hebrew. In *Pharaonic Egypt: The Bible and Christianity,* ed. Sarah Israelit-Groll, 157–61. Jerusalem: Magnes.

Rainey, Anson F. 1986. The ancient Hebrew prefix conjugation in the light of Amarnah Canaanite. *HS* 27: 4–19.

Regt, L.J. de. 1999. Macrosyntactic functions of nominal clauses referring to participants. In *The verbless clause in Biblical Hebrew,* ed. Cynthia L. Miller, 273–96. Winona Lake: Eisenbrauns.

Revell, E.J. 1985. The system of the verb in Standard Biblical Prose. *HUCA* 60: 1–37.

————. 1989. The conditioning of word order in verbless clauses in Biblical Hebrew. *JSS* 34/1: 1–24.

————. 1991. Conditional sentences in Biblical Hebrew prose. In *Semitic studies in honor of Wolf Leslau on the occasion of his eighty-fifth birthday,* vol. 2, ed. Alan S. Kaye, 1278–90. Wiesbaden: Harrassowitz.

Rosenbaum, M., and A.M. Silbermann. 1965. *Pentateuch with Targum Onkelos, Haphtaroth and Rashi's commentary: Numbers.* New York: Hebrew Publishing.

Schaper, Joachim. 2004. Rereading the law: Inner-biblical exegesis of divine oracles in Ezekiel 44 and Isaiah 56. In *Recht und Ethik im Alten Testament,* eds. Bernard M. Levinson, Eckart Otto and Walter Dietrich, 125–44. Münster: Lit.

Schellenberg, Elizabeth. 1993. Reader-response criticism. In *Encyclopedia of contemporary literary theory: Approaches, scholars, terms,* ed. Irena R. Makaryk, 170–4. Toronto: University of Toronto Press.

Schneidau, Herbert N. 1986. Biblical narrative and modern consciousness. In *The Bible and the narrative tradition,* ed. Frank McConnell, 132–50. Oxford: Oxford University Press.

Schneider, Wolfgang. 1985. *Grammatik des Biblischen Hebräisch.* 6th ed. München: Claudius.

Scholes, R., and R. Kellogg. 1966. *The nature of narrative.* New York: Oxford University Press.

Segal, M.H. 1967. *The Pentateuch and other biblical studies.* Jerusalem: Magnes.

Selden, Raman, and Peter Widdowson. 1993. *A reader's guide to contemporary literary theory.* 3d ed. Lexington: University Press of Kentucky.

Shklovsky, V. 1990. *Theory of prose.* Translated by Benjamin Sher. Elmwood Park: Dalkey.

Sklar, Jay. 2005. *Sin, impurity, sacrifice, atonement: The priestly conceptions.* Sheffield: Sheffield Phoenix.

Smyth, Herbert W. 1920. *Greek grammar.* Cambridge: Harvard University Press.

Snaith, N.H. 1966. The daughters of Zelophehad. *VT* 16: 124–7.

_____. 1969. *Leviticus and Numbers.* London: Oliphants.

Sprinkle, Joe M. 1993. The interpretation of Exodus 21:22–25 (*Lex Talionis*) and abortion. *WTJ* 55: 233–253.

_____. 1994. *The Book of the Covenant: A literary approach.* JSOTSup 174. Sheffield: Sheffield Academic Press.

Stackert, Jeffrey. 2007. *Rewriting the Torah: Literary revision in Deuteronomy and the Holiness Legislation.* FAT 52. Tübingen: Mohr Siebeck.

Stahl, Nanette. 1995. *Law and liminality in the Bible.* JSOTSup 202. Sheffield: Sheffield Academic Press.

Sternberg, M. 1987. *The poetics of biblical narrative: Ideological literature and the drama of reading.* Bloomington: Indiana University Press.

Strickman, H. Norman, and Arthur M. Silver, trans. 1999. *Ibn Ezra's commentary on the Pentateuch: Numbers.* New York: Menorah.

Talstra, Eep. 1978. Text grammar and Hebrew Bible. I: Elements of a theory. *BO* 35: 169–174.

_____. 1997. Tense, mood, aspect and clause connections in Biblical Hebrew: A textual approach. *JNSL* 23: 81–103.

Todorov, Tzevetan. 1977. *The poetics of prose.* Translated by Richard Howard. Ithaca: Cornell University Press.

_____. 1981. Analysis of the literary text. In *Introduction to poetics,* trans. Richard Howard, 13–58. Minneapolis: University of Minnesota Press.

Toeg, A. 1973. An halakhic midrash in Num 15:22–31. *Tarbiz* 43:1–20.

Tomashevsky, B. 1965. Thematics. In *Russian Formalist criticism: Four essays,* trans. and ed. Lee T. Lemon and Marion J. Reis, 61–95. Lincoln: University of Nebraska Press.

Vaulx, J. de. 1972. *Les Nombres.* Paris: Gabalda.

Watts, James W. 2007. *Ritual and rhetoric in Leviticus: From sacrifice to scripture.* Cambridge: Cambridge University Press.

Weingreen, J. 1966. The case of the daughters of Zelophchad. *VT* 16: 518–22.

_____. 1972. The case of the blasphemer (Leviticus 24: 10 ff.). *VT* 22: 118–123.

Weinrich, Harald. 1971. *Tempus: Besprochene und erzählte Welt.* Stuttgart: Kohlhammer.

Wenham, Gordon J. 1979. *The book of Leviticus.* NICOT. Grand Rapids: Eerdmans.

_____. 1981. *Numbers: An introduction and commentary.* Downers Grove: Inter-Varsity.

Westbrook, Raymond. 1986. Lex talionis and Exodus 21, 22–25. *RB* 93: 52–69.

Wevers, John W. 1997. *Notes on the Greek text of Leviticus.* Atlanta: Scholars Press.

Wevers, John W. 1998. *Notes on the Greek text of Numbers.* Atlanta: Scholars Press.

Wilder, Amos N. 1991. *The Bible and the literary critic.* Minneapolis: Fortress Press.

Wright, David P. 1987. *The disposal of impurity: Elimination rites in the Bible and in Hittite and Mesopotamian literature.* SBLDS 101. Atlanta: Scholars Press.

Index of Modern Authors

Fiddes, P.S., 292, 299
Fish, S.E., 29, 31, 284, 300
Fishbane, M., 8, 47, 49, 92, 159,
  277, 278, 279, 283, 295, 300
Fisher, E.J., 75, 300
Forbes, J., 47, 300
Fox, M.V., 193, 300
Frymer-Kensky, T., 75, 283, 300
Funk, R.W., 298
Geller, S.A., 216, 300
Gentry, P.J., 60, 208, 210, 213,
  228, 300
Gerstenberger, E.S., 56, 57, 124,
  135, 150, 300
Gese, H., 302
Goldenberg, G., 217, 300
Gray, G.B., 77, 90, 93, 94, 101,
  102, 108, 153, 155, 156, 159,
  165, 183, 187, 300
Green, D.E., xiv
Gregory Jones, L., 299
Greimas, A.J., 19, 20, 21, 22, 23,
  26, 34, 300, 301
Gross, W., 217, 219, 301
Gunn, D.M., 8, 301
Harris, R.L., xiv
Harrison, R.K., 45, 89, 91, 93,
  153, 156, 163, 301
Hartley, J.E., 45, 47, 67, 75, 119,
  124, 125, 128, 129, 151, 247,
  301
Hartman, G.H., 300
Hauerwas, S., 299
Heimerdinger, J.-M., 198, 199,
  204, 206, 301
Hoffmann, D., 66, 119, 137,
  301
Holzinger, H., 94, 108, 156, 159,
  179, 301
Houston, W., 120, 301

Howard, R., 297, 307
Iser, W., 1, 31, 39, 43, 113, 279,
  301
Israelit-Groll, S., 305
Jackson, B.S., 47, 75, 283, 301
Jacobson, C., 303
Janowski, B., 137, 301
Jobling, D., 21, 22, 23, 34, 302
Jöuon, P., xiii
Kautzsch, E., xiii
Kaye, A.S., 305
Keil, C.F., 6, 153, 156, 159, 302
Kellermann, D., 85, 87, 188, 302
Kellogg, R., 14, 15, 17, 18, 26,
  306
Kermode, F., 32, 299, 302
Khan, G., 217, 219, 302
Kirschner, R., 122, 302
Kiuchi, N., 119, 123, 125, 138,
  302
Knight, D.A., 299
Kotze, R.J., 55, 57, 302
Kroeze, J.H., xiii, 304
Lafont, S., 49, 302
Laughlin, J.C.H., 119, 302
Layton, M., 303
Lemaire, A., 93, 302, 305
Lemon, L.T., 307
Levine, B.A., 67, 77, 91, 92, 93,
  102, 108, 119, 137, 183, 259,
  302
Levinson, B.M., 8, 278, 283,
  302, 303, 306
Lévi-Strauss, C., 19, 20, 21, 23,
  303
Livingston, D.H., 66, 303
Lockshin, M.I., 159, 303
Longacre, R.E., 60, 61, 62, 82,
  202, 203, 204, 206, 207, 209,
  211, 212, 303

Lowery, K.E., 60, 202, 220, 303
Makaryk, I.R., 298, 306
Martin, J.D., 302, 305
McConnell, F., 306
McDowell, D., 300
Merwe, C.H.J., van der, xiii, 60, 186, 202, 303, 304
Milgrom, J., 45, 46, 47, 49, 57, 66, 67, 78, 89, 91, 94, 102, 123, 124, 125, 126, 128, 132, 137, 148, 153, 154, 160, 165, 166, 177, 179, 180, 184, 304
Miller, C.L., 305
Miller, R., 297
Mittwoch, H., 304
Muraoka, T., xiii, 304, 110, 132, 186
Murphy, R.E., 193, 304
Naude, J.A., xiii, 304
Nel, P.J., 283, 304
Niccacci, A., 54, 55, 57, 60, 61, 62, 63, 80, 82, 88, 174, 186, 204, 205, 206, 207, 208, 209, 210, 211, 212, 213, 217, 304, 305
Nielsen, K., 279, 305
Noth, M., 7, 77, 92, 93, 94, 101, 108, 109, 153, 155, 159, 305
Nunn, H.P.V., 137, 305
O'Connor, M., xiii
Olson, D.T., 6, 8, 9, 11, 12, 91, 93, 102, 153, 154, 155, 156, 161, 180, 184, 305
Otto, E., 306
Perron, P.J., 301
Polotsky, H.J., 212, 305
Propp, V., 20, 303
Rainey, A.F., 61, 305
Regt, L.J., de, 93, 305
Reis, M.J., 307

Revell, E.J., 80, 98, 216, 305
Ringgren, H., xiv
Rosenbaum, M., 159, 177, 305
Rosenblatt, J.B., 303
Rüger, H.P., 302
Sæbo, M., 305
Sauter, G., 297, 299
Sawyer, J.F.A., 301
Schaper, J., 279, 306
Schellenberg, E., 29, 306
Schleifer, R., 300
Schneidau, H.N., 288, 289, 306
Schneider, W., xiii, 200, 205, 214, 306
Schoepf, B.G., 303
Scholes, R., 14, 15, 17, 18, 26, 306
Segal, M.H., 123, 153, 306
Selden, R., 16, 20, 29, 306
Sher, B., 306
Shklovsky, V., 16, 17, 18, 20, 21, 25, 37, 306
Silbermann, A.M., 159, 177, 305
Silver, A.M., 307
Sitterson, J.C., 303
Sklar, J., 137, 306
Smyth, H.W., 71, 137, 144, 306
Snaith, N.H., 93, 94, 108, 154, 306
Sprinkle, J.M., 8, 10, 11, 12, 306
Stackert, J., 8, 279, 306
Stahl, N., 8, 11, 12, 306
Sternberg, M., 16, 307
Stott, D.W., 300
Strickman, H.N., 159, 307
Talstra, E., 200, 201, 205, 214, 307
Todorov, T., 24, 27, 30, 31, 34, 35, 36, 307
Toeg, A., 165, 307